A History of the

Evangelical and Reformed Church

PAUL PRESS, PRESIDENT OF THE EVANGELICAL SYNOD OF NORTH AMERICA, SHAKING HANDS WITH HENRY J. CHRISTMAN, PRESIDENT OF THE REFORMED CHURCH IN THE UNITED STATES, AT THE MERGER OF THE TWO CHURCHES.

A History of the Evangelical and Reformed Church

DAVID DUNN
PAUL N. CRUSIUS
JOSIAS FRIEDLI
THEOPHIL W. MENZEL
CARL E. SCHNEIDER
WILLIAM TOTH
JAMES E. WAGNER

INTRODUCTION BY
LOWELL H. ZUCK

90

The Pilgrim Press • New York

Library of Congress Cataloging-in-Publication Data

A History of the Evangelical and Reformed Church / David Dunn . . .
[et al.   ;   edited and] with an introduction by Lowell H. Zuck.
    p.   cm.
  Reprint, with new introd. Originally published: Philadelphia : Christian
Education Press, c1961.
  Includes bibligraphical references.
  ISBN 0-8298-0855-8 :
  1. Evangelical and Reformed Church—History.   2. Reformed Church
—United States—History.   3. United churches—United States—History.
I. Dunn, David, 1891–1970.   II. Zuck, Lowell H.
BX7465.H57   1990
285.7′34′09—dc20   90-33153
                                              CIP

The Pilgrim Press, 475 Riverside Drive, New York, NY 10115

Contents

INTRODUCTION TO THE REISSUED EDITION   ix
  • Lowell H. Zuck

FOREWORD   xxiii

THE AUTHORS   xxvii

PART ONE

THE REFORMED CHURCH IN THE UNITED STATES

1. EUROPEAN BACKGROUND—REFORMED   3
  • William Toth

2. ON THE FRONTIERS OF A NEW LAND (—1792)   23

3. THE SYNOD IN THE EAST (1793–1863)   53
  • David Dunn

4. THE ERA OF THE GENERAL SYNOD (1863–1934)   82
  • David Dunn

5. THE WINNING OF THE WEST (1824–1934)   115
  • Josias Friedli

PART TWO

THE EVANGELICAL SYNOD OF NORTH AMERICA

6. EUROPEAN BACKGROUND—EVANGELICAL   147
  • Theophil W. Menzel

7. FRONTIER BEGINNINGS (—1866) 158
 • Theophil W. Menzel

8. WESTERN CONSOLIDATION (1866–1883) 190
 • Paul N. Crusius

9. GROWTH AND OUTREACH (1883–1915) 222
 • Paul N. Crusius

10. THE POSTWAR ERA (1915–1934) 252
 • Paul N. Crusius

PART THREE

THE EVANGELICAL AND REFORMED CHURCH

11. JOURNEY INTO UNION (1929–1940) 279
 • Carl E. Schneider

12. THE NEW WITNESS (1940–1960) 296
 • James E. Wagner

STATISTICAL RECORDS 339

BIBLIOGRAPHY 343

INDEX OF NAMES AND PLACES 353

List of Illustrations

PAUL PRESS AND HENRY J. CHRISTMAN	Frontispiece
MARTIN LUTHER	Facing 18
PHILIPP MELANCHTHON	18
ULRICH ZWINGLI	18
JOHN CALVIN	18
FALKNER SWAMP CHURCH	19
FIRST CHURCH, PHILADELPHIA	19
SEAL OF COETUS	19
SEAL OF EASTERN SYNOD	19
MICHAEL SCHLATTER	19
PHILIP SCHAFF	50
LEWIS MAYER	50
JOHN H. A. BOMBERGER	50
JOHN W. NEVIN	50
J. J. BOSSARD	51
H. A. WINTER	51
HERMAN J. RUETENIK	51
JACOB STUCKI	51
HERMANN GARLICHS	82
LOUIS E. NOLLAU	82
FRIEDRICH SCHMID	82
GEORGE W. WALL	82

WILLIAM BINNER	83
ADOLPH H. BALTZER	83
JOSEPH A. RIEGER	83
ANDREAS IRION	83
JACOB C. LEONARD	114
JAMES I. GOOD	114
JACOB PISTER	114
JOHN ZIMMERMANN	114
DAVID B. SCHNEDER	115
ALLEN R. BARTHOLOMEW	115
JACOB GASS	115
PAUL A. MENZEL	115
LANCASTER THEOLOGICAL SEMINARY	146
EDEN THEOLOGICAL SEMINARY	146
MISSION HOUSE THEOLOGICAL SEMINARY	146
H. RICHARD NIEBUHR	147
GEORGE W. RICHARDS	147
JAMES E. WAGNER	147
LOUIS W. GOEBEL	147

Introduction to the Reissued Edition

THE YEAR 1990 has been a good one for church anniversaries. It marks the one hundred and fiftieth anniversary of the 1840 founding of the Evangelical Synod, an anniversary festively celebrated in St. Louis, as well as the two hundred and sixty-fifth anniversary of the 1725 founding, in Pennsylvania, of the German Reformed Church. The year also marks the fifty-sixth year since those two churches, the Evangelical Synod of North America and the Reformed Church in the United States joined in 1934 to form the Evangelical and Reformed Church. And it is the thirty-third anniversary of the 1957 merger between that church and the General Council of the Congregational Christian Churches, which formed the United Church of Christ.

Since the Congregational Christian side of the United Church of Christ is the larger and better known, it is especially important that this volume, which describes the twenty-three years of vibrant development and life of the Evangelical and Reformed Church, be reissued. This volume places the Evangelical and Reformed Church, as it became ready to move into the United Church of Christ, fully within both its European and American historical contexts. While the combined constituencies at the time of the union that formed the United Church of Christ were small by American standards, membership in the Evangelical and Reformed Church had expanded significantly. By 1934 there were 348,000 Reformed members and 282,000 Evangelicals, for a total E and R membership of 630,000. This was approximately two-thirds the size of the Congregational Christian Churches.

Their distinct heritages and strong regional loyalties made Evangelical and Reformed people proud of their ties to the Protestant Reformation. They had developed great respect for their traditions and were sustained by an ethnically based, family-like fellowship rooted in their German, Swiss, and Hungarian backgrounds. During the Revolutionary War, the German Reformed people, now sympathetic toward the American Revolution, had hidden the exiled Philadelphia Liberty Bell in their Zion Reformed Church in Allentown, Pennsylvania. In their new seminary in Mercersburg, Pennsylvania, two notable Reformed theologians, John Nevin and Philip Schaff, opposed the prevailing nineteenth-century revivalist trend among Protestants by sponsoring an "Evangelical Catholic" liturgical renewal that was rooted in both the Reformation *Heidelberg Catechism* and early catholic worship patterns.

The Evangelical *Kirchenverein* (or Church Association), begun in 1840 in the Midwest, was unique in America in that it combined the Lutheran and Reformed traditions into a not very creedal, liberal unionist Evangelical Synod patterned after the German Evangelical Church of the Prussian Union (1817). (That church still exists in Germany today as the largest German Protestant church and currently enjoys *Kirchengemeinschaft* [intercommunion] with the United Church of Christ.) More Pietistic than their Reformed cousins in the east, the Missouri-Illinois Evangelicals quickly published their own catechism, hymnal, liturgy, and church newspaper, and in 1850 established what became Eden Theological Seminary. The theological creativity of the Evangelical Synod is best illustrated by the fact that America's best known twentieth-century theologians, Reinhold, Richard, and Hulda Niebuhr, were born and educated in Evangelical parsonages and schools.

We can see, then, how these American descendants of Ulrich Zwingli and John Calvin were able to unite in 1934 with a later German group of Protestants of both Reformed and Lutheran backgrounds. No other American denomination so well represented the Reformed and Lutheran unitive tradition as did the Evangelical and Reformed Church. The original sixteenth-century unitive Protestant tradition had been overcome by a three-century long separation between the Lutheran and Reformed confessions. This special unitive characteristic was demonstrated again when they were able to carry out the first church union in the United States between denominations of differing ethnic and polity traditions, though a predominant Reformed theological background ran through all of the traditions that eventually united to form the United Church of Christ.

This book was written by seven historians of the Evangelical and Reformed Church under the sponsorship of its Historical Commission (now the Evangelical and Reformed Historical Society, an historical agency related to the United Church of Christ Historical Council). Published when the Evangelical and Reformed Church was coming to an end as such, the book, along with its companion volume, *The Faith We Proclaim*,[1] was intended to record the history and doctrine of "a church notable not so much for its denominational peculiarities as for its zeal for the unity of the people of God."

This volume, with the exception of this introduction and an updated bibliography, is reprinted unchanged and in its entirety. The first ten chapters tell of the European and American backgrounds of the people in both churches: their migrations to the New World and the development through succeeding centuries of their congregations, synods, colleges, seminaries, hospitals, other institutions, and ways of life. Carl E. Schneider, the historian of the Evangelical Synod, then traces the steps that led to the 1934 union and assesses its churchly and theological significance.

Finally, James E. Wagner, then President of the Evangelical and Reformed Church and Co-President of the United Church of Christ, traces the last twenty years of the Evangelical and Reformed Church (1940–1960), briefly noting the events that inaugurated the 1957 United Church of Christ. Recent documentation indicates that the propoasal for church union was initiated officially by a telegram sent in 1938 by Samuel D. Press, President of Eden Theological Seminary, to Truman Douglass, General Secretary of the Congregational Christian Churches, then meeting in their General Council at Beloit, Wisconsin. Wagner's chapter is of interest and value because of both his advocacy of Evangelical and Reformed viewpoints and his participation in the early years of the United Church of Christ.

I shall consider now the Evangelical and Reformed participation in the United Church of Christ through the past three decades in terms of (1) anticipations of the UCC; (2) perspectives contributed to the UCC; (3) three decades of progress toward unity (amid countervailing forces); and (4) "united and uniting," a conciliar ecclesiology.

Evangelical and Reformed Anticipations for the United Church of Christ

Different histories, traditions, and experiences meant that Evangelical and Reformed anticipations of further union were not the same as those of the Congregational Christians. The Congregationalists' early nineteenth-century "Plan of Union," undertaken in cooperation with the Presbyterians and designed to reach frontier Americans, had benefited the Presbyterians more because of their organization. The failure of the plan for the Congregationalists resulted in a loss of denominational identity, from which they did not recover until later in the century. Paradoxically, the Congregational recovery of national denominational unity was accompanied by increasing ecumenical interests and renewed liberal social concerns. Thus the Congregational willingness in 1931 to unite with the small Christian Connection represented this new ecumenical outreach. At the same time, the Congregational commitment to autonomy somewhat restricted their ability to unite with other church organizations.

Evangelical and Reformed people had had less experience with actual church union because of their confinement for a century or more within foreign language enclaves, although the German Reformed Church had been, from the beginning, influenced by a kind of Melanchthonian unionist movement within German Lutheranism. That had resulted, however, in a distinct Reformed stance that was unacceptable to the Lutherans. The German Reformed Church in the United States was never able to unite with its Dutch Reformed cousins; and mastering English was too much of an early barrier for union with the Presbyterians to occur, though later efforts were made to unite with both churches. A somewhat separatist Pietist movement that came out of the German Reformed constituency also helped begin the United Brethren Church (now part of United Methodism) and the small Church of God (Winebrennerian). The Evangelical Synod people in America, who had actually united Lutheran and Reformed traditions from the beginning, were eager, following attendance by their leaders at worldwide ecumenical meetings early in the twentieth century, to join with similar denominations, although an earlier possiblity had been for the Evangelicals to become merely another Lutheran synod in the United States.

Behind the Evangelical and Reformed union had been ecumenically minded Reformed leaders such as Samuel Press, John Baltzer, Julius Horstmann, H. Richard Niebuhr, Louis Goebel, and George W. Richards. As early as 1929, hopes were high that a "United Church in America" could bring together the German Reformed Church, the Evangelical Synod, and the United Brethren. When union with the United Brethren failed, negotiations quickly brought about a plan of union for the Evangelical and Reformed Church which stressed faith but did not produce a

Constitution. Six years elapsed (1934–1940) before the laboriously crafted Constitution of the Evangelical and Reformed Church was accepted—and then only after differences between Evangelical centralism and Reformed freedom were resolved, and the Evangelical and Reformed Church became essentially presbyterian but functionally congregational. This was a hint of what would later happen to UCC structure, although Evangelical and Reformed people had no historic commitments to congregational autonomy.

In spite of inevitable differences between the parent churches' practices and traditions, the new church struck a harmonious balance in size and strength between the two geographically separated, differently organized but essentially similar German-background churches of a common unitive Reformed type. After World War I, the leaders of both denominations took risks in moving toward further union.

In a similar way, the movement toward the United Church of Christ began in 1934 with ecumenical Bible and theology study groups in St. Louis, Missouri, held by Truman Douglass, Samuel Press, and other church leaders. At the same time, the ecumenical interests of the well-known neo-orthodox theologians Reinhold Niebuhr, Richard Niebuhr, and Paul Tillich made that denomination better known to Congregational leaders such as Douglas Horton and Truman Douglass, who were interested both in the new theology and in further ecumenical ventures.

Obviously, the denominations that were to become the United Church of Christ seemed to fit together less comfortably than had the earlier churches. Strong Congregational commitments to autonomy and a corporate, business-like organizational identity seemed out of accord with the more traditional churchly consciousness and presbyterian structure of the Evangelical and Reformed Church. Indeed, it is probably accurate to say that the possibility of a new United Church of Christ provoked an identity crisis for Congregationalists similar to the one they suffered after the breakdown of the Plan of Union in 1852. A lengthy period of litigation followed plans for the merger, and delayed and almost killed the emergence of the United Church of Christ. Some bitterness over those difficult days still remains among older Congregationalists bitterly opposed to merger. As more recent ecumenical participants, the Evangelical and Reformed people looked forward to becoming part of a larger church that they anticipated would be similar to the one they knew well. They were not fully aware of the radical nature of congregational autonomy held by many of their fellow believers in the other tradition. Thus, anticipations on both sides were confused, on one hand, by common hopes and expectations and, on the other, by completely different assumptions and commitments. One might argue that the degree to which the United Church of Christ has been successful (and, on the whole, it *has* been successful) would not have been predictable on the basis of its extremely rocky beginnings.

Evangelical and Reformed Perspectives Within the United Church of Christ

Because of the greater number of former Congregationalists in the UCC and because of the value they place on the principle of autonomy, one might wrongly assume that autonomy would characterize the UCC. And, in fact, section IV, paragraph 15 of the Constitution does indeed declare that every individual and entity within the UCC is autonomous and not subject to control by any other.

Yet there was general agreement between both groups of the need to (1) balance autonomy with accountability; and (2) develop a real union, one bound by a definite Constitution and By-laws, with regularly elected officers, and governed by a representative General Synod that would meet regularly. To maintain continuity between synods, an Executive Council was to be elected. The entire membership of the church was to be aided by autonomous but responsible Instrumentalities, and every part of the nation was to be reached through geographically appropriate Conferences and Associations. This organization existed to serve local congregations, themselves under the sole authority of Jesus Christ and the source of the other structures within the new church. Though some of these entities had names that recalled Congregationalism, the United Church of Christ was more structured than Congregationalism historically had been, and many of its characteristics were familiar to those who were accustomed to the Evangelical and Reformed presbyterial structures.

Evangelical and Reformed perspectives were included in planning for the United Church of Christ from the beginning. There were different emphases, however, between the Evangelical and Reformed Church and the United Church of Christ. The Evangelical and Reformed desire to exclude theological education, ministerial, and lay concerns from the powerful, autonomous Congregational Christian-oriented Board for Homeland Ministries led to struggles which erupted again in the 1980s, with a successful effort to have Health and Welfare concerns administered separately from the Board. The independence of the Board for World Ministries from denominational controls also troubled those from the E and R tradition. Both large boards have come recently to be more representative of the whole church.

In the midst of struggle, new instrumentalities were also created. One was an Office for Church Life and Leadership, which united both awkwardly and creatively earlier ministerial concerns with those formerly associated with women's and men's lay fellowships. A Commission for Racial Justice announced and advocated UCC social causes; and, slowly, a Coordinating Center for Women emerged.

Seminaries that had formerly been supported directly by the Evangelical and Reformed Church learned painfully to develop endowments on the Congregational Christian model, and to reach out for the support of local churches. Most disappointing from an Evangelical and Reformed perspective, the new church had no theological commission and not much of a desire for one, and devoted little attention to liturgy and worship concerns, although the Office for Church Life and Leadership published a *Manual on the Ministry* in 1977 and a new *Book of Worship* in 1986. Matters of historical importance were poorly supported by the denomination, with the happy exception of the Amistad Research Center in New Orleans; and little attention was paid structurally to ecumenical affairs. Their tradition of strong presidential leadership led Evangelical and Reformed people to wonder why so little authority was invested in top administrative positions, including the Presidency.

Yet these criticisms and reservations were but part of the growing pains of a fellowship seeking new ways to work and worship, and they were, in fact, very little different, except in emphasis, from Congregational Christian criticisms. There was a troublesome lack of communication between different entities within the United Church of Christ (evidence of a triumph of autonomy?), but there was growing goodwill and comfort among UCC members and agencies who felt themselves growing closer. Even the 1989 decision to move most church offices from New York City to Cleveland seemed to reflect increasing unity. At the same time, a host of mutually contradictory caucuses emerged, which one could perhaps expect to see more fully represented in a "liberal" religious group than anywhere else. The future was as always uncertain, but one can safely conclude that some Evangelical and Reformed perspectives, among others, were being haltingly adopted by the United Church of Christ, something new was emerging as well.

Three Decades of Progress Toward Unity

The United Church of Christ, begun in 1957 with an ecumenical commitment to church union, adopted the motto, "United and Uniting." This sentiment faced difficult times as UCC people have tried sometimes only halfheartedly to practice it through the past three decades and their cycles of tranquility, political protest against an unpopular war, and renewed conservatism accompanied by crises within mainline churches.

The United Church of Christ began in what many regard as an idyllic era—young men who had helped win World War II returned to begin families amid suburban prosperity and rapid, sometimes indiscriminate, church growth. Despite delays caused by both the war and litigation, the UCC moved ahead steadily to organize its new Conferences; and its national officers and agencies cooperated in restructuring, helping to meet needs in responsible ways.

The wide acceptance received by the 1959 *Statement of Faith* indicated the UCC interest in confessionally stressing "testimony" rather than "tests" of doctrine. Only later was the lack of inclusive language recognized there and in the church's 1974 hymnal. Feminist issues emerged somewhat slowly, in spite of the church's commitment to women's ordination, which can be traced to 1853 and pioneering Antoinette Brown. The discontinuance of national women's and men's church organizations by the UCC was not all gain, on the other hand. By the 1980s, a high 15 percent of UCC clergy and half of UCC ministerial students were women. Increasing leadership roles for women had brought about important changes in the denomination.

Responding to the civil rights movement, the UCC began modeling itself as a "justice church." Andrew Young, Ben Chavis, and others came to symbolize the empathy of many UCC people with Martin Luther King Jr.'s work. Later in the 1970s,

U.S. involvement in the Vietnam War troubled UCC folks, much as it did other Americans, and support was often expressed for the student protesters. In theological education and elsewhere, the activist stance of protesters temporarily changed the character of educational institutions as well as the nature of the church and ministry. At times, activism had the effect of encouraging both ministerial burnout and excessive criticism of traditional church life. Many recognized a certain lack of clarity and consistency in the theological perspectives of some UCC leaders and people in that era. The UCC sometimes became disillusioned because it had lost part of its Reformed and Puritan heritage, including a meaningful doctrine of the Fall. Nevertheless, the UCC attempted to maintain its up-to-date and even avant-garde attitude toward social concerns.

With the victory of the Vietcong and U.S. withdrawal from Vietnam, and with Ronald Reagan's election, the country faced a resurging "evangelical" movement, which was not well represented within the UCC. These events helped bring about an unprecedented collapse of the mainline church in terms of both morale and numbers. The United Church of Christ, Episcopal Church, and Presbyterian Church were especially adversely affected. One sign of the UCC effort to respond to the new situation was its effort to begin new congregations, which had stopped after the growth of the 1960s. More than two million dollars has been expended annually for new church starts in the 1980s. The Biblical Witness Fellowship movement has reacted against liberal stances of the denomination on social issues, and argues for maintaining solid theological foundations of the denomination in scripture and tradition.

Another way in which the UCC attempted to respond to societal changes was by recognizing openly the new pluralistic character of world and national society and churches, and being receptive to new people and new forms of social life. At the same time, there was a return to more traditional liturgical concerns, use of the lectionary in preaching, Bible study and exegesis, and experiments in small group religious life. Crises of the 1980s, while causing some discouragement, also provided an opportunity for the UCC to resume its responsive, activist role, and to call upon its reserves of church loyalty and stability, which many people at the grassroots level thought had been neglected for too long. Clearly, the UCC in the 1980s was seeking opportunities amid crises to carry on its mission.

But at the same time, the church's ecumenical outreach appeared to some to be less vital than in earlier decades, in spite of the powerful continuing growth of ecumenism, including a new covenant-style of cooperating with the Disciples/Christians. The future of the United Church of Christ continues to be uncertain, but changes, opportunites, and difficulties may be counted on to present themselves.

United and Uniting: A Conciliar Ecclesiology

A major issue throughout the history of the United Church of Christ and its predecessor bodies has been the nature of the church. In 1984, the report of official ecumenical conversations between the Lutheran and the Reformed churches[2] attempted to exclude the UCC from the conversation on the grounds that it is not one church and that it places creedal formulations under the authority of the local congregation. The 1989 UCC General Synod in Fort Worth, Texas, responded by saying that the United Church of Christ desires to continue those ecumenical conversations and is indeed one church in continuity with ancient creeds and confessions.

Gabriel Fackre among others attempted to support the UCC (especially E and R) conviction that a confessional perspective does, indeed, exist with the church. He described it as "in a *form* of a modest charter, occasional articulation, and broad ethos of belief, worship, and behavior, and in a *substance* of conviction focused on the classical narrative of faith with its call to join its Author and chief Actor in that epic, especially in its 'struggle for justice and peace.'"3

The late Louis H. Gunnemann, who until his death in November, 1989, was a spokesperson for the Evangelical and Reformed perspective on ecclesiology, described UCC polity as *polity-in-process*, shaped in the *covenantal* tradition and carried out in a *conciliar mode*.4 His first point stresses the UCC's engagement in a new and unfinished effort to organize the visible community of faith. (This repudiates the notion that autonomy is the one non-negotiable principle upon which the UCC is built.)

Gunnemann favored use of the familiar Congregational terminology of covenantal polity, by which he meant that it is the initiating act of God in Christ upon which the church depends. The covenant model thus accentuates the freedom that is to be exercised in responsibility to the community, in the manner of Christ. It requires living for the sake of the "other," in mutual accountability, in the spirit of Christ, and without vesting authority in any human institution or office. Where grace rules, coercive pressures of majority and minority concerns must give way to the commitment of the welfare of the "other."

Finally, Gunnemann thought that the United Church of Christ acts in a conciliar way, that is, subordinate to one another in Christ. In that mode, contingent authority is exercised by the congregation, which functions under the headship of Christ through the presence and work of the Spirit. Thus, magisterial authority is repudiated in favor of the absolute ministerial authority of Christ. Through the gifts of the Spirit, the life of the community is exercised as *communion*, in which order and freedom characterize the fulfillment of "the priesthood of every believer" in the manner of Christ's priesthood. Gunnemann believed that a proper emphasis upon conciliar church order expresses a fundamental principle of the gospel. It is encouraging that this principle has been approved universally in the modern ecumenical movement.

We can see, then, that the United Church of Christ is in touch with the basic truth behind ecumenism, and, rather than having a weak or wavering ecclesiology, affirms the basic authority of Christ ministering to all people in ways not limited even by the structures of democratic process. The ministering headship of Christ makes possible a developing, covenantal, and conciliar tradition ready to move toward further unity in the spirit of Christ, and based upon a sound emphasis on congregations finding direction under Christ's headship.

Like the Congregationalists, Evangelical and Reformed people have contributed notably toward developing this faith and polity, and it is in appreciation for their history, theology, and church life that this reissued volume appears.

LOWELL H. ZUCK
Webster Groves, Missouri
November 7, 1989

Notes

[1] *The Faith We Proclaim,* edited by Elmer J. F. Arndt (Philadelphia: Christian Education Press, 1960).

[2] *An Invitation to Action: The Lutheran-Reformed Dialogue,* edited by James E. Andrews and Joseph A. Burgess (Philadelphia: Fortress Press, 1984).

[3] Gabriel Fackre, "The Confessional Nature of the United Church of Christ," *New Conversations* (Winter/Spring 1988), 20.

[4] Louis H. Gunnemann, "The Polity of the United Church of Christ," *New Conversations (Winter/Spring 1988), 27.*

Foreword

IN THE PAGES of this book will be found the story of a body of American Christians with a tradition as long and ancient as that of any in all Christendom, but with a distinctive institutional history which has probably been shorter than that of any. For in less than a decade after the establishment of the Evangelical and Reformed Church was signalized on June 26, 1934 at Cleveland, Ohio, conversations had begun with representatives of the General Council of the Congregational Christian Churches which eventuated in the formal establishment of the United Church of Christ, again at Cleveland, Ohio, on June 25, 1957.

The life of the Evangelical and Reformed Church may thus be said to have covered the brief period of twenty-three years and one day. There were several years of negotiation and planning which preceded the beginning of that life. There would be a period of perhaps five years afterward until that life could be "translated" into the larger life of the United Church of Christ.

The record of that less-than-a-quarter-century of institutional existence will be found in the last two chapters of this book. But quite properly these chapters are preceded by ten which clearly reflect the rooting of the Evangelical and Reformed Church in the New Testament revelation of God in his Son Jesus Christ, and in the long history of the "people of God" at least as far back as the day Abraham "went out, not knowing whither he went."

More precisely, the first ten chapters tell the story of the European backgrounds of this church from the days of the Protestant Reformation in Europe and of the transplanting thereof onto

American soil through the migrations of the succeeding centuries. In that story it will become clear that the genius of the Evangelical and Reformed Church and its predecessor peoples is to be found in their stubborn insistence that the word of God in the Scriptures, as progressively revealed to his people through the guidance of the Holy Spirit, must be the ultimate authority for their life and faith, and that, however gratefully appreciative they are of the historic creeds, confessions, and institutions of Christian history, none of these may restrict the response of God's people to the further leadings of his Spirit.

There is an interesting provision in the Basis of Union and Interpretations on which the United Church of Christ was founded. It asserts (in *Interpretation f*): "In consummating this union the Congregational Christian Churches and the Evangelical and Reformed church are uniting without break in their respective historic continuities." This provision will mean different things to different people. Some will pass it over as ambiguous. Others will dismiss it lightly as a gratuitous recital of the obvious. Still others will discern in it an assertion of one great truth about the history of ideas and convictions and of the institutions in which they are clothed: for the human record and for as far as the human eye can see and the human mind discern, ideas, convictions, and institutions have no beginning and no end. They have their rise out of the fathomless depths of the past; they flow through a period which is relatively easy of definition and description; and then they lose themelves, yet in this also find themselves, by entering into, contributing to, and becoming part of something bigger than, but by so much not alien to, all that they were in the time of their observable existence.

All this is herein presupposed of the Evangelical and Reformed Church. It has rejoiced in its inheritance from the prophets and apostles, the saints and martyrs, from the whole Christian church throughout all the world, and from the holy life, redeeming death, and triumphant resurrection of the church's

Lord. It has been enriched by the doctrinal and devotional influences of Wittenberg and Geneva, by the unique admixture of German pietism and the humanism of Holland and its lesser counterpart in Switzerland, and by the ameliorating spirit of Melanchthon and the writers of the Heidelberg Catechism.

On American soil its pastors and teachers and its more devout and knowing laity appear to have kept instinctively away from every extreme of rigid rationalizing and the tendency to reduce Christian faith to a series of theological propositions. The Evangelical and Reformed Church and its predecessor communions have steadfastly contended that our experience of God in Christ is always greater than, and beyond, our descriptive powers, and that, therefore, the faith we proclaim is, as the bond of Christian fellowship and the basis of church union, prior, central, and superior to the doctrinal formulations and political forms which each succeeding generation give to that faith.

This is the heritage which the Evangelical and Reformed Church has rejoiced in. This is the treasure, albeit in earthen vessels, which the Evangelical and Reformed Church brings into the United Church of Christ.

For the sponsoring of this volume the church is indebted to its Historical Society, and for the writing of its chapters, with exception of the last, to historians who have been most active in the Society. It was they, especially through their present chairman and his predecessor, respectively David Dunn and Carl E. Schneider, who insisted that the President of the Church should write the story of the last twenty years, on the ground that, earlier as a member of the General Council, for three years as First Vice-President, for the past seven in his present office, he had taken part in the planning and decision-making which determined the direction the life and work of the church have taken.

He will only remark that it was far easier to live through the period than it was to reduce its portrayal to words—and fewer than fifteen thousand words at that. He will conclude with a doxology the substance of which he has almost invariably uttered in addressing local churches, synods, and the General Synod, and which the writing of the twelfth chapter again and again has recalled: the Evangelical and Reformed Church, often though it has failed its Lord or followed him only from afar, has infinite cause for gratitude and praise to Jesus Christ.

JAMES E. WAGNER

The Authors

BOTH THE Evangelical Synod and the Reformed Church had historical agencies before the union of 1934. George W. Richards, for forty years Professor of Church History at the Theological Seminary at Lancaster, had sparked the Reformed Commission, while Carl E. Schneider, who occupied the corresponding chair at Eden Seminary, headed the Historical Commission of the Evangelical Synod. From these two groups the merged church chose men to constitute its Historical Commission, with Dr. Richards as chairman. This commission was renamed the Historial *Committee* at the General Synod at Tiffin in 1953, and was given the task of preparing a history of the two uniting communions up to and including their coming together as one denomination. The successive periods in the lives of the two churches were assigned to members of the committee.

Dr. Richards died in 1955. Dr. Schneider, who succeeded him as chairman, was called to serve the ecumenical cause in Europe for a protracted period. The General Synod in 1956 at Lancaster made the Historical Society, founded in 1863 by the Reformed Church but after the merger expanded to include Evangelical interests as well, the official historical agency succeeding the Historical Committee. Dr. David Dunn, as president of the Historical Society, succeeded H.M.J. Klein, Emeritus Professor of History at Franklin and Marshall College, who served in this capacity for twenty-five years.

PAUL N. CRUSIUS, whose painstaking work in preparing chapters 8, 9, and 10, represents his last literary labor. He died on May 4, 1959. A native of Buffalo, New York, he received a Ph.D.

from Harvard in 1936 and a D.D. from Eden Seminary in 1955. His first and only pastorate was at St. Paul's Church, Downers' Grove, Illinois, from which he was called to the faculty of Elmhurst College in 1919; he served there until his retirement in 1956. His understanding and loving treatment of the Evangelical institutions and activities from 1866 to 1934 is quite expressive of his devoted and friendly life of service.

DAVID DUNN, author of chapters 3 and 4, was born in Huntingdon, Pennsylvania, July 15, 1891. He was a graduate of Franklin and Marshall College and of the Yale Divinity School. Graduate work was done at Edinburgh, Oxford, and Chicago. After pastorates in Turtle Creek and Harrisburg, Pennsylvania, he was called to the chair of Church History in the Theological Seminary at Lancaster in 1939 and served as dean after 1946. He retired from these positions September 1, 1961. Died September 4, 1970.

JOSIAS FRIEDLI, Emeritus Professor of Church History at the Mission House Theological Seminary, contributed chapter 5 on the Reformed Church in the West (i.e., west of the Ohio-Pennsylvania line). Born at Davos, Switzerland in 1877, he was educated in the Mission House Academy, College, and Seminary. After serving pastorates in Ohio, Indiana, and Wisconsin and as Secretary of Home Missions for the Synod of the Northwest, he was called to the professorship of Church History in the Mission House Seminary in 1925 and served until his retirement in 1952. After retirement, he supplied four Wisconsin churches in succession. Died January 19, 1969.

THEOPHIL W. MENZEL, author of chapters 6 and 7, a son of Paul A. Menzel of the Evangelical Synod's Foreign Mission Board, was born in Washington, D.C., in 1902. He was educated at George Washington University, Washington, D.C., and Washington University, St. Louis, Missouri, and received his theological training at Eden Seminary and at the Yale Divinity School.

After teaching at Elmhurst College and Eden Seminary, eight years in each school, he returned to the pastorate—at Bethel Church, Manchester, Michigan in 1948. He served as editor of *Daily Talks with God* and the *Daily Devotional Guide* and translated works of Wobbermin and Andrae. Died October 7, 1973.

CARL E. SCHNEIDER, who traced in chapter 11 our "Journey into Union," was Professor of Church History at Eden Theological Seminary. He was born at Jefferson City, Missouri, March 24, 1890, was educated at Elmhurst and Eden, and came to the faculty of the latter institution in 1918. Taking graduate work at Leipzig, Tuebingen, and Berlin universities, he received the M.A. degree from Washington University in 1934 and the Ph.D. degree from the University of Chicago in 1935. In 1939 was published his definitive history of the early period of Evangelical Synod history, *The German Church on the American Frontier.* Died July 29, 1981.

WILLIAM TOTH was born in Rath Bereg, Hungary, February 25, 1905. He graduated from Franklin and Marshall College and received his Ph.D. from Yale University in 1941. After pastorates in South Norwalk, Connecticut, and Harrisburg, Pennsylvania, he was called in 1946 to head the History Department at Franklin and Marshall College. His many contacts with the thought and life of the European continent qualified him to interpret the European background and early colonial period of Reformed Church history as he did in chapters 1 and 2 of this volume. Died June 21, 1963.

JAMES E. WAGNER, former President of the Evangelical and Reformed Church and Co-President of the United Church of Christ, supplied the Foreword, and reviewed in chapter 12 the growth and development of the merged Evangelical and Reformed Church. Born May 16, 1900 in Altoona, Pennsylvania, and a graduate of Findlay College and the Lancaster Theological Seminary, he served as pastor of St. Peter's Church, Lancaster,

for twenty-two years before being called to the leadership of the
denomination. With the aid of the Ecumenical Travel Fund he
traveled to the mission fields and to Europe and did much not
only to widen the horizons of the denomination but to make its
voice known and its influence felt in national affairs. Died October 20, 1985.

LOWELL H. ZUCK, author of the introduction to the reissued
edition, was born at Ephrata, Pennsylvania, June 24, 1926. He is
a graduate of Elizabethtown College, Bethany Theological Seminary, and Yale University, from where he received the Ph.D.
degree in 1955. He has taught at Eden Theological Seminary
since that time. Author of *Socially Responsible Believers* (1986),
he has been a member of the Evangelical and Reformed Historical Society executive committee since 1959, and is a member of
the United Church of Christ Historical Council.

PART ONE

The Reformed Church in the United States

1

European Background—Reformed

THE ROOTS of the Evangelical and Reformed Church lie deep in the soil of old Europe. Transplanting into the environment of the New World began before the end of the seventeenth century, a generation or so after the Congregationalists, Scotch-Irish Presbyterians, Baptists, and Anglicans of England had already blazed trails. Merchants in England, desiring to increase their economic possibilities across the sea and aware of the value of human labor, left the doors of the new continent wide open for people to enter. Toward the close of the century this open-door policy was not only proving advantageous in terms of economic gain; it was also moving in harmony with that humane outlook which permeated the reorientation of English life after the Glorious Revolution of 1688. Politically speaking, moreover, the control of immense territories in New England, along the Atlantic coastline to South Carolina, and westward into unexplored stretches of land bordering French possessions along the Mississippi, precluded any immediate possibility of being dislodged by any foreign powers. Thus, because of the relative security of life and property, beckoning hands were extended to one and all who were willing to seek their fortunes under the established authorities of the English government on this side of the Atlantic.

Our history begins with the German people who accepted the hospitality of these shores. Among them were Mennonites, German Baptists, Brethren, Dunkers, Amish, and Moravian groups that belonged to the fringes of German Protestantism. The majority stemmed from a Reformed or Lutheran background, which caused them to be designated as *church people* to distinguish them from the so-called *sects* that did not enjoy any official status in the homeland. Germans could be found among the earliest settlers—humble artisans in Jamestown, more vigorous individuals like the astute soldier and statesman Peter Minuit in New Amsterdam, adventurers and explorers like John Lederer in the Virginia colony, or scholars like Peter Fabian, a Swiss German who was a member of an expedition sent out in 1663 by the English Carolina Company to explore the Carolinas. Although a considerable sprinkling of Germans made their appearance early, the tide of immigration did not begin to flow until after the founding of Germantown in 1683 as a permanent settlement of Germans from the Palatinate.

German Immigration

From this time on, successive waves of German immigration touched our shores throughout the eighteenth century. A general idea of its force may be gained from the statistical picture in Pennsylvania. By 1727, when the migration became extensive, there were 20,000 Germans in Penn's colony; up to 1742, something like 18,000 were added. Six thousand more arrived by the end of 1748, and between 1749 and 1754 nearly 32,000 came through the port of Philadelphia alone. So numerous were the arrivals of these foreigners by 1727 that the Provincial Council deemed it necessary to require shipmasters to make lists of all immigrants and to have them sign an oath of allegiance to the

King of England. In a testimony before the British House of Commons in 1776, Benjamin Franklin declared that of the 160,000 white people in the province of Pennsylvania, about one third were Germans. A conservative estimate of the German population for the thirteen colonies at the outbreak of the Revolution has been set at 225,000.

How many Reformed people come in this vast migration? No one will ever know. Concerning the most populous settlements in Pennsylvania, it was reported in 1730 that "the Reformed holding to the old confession constituted more than one half of the whole number (of Germans), being about 15,000." In the middle of the eighteenth century, the estimate was 30,000 for Pennsylvania alone; at the end, the number of adherents in the organized church may have passed beyond 40,000. This much is known for a certainty, that while numerically the left-wingers surpassed the *church people* in the beginning stages, the Reformed element forged ahead as long as the migration was predominantly from Swiss and Rhenish lands. Their numbers lessened as other parts of Germany contracted the fever to move; then the Lutherans came to constitute the larger element. Not since the days of the early middle ages had such a shake-up of peoples taken place on German territory.

The area from which the migration poured was located chiefly along both sides of the Rhine River and its tributaries, the Main and Neckar rivers. It embraced territories extending from the junction of the Moselle and the Rhine south to Basel, Switzerland, and from Zweibruecken as far east as Bayreuth. Sections of the modern state of Bavaria, the districts of Spires, Worms, Hesse-Darmstadt, Zweibruecken, Nassau, Alsace, and Baden were heavily affected; also in Wuerttemberg, the districts of Darmstadt, Hanau, and Franconia. But the principal source was an area about the size of New Jersey called the Palatinate, which accounts for the name "Palatine" being indiscriminately used by colonial Englishmen to designate any German colonist. Mannheim, Worms, and Heidelberg were within its borders, the last an ancient city proud of being the capital and the home of one of the seven electors of Germany. From the Swiss-German population the most extensive outpouring was from the cantons of Basel, Lucerne, and Bern directly, as well as indirectly from among those who in the previous century had availed themselves of opportunities for new settlers in depopulated Germany. Another source has been traced to Emden in the North, which had early become a refuge for the uprooted Reformed of all lands. By the time of the Revolutionary War, scarcely a community existed among the German territories that was not making its swelling contribution of peoples to the varied enterprises of the English colonies.

The Reasons for the Great Migration

Along with their Protestant coreligionists, the Reformed people shared the motives—political, religious, social, and economic—which lay behind the great migration. The general climate of life in Germany, which was the cumulative product of centuries, had deeply impressed itself upon the character of all, and in a special way upon those who, out of a genuine sense of conviction and an inherited feeling of ethnic oneness, threw themselves into the ferment of historical forces. The Reformed people made a history and were, in turn, molded by the political, religious, and social factors of continental history that in their interconnectedness form a necessary backdrop to our understanding of the unique character with which they started a new life in a new country.

Politically, the European continent of the sixteenth century was being transformed from the universal Holy Roman Empire into national states. The German territories, constituting the last bastion of a vanishing political idea, naturally were tempted to yield to the contemporary current of nationalism. Aroused by fear or hate, a desire for adventure or security, or a hope for profit, the territorial rulers asserted their rights to power. This aim was supported chiefly by townsmen, long enemies of feudal decentralization and keenly sensitive to the advantages derived from centralizing the functions of government in the person of strong rulers. Using every opportunity to increase the lands, power, and prestige of their dynasty, princes of the land, over three hundred in number, began to form political combinations for the protection of gains achieved and the realization of ambitions strongly encouraged by unsettled conditions. The process of forming territorial sovereignties led to frequent armed conflicts, which resulted in mounting devastation of property. These fratricidal conflicts were supported by the religious preferences of the contending parties zealous to protect the Protestant reinterpretation of Christianity or to defend the old, and, to an equal degree, by the expanding capitalistic economy.

The high-water mark of this civil turmoil was the so-called Schmalkaldic War (1546-47), in which Protestants led by John Frederick of electoral Saxony and Philip of Hesse lined up against the Catholic princes under the leadership of Emperor Charles V. Inner political cleavages were not healed by the ensuing peace in spite of its assuring freedom to Lutherans, but were rather confirmed in the recognition of the territorial principle. This political fragmentation, all the more dangerous in its failure to accord rights to princes who had embraced the Reformed faith, subsequently turned Germany into the battleground of nations.

The many problems left unsolved at Augsburg finally erupted within the German state system and evolved into the most extensive and barbarous political struggle between Catholic France and the Catholic Hapsburgs. No part of Germany remained unscathed, and after thirty years of unceasing warfare, involving plunder, rapine, intrigues, and constant death, all Germany lay prostrate. Business had succumbed completely; schools and churches were left without leaders; cities and villages smoldered in ashes; and once-fertile farms sank into unbelievable neglect. The extent of physical destruction staggers the imagination, and the toll in human lives remains forever unknown. Contact with the French brought into the country French manners and customs, much that was alien to the old German outlook, and accelerated the process of an inner spiritual disintegration that war by virtue of its character had inevitably quickened. Historians agree that the aftereffects of this war thwarted German life for a hundred years.

One reassuring feature offset this national paralysis, namely, that the Peace of Westphalia (1648) formally settled the major religious conflicts that had originally provided animus for the undergirding of political aspirations. The Reformed faith received recognition at last and the right to change religion was permitted, with the significant provision that in the event of change the minorities of the other faith which had existed before 1624 were to be tolerated. Religious allegiance, at least on paper, was finally separated from political interests and considered a matter of individual conscience, although churches continued to remain under state control. This religious solution served as the pathmaker for a later, more pronounced individualism. The precarious balance of power established by the Peace of Westphalia did not insulate the German people against possible attack on the part of an ambitious absolute sovereign, who was ready and willing to take advantage of a crippled "state" and who had at his beck and call a bureaucracy subservient to his princely aspirations for power and aggrandizement.

Such a one Louis XIV of France proved to be before the seventeenth century had run its course. Imbued with the idea of divine-right authority, he challenged the political security of Europe with an aggressive policy bent on obtaining wider boundaries and greater prestige. Among the objects of his quest to realize France's "natural boundaries," Rhenish Germany lay astride his path. As early as 1686 the League of Augsburg was formed by Bavaria, Saxony, and the Palatinate, which sought, with the aid of other European countries, to counterbalance Louis' designs. On the strength of a dubious claim to some areas and a trumped-up charge of impending Hapsburg aggression, Louis' armies invaded the Palatinate with some 50,000 men under General Montclas and, later, with the forces under command of General Melac.

The war was carried on with varied success and loss, but in the end what could make up for the fact that the French generals made the German soil alone the field of their operations? Worms, Spires, Frankenthal, Alzei, Oberwesel, Andernach, Kochheim, and Kreuznach were reduced to ashes. In 1689 the cavalry of General Melac surrounded the country around Heidelberg and set fire to the towns of Rohrbach, Nuszloch, Wislocj, Kirchheim, Eppenheim, Neckarhausen, and many others. Heidelberg suffered greatly, but the castle held out. Stuttgart and Asperg, after a fruitless resistance, were taken. Five columns overwhelmed the German borderlands with fire and sword. More than 1,200 communities, Catholic and Protestant indiscriminately, fell victim to wanton devastation. An historian writes:

> The most cruel of these plunderers was the infamous General Melac. . . . The scheme of turning the Palatinate into a desert was fulfilled. Not merely the houses and cottages were burnt down, but everything which could serve for support was destroyed; all the vines were torn up, the fruit trees all cut down. Four hundred thousand inhabitants of Baden and the Palatinate were rendered entirely destitute, the women subjected to brutal treatment; the men who attempted to defend their wives and daughters or sweethearts were massacred, others driven from their towns and villages into the snow and ice of the winter to look for shelter.

By the Treaty of Ryswick (1697) military operations were replaced by the French occupation of the Palatinate, Breisach,

Freiburg, Phillipsburg, and Strassburg. The French language took the place of Latin in the transaction of official affairs. The Jesuits redoubled their efforts to win back Protestants to their faith, if necessary, by force. Philip, the Catholic puppet ruler of the Palatinate, enforced his right to impose his religion throughout his new possessions, especially since over 1,922 places in the Palatinate had already been re-Catholicized during the course of the war. His court, dominated by the Jesuits, appealed to the ancient principle of *cuius regio, eius religio* (the ruler determines the religion of a territory) to thrust disabilities upon all who would not willingly surrender their faith. New mistrust and religious discord were again quickened in the wake of political changes.

After a brief interval came the War of the Spanish Succession (1701-14), during which western Germany once more experienced the devastations of armed conflict. Much fighting took place in this area with movements of troops back and forth. The French under Claude Louis Hector de Villars ravaged the Upper Rhine and Swabia with impunity. The gallant but old and ineffective leader of the Germans, Louis of Baden, failed to rally sufficient support to cope with the French. The terrible winter of 1708 and 1709, in which the olives and vines were killed by the frost, together with the failures of summer harvests, added to the distress of the people. Particularly the Rhenish provinces were exhausted. The victory of Marlborough over Villars at Malplaquet in September, 1709 practically finished the war.

In the commotion of the times little attention was excited by the bands of German peoples who were quietly leaving the Rhenish provinces. Variously estimated from 2,000 to 32,000, they sought refuge in London between May and November of 1709, joining the fifty who had earlier spearheaded this exodus. Among them were people of the Reformed faith, who would be followed in increasing numbers throughout the century.

Religious Backgrounds

These Reformed people, in their religious backgrounds, could look back to a heritage historically as old as, if not older than, that of many English religious groups in the colonies, with the exception of Roman Catholics. Their religious complexion, in distinction from that of the various streams of people in the English colonies, may be said to have been derived mainly from the Swiss and German modifications of Protestant reform in the sixteenth century.

Both in Switzerland and in Germany common elements of faith and practice bound together the various shades and gradations among those who, early in the sixteenth century, were roughly distinguished from Lutherans by the name "Reformed." They held the Lord's Supper to be a memorial act as understood by Ulrich Zwingli or, following John Calvin, a sign and seal of the spiritual presence of Jesus Christ. They encouraged laymen to think for themselves and claim their rights in church government. In disesteem they toned down the significance of liturgical forms and highlighted, in one form or another, the doctrine of predestination. They considered discipline important for both clergy and laity; they therefore organized on the congregational level a body known as the *consistorium,* made up of pastors, teachers, elders, and deacons, and on a regional level a jurisdictional body generally referred to as a classis or synod. The concept of the priesthood of all believers was interpreted to imply the assumption of solemn responsibilities by church members in affairs of church and state. Yet no such entity as a German Reformed Church can be found in the Reformation period. There existed only territorial organizations exhibiting basic similarities of belief and spirit with regional modifications of both.

The Swiss-German church developed its genius out of the religious resources of Zwingli, a German, and Calvin, a son of France. The former initiated the movement, while the latter provided a directional force, in doctrine and organization, that led to consolidation. Organized on a cantonal basis, the synods maintained fraternal relations, resisted Lutheranism and Catholicism, elaborated upon the inherited doctrines, and generally supplied a theological leadership which was transferred to the Reformed centers of Holland only in the early seventeenth century. The *Second Helvetic Confession,* predominantly Calvinistic and adopted in 1566, was considered by all the Swiss Reformed churches as a guide to doctrine and practice. Among other things, the confession took a strong position for simplicity in worship on the ground that the multiplication of rites reduces the liberty of a Christian and supplants faith by ceremonies.

The waves of Protestant scholasticism, so strong in the seventeenth century, did not leave the Swiss churches unaffected. The philosophical methods of René Descartes invaded Protestant theology, and the result was an emphasis on the form of doctrine rather than upon the life in it. In the ensuing crisis the Swiss churches adopted the *Helvetic Consensus* (not to be confused with the *Confession*), sharply accentuating its opposition to the current popularity of the doctrine of general atonement. This so-called scholastic Calvinism, after about fifty years, gave way partly to the religious tendency of pietism and partly to the movement triggering an ecumenical approach to resolve the disunity existing over dogmatic differences among Christians. The vitality of one's faith was to be regarded as the test of Christian fidelity, according to the Pietists. Young Samuel Guldin, destined to be the first Reformed minister to arrive in the English colonies, was among the enthusiastic propagators of this view and wrote in defense of it. At the end of the century, when migrations from German-Swiss areas began, the religious atmosphere was electric with controversy over these matters. But this situation would not have driven the masses from their beloved country so much as burdens of a social and economic character.

The second and major stream of German emigrants issued from German lands proper where a distinct brand of the Reformed faith had come into being. This unique religious development was associated, in western Germany, chiefly with the electoral principality of the Palatinate, which in the course of the economic revolution of the times emerged as a new frontier in Europe. Western Germany had developed into a focal point of trade from the east and the point of contact for movements both eastward and to the promising New World markets beyond the mouth of the Rhine. The elector of the Palatinate enjoyed a commanding position politically and culturally.

Martin Luther's views quickly won currency in this area but in their adoption underwent a modification by virtue of the nearness of Strassburg, where Martin Bucer held forth, in favor of the more conciliatory religious position of Philipp Melanchthon, a native of these parts. Geographical and cultural ties with German Switzerland opened the way for Zwinglianism and Calvinism. Zwingli had many friends and admirers here, especially the Landgrave, Philip of Hesse, whose labors to reconcile the contending religious parties are well known. Democratic elements in the free cities of southern Germany sensed in the views of Melanchthon a middle ground that retained the essentials of reform without yielding to Romanists or left-wing radicals and the promise of assuring the prosperity of citizens in a climate of religious agreement.

The attempt to clarify the Protestant position, however, resulted in theological discussions which reached disquieting proportions. The nature of the Lord's Supper was the chief element of contention. Extreme Lutherans, led by the fanatical Hesshus, professor at the University of Heidelberg, insisted that Christ was in the elements—"in, with, and under"—a formula to which his ardent supporters added "round and round," while Melanchthonian and Reformed loyalists stressed the necessity of faith as a basis for communion with Christ. Hesshus snatched the communion cup from the hand of Klebitz, the Reformed deacon, and when Elector Frederick William III returned from the Diet of Augsburg in the summer of 1559 he found his country seething with the "madness of theologians."

To allay the resultant confusion the elector invited new leaders, among others Zacharias Ursinus and Caspar Olevianus, whose task was to establish reconciliation. Both were ideally suited, by temperament and training, to create a religious climate in harmony with Frederick's policies. The resultant church may be regarded as the "mother" of the German Reformed type, which gradually secured adoption elsewhere—Nassau (1571), which had strong connections with the Netherlands through the House of Orange; Bremen (1581), Zweibruecken (1588), Anhalt (1597), Lippe (1600), Hesse-Kassel (1604), Cleves, Julich, and Berg, and most significantly for future developments, electoral Brandenburg (1613). Neither Geneva nor Wittenberg could claim victory in molding the spirit and thought of the German Reformed people; rather, something new emerged which reflected carefully screened elements from both sides in a uniquely different pattern. The main outlines are contained in the *Heidelberg Catechism* (1563), the *Palatinate Liturgy* (1563), and a consistorial order published in 1564.

The Heidelberg Catechism, often regarded as "the fruit and flower of the whole German and French Reformation," stimulates the conviction that Christianity, vastly more than a system of doctrine, must be a Godward orientation of the soul of man that culminates in the transformation of human activities according to the designs of God. Its genius lay in the irenic spirit that cultivated the love of essentials—beyond the churches the church and beyond the scriptures the historic stream of faith and experience. "It was Lutheran inwardness, Melanchthonian clearness, Zwinglian simplicity, and Calvinistic fire, harmoniously blended."

Quickly adopted even beyond the Rhine region, the Catechism fulfilled a threefold office as a book of instruction for the young, a confession of faith for the community, and an introduction to theology.

The Palatinate Liturgy prescribed the manner of worship. With a remarkable spirit of independence, it borrowed from the forms prevalent in Holland and Geneva. To directions for worship in the churches on ordinary and holy days specific forms were added. Readings from the Catechism were made mandatory preceding the sermon. Tables were to be used in place of altars, zinc vessels instead of baptismal fonts, ordinary cups rather than chalices, and broken bread instead of wafers in the Lord's Supper. Heavy and didactic in style, the Liturgy, unlike the Catechism, did not win universal acceptance; but it was instrumental in consolidating the realm of Frederick William.

The government of the church was based on the *Kirchenrathsordnung*, or order of the church council. This made the Elector responsible for the spiritual and ecclesiastical life of his people. Church affairs, however, were administered by a consistory, composed of six persons—three religious and three secular, appointed by the Elector. Each district or classis was under the special oversight of a superintendent. Synods, comprised of preachers and two lay and two ministerial delegates of the *Kirchenrath*, met annually for the purpose of reviewing the general work of the churches. A General Synod of all the superintendents assembled at the instance of the *Kirchenrath*. This polity, with some unessential deviations, was followed elsewhere in German Reformed regions.

The foundations were thus laid, but the building did not proceed without difficulties. Attacks and counterattacks, surcharged with fire, appeared in theological circles between Lutherans and Reformed. The Lutheran *Formula of Concord* (1580) failed to bring religious peace. Noteworthy in this period is the publication of *Irenicum* (1614-15) by the Reformed theological professor at Heidelberg, who offered a detailed proposal for Protestant union through a universal synod, in which individual religious groups would be represented by "the best and weightiest men from every province and nation of the Christian world." The Protestant cause, by virtue of the unfriendly relations of Lutherans and Reformed, was exposed to irreparable losses in the Thirty Years' War (1618-48), somewhat significantly compensated, however, by the legal recognition of Calvinists on the same basis with Lutherans in the Empire.

A half-century of peaceful coexistence, dictated largely, but not entirely, by the paralysis that resulted from the war, was followed by the terrible persecutions to which reference has been made in sketching the political backgrounds. The people lost their churches, schools, and cemeteries in addition to personal possessions that had vanished in the wars. As a result of governmental policies, an electoral edict in 1719 forebade them to use the Heidelberg Catechism and forced them to surrender the Church of the Holy Ghost at Heidelberg, which had stood as a venerable symbol of the Reformed faith for generations. In short, they were completely at the mercy of the Jesuits who controlled the Catholic electors. During the reign of Elector Charles Phillip (1716-42) such oppressions obliged one fourth of the population to emigrate to other lands, many to the English colonies in North America. Princes were determined to use the state-church principle as an instrument of social control; a growing sectarian movement was challenging the power of the state church; and the persecuted elements sought refuge where it was offered. Around the year 1700 people might still quarrel about salvation by faith, election, grace, and good works; religious contestants still hurled their barrages of anathemas and cannon balls. But the age was changing; the destiny of peoples was being determined more and more by politics and economics.

Political and Economic Conditions

Politically, the German princes had been pawns in the hands of foreign powers in the last century and a half. Repeated military defeats, the ravishment of the lands, and the blasting of hopes for improvement should have taught people the futility inherent in political disunity. Blindly the rulers sought a remedy, partly by working to revitalize the outmoded feudal institutions associated with the great landed nobility, and partly by centralizing a greater measure of authority in a bureaucratic court system.

Their chief interests were the practical ones of finance, justice, and police—in other words, maintenance of their power. To this end, like their ancestors before them, these princes were above all feudal lords, the ideas particularly of the lesser ones being little removed from the thinking of the medieval world. The state of Brandenburg-Prussia, to be sure, was gradually adopting a more modern political system, in which fundamental human rights were extended out of expediency; but the petty units, too small to build armies, to subsidize industry, and to enter the channels of world trade, stood their conservative ground as best they could. The cameralist school of economic thinking sought to emphasize that a Christian prince must rule his lands in the interests of his subjects, but actually, with the notable exception of Frederick William, elector of Brandenburg-Prussia, and his successors, the petty princes exhibited few traces of paternal concern for the welfare of the masses.

They exacted revenues due them as feudal lords, imposed the direct taxes, usually called "contributions," and depended for additional income on the excise taxes collected on liquor, beer, wines, soap, meat, candles, and many other commodities of popular consumption. Political decentralization prevented any vigorous commercial and industrial policy on a national scale. Efforts to establish a common monetary system, in 1660 and again in

1738, failed. How great was the monetary confusion may be inferred from a single fact, namely, that the lower Rhenish region alone had more than sixty mints. The free development of trade and industry was further handicapped by state and guild monopolies of the manufacture and sale of certain items.

Needless to say, this policy weighed heaviest on the shoulders of the agricultural class, especially those with medium-sized and small farms, and urban merchants and professional groups. Three decades of warfare at the turn of the century left these social classes at the end of their resources. Certain areas and cities suffered frightful damage. The years 1701 to 1706 brought excellent harvests and resulted in a drop of about 20 per cent in grain prices everywhere; but from 1708 to 1710 the prices of grain again skyrocketed to heights not reached for three decades before or after. Scarcities increased human misery. This was only multiplied by the bureaucratic shortsightedness that sought the relief of its own impasse by making feudal exactions even more oppressive.

Commerce within the system of German states was hampered by innumerable tariff barriers, and competition with the unified national states of Europe was out of question as long as each of the rulers of the three hundred odd German states pursued his own selfish, independent policy. The wars consumed a great measure of what the masses earned, but the tax collectors, in addition to the depredations of soldiers, were chiefly responsible for blighting trade and commerce and, no less, for discouraging the cultivation of the soil. Mounting taxes made it impossible in many cases, to hold on to lands or to buy additional acreage. German-Swiss immigrants on arrival here did not cease to complain of the restrictions and burdens to which they had been subjected in the homeland—tithes, the *fronungen* or statute-labors, the inability to dispose of property, especially of real estate, which could take place only at a public sale and with the

MARTIN LUTHER

PHILIPP MELANCHTHON

ULRICH ZWINGLI

JOHN CALVIN

FALKNER SWAMP CHURCH

FIRST CHURCH, PHILADELPHIA

SEAL OF COETUS

SEAL OF EASTERN SYNOD

MICHAEL SCHLATTER

consent of the government, and the exorbitant rates of interest on borrowed money.

Peasant dissatisfaction, if it became overt as among the German-Swiss, was as a rule put down by coercive means. The accounts of immigrants speak too often of limited means, debts, and bankruptcy not to be a general symptom. This depressed economic status is graphically summed up in a contemporary account from southern Germany, thus: "If a man beats his dog the whole day it will run away and seek another master that will treat it better. Now every one beats the common people. The duke beats them, the soldiers beat them, the huntsmen beat them. This they will not endure, but run away."

Little wonder that people cupped their ears to the stories of a different way of life in the New World. The Germans, always avid travelers, responded to the lure to know the diverse peoples and civilizations of the earth which was so strong among Europeans in that age. The accounts of these travelers, made available by the printers of the age, increased markedly throughout the sixteenth century. To them were added the letters written by occasional immigrants to their relatives. Information regarding the open doors of new life in new places circulated everywhere and stimulated the desire to launch out on a different life no matter how formidable the obstacles. These obstacles were minimized, and the benefits to be derived were usually exaggerated by the enticing advertisements of English proprietors of the colonies in America who engaged professional agents to work among the people of the Rhine Valley with the purpose of recruiting them.

Pennsylvania was the best advertised colony and William Penn, without a shadow of doubt, the most successful advertiser. The words of Pastor Joshua von Kocherthal and Francis Daniel Pastorius, writing from New York, gave weight to all good reports. Queen Anne's government, sensing the economic importance for England that its colonies should be populated, passed a bill granting citizenship to Protestant German immigrants. Harassed Germans were not slow in reaching out to obtain those liberties which were denied them at home. Legal and extra-legal barriers thrown in the path of prospective emigrations by German and Swiss authorities proved ineffective in stemming the population tide that moved toward the land of "golden promises."

Social and Cultural Backgrounds

The social and cultural life of Germans around 1700 was also in a state of ferment. The aristocracy as well as the gentry fell under the influence of France, like their peers elsewhere on the continent. French customs, manners, etiquette, and standards of taste penetrated the life and culture of the upper classes and spread to the wealthy bourgeoisie in the towns and cities. Cultural life, having declined after the Thirty Years' War, slowly began to show signs of reinvigoration. Johann Kepler and Gottfried Wilhelm Leibnitz had attracted attention in intellectual circles. German scholars, immersed mainly in theological disputation, confined their energies to sterile religious discussion. In the wake of the pietistic movement, a stimulating new hymnology was initiated by Joachim Neander (1650-80) in the Reformed churches and a long-neglected field was to grow into a veritable revival. By 1700 the cantatas, passions, and oratorios had assumed the styles that were to be further developed throughout the century. German writers were beginning to discard Latin and were using their own tongue to please the literate middle class.

In 1688 the first German monthly journal was published and blazed the trail for others in the German language, which gradually was vindicated as a keen-edged tool for transmitting new, often revolutionary, ideas. Before very long, brilliant men like Lessing, Goethe, Herder, and Schiller were to usher in Germany's most creative literary period, and musicians of the stature of Bach, Gluck, Haydn, Mozart, and Beethoven appeared on the horizon. Princes were patronizing literature and the arts and, inevitably, the effects of this vigorous cultural revival pervaded all classes.

Schools also were entering a period of renewed strength and vigor so that they were steadily whittling down the rate of illiteracy among Germans. A study of the lists of German immigrants in the first half of the eighteenth century shows that 74 per cent of the male immigrants were able to write. This high rate of literacy, unusual among Europeans at that time, was neither accidental nor incidental. It was rather the result of a long tradition of commitment to the idea of education embodied in the support of higher schools of learning as well as parochial schools. Protestant princes took the initiative in fostering education. As early as 1559 a state-church school system had been organized in Wuerttemberg, followed by Brunswick in 1569, Weimar in 1619, and Gotha in 1642. By the middle of the seventeenth century most of the German states had adopted some state-church plan of education.

As a rule, both Lutheran and Reformed churches were accustomed to engage a minister as well as a schoolmaster—providing them with a stated salary and a home—and to set up high educational standards. The effectiveness of these schools, of course, fluctuated with the vicissitudes of the times, but never waned completely. Whenever the state failed to provide the necessary schools, the churches rallied to the challenge involved in maintaining the standard of literacy among their numbers. Educational leadership came from the universities, which generally were a special responsibility of the rulers. At the beginning of the eighteenth century universities, like those at Heidelberg, Herborn, and Marburg, came to new life, and others, like the one at Halle in 1691, were founded. The German-Swiss universities of Zurich, Basel, and St. Gall stood high among European institutions devoted to the cultivation of learning. The foundations for an aggressive educational leadership in later periods were thus substantially laid.

2

On the Frontiers of a New Land

THE ENGLISH COLONIES in North America were entering a new and exciting era as more and more Germans decided to exchange the Rhine lands for those of the Hudson, the Delaware, and the Schuylkill valleys. The Glorious Revolution over, English trade responded to the refreshing atmosphere of peace and greater democratic ideals within a political framework nowhere matched at the time. Over four million Englishmen were "engaged in manufactures" at the turn of the eighteenth century in the British Isles, working in their cottages under the "domestic" system and, as employees of merchant capitalists, creating a tremendous stockpile of woolen and leather goods, copper, iron, lead, and tin articles; and considerable paper, glass, porcelain, silk, and linen items.

Parliament, though still dominated by the upper classes, instinctively responded to public demand in providing commercial outlets for this industrial activity. Royal authority over at least parts of the colonies had been strengthened by creating the Dominion of New England, to be sure, but the work of Charles II and James II was undone by the Glorious Revolution, and the new colonial policy had to take into consideration the independent spirit of the colonial assemblies that had developed during a long period when the colonies were left to shift for themselves. The colonies, proprietary for the most part, desired to share in the rights won by their compatriots at home, and were stimulated to take a greater hand in the management of their own affairs. Colonial self-consciousness was dawning, although no two colonies were to follow the same pattern of growth. All of them, however, benefited from the protracted period of isolation that strengthened the spirit of independence and freedom, the economic expansion in England resulting in an access to goods that relieved the asperities of frontier living, and a gradual shift away from an agricultural to an industrial economy. Those who still loved the soil but found diminishing returns in it at home came to swell the numbers of the pioneer colonists.

By the beginning of the eighteenth century the destiny of the colonies received further direction from the impact of fresh waves of diverse immigrants. One of these consisted of the Scotch-Irish, forced out of northern Ireland; the other equally important one was the German migration from western Germany and northern Switzerland, which was destined to reach its peak only in the middle of the century. All the colonies extended a welcome hand to these new peoples, but since they were primarily interested in agriculture they found little promise in New England's rocky soil, among New York's patroon estates, and in the plantation system of the South. Thus, most of this immigration flowed through Philadelphia and then spread out along a path that moved southwest along the fringes of the Appalachians into the back country of Maryland, Virginia, and the Carolinas.

There was nothing spectacular or unusual in the arrival of the early Germans. The clearly defined upper class, consisting principally of wealthy merchants in the North and planters in the South, together with the dominating professional class of lawyers and, within limits, the clergy, saw no social or economic threat but only advantage in their coming. The bulk of the population was of the "lower middle class," independent farmers, small merchants, retail tradesmen, and skilled artisans; below them were the struggling town laborers, ordinary seamen, tenant farmers; and still further down, the white indentured servants and the slaves. These were too preoccupied with making ends meet to analyze the social and economic significance of the swelling tide of new peoples. Most of them were farmers, but there were many mechanics, who brought along a knowledge of the arts that were necessary and useful, such as weavers, tailors, tanners, shoemakers, combmakers, butchers, papermakers, watchmakers, bakers, and smiths of all kinds.

The religious culture of the colonies where these new people settled reflected the greatest degree of toleration existing anywhere in the world at the time. By 1646 the gospel was being preached in eighteen different languages along the Hudson River alone. Maryland under the Calverts offered unrestricted religious liberty, a latitude officially not granted in New England and Virginia, although in the latter region accommodations to religious diversity were creeping in gradually. In Pennsylvania the "holy experiment" of the Quaker William Penn, intent "to lay the foundation of a free colony for all mankind," was well on the way to concrete expression in a constitution and a body of laws which guaranteed civil liberty, religious freedom, and economic opportunity to all inhabitants, without discrimination of any sort.

The time had passed when any colony could draw the lines of orthodoxy so sharply as to discourage the much-needed increase of population. Incoming peoples, however heterogeneous racially, religiously, or socially, were readily accepted around 1700. The Germans were being hospitably received and they rejoiced to find, especially in Pennsylvania, what a European traveler, Peter Kalmes, reported in mid-century: "I wish to place further emphasis on the prosperity of this country. Much of the land is tax free or taxed so lightly one could hardly consider it a tax; due to the freedom which is enjoyed here, every man may be said to be a king on his own land and in his own home. There are no customs, no taxes; there is complete religious freedom, and the country is not in danger of enemy attack." The head tax required to enter the colony, which was enacted in 1729 by the Pennsylvania legislature, or the English law requiring an oath of allegiance to the Crown constituted no major obstacles to Germans seeking a new home, for Governor James Logan reports about the same time: "We are daily expecting ships from London, which bring over Palatines." Another official warns the Pennsylvania Assembly: "Should any discouragement divert them from coming hither, it may well be apprehended that the value of your lands will fall, and your advances to wealth be much slower; for it is not altogether the goodness of the soil, but the number and industry of the people that make a flourishing colony."

Three factors might easily have discouraged a people made of less stern stuff: the voyage across the Atlantic, the hardships of the frontiers, and the redemptioner's status that, of necessity, many accepted. Amidst unbelievable hardships of travel, many lost property and health; sometimes nearly one sixth would die from ship fever that was generally known in Philadelphia as "Palatine fever." In the lonely parts of southeastern Pennsylvania they shared the common abode of most American pioneers, the caves and sod houses; but these soon gave way to the well-known log cabins—small, rude structures, with little light or ventilation, few conveniences, and no comforts—followed by the highly appreciated Pennsylvania Dutch stone farmhouses still in evidence around Doylestown, Easton, Bethlehem, Allentown, Lancaster, and Reading.

To sell one's services as an indentured servant was a socially acceptable means of obtaining passage and of finding employment. During the term of servitude few rights were enjoyed, but, once freed, one acquired the same status as anyone else possessed; in fact, the period of indenture, especially in the case of young people, often proved to be preliminary to substantial advancement as farmers or craftsmen in most communities. Their language, their customs, and their ways of living may have seemed strange, if not crude, to their English and Scotch-Irish neighbors; but these Germans, once settled in Penn's Woods and elsewhere as individuals, families, or groups of a hundred or more, set themselves to make a living, and—most of them—a life true to those religious convictions that sustained them amidst hard and trying conditions.

No record has been found to indicate that any of the colonial German immigrants were unbelievers. The first colonists belonged to the left-wing elements, but by the beginning of the century the "church people"—Lutheran and Reformed—forged ahead, and after a quarter century the report presented to the Synod of South Holland, convened at Breda in 1730, stated that "the Reformed holding to the old confession constituted more than one half of the whole number (of Germans), being about 15,000." These were scattered over a wide territory beginning along the Hudson River and extending from Germantown west to Reading and east to German Valley, New Jersey; south into Lancaster County, across "Wright's Ferry" into the present York and Adams counties; farther yet, across the Potomac into Maryland and the rich and beautiful Shenandoah Valley of Virginia, soon making a connection with independent settlements in South Carolina. Along this route the religious spirit of these settlers might have been observed by travelers—first in the manner of their life, then in the more formal religious services. Let us briefly survey these earliest frontiers.

Along the Hudson River

The earliest settlers in New York, having come from Holland, were members of the Dutch Reformed Church. In 1626 Peter Minuit arrived as the governor of the colony under appointment from the Dutch West India Company. Minuit, born in the city of Wesel in Germany, had served as a deacon in the German Reformed church of his home community and actively participated in the religious work of the Dutch church. While practically one third of this congregation was of German origin no separate German services were held until the arrival of the Reformed minister, John Frederick Haeger, in June, 1710, along with the Lutheran pastor Kocherthal and nearly 3,000 Palatines. The Society for the Propagation of the Gospel in Foreign Parts had engaged Haeger to "be the Society's missionary to such parts of the Province of New York, where Her Majesty shall think fit to settle the poor Palatines, provided he be Episcopally ordained and that said Mr. Haeger do qualify agreeable to the orders of the Society about missionaries." Almost at once he began divine services.

By order of Governor Hunter, the Germans were moved north along the Hudson River to produce tar and pitch on the crown lands. Haeger followed his people. When many of them moved away to settle along the Swatara near present-day Lebanon, Pennsylvania, Haeger continued to serve the 329 families of his parish, preaching mostly under the open sky. In spite of an apparently successful ministry, the Society in 1717 cut off Haeger's salary; amid privations he died in 1721.

His successor John Jacob Oel, ordained by the Bishop of London, took up the threads of this ministry in Schoharie and extended his labors along the Mohawk River. Subsequently German Reformed people were served by George Michael Weiss, John Casper Rubel, and John Jacob Wack, who were loosely associated with the Dutch Reformed Church. The interesting feature of this work is that people as well as ministers, although nominally linked with other communions, were regarded as being of the German Reformed faith. These congregations in time were absorbed by the Dutch Reformed Church.

In Virginia

The first German colony was brought to Virginia through the agency of Governor Alexander Spotswood and Christopher von Graffenried, a Swiss baron, who had earlier led the ill-fated Swiss and Palatine immigrants to New Berne, North Carolina. The settlers were experienced miners from Siegen. Graciously treated by the governor, these Germans established themselves in a place called Germanna on the southern branch of the Rappahannock, where they were joined in 1714 by the patriarchal Reverend John Henry Haeger, then seventy-five years of age. From a contemporary journal we read this first written account of religious services among German Reformed people on this continent: "They make use of this blockhouse for divine service. They go to prayers constantly once a day, and have two sermons on Sunday. We went to hear them perform their service, which was done in their language, which we did not understand; but they seemed to be very devout and sang the psalms well."

This German colony mined ore, built a furnace, and manufactured iron; on an 1,800-acre area they developed a community that set aside a choice ten-acre plot for the support and enjoyment of their pastor. Sometime after 1718 the German Reformed part of this community founded Germantown, in Stafford (now Fauquier) County, on the Licking Run, about eight miles south of Warrenton, the present county seat. The government in 1730 passed an act "to exempt certain German Protestants in Stafford from the payment of parish levies." This shows that they scrupulously refrained from meddling in secular and ecclesiastical politics and enjoyed the benefits of pragmatic separation of church and state long before Jefferson's days. They built both a church and a schoolhouse.

The urge to expand split the community in half, a small party settling about ten miles south of the Little Fork of the Rappahannock, where they erected a "pretty and well-built, but little clapboard church." Unable to obtain a regular minister after the death of Haeger, these communities were served by "readers" or by traveling ministers, among them John B. Rieger from Lancaster and Michael Schlatter. With the second generation, the people seemed to have been absorbed by the English.

In North and South Carolina

Two Swiss gentlemen, Graffenried and Michel, founded New Berne, North Carolina, with Swiss and Palatine immigrants in 1710. Graffenried had been "licensed by the Bishop of London to read the service to the colonists" who were to enjoy "perfect religious freedom." An Indian massacre almost wiped out the community, and the remnant joined other churches. Their places were filled by German settlers who began moving southward from Pennsylvania around 1745. A long time elapsed before they were able to build churches, and on Sundays they gathered to listen to sermons read by German schoolteachers. Lack of ministers prevented the formation of lasting congregational life until the beginning of the nineteenth century.

In South Carolina five German settlements may be noted between 1732 and 1755: Purysburg, Orangeburg, New Windsor, Saxe-Gotha, and Amelia townships. Some of the people were farmers and some, tradesmen. Their religious needs were satisfied largely by French-Swiss ministers ordained by the Bishop of London. At least eleven Reformed ministers are known to have labored in these duly constituted congregations.

An unusual characteristic of religious life among the Germans of these areas was the tendency toward close fellowship between

Reformed and Lutherans, who cordially accepted the services of their respective pastors and even of Moravian, Presbyterian, and Episcopalian ministers.

In Maryland

Lands along the Monocacy River were settled by Germans of the Reformed faith who migrated from Pennsylvania about 1729. Their community in the village of Monocacy was the first and most important settlement of white people in western Maryland. A "log (*holzerne*) church" was built between 1732 and 1734 and used jointly with the German Lutherans. Its congregational life earned this description by an observer in 1748: "It appears to me to be one of the purest in the whole country, and one in which I have found the most traces of the fear of God."

Little is known of the German settlement on the Conococheague. Fredericktown welcomed Palatinate Germans as early as 1735 under the leadership of John Thomas Schley, whom Schlatter called "the best schoolmaster that I have met in America." The log church built in 1748 housed a congregation that became one of the most prominent, not only among the Reformed churches in Maryland, but among all the churches in the denomination.

In New Jersey

The first Palatines appeared in New Jersey between 1710 and 1713 and came from New York. They settled in the northern and northwestern part of the province on lands between Lambertville and Newton, and between the Delaware and Bound Brook. The first Reformed minister was John B. Rieger who settled at Amwell in 1735. Scanty documentary information reveals that other thriving congregations were established at Fox Hill, Rockaway, German Valley, and elsewhere. The deed of the land for the Amwell church was given to "trustees to and for the Calvinistical High Dutch congregation." Highly interesting "articles of Order and Discipline" were adopted on the day of the dedication of the church, December 1, 1749. No minister was to be allowed to preach in the church unless he belonged to Coetus. No one was to be a member who was not devoted "with mouth and heart" to the doctrines of the Heidelberg Catechism. No child was to be baptized, except in case of sickness, unless it be brought into the church, and only parents could present it, and they only if they had been confirmed. The dead were to be buried with appropriate ceremonies. All the members were to contribute for the support of the church. These congregations also, in the absence of regular ministry and effective organization, were lost to other denominations.

In Penn's Woods

Germans who came early to the port of Philadelphia spread out over lands of the frontiers. Here at points called Neshaminy, Skippack, and Whitemarsh, as well as in Germantown, the Dutch pastor Paulus Van Vlec preached and baptized between 1710 and 1715. Samuel Guldin, a Reformed pastor evicted from Switzerland because of his pietist views, bought a tract of land in Roxbury, Philadelphia County, at this time, and although he devoted himself primarily to land transactions, tradition has it that he preached occasionally but founded no congregation anywhere.

The first regularly organized congregation in Penn's Woods was the work of John Philip Boehm, who took up land among the Palatines of Whitpain Township in the fall of 1720. Formerly a schoolmaster at Worms, he at once attracted attention and was prevailed upon to hold services such as schoolmasters had been authorized to do in the old country. People came to hear him from miles around and, to use his own words, he "maintained the ministry of the Word to the best of my ability, and to the great satisfaction of the people, for five years, without any compensation." People "with tears in their eyes" begged him to baptize their children and to administer the Lord's Supper. Reluctantly he acceded to their entreaties, and "there communed for the first time on October 15, 1725, at Falkner Swamp, 40 members; in November, at Skippack, 37 members; on December 23, at Whitemarsh, 24 members." Here the foundation of the German Reformed Church was laid in the colonies. Altogether Boehm later served thirteen congregations scattered over a territory now comprising eight counties. One, bearing the name "Falkner Swamp," has survived to this day.

At this point our history is intertwined with similar beginnings in Lancaster County. Here Conrad Templeman, a pious tailor from Heidelberg, had been a "reader" and, like Boehm, leading "small gatherings in houses here and there, with the reading of a sermon, with songs and prayer, according to the High German Church Order, upon all Sundays and holidays." Templeman's services radiated over a territory embracing modern Lancaster and Lebanon counties with seven congregations founded or served in his early ministry. In 1732 he first administered the sacrament of baptism. He enjoyed the encouragement of Boehm, who visited his Conestoga church in 1727 and gave communion there.

Having been duly elected pastor in his congregations, Boehm at once proposed a church constitution and effected an organization after the Reformed custom. This constitution embodied the principles of polity handed down by the Reformed tradition of the Rhineland. It provided for a consistory, for strict church discipline, for the instruction of children, for adherence to the Heidelberg Catechism, for the burial of the dead according to ancient custom, and for the proper administration of the temporal and spiritual affairs of the congregation. No church officer was installed until he had subscribed to this law and order in his "own handwriting." Similarly adopted by other congregations, this constitution served as a pattern that molded the character of later developments.

Progress in church organization by no means proceeded smoothly. The arrival of other ministers caused troubles. George Michael Weiss objected to the irregularity of Boehm's work; reconciliation ensued only when Boehm was officially ordained into the Christian ministry by the Dutch Reformed Church. John Peter Miller, another highly trained minister, objected to the subordination of the German churches to the Classis of Amsterdam, whose interests Boehm courted and desired in terms of material support; and Miller scattered thistle into the plantings of Boehm everywhere until his own dramatic departure into the fold of the Ephrata Brethren. The maladministration of funds collected abroad by Weiss and Elder Hans George Reiff for the assistance of German congregations led to the recall of Boehm to Philadelphia. He had scarcely calmed the ruffled waters when he was embroiled with a young hothead, John Henry Goetschy, and an ambitious newcomer, Peter Henry Dorsius, who designed to take over the field entirely. Orderly church life, however, once more triumphed.

Real as these crises were, they pale into insignificance when compared with that generated by the coming of Count Nicholas Ludwig von Zinzendorf, the Moravian, into the center of the paradise of sects. His intention was to unite the many German groups, confessionalists and pietists alike. His purpose was fine and laudable. Pennsylvania Germans of diverse religious persuasions had organized in the Perkiomen Valley as early as 1736 with plans to meet every four weeks, as the Associated Brethren of Skippack, for the purpose of deepening their spiritual life. Five years later after consultation with Zinzendorf, Heinrich Antes, a leader of the Reformed at Skippack, sent out a call for united action "to remedy the frightful evil wrought in the church of Christ . . . through mistrust and suspicion" and to ascertain "whether it would not be possible to appoint a general assembly, not to wrangle about opinions but to treat with each other in love on the most important articles of faith, in order to ascertain how closely we can approach each other fundamentally, and, as for the rest, bear with each other in love on opinions which do not subvert the ground of salvation."

Zinzendorf's plan, as it unfolded, allowed the participating members to retain their denominational membership. Creating a religious fellowship within an organizationally federated system, they were to express their oneness in Christ in the practical work of evangelization among the Indians, in the interchange of ministers and devotional literature, and in intercommunion. The motivating force behind this first American ecumenical endeavor is as modern as anything to be found in our contemporary movements.

Unhappily, the synods that met to implement this ideal became an arena of "vindictive shadowboxing." Among the Reformed ministers, John Bechtel went so far as to allow his name to be used in connection with the authorship of a catechism, actually written by the count, and accepted ordination as well as an appointment by Zinzendorf as inspector over all the Reformed congregations in Pennsylvania. Violent opposition developed against what was considered an unwarranted interference in the affairs of a denomination outside of the count's jurisdiction. Boehm considered the Catechism abominable. He wrote: "There is in it from beginning to end not a word of the articles of our Christian faith (that is omitted because the Herrnhuters do not want to pray to God the Father, but only to the Savior, as has been stated before). Nor is there in it a word about Holy Baptism or Holy Communion, no word about the most holy prayer, which our Savior has taught us to pray." The attack on the floor of the Synod against the Classis of Amsterdam convinced Reformed people that the real objective was "to create a division and to take the Reformed people away from the control and the supervision of the Church of Holland."

Boehm received the support of Samuel Guldin, who had attended the first Synod, and wrote a book entitled *Unpartisan Witness on the New Union.* You cannot have a union among diverse elements of Christians, this polemic argued, until they first achieve union with Christ; and union must primarily come from above and not as a result of men's machinations. This unionist movement, more than a century ahead of the times, failed and, when the crisis passed, left the Reformed elements markedly strengthened in their denominational consciousness.

The aggressive position taken by Zinzendorf's supporters necessitated a similarly positive stand on the part of the "church people." Bechtel joined the Moravians; other pastors, like Henry Rauch and Jacob Lischy, were active fellow travelers of the Herrnhuters. Similar emotional groups—Independents, Puritans, New Born, Saturday-Folks, Labadists—were depleting the ranks of nascent Reformed congregations by means of enthusiastic proselytizing. A precious heritage of creeds and customs was exposed to grave dangers of what seemed to be clearly erroneous beliefs and practices. Weiss, as early as 1729, had published a small booklet attacking the sect of the New Born; now, representing the same antipathy toward "enthusiasts" that "church people" had brought over from the other side of the Atlantic, Boehm wrote a booklet of one hundred pages, followed by another smaller one, in which he focused his attack on the unionist movement as belonging to the same category. Boehm and Weiss, pious men but not pietists, succeeded in saving their congregations, but not all the people. Pietism, with its tremendous emotional appeal, specifically among the Germans and more generally among those touched by George Whitefield's preaching and the first breezes of the Great Awakening, was on the march and making inroads upon the frontier life of orthodoxy everywhere.

The Safeguard of Organization

The most effective safeguard under prevailing conditions was regarded, now for over a decade, to lie in organization headed by one with authority. The ministers, however, were unable to see eye to eye in spite of advice from the Classis of Amsterdam to whose care the church of the Palatinate had recommended its colonial members. This body in 1741 next suggested union with the Presbyterians. Extended discussions in this direction ended by refusal on the part of the German Reformed people on the grounds that such a step would mean "a change of religion."

These negotiations were proceeding through the slow channels of communications possible at the time, when the arrival of Michael Schlatter, on the first day of August, 1746, changed the picture completely. If Boehm was the organizer of the scattered coreligionists, Schlatter deserves the honor of consolidating the congregations into a definite denominational mold.

Schlatter possessed admirable qualifications for his task. Not only had he come from a distinguished family of St. Gall, Switzerland, and enjoyed the best educational opportunities of the day, but he also embarked upon this undertaking with the full confidence of the deputies of the Holland Synod. After an interview with the church authorities, the clerk recorded: "The deputies, seeing his promptness, heartiness, and Christian disinterestedness, combined with Christian humility, modesty, and friendliness, were profoundly rejoiced that they had encountered so worthy and capable a subject." They gave him $242 and a written list of instructions as to what he was to do—consult with the German and Dutch ministers, visit the churches and congregations, organize local consistories, call the first Coetus and, afterward, be free to accept the pastorate of any congregation he preferred, serving it as long as he wished.

With his commission in hand, Schlatter, upon his arrival, visited forty-six congregations up and down the colonies, distributed gifts of books and money from abroad, and made the acquaintance of ministers. On the twenty-ninth of September, 1747, thirty-one delegates, of whom only four were ministers, convened in Schlatter's house and in the old church in Philadelphia and formally organized the Coetus of the Reformed Ministerium of the Congregations in Pennsylvania. This was the beginning of a genuine institutional life that was to last in this form until after the Revolution. The plan followed the lines of a similar organization in use among the ministers of the Dutch Reformed Church in New York. The constitution, adopted in the following year, closely adhered to the model which was drawn up in 1725 by Boehm for his congregations. A few necessary additions were made; for example, that no minister would be acknowledged as regular without the approval of the Classis of Amsterdam.

This organization definitely separated "regular" ministers from those independents who continued in free-lance manner to preach wherever they found hearers. While neither all the Reformed churches nor all the ministers were ever included, nevertheless, orderly church life ensued. The transactions of Coetus, as well as its correspondence with Holland, leave the impression that the annual meetings were thoroughly dignified. Writes one of our historians:

> The members generally met at the schoolhouse and marched in solemn procession to the church, where the Praeses of the preceding year preached the opening sermon. The letters from Holland were then read, and the state of the churches minutely considered. Then the elders were for a time dismissed, and the *censura morum* was held, at which the character of individual ministers was investigated and advice given with regard to future conduct.

Schlatter has left us a collective portrait of these ministers:

> I plead for the few ministers who are now in this country, and for those who may yet be able to come to their brethren and fellow laborers. . . . They have cheerfully set aside personal gain and

advantage; they seek not to heap up treasures; let not your brotherly love permit them to languish under this heavy labor for the want of fellow laborers . . . nor let them be compelled to waste their precious time in digging and plowing the fields which they desire to spend in the vineyard of the Lord.

Forward Under the Coetus

The epoch-making character of the step taken in 1747 is revealed in the light of the activities of Coetus throughout the ensuing decades of the century. The German Reformed people gradually ceased to be merely a collection of unrelated congregations and developed into a self-conscious denomination. To this end the Coetus supervised the work of the ministers, settled disputes, and regulated the ordination of newly trained ministers. It supervised the equitable distribution of funds from Holland and provided for the widows of deceased pastors. It supplied vacant charges with pastors, reproved those who stepped out of bounds, healed breaches in congregations, and set up safeguards against the inroads of doctrines unsupported by the Heidelberg Catechism. Through its secretary it sent the minutes of meetings, together with elaborate reports on prevailing conditions, to the authorities in Holland with whom cordial relations were at all times desired. The success of this organization is only partially yet very dramatically reflected in the fact that at the time of the dissolution of the Coetus in 1793, its ministers had increased from 4 to 24, and the congregations, growing from 50 to approximately 150, embraced nearly 15,000 communicants. In this period a total of 37 missionaries had been sent from Holland; 27 had been educated in Pennsylvania, making a total of 64 constituent members of the Coetus.

The nature of their parochial work may be gathered from the statistical report of a pastor in 1792. Serving seven congregations, John Henry Helfferich looked after 246 families for whom in that year he baptized 76 and after catechization confirmed 76 children; in addition, he supervised five schools with 241 students. Distances between churches and the homes of members entailed considerable travel over primitive roads, mainly on horseback. He preached twice on three Sundays and once on the fourth. Catechetical instruction went on throughout the summer in each congregation. While baptism of children occurred in the church at the time of his preaching engagement, most of the marriages were solemnized at his house in Weissenburg, although occasionally some would insist upon a church wedding. Funerals caused him the hardest problem, but he reports: "If my members cannot accommodate themselves to me, they ask the Lutheran minister, as I have many Lutheran funerals." Excessive work, continual travel, and increasing age were beginning to tell. Hence, in words that serve as a mirror of the spiritual life of our forebears, ministers and laity, he said: "I often intended to give up some congregations, but neither through kind words nor earnest remonstrances was I able to gain my purpose. The continued petitions, the touching representations, and the great love of the people to me always frustrated my plans."

Pressing Problems

A relatively close-knit denominational life emerged from the frontier soil. The German Reformed Church thus represents a significant element in colonial Christianity. To achieve this status tremendous adjustments had to be made to the new and strange conditions of a world in the wilderness. Let us consider some of the most pressing problems.

Foremost for the welfare of the churches was the need to regularize the ministry. Church people had been accustomed to a ministry established according to theologically well-grounded principles. They respected and honored the profession as necessary in the scheme of salvation and indispensable for the religious and intellectual leadership of the Christian community. The

radical sects, with their easy recognition of self-appointed preachers, scandalized many who saw in the practice the road to
religious anarchy. But they were even more shocked at the
behavior of certain representatives of the cloth.

Of ministerial vagabonds and impostors there were plenty, to
be sure. Congregations, eager for ministers, often elected the
first educated man who came along, without asking for certif-
icates of recommendation. Moreover, frontier life was without
fences; old world conventions were ignored among laity and
clergy alike. Christopher Saur's German paper delighted in ex-
posing clerical offences, but, for that matter, the minutes of
Coetus provide ample information on this theme. Intemperance,
marital infidelity, implication in the Fries Whiskey Rebellion,
murder, and ungovernable temper appear among some of the
charges.

Investigation proved some to be false, others to be true, but
the records show that Coetus acted in a firm and positive manner
concerning every complaint. A few men were unfrocked, which,
unfortunately, did not result in putting a halt to their irregular
activities in regions beyond the jurisdiction of Coetus; others,
though vindicated, were removed to serve elsewhere. Confronted
with a problem that was common among all frontier churches,
Coetus exercised unrelenting vigilance in weeding out the scan-
dalous by means of an increased emphasis on discipline, and the
results measured more than favorably with those achieved by
other frontier churches. The trouble, of course, was rooted in
the loosening of social conventions characteristic of frontier
living, in the spirit of unbridled opportunism, but especially in
the lack of trained ministers to meet the extensive need in rapidly
growing areas. Coetus took a positive approach to the problem
by instituting the *censura morum*, a kind of moral self-examina-
tion among the ministers; by strictly requiring proper ordination,
election, and installation steps in every case; and by continually

encouraging the interest of young ministers abroad to dedicate themselves to work in the colonial wilderness. The undivided love and esteem won by certain ministers caused many a congregation, again and again, to request their return from other fields of labor.

Educational Efforts

Naturally a more direct way of handling the situation would have been through the creation of a native ministry. To avail themselves of the several theological schools already founded by other denominations seemed entirely out of the question; their own resources also precluded such action. The situation reached a crisis in 1764. Important places like Lancaster, Reading, York, Tulpehocken, Whitehall, Easton, and Goshenhoppen joined plaintively to "request, beg and pray" for at least five or six ministers, else they would be "compelled to give up the Coetus." But, probably because of the economic confusion attendant upon a general European war, Holland desired to reduce its own burdens and even suggested self-support.

As early as 1730, Dr. John Wilhelmius of Rotterdam urged that "two young men must be selected . . . and educated with their money for the ministry of the church." Sons of ministers taught by their fathers and schoolmasters receiving instruction from their pastors had been duly ordained by consent of the Holland authorities. Capable ministers, like George Michael Weiss, Peter Henry Dorsius, William Hendel, Sr., Daniel Gros, John George Alsentz, and others, undertook to give private instruction. The Coetus of 1755 resolved that Philip William Otterbein and William Stoy be proposed "as fit persons" for this purpose.

But an organized educational effort seemed inevitable. Partly in answer to this need Michael Schlatter accepted the superintendency of schools being established in Pennsylvania by an

English society. Coetus at first approved the project but quickly rescinded its action. The minutes of a special meeting in 1755 briefly state: "The gymnasium (college) for which we hoped has come to naught." Hopes in this direction were revived again after the Revolution, when in 1787 Lutherans and Reformed joined to found Franklin College in Lancaster.

German Reformed people had been traditionally committed to the educational ideal. On the premise that only an informed church can be truly Reformed, they regarded education as an auxiliary function of the church. Prior to 1730 few schools existed among them in the colonies, although schoolmasters are known to have come here. Even in 1734 Boehm claimed that because of the distances children would have to travel few schoolmasters could make a living. Shortly, however, a school appeared in Old Goshenhoppen, Montgomery County, and by 1741 five schools were in operation.

The time between 1745 and 1775, however, was marked by an increase in both the influence and numbers of these schools. The early vicissitudes of pioneer life over, congregations could devote increasing attention to the educational task, which grew more pressing as the young people were exposed to English influences and the proselytizing of sects. Following Schlatter's first visit to Holland in 1751, considerable financial aid for this purpose also came from Holland and West Friesland. In 1760 eighty-four church schools were being conducted. Fear of the Anglicizing influence of the charity schools stimulated the congregations to provide adequate educational facilities for the young. In spite of lack of funds and good schoolmasters, schools of the church appeared for the first time in Northampton, Bucks, York, Chester, and Adams counties, and even in Westmoreland County. Their numbers increased almost sevenfold. When the charity schools ceased in 1763 for lack of support, the educational work of the church received a new impetus culminating in the existence, as far as we know, of 124 schools by 1799. This educational work was undergirded by the so-called neighborhood schools, which came under the influence of German Reformed people. When James Logan proposed the secularization of schools in 1800, the idea was vigorously opposed by the people of the Reformed Church.

The nature of this general education varied from time to time and from place to place. Normally, the supply of teachers was inadequate, partly on account of low salaries. The instruction was in German, although English was often taught. Money to erect schoolhouses was often raised by means of a lottery. Schoolmasters were expected to act as precentors and to give catechetical instruction, and were subject to the jurisdiction of the consistory, with the pastor acting as principal. Attendance was voluntary and tuition fees were exacted except in the case of the very poor. We may safely conjecture that qualitatively this educational effort did not fall below the standard of other church groups in the eighteenth century. Undoubtedly colonial Germans were sufficiently literate to support several newspapers in their language and bookstores with stock that came from their own presses as well as from abroad. In the perpetuation of the German language the German Reformed Church played no small part.

Relations with Other Churches

We are not to suppose that the people of our congregations, isolated through customs, language, and religious tradition, could remain completely aloof from the general life of the colony. A sense of belonging developed early. They began to identify their destiny with that of their neighbors.

Cordial relations with the Dutch Reformed Church went on unabated. When a delegate from the Coetus of New Jersey and New York appeared before the Reformed Coetus in 1767, his purpose was to "seek more fellowship." The means toward this end was the material support of a prospective college in New Jersey. The Germans were ready to accept the proffered friendship and enter into a closer fellowship. When Queen's College (now Rutgers) was organized, its location at New Brunswick was agreed upon partly to accommodate the German churches in Pennsylvania and two German ministers were named in the charter as trustees. So close was this association that in 1768 the Dutch sent a delegation to the Germans for the purpose of bringing about a union of the two churches. Closer accommodation was deemed of "great service for the advancement of the Reformed Church in this country," but the Germans held back from this drastic step for fear of offending the church authorities in Holland. However, even in 1794 some were thinking of this union as a "desirable consummation."

As might be expected, the relationship of the German Reformed and the Lutherans was by and large a happy one. This friendship, in spite of significant distinctions in piety, was nurtured by a common linguistic and national background, common tasks, a similar church polity, and particularly by intermarriages. Their close practical cooperation revealed itself most forcibly— particularly after 1760 — in the increasing number of union churches. What at first was exceptional now became an accepted thing.

Practical economic necessity prompted this common enterprise. In Pennsylvania and in other German communities they solved what at the time was singly an insurmountable problem by joining hands to own and to use church property jointly. Sometimes the arrangement was one of simple partnership in owning property, with separate services and a separate consistory, and sometimes church and school were owned and supervised by a common consistory. Often ministers of the two denominations were paid out of a common treasury; they performed sacramental functions without regard to denominational lines. Instances are frequent when the denomination that was first in the field generously and without cost presented one half of its real estate to a newly organized congregation of the other confession. Union parochial schools were maintained; union hymnals were produced by the end of the century; and church records were frequently kept in common. Between 1789 and 1798 four union churches were erected in Berks County alone. Cooperation was not limited to union arrangements, but was general, as, for example, when the Lutheran church in Philadelphia was destroyed by fire in 1794, the Reformed congregation not only opened their building for Lutheran services, but also raised a subscription of several hundred pounds to aid their distressed Lutheran brethren, though they themselves were in the midst of an extensive building project. The local history of many of our most prominent congregations gives ample evidence of this congenial, warmhearted, fraternal intimacy between the two leading German denominations.

The First Great Awakening

No colonial church could avoid coming in touch with the successive waves of revivalism, so marked a feature of eighteenth-century religious life; and ours was no exception. We have seen that in the first half of the century our religious leaders, for the most part, adamantly opposed the pietism of many German sects —the *Schwaermerei*—and also remained cool toward the early "new lights" of Presbyterianism. They were pious but not pietistic and insisted upon uncompromising adherence to doctrinal standards based on the Word of God and inherited traditions. They felt that vital religious living must be worked out within this framework. This mode of religious community life, however, soon became impossible on the new frontiers, where a regular ministry could not be maintained but where religious needs were still pressing. Many people felt out of touch with the churches and were exposed to a pernicious laxness in morals and the letting down of standards, and more particularly to the rising tide of "infidelity." The spiritual welfare of these Germans on the frontier fringes deeply concerned certain members of the Coetus, who, accordingly, were inspired by the spirit of the movement now known in American church history as the First Great Awakening.

The earlier phase of this religious revival stressed the importance of a correct understanding of evangelical doctrines as the source of vital personal religious living. Philip William Otterbein, a very pious, quiet, but hard-working minister, who had come from the Reformed University of Herborn with Schlatter in 1752, expressed this position in a sermon preached in Philadelphia in 1760 under the title "The Incarnation and the Victory of Jesus Christ over the Devil and Death." As pastor in Frederick, Maryland, his travels took him into the depth of the frontier and he traversed as much as 180 miles at a time. He gained a thorough knowledge of the needs, as well as an insight into the techniques effectively used by frontier preachers. Upon taking up his work in Baltimore, he introduced the idea of forming societies and organizing class meetings, venerable pietistic techniques of practical church work long familiar among Palatines.

Five members of the Coetus were willing to associate themselves with Otterbein in an effort to extend this type of evangelism in the scattered congregations. They were Benedict Schwope of Pipe Creek, Jacob Weymer of Hagerstown, Frederick L. Henop of Frederick, Daniel Wagner of York, and William Hendel, Sr., of Tulpehocken, Pennsylvania. United in a common effort to promote a deeper devotional life, they held a series of at least five meetings between the period of May, 1774 and June, 1776 in various Reformed congregations.

These revival meetings were serious, dignified, and surcharged with evangelical fervor. They organized class meetings with appointed lay leaders for the continuation of these gatherings. These groups were to meet in the weekdays and were to support the regular divine services when held. The objective was clearly outlined in the minutes of the first assembly:

> The ground and object of these meetings is to be, that those thus united may encourage each other, pray and sing in unison, and watch over each other's conduct. At these meetings they are to be especially careful to see to it that family worship is regularly maintained; all those who are thus united are to take heed that no disturbances occur among them, and that the affairs of the congregations be conducted and managed in an orderly manner.

The continuing effects of this revivalistic zeal are hard to measure as far as the internal life of the German Reformed group is concerned. With some hesitancy Coetus ordained some of the outstanding class leaders to the Christian ministry, subsequently evicting one of them, George Adam Gueting, for "disorderly conduct." Together with his first associates Otterbein remained with the Reformed Church till his death. An intimate friend in this revival program has said of Otterbein:

> His preaching was sharp and powerful. He was a great friend of revivals, but of his own kind; he would have no noise; this he never could bear. He always made great account of the Catechism, and never thought of leaving our church—had no design of forming a new organization. I often heard him say to his audience in his appeals: "I ask you not to leave your church. I only ask you to forsake your sins."

The coetal letter of 1788 pays this tribute to him: "He has done a great deal of good, he has labored earnestly for the salvation of many souls, and the purpose of his ministry—though it may not in the strictest sense have always accorded with the opinion of everyone—was edification and blessing—for what else could it be?" It is true that his congregation, after his death, joined the conference of the United Brethren, but no other congregation followed this example, although individuals undoubtedly did. Those who remained were caught in the upsurge of a new life within the denomination following the achievement of national independence.

The Process of Americanization

At first, preoccupied with letting down their roots in the new soil, German immigrants kept aloof from colonial affairs. A certain measure of nostalgia for the native land, as well as their strange language and customs, bound them to an island of isolation. On the edges of civilization this position might be maintained, but as their property increased and as the political disturbances of the 1740's and 1750's brought their very lives into jeopardy, a change in the climate of feeling came. Lutherans in conformity with their principles might take a neutral position toward the affairs of the state, but the Reformed, like their co-religionists of the Dutch Reformed and Presbyterian churches, were bound in conscience to fulfill certain obligations in the temporal sphere. They were willing to make the inevitable sacrifices. Out of this participation in the political struggle of the colonies grew a consciousness of separateness from the old world and its institutions, developing parallel with similar ideas in the minds of such colonial leaders as Benjamin Franklin. So the German Reformed identified their destiny with that of the colonies.

Almost without exception the German Reformed clergy was to be found supporting the war against Great Britain, however deeply they felt gratitude for previous favors. John Conrad Bucher and Michael Schlatter had already distinguished themselves in the French and Indian War as chaplains, and they again enlisted. The Reverend John W. G. Neveling converted his entire estate of 5,000 pounds into a loan to Congress. The Reverend Henry Hertzler of Reading, Pennsylvania eloquently demonstrated the meaning of the new freedom for which the colonies were fighting by demanding that the authorities release the pacifistic Mennonites whom they had imprisoned. The independent German Reformed minister, John J. Zubly, of Savannah, Georgia, tried to steer a middle course of compromise, declaring, "I do not regard independence as a remedy for our troubles." Although there was much truth on his side, he found himself out of tune with his coreligionists.

During the Revolution, the Tory-minded Michael Kern and John Casper Rubel no longer enjoyed the recognition of their colleagues of the Coetus, who were of one mind to build a new nation, even as their members supported the cause on the field of battle. Every congregation of the Coetus had its list of patriots who died in the cause of freedom. Every congregation was in the fight. When the British Army was approaching Philadelphia in 1777, Zion Reformed Church in Allentown ripped up the floors of its church to hide the Liberty Bell until the city was evacuated by the British. Michael Hillegass, an elder in the Reformed Church, served as treasurer of the colonies from 1775 until the establishment of the Treasury Department in 1789.

The ministers keenly felt the effects of prolonged strife. "Alas! on account of the sad war," their minutes complain in 1777, "many a praiseworthy observance is omitted, especially in regard to the keeping of the sabbath day and Christian exercises in the families at home. People at present think more of arms than of God's Word." This situation demands a resolution: "Every minister shall take good care in his congregation to observe and to preserve everything which agrees with the duties of a Christian." To some Hessian prisoners one minister preaches on the text "For thus saith the Lord, Ye have sold yourselves for nought; and ye shall be redeemed without money" (Isa. 52:3, KJV), and again on the text "If the Son therefore shall make you free, ye shall be free indeed" (John 8:36, KJV). At last the Philadelphia

PHILIP SCHAFF

LEWIS MAYER

JOHN H. A. BOMBERGER

JOHN W. NEVIN

J. J. BOSSARD

H. A. WINTER

HERMAN J. RUETENIK

JACOB STUCKI

session of Coetus in 1783 could rejoice "on account of the blessed times of peace, whereby the Lord has crowned the physical and spiritual struggle of true Republicans." The ministers now began to refer to themselves as "American ministers." A spirit of hope prevailed. And they were prompted in 1789 to send an address of congratulations to President George Washington for "the happy and peaceable establishment of the new government" which inspired their souls "with new and most lively emotions of adoration, praise, and thanksgiving to God's holy name."

Only one more step was left to complete the formal process of Americanization—to sever the moorings that bound them to the Classis of Amsterdam in Holland, as other denominations had done with their old world connections. The time had fully matured for action. The first generation of preachers was disappearing; the problem of replacement was continually becoming more acute. The accreditation of newly trained ministers, so that vacant churches might be supplied, so often rudely interrupted or delayed on account of uncertain shipping service, created unusual irritation. Hence, at the Coetus assembly of 1791 "it was resolved that the Coetus has the right, at all times, to examine and ordain those who offer themselves as candidates for the ministry, without asking or waiting for permission to do so from the Fathers of Holland."

The result was the transformation of the Coetus into *Der Synod der Reformierten Hoch Deutschen Kirche in Den Vereinigten Staaten von America* (Synod of the Reformed German Church in the United States of America). The separation was made complete in 1793 at Lancaster, Pennsylvania by the adoption of a constitution or *Synodal-Ordnung*. Its preamble breathes the spirit of a precious American document adopted by the nation a few years before: "The ministers of the Evangelical Reformed Church in Pennsylvania and adjoining states have deemed it necessary to establish among themselves a wholesome Christian Discipline and to observe the same, not with a view to invade the rights of the civil authority, but that, governing themselves, they may not be exposed to the censure of others."

At the same time the president asked the usual questions from the ministers and elders present and received the unanimous response that "outward peace and harmony prevail in the churches, and that the office which proclaims reconciliation is not without fruit and profit."

But what of the days ahead, now that they were thrown altogether upon their own resources? The destiny of the Republic trembled in the balance. And across the seas the future in 1793 was no more certain. Wrote one of the pensive leaders of the new-born church: "The condition of Europe is dreadful; whether the French will be able to maintain their republic cannot be foretold. I do not believe that the united powers of Europe will be able to conquer them, but I fear they will destroy themselves. If the war continues a while longer the Palatinate will suffer greatly. Have we not every reason to regard kings and princes as scourges of the human race, or at least of the Christian church? Did not God give Israel a king in his wrath because they had rejected him?"

Undaunted and fully determined to implement their freedom along with the other independent religious bodies of the new nation, the successors of Zwingli and Calvin, Olevianus and Ursinus, Boehm and Schlatter faced forward to the days ahead.

3

The Synod in the East

So it was that at Lancaster on April 27, 1793 the German Reformed churches in Pennsylvania and adjacent states entered upon a new stage of their history and became an American denomination, a free church in a free country. They had been organized as a *Coetus;* they had now become a *Synod.* The two words, the former of Latin, the latter of Greek, derivation, mean literally the same: a coming together. In church usage both words imply the nature and purpose of such assembling, namely, conference and action by members of the assembled group in their common interests. As a coetus the German Reformed churches in America had been dependent on the Reformed Church in Holland for ministers, books, and financial help, as well as for final approval of their actions and for ordination of their ministers. As a synod they were "on their own," independent of all supervision and control.

As one scans the minutes of the meetings in this transition period, he is struck by the seemingly incidental and inconspicuous references to the step that was being taken. The "fathers and brethren" were too busy making history to be very history-conscious. Men were sorely needed for the ministry, and their preparation, examination, ordination, and settlement in needy fields, as well as the smoothing out of difficulties among pastors and congregations, were the matters of immediate and important consequence. The *Synodal-Ordnung* (Church Discipline) regulated mainly the conduct of the sessions and the relations with pastors and charges. Prepared by William Hendel, Sr., and Abraham Blumer, it was amended, approved, and subscribed to by the thirteen ministers and their delegate elders, whose names are not given. The first officers were John Henry Winckhaus, president, and Caspar Wack, secretary. William Hendel, Sr., was the commonly recognized leader. Joseph H. Dubbs estimates that at this time *Der Synod der Reformierten Hoch Deutschen Kirche* consisted of 178 congregations, 55 of them vacant, 15,000 communicants, and 40,000 adherents. In addition to these, there were independent ministers and congregations, that is, those not affiliated with the Synod, who for one reason or another, shied away from any overhead organization.

A new hymnbook and a new edition of the Heidelberg Catechism were among the first projects of the new Synod. The Marburg Hymnal, brought along by many of the Reformed settlers and by that time out-of-print, was used by the Synod's committee as the basis for the new one which, because of Hendel's part in its preparation, came to be known as "Hendel's Hymnbook."

Attitudes of "the fathers" toward current questions in the closing years of the century are shown in two interesting actions taken at the 1796 meeting. One was in response to a report by Dr. Hendel of "the sad consequences ... caused by the publication of the blasphemous works, especially those of Thomas Paine." Synod resolved "that the ministry endeavor to operate against these results by watching and prayer according to the example of apostles" (Article 8). Hendel also "called attention to the proposition in the House of Representatives, threatening the overthrow of the instruction of the youth in the true Christian religion" (Article 11). The first moves toward a public school system in the commonwealth were evidently regarded as endangering the church's right to instruct her children in parochial schools.

H. M. J. Klein comments on the minutes of 1795 that "not a word is recorded concerning the yellow fever epidemic in Philadelphia which terrified the whole state." Pastor Winckhaus died of this disease in 1793, as did his successor, William Hendel, Sr., in 1798. Both men "heroically remained at their post of duty throughout the epidemic."

It would seem that the scarcity of references in the Synod minutes, especially in these earlier years, to contemporary events, particularly in the political realm, reflects an attitude resulting from convictions as to the separation of church and state. This may well represent a reaction from the situation in the fatherland, where the relationship between the two was regarded as too close for the welfare of either.

The Call of the Frontiers: Missions

The minutes of this early Synod are sadly punctuated with appeals from "outlying regions" to the heartland of the church in eastern Pennsylvania. From western New York, Virginia, the Carolinas, the land across the Alleghenies, and Ohio came pleas to "send men to help us." Communications from Hardy County, Virginia and from Guilford County and Rowan County in North Carolina were received by the Synod of 1797, begging for "faithful ministers" and financial help. As pastors for the northern circuits were few, the best that could be promised was occasional visits by Pennsylvania pastors and ministers of their own "as soon as practicable." According to a resolution of 1813, "in the future all young men who are licensed shall, prior to taking charge of congregations, make a missionary tour to distant destitute regions and devote to this important and necessary work as a missionary a period of two or three months." The added clause, "except only in such cases where there shall be sufficient cause for not complying," seems to have been more effective than the principal action. In that year, however, James Ross Reily was commissioned to go on a missionary tour of the North Carolina settlements. He was gone three months, confirmed 169 and baptized 113, and brought the southern field closer to the conscience and fellowship of the church in the North.

Before this, several young men had gone to North Carolina, notably Andrew Loretz, the first to establish the church in the western part of the state. Jacob Larose, Jacob Christman, and Samuel Weyberg also served in that region but moved on westward—the first two to Ohio, the last to Missouri. George Boger, who lived, labored, and died in the Carolinas, held the line with some help from Albert Hauck and John Rudy, until the coming of John Christ Fritchey in 1828.

Into the Shenandoah, "the Valley of Virginia," German Reformed people from Pennsylvania and Maryland had been moving in growing numbers since before the Revolution. Ministers had come too late to serve the earliest congregation of Germanna Ford and Germantown. Bernard Willy and Henry Giesy preached in these parts, and Coetus ministers, for example, Philip William Otterbein, had made evangelistic journeys. But the man who really saved the valley for the Reformed Church was John Brown, who, beginning in Rockingham County at the turn of the century, was the only permanent Reformed pastor in Virginia for thirty-five years. "Father" Brown, as he was fondly known, published about 1818 at Harrisonburg a "Circular Letter to the Germans," which is said to have been "the first published discussion of slavery by anyone in our church."[1]

---

[1] *History of the Reformed Church in the Nineteenth Century* by James I. Good, p. 197.

At the beginning of the synodical period the only Reformed minister laboring in western Pennsylvania was John William Weber. His labors and trials are vividly described in a document written by him in 1814, which Henry Harbaugh quotes in his *Fathers of the German Reformed Church in Europe and America* (Vol. II). Other pioneers west of the mountains were Giesy, who came to Somerset County in 1794, and John Peter Mahnenschmidt, who came from and returned to Ohio, laboring in Washington County, Pennsylvania, 1806-12. At the Synod of 1811 he expressed penitence for having baptized without being ordained and, being forgiven with censure, was licensed as a catechist and later (1817) received ordination. About 1819 Nicholas P. Hacke and Henry Koch crossed the mountains into western Pennsylvania. Koch went into the Clarion region, while Hacke organized churches around Greensburg, where he served as pastor until 1877 (probably a record for ministers of the denomination).

The phrase, "lost churches," is usually applied to those of South Carolina and western New York. After the death of Christian Theuss, the most active Reformed pastor in South Carolina, the congregations there had only occasional service by men from North Carolina or from other denominations. Eventually, when the Synod could not answer their appeals, these groups disintegrated and their members joined the congregations of other communions.

In 1802 Anthony Hautz was called by a settlement of Pennsylvania Germans in the Finger Lakes region of New York State to be their pastor. He served them until his death in 1830. The Reverend Dietrich Willers, a veteran of Waterloo, who was to become the first president of the Board of Foreign Missions, succeeded the Reverend John Pulfish in this general region. Willers wrote earnest appeals in *The Messenger*, but there were no responses, and this part of the state had to wait for the later nineteenth-century migration of Germans for the establishment of congregations with pastors to serve them.

German Reformed groups in Nova Scotia and Maine gradually turned to Presbyterian or Congregationalist fellowships for want of ministers to lead them in the church of their fathers. For the same reason, congregations in New Jersey, at first represented in Coetus and Synod, went over to other denominations.

From 1819 to 1826 the Synod had only a home missions committee, but in 1826 a missionary society was organized at Frederick, Maryland, and auxiliary societies were formed in different sections of the church. In 1832 the Synod took the work of the general committee under its immediate supervision as a Board of Missions, but by that time the classes (small regional organizations of churches—pronounced classees) tended to do their own home mission work, and that of the Board had little scope or success.

The Language Question

In the early decades of the new century, and before the doctrinal and liturgical controversies began to loom, four problems vexed the German Reformed Church and interfered with her normal growth as an American denomination: language, revivalism, organization, and the supply of ministers.

With the exception of a small minority of French Huguenots, who came to America via Germany and Holland, and whose very names and thought patterns were considerably affected by Teutonic influences (for example, De la Coeur becoming Dallicker), the great mass of the Reformed immigrants was of German extraction and culture and used the German tongue. The transition to English was slow and gradual. English began to be used in the churches in New Jersey, where Germans were far less numerous and under the influence of the Dutch Reformed, who had made the change much earlier and less painfully. West of the Susquehanna and in Maryland, English soon prevailed. In general, the conflict over language in the churches seems to have been far less violent in the open country than in the larger towns, where the Germans, especially the young folks in their community relationships, had much more contact with English-speaking people.

The classic case, which was soon to reach the floor of the Synod, was that of the Race Street Church in Philadelphia, of which the redoubtable Samuel Helffenstein was pastor from 1799 to 1831. The first action of the Synod was in 1804 when "a petition was read begging Synod to come to their assistance in their present sad condition inasmuch as a total separation is to be feared from the fact that there is a strong party among them who desire a sermon in the English language every two weeks."

The Synod contented itself with a general appeal to both factions to exercise forbearance and brotherly love, but the struggle in Philadelphia continued. Helffenstein, faced by a tie vote in the consistory, cast his vote against the introduction of English, with the result that those who wanted it withdrew and founded a new congregation that soon affiliated with the Dutch Reformed. But the number of those desiring English grew again within the congregation, and they reached Synod in 1805 with their appeal, whereupon Synod resolved that they be permitted to have services in English "upon condition that no minister not connected with a Presbyterian synod be permitted to enter the pulpit and none without the consent of the German minister." During the next decade, the battle was resumed. By 1817 "the English" had Pastor Helffenstein with them and attained a majority. Then "the Germans," reinforced by tides of immigration, withdrew and formed a church on John Street that mothered a group of congregations which were later to organize as the German Synod of the East.

St. Paul's and First congregations in Lancaster, Pennsylvania, now almost straight across the street from each other, experienced similar separation. Other solutions were found elsewhere. In some communities occasional or even alternating English services were provided. In Frederick, Maryland an assistant conducted the English services.

As for the church at large, German was used in Synod and in many classes until well toward the mid-century. As late as 1826 the president of Synod rebuked a member who presumed to address that body in English. It was strongly felt and expressed by the older men that only the German language was capable of rendering deep theological thought and dignified ecclesiastical procedure. The first English minutes were printed in 1825, but both languages were used in publishing minutes for several years thereafter.

The conclusion can hardly be avoided that the tenacity with which large sections of the German Reformed Church clung to the language of their fathers had much to do with the slow pace at which consciousness of being an American denomination developed. It surely had something to do with the reluctance and opposition with which the more dyed-in-the-wool German sections of the church met the challenges to educational and missionary enterprise that the new century presented. The loss of congregations, families, and individuals to English-using denominations, while it cannot be measured in statistics, was undoubtedly very large.

Revivalism: The New Measures

The German Reformed Church could not keep from being affected by that wave of religious interest and activity known as the Second Great Awakening. As the first one, in the eighteenth century, led by George Whitefield, Jonathan Edwards, and the Tennents, had divided religious groups as, for example, the Presbyterians, into "Old Lights" and "New Lights," the revival of religion in the teens and twenties of the nineteenth century brought similar divisions to many Protestant groups in America. the German Reformed among them.

James I. Good, in his chapter on "Revivals" in *The History of the Reformed Church in the Nineteenth Century*, brings together considerable evidence to prove that the leaders of the Reformed Church in this period were not opposed to experiential religion nor to real revivals, but only to some of the excesses and extravagances that obtained in certain quarters. The influence of German Pietism on both the Reformed and Lutheran colonial churches can hardly be gainsaid. Henry Melchior Muhlenberg came from Halle, the center of German Lutheran Pietism. William Hendel, Jr., Daniel Wagner, and others of the Reformed leaders held prayer meetings, sought conversions, and followed what seems to have been the pietistic rather than the confessionalistic pattern.

One case involving synodical action was that of John Dietrich Aurandt. As a young man he had been associated with John G. Pfrimmer, a leader of the New Measures movement, and attended some of the "big meetings." When the Reformed congregations of the Buffalo Valley asked for his ordination, it was brought out that he had already done some baptizing. At his own request his examination was postponed, and he was ordered by the Synod of 1801 to abstain from administering the sacraments and from attending the big meetings, as well as to pursue his studies under the direction of a Synod minister. He complied with all of these injunctions and later served valiantly as the pioneer missionary in south-central Pennsylvania.

The expulsion of George Adam Gueting from the Synod in 1804, because of new measure excesses, contrasts with the respectful and appreciative dealings with Otterbein, who remained all his life a minister of the Reformed Church. His congregation, the Second Church of Baltimore, seceded to the United Brethren after his death.

The so-called new measures were a nationwide reaction from the coldness and formality that had characterized so much of American church life at the turn of the century. Like the First Great Awakening, this nineteenth-century movement led to the establishment of educational institutions and a deepened interest in missionary and benevolent enterprises. In the congregations the results included prayer meetings, emphasis on the family altar, more students for the ministry, and an increase in the number of Sunday schools, which at first were opposed by many ministers who feared these schools would become substitutes for catechetical instruction. (The first Sunday school organized by a Reformed congregation was reported from Philadelphia in 1806).

The most reasonable conclusion seems to be that our church leaders distinguished between sound and disorderly revival methods, approved the former and warned against the latter. Even John W. Nevin, at least in his earlier days, while denouncing the anxious bench and similar concomitants and paraphernalia of big meetings, approved the true revival of church and individual life, though he was not so ready to attribute it to the Second Awakening.

The Reformed Church suffered several defections from her ranks during this period. The largest involved Philip William Otterbein, leader of the United Brethren, sometimes called the New Reformed. Another, which drew perhaps more from Lutheran than from Reformed circles, was led by Jacob Albright and became eventually the Evangelical Association, whose members were known as *Die Albrechtsleute*. Then there was John Winebrenner, pastor at Harrisburg, who, when locked out of his church by a hostile consistory, met with his followers in private homes and organized the denomination now known as the Churches of God. The Reformed Synod at Mifflinburg in 1828 announced that Winebrenner had refused to respond to its citations and was preaching against infant baptism, whereupon his name was erased from the Synod roll.

It is tempting to speculate how much larger the Reformed Church would have been if its leaders had been more tolerant of the more pietistic groups, and if the latter had been less radical in some of their practices. But as God "maketh the wrath of men at times to praise him," we may well think that even the divisions in his churches may have resulted in reaching and ministering to wider circles of his people. Paul and Barnabas, once separated after their first journey together, may have covered more territory and won more converts than they would have gained had they continued to travel in each other's company. At any rate, we may be thankful that the tide of Protestant division has turned and that in federation and cooperation, if not always in organic union, God's servants are laboring together to evangelize mankind.

Organizational Developments: the Classes; the Free Synod

The Synod at Lancaster in 1819 heard and accepted the report of a committee appointed the year before to consider the division of the Synod into classes (singular, classis; plural, classes). The report began:

> Because of the rapid growth of the population of the United States many Reformed congregations have been organized, and because it is our great desire that all regular ministers of our church in the United States shall be united by an inseparable bond of union, and because our church has spread far and wide, thus making synodical activities ever more difficult, and because some of the brethren have great distances to cover . . . Synod shall be divided into classes.

The first eight classes, with their districts defined according to states, Pennsylvania counties, or parts of counties, were then listed: Philadelphia, Northampton, Lebanon, Susquehanna, West Pennsylvania, Ohio, Maryland, and Zion (the York region).

Articles followed, defining the rights and activities of the Synod in relation to its classes. The first meetings of these classes were appointed for the fourth Sunday after Easter, 1820 and the places of the meetings were designated.

Changes in the setup preceding the General Synod of 1863 were as follows: Ohio Classis separated from the mother Synod in 1824 for much the same reasons that the Coetus had for breaking relations with the church in Holland—distance and the right to ordain ministers. Then, as Ohio Synod, it organized its own classes, including Westmoreland (1841) and Clarion (1850) in Pennsylvania, but transferred the latter to the eastern Synod[2] in 1857.

New classes organized included Virginia, 1824; East Pennsylvania, 1826; North Carolina, 1831; Mercersburg and New York, 1840; Goshenhoppen, 1841; Lancaster, 1852; Susquehanna divided into East and West, 1856; St. Paul, 1861.

The Synod that met at Hagerstown in 1820 was known as a "General Synod" and consisted of the delegates elected by the various classes. A "Convention Synod" was one in which representatives of the congregations constituted the Synod.

The Synod of the Free German Reformed Congregations of Pennsylvania, later called the German Reformed Synod of Pennsylvania and Adjacent States, represented a "walkout" of certain ministers and congregations, most of them in eastern Pennsylvania. It was caused chiefly by opposition to the plan for a seminary and was aggravated by the personal grievances of Lebrecht Frederick Herman, whose teaching of theology in his "Swamp College" at Falkner Swamp had been forbidden by the Synod, and whose son, Frederick, had been suspended by the

---

[2] It was not until 1889 that this Synod in the eastern part of the country was officially called the Eastern Synod. References to the history of the Synod preceding that date therefore use "eastern"; and references to its history from 1889 on use the capital "e."

Synod in not too gentle manner. As many as fifty-seven ministers and one hundred congregations belonged to this dissident group at one time or another. But time tended to heal the wounds, and at its meeting in Philadelphia in 1836 the Free Synod made overtures to return to the fold. Their delegates to the mother Synod, meeting at Baltimore that year, were welcomed with open arms; and the reunion was effected in 1837.

Provision and Preparation of Ministers: Seminary and College

Probably the church's most serious problem from the very first was that of providing for the congregations an adequately prepared clerical leadership. With the separation from Holland tutelage the supply of young Germans and Swiss through the help of the Reformed Church there came to an end. Several young men, notably the younger Hendel, were prepared in seminaries of other churches on this side, New Brunswick and Princeton. But the great demand and the scant supply led to a makeshift in theological education which surely helped to save the day, namely, private instruction in the homes of older and more experienced ministers. Samuel Weyberg, Abraham Wagner, and William Hendel, Sr., had done some of this work before the synodical period began, and in the early years of the new century it was continued, most of it, by three outstanding pastor-teachers: Christian L. Becker, first at Lancaster and later at Baltimore; Lebrecht Frederick Herman at Falkner Swamp; and Samuel Helffenstein in Philadelphia. The young student would live as a member of the minister's family, would help him in his rounds of pastoral labors, and at stated times would be given instruction in the languages and in philosophy and theology.

With the passing of the years and the multiplying of the church's problems and opportunities, the critical need of a theological institution became more apparent. The Synod of 1817 appointed a committee to confer with Lutherans and Dutch

Reformed in regard to a joint project, but John H. Livingston, the capable and respected leader of the latter church, presented to the Synod 150 copies of his "Address to the Reformed German Churches in the United States," urging them to found a seminary of their own. Maryland Classis took the lead in agitating for such a school.

The Synod at Hagerstown in 1820 turned from discussion to action—at least action on paper. A plan was adopted for the founding and the control of the institution. Twelve ministers were chosen as "superintendents." Philip Milledoler, then pastor of a Dutch Reformed church in New York, was elected president (and professor) at a salary of $2,000. Frederick, Maryland was favored but not quite chosen as the location, and action was taken forbidding theological teaching in the homes of pastors.

Opposition at once arose and increased, particularly in the eastern sections of the church. Milledoler, doubtless sensing it, after considerable wavering declined the appointment. Pledges of support, contingent upon the assuming of his duties, were withdrawn, and the first stage of the effort closed with little result except the secession of the Free Synod. The years of reaction and uncertainty that ensued could not quench the spirit of the little group of stalwart proponents of a seminary. At the Bedford Synod in 1824 an invitation by Dickinson College, then Presbyterian, to house the infant institution in its buildings at Carlisle, was accepted. The opposition to the beginning of the seminary was so strong that, according to the account of some who were present, there was a tie vote requiring a decision from William Hendel, Jr., the presiding officer, who was pastor at Womelsdorf in an anti-seminary region. Then came his words, probably measuring—and that accurately—the personal results that would come to him: "I vote for the seminary. I have broad shoulders and can carry much." At the same meeting, Lewis

Mayer was elected professor at a salary of $700 after Samuel Helffenstein had declined to serve.

So on March 11, 1825 the seminary opened at Carlisle with five students, one hundred volumes in the library, and $300 in funds. The outlook was very dark. Dr. Mayer reported for the year 1826 that only four ministers had taken offerings for the school, amounting to but fifty-eight dollars. Then came help and new hope through what some at first regarded as a quixotic expedition by James Ross Reily, then pastor at Hagerstown, whose missionary journeys south and west had marked him as an adventurous and devoted spirit. With the credentials of the Synod but at his own expense he journeyed to Holland, Germany, and Switzerland, telling the story of the German Reformed Church and its sorely needed "school of the prophets." The response was generous in money, in books, and in deepened interest on the part of the older Reformed churches in their brethren on this side of the sea. It gave "a shot in the arm" to the church in America, whose interest in the school had been waning, and contributions began to increase.

In 1829, due to unsatisfactory conditions at Carlisle, where the Scotch-Irish college students showed little interest in Mayer's German course offerings and much more interest in tormenting him and his scholars, the Synod moved the school to the more German atmosphere of York, where Dr. Mayer had formerly been pastor. The Reverend Daniel Young was elected a second professor and editor of *The German Reformed Church Magazine*, the first church paper of the denomination, but he died in 1831. Mayer was more and more impressed by the lack of scholastic preparation for theological training on the part of the students in the seminary and applicants for admission. So in 1829 he asked Synod "for the privilege of connecting with the seminary a literary and scientific institution in which Latin, Greek, Hebrew, natural sciences, mathematics, logic, geography, history, and composition should be taught." Out of this need came the "Classical School" or "High School" in a building on George Street in York, after that city was chosen for the seminary, rather than Lancaster, where some had proposed the use of Franklin College for this purpose. Frederick Augustus Rauch was elected principal in 1832; he presented his plan of instruction and began his work in 1833. After studying at Heidelberg, Giessen, and Marburg in Germany he had come in 1831 to Easton, Pennsylvania where he impressed the pastor, Thomas Pomp, by his learning and spirit, and where he taught for a short while at Lafayette College.

Two factors led to unrest about the York location of the church's schools. The Germans of that city did little better than Carlisle by way of financial support, and the growth of the Classical School called for more commodious quarters. So in 1835 the Synod resolved to move both institutions to Mercersburg, a village in the foothills of the Alleghenies, where the Reformed pastor, Jacob Mayer, had incited the community to make the best offer—$10,000 plus ground for a building and a house for the professors until one could be built. The Classical School moved immediately and received its charter as Marshall College in 1836. The seminary followed in 1837, but at first without Dr. Mayer. Soon, however, he was persuaded to withdraw his resignation and come to Mercersburg, where he served until his second resignation in 1839.

Following long negotiations and against considerable opposition on the part of those who wanted to keep it in Mercersburg, the college was moved to Lancaster in 1853 and united with Franklin College to form Franklin and Marshall. James Buchanan, later to become President of the United States, was the president of the first Board of Trustees of the merged institution. John W. Nevin had resigned from the seminary in 1851 and had moved to Lancaster. He was active in the movement to bring the college there, but refused to accept the presidency. The Synod would not release Philip Schaff from his seminary professorship. So Emanuel Vogel Gerhart was challenged to come from Heidelberg College in Ohio. He accepted and labored and suffered through the period of war and reconstruction to put the college on a firmer academic and financial footing.

Relations with Other Churches

The three sister denominations with which the German Reformed Church had closest contact and most intimate relations were the Dutch Reformed, the Lutheran, and the Presbyterian. The factors that drew her closer to one or another of these were different, as were the obstacles that prevented the consummation of union.

Cordial relations with the Dutch Reformed were sustained throughout the first half of the century. The common relationship with the church in Holland and similarities in polity and doctrine make this quite understandable. In 1803 John H. Livingston, in a letter to the Reformed Synod, asked for two things: (1) for ministers to be sent to the spiritually destitute Germans in New York State and (2) for a fraternal correspondence between the two communions. Until 1813 this correspondence was carried on by letter and in the following years by delegates. In 1818 an invitation was extended to join with the Dutch in their seminary at New Brunswick. In 1843 a plan was drawn for even closer relations through triennial conventions of the two German synods (Eastern and Ohio) and the Dutch synods. The first convention was held the next year in Harrisburg, at which the Dutch contributed $10,000 for the domestic missions of the German church.

James I. Good attributes the withdrawal of the Dutch Reformed from this cooperative relationship to their suspicions of the Mercersburg theology, but there were reasons other than their feeling that the German Reformed were not thoroughly Calvinistic. The German church regarded the Heidelberg Catechism as symbol enough, without adding the Belgic Confession and the Articles of Dort. Moreover, the two groups lived in rather distinct geographical territories, and the Dutch acceptance and use of English had antedated that change on the part of the Germans. It is quite probable, too, that some of the Dutch Reformed in their well-endowed churches in and around New York looked a bit askance at their "poor relatives" in Pennsylvania.

As for the Lutherans, they were "kith and kin" of the Reformed, of the same stock, occupying much the same territory, much intermarried, and often members of "union churches." Helmuth's *Evangelical Magazine* (1812) and the *Gemeinschaftliche Gesangbuch* (1817) had been approved by the Reformed Synod and were widely used by both churches. Yet there were historic doctrinal differences, deeper than that between *Unser Vater* and *Vater Unser* in the Lord's Prayer. Memory of the conflicts in the fatherland dating from as far back as the Marburg Colloquy (1529) still lingered. Differences in the interpretation of the Lord's presence during his Supper continued to figure in the minds of many leaders of both churches. The Evangelical Union of Prussia in 1817, and the following of its pattern in other German states, could not help but make an impression on this side of the Atlantic, but Benjamin S. Schneck's report on the German situation, "outward union with inward disunion," coupled with the immigration of many Germans who were out of sympathy with the unionistic movement, kept the two churches apart.

The chief cooperative venture in the field of education was, of course, Franklin College, whose founding in 1787 has already been noted. Its vicissitudes through the early years of the nineteenth century were due in some small part to dual ownership and control. By mid-century both Lutheran and Reformed seemed convinced that one should buy out the other. As the Reformed had the larger financial interest (two-thirds), and as union with Marshall College at Mercersburg was imminent, it was finally agreed (1850) that the Lutherans should give up their share in return for about $15,000, which was used to found a professorship in their college at Gettysburg.

There were negotiations with the Presbyterians as early as 1822. Committees appointed to explore the possibilities of closer union met in 1828 and concluded that organic union was not possible. After the Old School-New School divisions of the Presbyterians, a yearly exchange of delegates was maintained with both bodies. Maryland Classis in 1833 took action, refuting the claims being made by some Presbyterians that they and the Reformed were really the same, and ordered the preachers to discuss the differences from the pulpit.

The Mercersburg Movement

We have seen that in 1837 the little Reformed Church Seminary moved to a Franklin County, Pennsylvania village, nestled at the foot of the Blue Ridge and named for General Hugh Mercer of Revolutionary War fame. This was to give a label to a particular trend or type of Christian thought and cultus, interest in which seems to have widened and deepened with the years. Many, whether or not they have favored and followed its ways, have regarded it as the unique contribution of the German Reformed Church in America.

Movements begin with moving men, of whom in this case there were three. We have already noted the coming of Frederick Augustus Rauch to head the Classical School at York, soon to be transferred to Mercersburg. With this he assumed the second or "German" professorship in the seminary. It may be said that he brought *the philosophical initiative* to these schools and to the school of thought that was to develop in them.

Greatly influenced by Hegel, he has been considered a pioneer in the field of psychology in America. Regrettably but inevitably his teaching clashed with that of Dr. Mayer. The students followed the line of Rauch, and Mayer resigned a second time in 1839. His successor, John W. Nevin, was elected by the Chambersburg Synod of 1840. A native of Franklin County, of Scotch-Irish extraction and a Presbyterian, he had graduated from Union College, Schenectady, New York and from the Theological Seminary at Princeton. He was at the time a teacher in the Western Theological Seminary at Allegheny, now Pittsburgh, North Side. He had been studying German theology and now applied himself to the Heidelberg Catechism. His all too brief association with Rauch quickly bloomed into a deeply appreciative mutual regard. Nevin was soon to become the *theologian* of the movement that was now taking direction and form.

Rauch died in 1841 at the age of thirty-five. The need of a "German professor" to succeed him directed the eyes of the church to the fatherland. After the first choice, Frederick William Krummacher, had declined the invitation, Philip Schaff, a young private docent of the University of Berlin, "a republican Swiss," was challenged. He accepted and at the age of twenty-five crossed the Atlantic in 1844 to serve as professor of Historical and Exegetical Theology in the seminary at Mercersburg. Thus came the *historian* and the *liturgist* into the beginnings of the movement to which he was to contribute much.

To understand the issues in the controversies that were to enlist the men of Mercersburg, we need to recall some of the trends and currents in American Christendom in the thirties and forties of the nineteenth century. The Second Awakening had set in motion waves of revivalism and sectarianism that had quite thoroughly inundated both cities and countryside. Puritanism and Methodism, stressing the "gathered churches" and individualistic piety, were riding high. Anti-Roman Catholicism was militantly expressed both in political and in religious circles. There was considerable resentment and resistance to ideas from Europe, such as were represented, for example, in German theology and in the Oxford Movement in England.

Before Schaff came, Nevin had published in 1843 *The Anxious Bench,* an elaboration of his original protest against some of the techniques of current revivalism. In this he pleaded especially with the churches of German extraction to cultivate the true kind of revival, centered in the life of the church and nourished and guided through the catechetical system. A number of vigorous retorts came from various quarters, most of them accusing him of trying to "quench the Spirit."

Schaff's inaugural address, delivered in First Church, Reading, Pennsylvania on October 25, 1844 was entitled "The Principle of Protestantism" and was a discussion of the nature of the church as *one, holy,* and *catholic.* Though corrupted and distorted by Rome, the church, Schaff believed, was continuing and developing, with the divine life flowing through its members, making it a divine organism and a proper object of faith, as in the Creed. In the anti-Roman atmosphere of the times this position drew sharp attack. Nevin translated and edited the address and defended it as true gospel. Philadelphia Classis, led by Joseph F. Berg, demanded an investigation of the new professor and his doctrine, and what is sometimes called "Schaff's heresy trial" was held in connection with the Synod at York in 1845. The vote of vindication was forty to three.

Here then began what some have called "the thirty years' war." It passed first through a mainly doctrinal phase and then through more liturgical stages to the work of the Peace Commission in 1878. On the one side were the two Mercersburg professors and a loyal following of their students and friends; on the other, their challengers, who were wont to call themselves the "Old Reformed." The latter claimed that they were faithful to the Reformation fathers, to Ulrich Zwingli in particular, while their opponents were dangerous innovators. The Mercersburgers claimed to take into consideration the ancient as well as the Reformation creeds. They called themselves Christocentric, not bibliocentric, insisting that in their thought they made the whole person of Christ basic, not just his teaching, his work, or his death.

In three writings of the late forties, Nevin presented the Mercersburg position. In *The Mystical Presence* he interpreted John Calvin's doctrine of the spiritual real presence of Christ in the Eucharist in a way that was challenged by his former teacher, the Princeton Calvinist Charles Hodge. In *The History and Genius of the Heidelberg Catechism* he appealed to that symbol for support, while in *Anti-Christ, or the Spirit of Sect and Schism* he combated the extreme individualism of the sectarian, which had brought forth such a proliferation of religious groups, all claiming to be the true church. Philip Schaff in his treatise *What Is Church History?* stressed the objective factor in man's salvation as represented by the church with the Word and the Sacraments. Accused of "Romanizing" and "Puseyizing," that is, following the Roman Catholic and Anglo-Catholic line, Nevin and Schaff endeavored to explain the differences between their position and the positions of Rome and Oxford. Their chief literary medium was the *Mercersburg Review*, a magazine established in 1848 by the alumni and students of Marshall College.

To the "battles and sieges" of this conflict James I. Good devotes 376 pages in his *History of the Reformed Church in the United States,* with many references in other sections of the book, all definitely slanted from the Old Reformed partisan side; while Joseph H. Dubbs, the historian in the Mercersburg tradition, deals with the subject more calmly and in less detail. It was a stage in our denominational history that many on both sides have deplored and tried to forget. There were defections from the Mercersburg camp to the Roman and Anglican churches and from that of their opponents to the Presbyterian and Dutch Reformed. North Carolina Classis dissociated itself in 1853 from the mother Synod for a period of years because of suspicions regarding the orthodoxy of the seminary. Interest and activity in missions were diverted into channels of controversy. Yet the losses were not unmixed with gain. Clergy and laymen alike were moved to examine the faith that was in them. Historical research regarding ancient and Reformation men and ideas and the leaders and pioneers of the church in America, was strongly incited. Who but the Supreme Judge himself can truly assess the results of such differences and conflicts among his children?

Liturgical Rumblings

While the second and mainly liturgical stage of the "Mercersburg controversy" did not come to a head until the General Synod period, its beginnings may be readily noted in the earlier decades. The question as to whether there was any great need or demand for a liturgy in those times is itself one of the moot questions of historical interpretation. The general impression persists that, though the Palatinate Liturgy had been brought over by some of the first Reformed immigrants, it had never attained widespread use, and that, as a rule, every pastor was a law to himself in regard to the amount and kind of ritual he used. A liturgy prepared by Lewis Mayer was published by the Synod in 1841, but it had rather limited acceptance in the church. In 1847 East Pennsylvania Classis overtured Synod to take steps toward a new liturgy, and a committee was appointed the following year with Nevin as chairman and such "low church" leaders as Joseph F. Berg and John H. A. Bomberger as members. Schaff soon replaced Nevin as chairman, and after many meetings and much discussion the committee presented what came to be known as "the Provisional Liturgy" to the Synod of 1857. It was based on certain liturgical principles that Schaff had offered to the Synod at Baltimore in 1852. This liturgy was offered by the Synod to the churches for optional and experimental use. Criticisms and demands for its revision began at once to pour in. Synod then turned it back to the committee for revision "in a way that shall not be inconsistent either with established liturgical principles or with the devotional and doctrinal genius of the German Reformed Church." About this time Nevin published his treatise on *The Liturgical Question,* espousing an altar liturgy, and Bomberger made reply, insisting that this was contrary to the cultic heritage of the Reformed Church.

The Tercentenary, celebrating the formation and adoption of the Heidelberg Catechism, was held in Philadelphia in 1863. This was a high spot in the history of the German Reformed Church in the nineteenth century. For a brief time the liturgical argument was recessed.

"Congregational singing," writes Joseph H. Dubbs, "had in some parts of the church almost become a lost art." In 1830 *Psalms and Hymns,* prepared by a committee of Maryland Classis, was adopted for "English" churches, and in 1857 a small collection of English hymns was published by the Liturgical Committee. Dr. Schaff made a collection of German hymns that was adopted in 1859 by both the eastern Synod and the Ohio Synod.

Publications: Church Papers

The first annual report of the Missionary Society of the Reformed Church to the Synod at York in 1827 proposed that, as a means of keeping the members informed about the educational and missionary work of the church, "The Religious and Missionary Magazine of the Reformed Church" be published. Lewis Mayer was named editor and the Reverend Daniel Zacharias, the agent for securing subscribers. The first issue appeared

in 1828 at Carlisle; in 1831 it was removed to York, whither the
seminary had gone, was changed from a monthly to a bimonthly
issue, and named *The Messenger of the German Reformed
Church.* Daniel Young was in charge of the paper until his untimely death in 1831.

As the church was still largely German, papers in that language were necessary. Following several private ventures of
limited duration, the *Christliche Zeitschrift,* later the *Reformierte
Kirchenzeitung,* served the German constituency and was subsequently moved to Cleveland, Ohio.

At the same synod meeting which elected Nevin (1840), it
was announced that a printing business had been established
at Chambersburg, Pennsylvania and was in successful operation.
Messenger subscribers at this time numbered 2,300; those of the
Zeitschrift, 1,700. In 1844 this interest was turned over to a
newly organized Board of Publication, under whom the business
deteriorated to a point where a firm, known as M. Kieffer and
Company, consisting of the Reverends Moses Kieffer, Samuel
R. Fisher, and Benjamin S. Schneck, saved it from bankruptcy
by taking it over, reduced its debts, and paid an annual sum to
the Synod. In 1854 a half-interest and, a decade later, the balance, were sold back to the Synod, just before the destruction
of the property by a Confederate army in 1864.

The Church and the Civil War

The reader of the synod minutes is struck by the few references to the national crisis through which the nation was passing.
The Easton Synod meeting in 1861 noted the President's call
for "A Day of Humiliation, Fasting, and Prayer" and set aside
the second day of the sessions for this purpose. The Reverend
Thomas C. Porter preached the sermon. The next annual meeting (1862) at Chambersburg was held close enough to the battle-
front to cause considerable anxiety and alarm. In fact, the

"rebels" under "Jeb" Stuart had been through the town just four days earlier, and Stonewall Jackson was reported to have crossed the Potomac and to be on his way northward. Benjamin Bausman, pastor at Chambersburg, on account of "exaggerated reports in regard to the state of things in this place in consequence of a raid made through this section of the country on Friday and Saturday last, by a portion of rebel cavalry," felt it necessary to send out a circular to the delegates, assuring them that they "can come to Synod with perfect safety, and that every preparation has been made by our citizens to give them a proper reception."

The Synod met as planned. "The attendance," according to one account, "though not so large as it would have been had not this place been the center of much alarm and excitement, was tolerably good." Henry Harbaugh preached the opening sermon on the text, "Can ye not discern the signs of the times?" Emanuel V. Gerhart was elected president. Three services were held by the members in army hospitals. The fathers and brethren went calmly about their business, listening to opposing reports on the Provisional Liturgy and making plans for the observance of the Tercentenary in the following year.

Students in the seminary at Mercersburg were evidently not quite so much at ease; they petitioned the Synod for "a temporary removal of the school to Lancaster or some other place less exposed to personal danger and disturbance of study by rebel invasions." In the Board of Visitors' report to the Synod at Carlisle, 1863, it was stated that the school was closed on June 16

on account of the rebel invasion under General Lee. On the fifth of July the seminary building was taken possession of by order of Colonel Pierce and Dr. Elliot, for government hospital purposes. Between six and seven hundred wounded rebel officers and privates were captured on that day . . . and the great majority of them were left in the seminary. This prevented the seminary from resuming its regular exercises for the remainder of the session. The wounded however were gradually removed and the building cleansed and prepared for the next session which was ordered to open on the eighth of September. With the exception of this interruption, the students have pursued their studies unmolested, though exposed to some distraction by the unsettled state of affairs in the country.

At the eastern Synod meeting in 1863 at Carlisle, an agent of the United States Christian Commission reported on its work among the soldiers and urged the distribution of the church papers among them. The new General Synod of the same year, meeting at Pittsburgh, received the appeal of the commission "for funds for the supply of hospital stores, blankets, and so on, for the sick and wounded soldiers and sailors of the hospitals and asking the clergy to take up collections in aid of these objects on Thanksgiving Day." The General Synod heartily approved the work of the commission and urged the collection as requested.

An overture from an anonymous source on the subject of ministerial conscription was answered by the rather brusque statement that this subject was "of such a nature as to be inexpedient to engage the attention of Synod." It would seem that ministers, as well as laymen, were subject to the military draft and had to "buy their way out."

The report on "Religion and Morals," presented by Thomas G. Apple to the Synod of 1864 at Lancaster, called for

devout gratitude that during the ecclesiastical year nothing has occurred to interrupt seriously the general operations of the church, except perhaps within the bounds of the two classes not represented in Synod (Virginia and North Carolina). This is remarkable when we consider that during this period the civil war which convulses the nation has continued to rage with unabated fury. . . . While some classes have been the scene of actual hostile conflict, all of them speak of the influence upon the church of the awful curse of . . . war. The church has not only held its own but enjoyed a very encouraging increase during a year of extraordinary trial and peril. . . . The demoralizing influences of an unnatural war, intense political excitements and prejudices . . . these have continually thrust themselves forward to disturb the peace and prosperity of the church.

The Synod of 1865 sent a fraternal letter of greeting to the two southern classes referred to above, declaring, "we have learned of your sad and distressed condition and desire to express to you and the people under your care our most hearty feelings of regard, Christian sympathy, brotherly kindness, and charity." More than words was sent—clothing, household supplies, and money—to the destitute and scattered congregations of these two classes. There can be little doubt that this had much to do with the rather prompt return of the brethren of these two classes to the councils of the Reformed Church.

In the Tuesday morning session of this same Synod (1865), a "solemn service of Thanksgiving" was held, recognizing "the victorious re-establishment of the authority of the national government over the entire union and the restoration of peace."

In the absence of much reference to the war and war conditions in the official minutes of Synod, the personal diaries of the Reverends Benjamin Bausman, Henry Harbaugh, J. Spangler Kieffer, Emanuel V. Gerhart, William Rupp, and of Elder William Heyser and others have proved to be real treasures in the effort to look at those times through the eyes of contemporary churchmen. They give the impression that there were wide differences of opinion as to the necessity of the war, Lincoln's conduct of it, and many other matters. An address of Dr. Nevin in March, 1861 advocated "peaceful separation." Dr. Gerhart was much more devoted to union, even at the cost of war. Name calling ("copper-head," "abolitionist") was heard in seminary halls as well as among the ministers and laymen of the time. A procession in Lancaster, honoring the return from Washington of ex-President Buchanan, was met with acclaim except by some radical Republicans.

Some northern congregations were divided and weakened through the excessive partisanship of their ministers. There was an exodus from the Reformed to the Lutheran church at Huntingdon, Pennsylvania due to pulpit attacks by the pastor, S. H. Reid, on one of the political parties of the day for alleged failure to support Lincoln as President.

The assassination of Lincoln soon after the close of the war caused shock and grief that are reflected both in official records and in private diaries, and that helped to induce a sense of unity among churchmen, which was only partially dispelled by the bitter political quarrels of Reconstruction days.

It is rather noteworthy that the obvious line of division between the synodical period, during most of which the "eastern" and "western," or "mother" and "daughter," synods carried on their work, separated but not estranged, and the period of the General Synod, after their reunion, should run right through the middle of the Civil War period in American history.

4

The Era of the General Synod

IT HAD BEEN PROPOSED in 1857 that the three hundredth anniversary of the Heidelberg Catechism be observed six years later as "a sublime festal service to God." Another proposal, made at about the same time, was that the two synods (in the East and in Ohio) unite to form a General Synod. Joseph H. Dubbs records that at first few were hopeful that such a union would be possible, due to differences that had developed between the two sections of the church, but he feels that the common veneration for the Catechism and for the heritage that it symbolized was the factor that paved the way for the union. He writes of the celebration as marking "the close of a formative period and the beginning of an epoch of united endeavor."

The first General Synod was convened at Pittsburgh on November 18, 1863. John W. Nevin was elected president. The celebration had opened with the Tercentenary Convention in Philadelphia on January 17 of that year and was formally closed by a convention at Reading, Pennsylvania, May 21-25 of the following year. Henry Harbaugh was chairman of the Tercentenary Committee, while Emanuel Vogel Gerhart edited *The Tercentenary Monument*, a large volume including addresses and articles contributed by leading Reformed scholars in Europe and

HERMANN GARLICHS

LOUIS E. NOLLAU

FRIEDRICH SCHMID

GEORGE W. WALL

WILLIAM BINNER

ADOLPH H. BALTZER

JOSEPH A. RIEGER

ANDREAS IRION

America. A new edition of the Heidelberg Catechism was published also. The members of the denomination were enrolled, and freewill offerings for the work of the church amounted to $108,126.

This great year was marked by other beginnings. Emanuel Boehringer, a pastor of the mission church in Bridesburg, Philadelphia gathered into his own home several orphans found on the city streets. By the end of the year he had twelve under his roof—five of them the children of soldiers. Thus began the *Waisenhaus*, which later became Bethany Orphans Home and was moved to Womelsdorf, Pennsylvania in 1867. Another beginning was that of the Historical Society, proposed by Thomas G. Apple, after his tercentenary address appealing for loyalty to the church's heritage.

Continued Controversy

The war between the states was over. The Synod at Lewisburg in 1865 acknowledged and thanked God for peace and the re-establishment of federal authority. But the war within the church was about to break out again, and the unity and inspiration of the tercentenary celebration seems to have been just a happy interlude between campaigns. The argument over liturgy was resumed and was given new point and heat when, in 1866, the "Revised Liturgy" was presented by the majority of the committee as an "Order of Worship" for the church. The Synod in the East resolved that this liturgy be approved for optional use until the General Synod should take action. By that time John H. A. Bomberger, emerging as the leader of the opposition, had published his critical treatise on *The Revised Liturgy,* and Dr. Nevin had replied with his *Vindication of the Revised Liturgy.*

At the General Synod meeting the battle lines were formed. Most of the western church, together with that of North Carolina, joined the low-church minority in the East. This made the two parties about equal in strength. The General Synod's action was something of a compromise. The western Synod was encouraged to continue its labors in preparing a liturgy, the Order of Worship (1866) was allowed for use in congregations and families, and the freedom of all ministers and congregations in regard to the liturgy was emphasized.

The eastern Synod, its classes with the exception of Philadelphia and Zion dominated by Mercersburg men, proceeded to promote the use of the Revised Liturgy. *The Messenger* with its dynamic editor, the Reverend Samuel R. Fisher, and of course, the *Mercersburg Review*, later the *Quarterly Review*, expressed the arguments and sentiments of this majority party. The low-churchmen, the minority in the East, called a convention in Myerstown, Pennsylvania in September, 1867 that directed a protest against the Synod's espousal of the Revised Liturgy and the moves to implement its use in the churches. Steps were taken toward the publication of a journal and the establishment of a school that would represent what they considered the historic Reformed faith. When the Synod denounced the convention as illegal and schismatic, the Old Reformed party proceeded to take the threatened steps. *The Reformed Church Quarterly* appeared in January, 1868 with John H. A. Bomberger, Jeremiah H. Good, and J. H. Klein as editors; and in January, 1869 Freeland Seminary, in what is now Collegeville, Pennsylvania was purchased. Ursinus College was incorporated on February 5 and formally opened September 1, 1870 with six professors and fifty-nine male students. Dr. Bomberger was its first president, continuing in that office until his death in 1890.

The two most important questions in the councils of the church concerned the right of the Ursinus professors to teach theology without the authorization of the Synod and the right of congregations to send beneficiary education money to institutions other than those sponsored by the synods. When the Synod ruled against the low-churchmen on both these points, censuring Bomberger in particular for teaching theology without synod sanction, appeals were made to the General Synod at Cincinnati in 1872. That body, by small majorities, reversed the actions of the eastern Synod. It also upheld Bomberger as a teacher of theology at Ursinus and sustained the consistory's right to designate funds not earmarked by the givers.

Some of the Mercersburg party then questioned the authority of the General Synod and even suggested the formation of synods based on differences of cultus. But cooler heads prevailed, and the way toward a more peaceful solution was soon indicated. Men on both sides were tiring of the conflict and were realizing that it was interfering with the main work of the church. A peace commission was appointed at the General Synod at Lancaster in 1878, representing both points of view and all sections of the church. Dr. Bomberger was named president of the eastern Synod at Easton; the action of 1873 against him was withdrawn, and Ursinus College was commended.

The Peace Commission issued in 1887 a "Directory of Worship," designed to compromise the differences between the two parties to the long conflict. It was adopted by the church but never attained widespread use. Many churches, especially in the East, continued to use the Order of Worship of 1866 until the publication of the new *Book of Worship* of the merged Evangelical and Reformed Church. The spirit of "worship and let worship" came more and more to prevail.

So the hatchet was buried, though some of the wounds remained open and festered through a good many years. The commissioning in 1879 of the Reverend and Mrs. Ambrose D. Gring as missionaries to Japan signalized a union through common labors, the most effective road to peace.

Reviewing the controversy, we may note that its earlier stage centered around the alleged innovations introduced by the Mercersburg theologians—the conception of the church as an organism, the idea of historic development, the stress on the objective character of church and sacraments, and the function of the minister as priest rather than prophet. The Old Reformed element espoused Ulrich Zwingli as their special founding father; the Mercersburg men made more of John Calvin, especially of his eucharistic doctrine of the spiritual real presence. The later, post-Civil War stage of the argument was more concerned with liturgy and church practice. Mercersburg favored an altar-centered liturgy, with responses and chants, forms for the church year, read prayers, and more formal garb for minister and choir; while the Old Reformed favored a pulpit-centered service, "free prayer," and a minimum of ceremonial. As the conflict continued, differences in polity were accentuated. Mercersburg stressed the authority of the Synod over classis and congregation and the institutions of the church, as well as the minister's authority over the local church order. Opponents stood for congregational autonomy and the consistory's control of the church's order of service.

The sincerity of the leaders on both sides cannot be questioned, but as the struggle continued they let personalities enter into it and failed at times to speak and write in love the truth as they saw it.

The Church in the South

The North Carolina Classis was organized in 1831, pursuant to the instructions of the Synod at Hagerstown in the previous year, with four ministers and four elders meeting at Clapp's Church in Guilford County. Hampered by a lack of pastors and separated from the main body of the denomination, these Carolina churchmen nevertheless kept in touch with the Synod and its institutions. Their concern for the slaves in the earlier period was manifest in the actions of Classis; for instance, urging all churches in

1838 to provide place and instructions for them, as evidently the majority of the congregations had already done, thus "opening a door for their reception into the communion of the church whenever their knowledge of the truth and personal piety shall render them fit subjects for Christian communion."[1] Following the war, the Classis (November 7, 1865) resolved "to render hearty thanks to almighty God for the restoration of peace to our divided and suffering country, and for the preservation of the precious lives of so many of our brethren exposed to death."

It was not the war, however, nor differences in regard to slavery, that caused the temporary withdrawal of the Classis from the Synod. Rather it was "doubt . . . as to the soundness of the theology taught in the seminary," that is, the Mercersburg theology. A committee was appointed in 1853 to investigate, and upon receiving their report, the Classis expressed itself as not in sympathy with the Mercersburg teachings and declared itself independent of the Synod "until satisfied that the alleged heresies were no longer held." Efforts on the part of the Synod to woo back the "separated brethren" continued through the fifties. There was some negotiation on the part of the southern churchmen looking toward union with the Dutch Reformed and Presbyterians, but loyalty to the Heidelberg Catechism, aided by letters of sympathy from the North during and at the close of the war, prevailed. Delegates of North Carolina Classis attended the Synod at Baltimore in 1867, and former relations were resumed.

The war caused extreme desolation and impoverishment in the church of North Carolina. A pastoral letter at the close of the war exhorts the members of the congregations to endure the great trials and to bear the burdens of the victims of the struggle:

> We have almost as many orphans in the church as children whose parents live, almost as many widows as wives. . . . So far as we

---

[1] *The Reformed Church in North Carolina* by Jacob C. Leonard, p. 61.

can see, there is not one word or act in the records of our Church North that is marked by bitterness, but our churches have been hailed with delight on the return of peace. . . . A large number of those formerly slaves are now cast upon the country uneducated, without the means of life. . . . Let all seek to be faithful in this new relation in which we are placed to the colored race.

The recovery of the North Carolina churches from the war and its aftermath was slow but sure, and it gathered momentum as the nineteenth century years came and went. The southern church was characterized by the use of Sunday schools, prayer meetings, revival services, and even camp meetings held within orderly bounds—all without neglect of catechetical training. These had developed a type of piety and church loyalty that greatly aided in the recovery. They also had something to do with the anti-Mercersburg attitude of the southern churches, their orientation toward Ohio, and the attendance of their theological students at Central Seminary in the earlier years of the twentieth century.

The Organized Church

George W. Richards in his history of the seminary[2] quotes from the report of the Committee of the first General Synod (1863) on the State of the Church:

We find the church of the Heidelberg Catechism in this country unified with sound, healthy life. Rationalism and Romanism have alike failed to corrupt her; schism has in vain tried to ruin her. . . . We have one General Synod, two District Synods, twenty-seven Classes, in round numbers about 500 ministers and 1,200 congregations, about 100,000 baptized members yet unconfirmed, and about 130,000 confirmed members, about 1,000 Sunday schools, 2 theological seminaries, 1 mission house, 4 colleges, 7 religious papers, 4 of which are German, 1 monthly magazine, 1 quarterly review, a board of home missions, a board of foreign missions, a

---

[2] *History of the Theological Seminary of the Evangelical and Reformed Church at Lancaster* by George W. Richards, pp. 331-332.

widows' fund, and an orphans' home; and the amount collected during the year for benevolent purposes will no doubt be considerably more than $100,000.

It was proposed in 1867 that the word "German" be dropped from the denominational name; when this had received approval by the classes, it was so declared in 1869.

The coming of many German Reformed immigrants, especially in the period from 1840 to 1870, resulted in the formation of German district synods in which the language of the fatherland continued to be used. First, the German Synod of the Northwest was organized at Fort Wayne, Indiana in 1867. Then came the German Synod of the East, organized in 1875 at Philadelphia. The Central Synod (Galion, Ohio, 1881) and the Synod of the Southwest (Louisville, Kentucky, 1914) were next in order. In the meantime, the "English" synods, both the mother Synod in the East (officially the "Eastern Synod" after 1889) and the Ohio Synod were growing and dividing. Pittsburgh Synod (Pittsburgh, Pennsylvania, 1870) and Potomac Synod (Frederick, Maryland, 1873) were formed, the latter stretching all the way from south-central Pennsylvania to North Carolina. The Synod of the Interior was carved out of the Ohio Synod at Kansas City in 1887.

The early twentieth century proved to be a period of union rather than of division of synods, the German and the English ones merging in three regions of the church: the Interior and Southwest to form the Midwest (Freeport, Illinois, 1921), the Ohio and Central to be the Ohio (Canton, Ohio, 1923), and the Eastern and the German of the East to be the Eastern (Schuylkill Haven, Pennsylvania, 1932).

The stated clerks of the synods, who kept the ecclesiastical wheels turning smoothly through the years, deserve a word of tribute. Presidents came and went each year, but many of the stated clerks served through long periods of time, preserving a continuity of thought and action. One thinks of men who served the Synod in the East—Samuel R. Fisher, 1840-81; John Philip Stein, 1881-1908; and his nephew, J. Rauch Stein, 1909-39 (who served during the same period for the General Synod); Lloyd E. Coblentz in the Synod of the Potomac, 1906-38; and J. Harvey Mickley in the Pittsburgh Synod, 1894-1937. Stated clerks of classes, too numerous to mention, performed similar duties within narrower bounds.

Four Hungarian classes were established in the following synods of the Reformed Church: Eastern Hungarian in Eastern Synod, Lakeside Hungarian in Ohio Synod, Central Hungarian in Pittsburgh Synod, and Zion's Hungarian in the Synod of the Midwest. These were later combined in the Magyar Synod of the Evangelical and Reformed Church. Some Hungarian churches have chosen to belong to the English-speaking synods in which they are located.

Educational Institutions

The liturgical controversies were to play an important part in the beginnings of some schools and in the development of others.

THE SEMINARIES

Mercersburg-Lancaster. To the earlier period belongs the story of the founding of the first theological seminary, its shift of location from Carlisle to York to Mercersburg, and of the establishing at its side in York of the Classical School, soon to move to Mercersburg as Marshall College. To this period also belongs the account of the removal of the college to Lancaster in 1853 to be joined with Franklin College, thus becoming Franklin and Marshall. The seminary remained at Mercersburg for eighteen more years. Dr. Nevin retired in 1852 and was succeeded by Bernard C. Wolff, whom Charles E. Schaeffer has celebrated in the biography entitled *A Repairer of the Breach,* which describes how this layman, turned clergyman and theologian, came to the rescue of the educational institutions of the church at several critical times. As Dr. Wolff did not begin his work at once and Philip Schaff was in Europe on leave of absence, the school was closed for the year 1853-54, but it resumed operations in the fall of the latter year. Schaff and Wolff were the faculty, and William M. Reily was added as a tutor in 1861. In 1862 Schaff asked for another leave. He never returned to his Mercersburg professorship, and Bernard Wolff resigned in 1863; hence the seminary had to be closed again for lack of teachers, and the buildings were taken over for a while as a government hospital following General Robert E. Lee's invasion. At this point we enter the period of the General Synod. We find the eastern Synod electing Henry Harbaugh to succeed Wolff and in 1864 choosing Elnathan Elisha Higbee to succeed Schaff.

In 1866 and 1867 the faculty consisted of Harbaugh, Higbee, and Tutor J. B. Kerschner. After Henry Harbaugh's death at the age of fifty, in 1867, Emanuel V. Gerhart, professor at Franklin and Marshall College, was called to succeed him; and in 1871 he returned to Lancaster with the seminary. Elnathan Higbee chose to remain in Mercersburg to teach in Mercersburg College, which had been founded there in 1865 following the departure of Marshall College. He served as its president until the suspension of its work in 1880, and the next year was named State Superintendent of Public Instruction; in that capacity he served under three governors. Thomas G. Apple, who had been presiding over Mercersburg College, was elected to succeed Higbee in the Church History chair, which he filled until his death in 1898.

The Reverend Frederick A. Gast, then teaching at Franklin and Marshall College, was named as tutor in 1870, and in 1874 when the tutorship and the tercentenary professorship were combined, he became the first professor of Hebrew and Old Testament. George W. Richards points out in his history of the seminary that "for the first time in the history of the institution, three professors (Gerhart, Apple, and Gast) taught without interruption for thirty years."

By that time the three eastern synods into which the mother Synod had divided had taken over the control and support of the seminary. The college trustees had given a plot of ground for a main seminary building and two professors' houses were erected, but "Old Main" of the college had to provide the seminary with classrooms and library for twenty-three years.

The last decade of the nineteenth century witnessed marked progress in the provision of buildings and a larger faculty. The Synod of the Potomac elected the Reverend John C. Bowman to teach New Testament Exegesis. The endowment of the Pittsburgh Synod professorship was completed in 1892 for the chair of Practical Theology, and William Rupp was chosen as the professor. On May 10, 1894 the first group of buildings was dedicated, and the seminary moved to its own campus home. The Reverend George W. Richards was elected in 1899 to succeed Thomas G. Apple as professor of Church History. Following the deaths in 1904 of William Rupp and Emanuel V. Gerhart, Dr. Bowman was transferred to the department of Practical Theology to succeed Dr. Rupp. The Reverend Christopher Noss was brought from Japan to teach Systematic Theology, and William C. Schaeffer was chosen professor of New Testament. Irwin H. DeLong, appointed tutor to assist Frederick A. Gast in 1904, followed him as professor of Old Testament in 1909. After the election in 1910 of Theodore F. Herman to succeed Professor Noss, who returned to Japan, the ranks of the faculty were preserved intact for over a decade. Changes then took place in the departments of New Testament and Practical Theology, the Reverends Oswin S. Frantz and Edward S. Bromer, respectively, succeeding William C. Schaeffer and John C. Bowman in 1921.

In 1928 the Reverend Nevin C. Harner was elected to the newly created department of Christian Education, first as instructor and then in 1930 as professor.

A permanent instructorship in Sacred Music and another in Rural Church Work that was turned into a professorship in the mid-twentieth century, were also provided. A dormitory, refectory, and library annex were dedicated in 1918.

Presidents of the seminary in the later period have been as follows: George W. Richards, 1920-39; Theodore F. Herman, 1939-47; Allan S. Meck, 1947-57; Robert V. Moss, Jr., 1957—.

Ursinus. A theological department of Ursinus College was authorized by a resolution of its board of directors in June, 1871 and the first class was graduated the following year. Opposition to the teaching of theology in any other school than one officially sponsored for that purpose by the Synod was overcome in the General Synod at Cincinnati in 1872, and the theological department was definitely organized as the Ursinus School of Theology in 1874 with a faculty separate from that of the college. John H. A. Bomberger was named professor of Systematic and Practical Theology, Symbolics, and Exegesis; H. W. Super, professor of Church History, Biblical Literature, and Homiletics; and J. Van Haagen, professor of Hebrew Language and Literature. A visiting committee was chosen, but the effectual control remained in the hands of the college board of directors. Later members of the faculty included Evan M. Landis, Francis Hendricks, George Stibitz, William J. Hinke, Moses Peters, and James I. Good. Dr. Good became dean after Dr. Bomberger's death in 1890. John H. Sechler began to teach in 1895.

The school continued to have the backing of Philadelphia and Zion classes and of individual ministers and congregations in other sections, east and west. It was approved by the General Synod at Fort Wayne in 1875 and finally by the eastern Synod at Easton in 1878—one of the fruits of "the pacification." In Sep-

tember, 1898 the school was moved from Collegeville to Philadelphia, where Philip Vollmer and Edward S. Bromer were
added to the faculty in 1898 and 1905, respectively. James I.
Good lodged the school in his Philadelphia home and gave it
other financial support. In 1906, the last year of the separate
existence of the School of Theology, there were twenty-seven
students, while the college enrollment was 102. An effort in 1906
to unite the Lancaster and Ursinus theological schools failed,
but success crowned a similar plan to merge the Ursinus and
Heidelberg schools of theology into Central Theological Seminary at Dayton, Ohio.

THE COLLEGES

At the time of the organization of the General Synod in 1863
four continuing colleges of the Reformed Church were in operation. Heidelberg at Tiffin, Ohio and Mission House near Plymouth, Wisconsin had been started in 1850 and 1862, respectively,
to serve the needs of the western church.

Catawba College traces its beginnings to the year 1851. On
December 3 a school was opened at Newton, North Carolina
with C. H. Albert as principal and with thirty-two pupils.
The name Catawba was taken from the river and the county of
that name. Professor J. C. Clapp headed the institution before
and after the war. In 1889 the first class of the college was graduated. It consisted of three men, one of whom, Jacob C. Leonard,
was to become the outstanding leader of the North Carolina
church and president of the General Synod of Hickory, North
Carolina in 1923. This Synod authorized the transfer of the college to Salisbury and a financial campaign throughout the whole
church to undergird and support the institution. Elmer Rhodes
Hoke became the first president at the new location where the
college was formally reopened September 15, 1925. He died in
1931 and was succeeded by Howard R. Omwake and he, in turn,

by Alvin R. Keppel in 1942. Under these three successive presidents the college made steady progress.

Franklin and Marshall College began its career in 1853 at Lancaster, Pennsylvania with the union of Franklin College in that city and Marshall College, removed from Mercersburg. After Philip Schaff declined to leave the seminary to be the college president, Emanuel V. Gerhart came from the presidency of Heidelberg College and served as head of Franklin and Marshall from 1855 to 1866.

Following the Civil War when the affairs of the college were at low ebb, John W. Nevin responded to the challenge to assume the presidency and served for a decade. Then for twelve years Thomas G. Apple, professor on the seminary faculty, discharged the duties of college president as well. Soon after Dr. Apple's death in 1899, John S. Stahr was named president and served until his resignation in 1909. Later presidents were: Henry Harbaugh Apple, 1909-35; John A. Schaeffer, 1935-41; Theodore A. Distler, 1941-54; William W. Hall, 1955-56; Frederick deWolfe Bolman, Jr., 1956—.

The emergence of Ursinus College as one of the products of the liturgical controversy has already been noted. Freeland Seminary at what is now Collegeville, Pennsylvania was purchased in 1869 and was incorporated on February 5 of that year. John H. A. Bomberger was elected its first president. The college was established, so declared an advertisement, "to represent that tendency in the Reformed Church which maintains the historical principles and practices of the church in opposition to all high church tendencies." It opened with two departments, the academic and the collegiate; the program of the preparatory school was continued until 1910. The college became coeducational in 1881.

The eastern Synod at Easton in 1878 commended the work of Ursinus College, one indication of the end of active controversy.

Ursinus has never been connected in any legal way with the synods of the Reformed Church or the Evangelical and Reformed Church, but has long since come to be recognized as one of the colleges of the denomination.

Several presidents followed Dr. Bomberger for brief terms. Then George Leslie Omwake served from 1912 to 1936, Norman Egbert McClure from 1936 to 1958. Dr. McClure was succeeded by Donald L. Helfferich.

At the Eastern Synod meeting in Reading, Pennsylvania in 1894 the Reverends Joseph Henry Apple and J. William Knappenberger shared in the presentation of a program entitled "Education for Women." They represented the interests of the two institutions for such education that had grown up within the bounds and with the support of the church in the East. We shall consider each of these institutions under the name by which it is known today.

Cedar Crest College was founded in 1867 at Allentown, Pennsylvania as the Allentown Female Seminary. In 1915 it moved to a fifty-three-acre campus on the fringe of that city and came to be known by its present name. In the larger development of this school for girls under the control of the Eastern Synod of the Reformed Church, William F. Curtis, president from 1908 to 1941, took the leading part. He was succeeded by Dale H. Moore.

Hood College for women was established in 1893 by the transfer of the department for young women of Mercersburg College to Frederick, Maryland where it was merged with the Frederick Female Seminary. Named in 1913 for an early benefactress, Mrs. Margaret E. S. Hood, it had the able guidance of Joseph H. Apple as president from 1893 to 1934. Pittsburgh Synod joined Potomac Synod in 1916 in direction of the college. Henry Irvin Stahr served as president from 1934 to 1948 and was succeeded by Andrew Gehr Truxal.

PREPARATORY SCHOOLS

The question whether Franklin and Marshall College or Franklin and Marshall Academy had a right to the founding date of 1787 was occasionally discussed until the closing of the latter in 1943 by the college trustees. The buildings were used for three years by the college Navy V-12 unit and after September, 1946 as a freshman dormitory and refectory. In one respect the academy had the better right to the original date, since the school, as first founded, was referred to as a "high school" and was more like a preparatory school than a modern college. Under the headmastership of Edwin Mitman Hartman the Academy enrolled 3,600 boys, 2,000 of whom entered colleges and universities.

After the removal of Marshall College to Lancaster in 1853 an educational institution was continued at Mercersburg, known for a while as the Collegiate Institute, and later as Mercersburg College. Beginning in 1893 it became a preparatory school for boys only, and was destined to become one of the best known academies in the country. William Mann Irvine, its first headmaster who served until 1928, was the primary factor in its growth and service.

Massanutten Academy, the youngest of the Reformed Church institutions, was established by Virginia Classis at Woodstock, Virginia in 1899. At first coeducational, it became a boys' school with military training. It stands as a living monument to the devoted labors of its headmaster, Colonel Howard Johnston Benchoff.

Benevolent Work

Doubtless due to differences in background and to the differing needs of the periods in which they settled in this country, the Reformed churchmen organized fewer agencies of charity and mutual help than did those of the Evangelical Synod.

We have noted the founding of the first orphanage in Brides-
burg, Philadelphia in 1863, and its removal to Womelsdorf as
Bethany Orphans Home in 1867. In the latter year, St. Paul's
Orphans Home was established at Butler for orphans of western
Pennsylvania; it was moved to Greenville, its present location, in
1908. In 1906 and 1910 orphanages were founded in North
Carolina and south-central Pennsylvania, respectively: the Naz-
areth Orphans Home at Rockwell, North Carolina and the
George W. and Agnes Hoffman Orphanage near Littlestown,
Pennsylvania.

The need for homes for the aged increased as that for orphan-
ages decreased. The first such home to be established by the
Reformed in the East was Phoebe Home for the Aged at Allen-
town, Pennsylvania in 1903. The next was the St. Paul's Old
Folks Home at Greenville in 1927, later to be joined with the
Evangelical Home at Dorseyville under one superintendent, responsible to the Pittsburgh Synod. In 1928 the Philadelphia
Synod founded a home at Wyncote in suburban Philadelphia.
In 1932 the Homewood Church Home was started at Hagerstown, Maryland and later developed in three units, situated at
Williamsport, Maryland and at Carlisle and Hanover in Pennsylvania. In 1956 the Devitt Sanitarium near Allenwood, Pennsyl-
vania was taken over as a second unit of the Phoebe Home.

Alexander Kalassay was instrumental in organizing in 1896
the Hungarian Reformed Federation of America, a mutual help
agency of the Magyars in this country which in turn founded the
Bethlen Home at Ligonier, Pennsylvania with him as its first
superintendent. This home later made provision for aged folks
as well.

Ministerial Relief and Sustentation

The concerns evidenced in the founding by the Coetus in 1755
of the Society for the Relief of Ministers and Their Widows received more or less recognition by the various synods through-

out the nineteenth century. It was not until 1905 that General Synod's Board of Ministerial Relief was organized. The causes of sustentation and relief were given an impetus by the Forward Movement and brought into a conjunction that was to issue in the Board of Pensions and Relief of our merged church.

The Jericho Road

Though Church World Service on a wider scope and in a more organized form had to wait for a later day, the synods and General Synod took notice from time to time of catastrophes and emergencies and laid them upon the hearts of the people of the church. The massacres of the Armenians, the plight of the Near East, the San Francisco and Tokyo earthquakes, the Johnstown flood, and other disasters elicited appeals for the support of the Red Cross and other united agencies of organized benevolence.

Christian Education and Publication

Following the burning of Chambersburg in 1864, the publication headquarters of the Reformed Church were moved to Philadelphia. Samuel R. Fisher was in charge and had the church papers in the subscribers' hands again in four weeks. In 1863 the first General Synod authorized a Sunday School Board, and in 1878 one for the eastern Synod was appointed, indicating the deepening interest of the church leaders. Upon Dr. Fisher's death in 1881 his son, Charles G. Fisher, took over as superintendent of publications.

In 1893 the General Synod provided for a General Sunday School Secretary. Rufus W. Miller was elected to that position, and with him a new era in this field began. Dr. Miller's leadership continued for thirty-two years. During that time Sunday school membership more than doubled; the teacher-training class, the Home Department, the Cradle Roll, and other features of the program were developed; and about six and a half million lesson papers and periodicals were sent out. In 1908 the Reformed Church Building at Fifteenth and Race Streets, Philadelphia was dedicated and became the headquarters of the denomination. In 1923 the thirteen-story addition and the new name, "The Schaff Building," proved a further realization of Rufus Miller's vision and enterprise.

The General Synod at Dayton in 1896 commended "the efforts of the young people in their endeavor to develop piety and devotion to their church; in making more effective our methods of church work and in opening and securing larger opportunities of usefulness to the people of our several congregations." The same Synod approved the Heidelberg League, along with other young people's societies, the majority of which were affiliated with the Christian Endeavor movement. Most of these youth groups were eventually to become Youth Fellowships, according to the approved pattern of the denomination, under the general supervision of the Board of Christian Education and Publication. The youth of the church were pathfinders in movements toward union and progress.

Later years saw the summer school and camp program develop. Camp Mensch Mill was founded by the Eastern Synod in 1928 as the pioneer summer camp in the East, with Fred D. Wentzel as the guiding spirit; other synods were not long in following this example.

In the days of controversy *The Messenger*, under the editorship of Benjamin Bausman, Samuel R. Fisher, Thomas G. Apple, and others, served as the popular organ of the Mercersburg party. This led many of their opponents in the East to subscribe to the *Western Missionary*, founded in 1854, and to its successor, *The Christian World*, published in Dayton, Ohio first, and later in Cleveland, from 1867 to 1936. Complaints were made against the partisanship of *The Messenger*, which was supposed to represent the whole church. Consequently, as early as 1874, controversial subjects were avoided and perhaps for that reason the size of the paper was reduced.

In 1896 Cyrus J. Musser became the editor. He was followed in 1917 by Paul S. Leinbach, who served ably until his sudden death on Pearl Harbor Day, December 7, 1941. Since the merger with the *Evangelical Herald* in 1936 Leinbach had shared the editorship with Julius H. Horstmann, editor of that journal. David D. Baker assumed the editor's chair and was succeeded, after his fatal automobile accident in 1950, by Theodore C. Braun.

An independent paper with considerable circulation in eastern Pennsylvania was the *Reformed Church Record,* edited and published most of the time from 1908 to 1943 by the Reverend I. M. Beaver at Reading, and dealing chiefly with news notes from local congregations.

For forty years (1850-90) Henry Harbaugh and his successors as editors circulated *The Guardian,* a magazine "devoted to the social, literary, and religious interests of young men and ladies."

From 1909 to 1942 the two boards of missions and the Woman's Missionary Society published the *Outlook of Missions,* designed to bring information and inspiration from the mission fields into the homes and hearts of Reformed Church people.

The *Reformed Church Almanac,* which first appeared in 1864 and later added the title "Year Book," brought statistics and general information about the personnel and work of the denomination. Its last issue was at the time of the merger, 1934, after which it became *The Year Book and Almanac* and, later, just *The Year Book of the Evangelical and Reformed Church.*

In the more scholarly field, the *Quarterly Review* succeeded the *Mercersburg Review* in 1879 as the theological medium for the Mercersburg-Lancaster party, while the *Reformed Church Quarterly* was published by their Old Reformed (Ursinus) opponents from 1868 to 1876. As the zeal of controversy slackened the latter journal ceased, and in 1896 the former became the *Reformed Church Review*, which continued until 1926 under the aegis of the Lancaster Seminary. Later the *Bulletin* of that school fulfilled some of the purposes of the *Review*, from 1930 to 1957, and was succeeded in 1958 by *Theology and Life*, representing the faculties of all three seminaries of the Evangelical and Reformed Church.

Auxiliary Organizations

Men's and women's work in the local congregations was carried on through the years in many forms and under many names. The beginnings of organization on a denominational level came in the latter years of the nineteenth century. These organizations· were separate from but worked in cooperation with synods and classes. The movement among the women started in 1877 with the first known congregational society, organized in the church at Xenia, Ohio (S. B. Yockey, pastor). The first official recognition was given by Pittsburgh Synod in 1883. Then at the General Synod at Akron, Ohio in 1887, twenty-five women, representing five synods, organized the Woman's Missionary Society of the General Synod, with Mrs. Yockey as the first president. By this time thirty-one congregational societies, five classical societies, and one synodical society (Pittsburgh) had been organized. Thus began the movement of devoted women that proved such a stalwart support of the mission enterprise of the Reformed Church and that later joined the Women's Union of the Evangelical Synod to constitute the Women's Guild.

Two movements channeled the activity of the men of the church into the Reformed Churchmen's League of 1928. One was the Brotherhood of Andrew and Philip, suggested and founded by Rufus W. Miller. The other was the Laymen's Missionary Movement under the chairmanship of Elder William W. Anspach and the general direction of William E. Lampe. These movements, though of a temporary character, developed a leadership among laymen and an interest in missionary and educational progress that found expression in the Churchmen's League. The General Synod of 1929 at Indianapolis recognized the League as the official men's organization of the church, and in 1936 it united with the Brotherhood of the Evangelical Synod in the Churchmen's Brotherhood of the Evangelical and Reformed Church.

Foreign Missions

The first organization of the Reformed Church for missions, "The American Missionary Society of the German Reformed Church," was founded by the Synod of Frederick in 1826 "to promote the interests of the church within the United States *and elsewhere.*" Eight years later, Susquehanna Classis addressed this question to Synod: "Is not the time at hand when the Reformed Church, instead of giving its contributions as heretofore to other churches for the spread of the gospel among the heathen, should think of establishing an institution of its own for the purpose?"

The Synod of 1838 decided to form the Board of Foreign Missions and to unite in the work of the American Board of Commissioners for Foreign Missions, which had been organized in 1810 by the Congregational Association of Massachusetts and was the first board of its kind in America. Through it for twenty-seven years the Presbyterians, the Dutch Reformed, and the German Reformed worked with the Congregationalists. Then, one by one, they formed boards of their own. The German Reformed withdrew in 1866; but for twenty-eight years preceding that date they had, on paper at least, their own Board of Foreign Missions, which cooperated with the American Board and was represented on it from 1840 to 1865 by none other than John W. Nevin. The American Board acknowledged gifts amounting to $28,000 from Reformed Church sources.

Since no volunteers from the Reformed Church were in view, the Synod of 1840 requested that the Reverend Benjamin Schneider, reared in that church but then a Presbyterian missionary at Broosa in Asia Minor, return to the church of his fathers and be supported by it as a missionary of the American Board. The Schneiders accepted the challenge and served at Broosa under the American Board from 1842 to 1849, and at Aintab, on the northern border of Palestine, from 1849 to 1866. In 1866 the German Reformed Church withdrew from the American Board and began to look for a field and missionaries of its own.

During the interim of years before such were found most of the money raised for foreign missions in the Reformed Church was contributed to the German Evangelical Missionary Society for its work at Bisrampur in India, where two missionaries from the Reformed Church, the Reverend Oscar Lohr of New York Classis and the Reverend Jacob Hauser of Sheboygan Classis, were working under the Society. This was the mission taken over by the Evangelical Synod in 1884. It is interesting to note that these early contacts and cooperation with the Evangelicals and the Congregationalists anticipated the unions of 1934 and 1957 respectively.

Attention was first called to Japan by the Reverend J. M. Ferris of the Reformed Church in America. That land was definitely chosen by our Board in 1873, and the first candidates presented themselves in 1878. From among them, the Reverend Ambrose D. Gring was selected, and he and his wife sailed in May, 1879, reaching Yokohama the following month. Once having entered Japan as her first foreign mission field, the Reformed Church sent out a succession of able and adventurous men, most of them accompanied by wives just as courageous and resourceful. The Jairus P. Moores went in 1883, William E. Hoy in 1885, the David B. Schneders in 1887, the Henry K. Millers in 1892, the Christopher Nosses in 1895, Paul L. Gerhard in 1897; and others followed.

The Reformed Church mission, almost from its beginning in Tokyo, was part of a union enterprise, which became the Church of Christ in Japan. After a few years of labor in the capital city, it was expanded to Sendai in North Japan. Here the work was of two kinds, educational and evangelistic. The latter had been begun by two Japanese Christian ministers, Masayoshi Oshikawa and Kametaro Yoshida, before the coming of the missionaries. In 1886 Elizabeth R. Poorbaugh and Mary B. Ault (soon to become Mrs. Hoy) founded Miyagi (Girls') College, while William E. Hoy and Masayoshi Oshikawa in the same year laid the foundations of Tohoku (North Japan) College for Boys, soon to be developed by the Schneders. In the meantime the Moores, the Nosses, and their colleagues pressed the evangelistic work in the outlying districts.

A new field was opened in the Hunan Province of China, where the mission board was instructed by the General Synod of 1899 at Tiffin, Ohio to open a second mission. Dr. and Mrs. Hoy were the pioneers there and took over some of the property of the London Missionary Society. They were soon conducting evangelistic work in Yochow and Shenchow. A Hunan Classis was organized, but dissolved with the consent of Eastern Synod of which it was a mission branch, in order to join Presbyterian and Congregationalist groups in forming the Church of Christ in China. Schools for boys and girls were started, and early in this century Huping Christian College was opened. The Reverend William A. Reimert taught there. Later he became a martyr in his Lord's service. The need for primary and secondary schools was very great, and the two Eastview schools, the Ziemer Memorial Girls' School and the Shenchow Girls' School, were opened in rapid succession. Medical work was started in 1902 by Dr. and Mrs. J. Albert Beam in Yochow. Dr. William Kelly, who had begun independent work in Shenchowfu was taken into the mission in 1904. The medical work was carried on through the years by a devoted group of doctors and nurses. In spite of wars and revolutions the work in China continued, and we may well believe that even though the last members of the mission have been expelled by the Communist regime, the seeds that were sown will bear eventual fruit in the China of the future.

In April, 1924 representatives of the two Reformed churches (of German and Dutch origin) and of the northern Presbyterian Church organized the United Mission in Mesopotamia (now Iraq). Dr. and Mrs. Calvin K. Staudt arrived on the field in March, 1924 as the first missionaries of our church. Schools were opened in Baghdad, one for girls in 1924 and one for boys, no longer in existence, in 1925, in both of which youth of various races and religions have been enrolled. Evangelistic work was carried on by the Reverend and Mrs. Jefferson C. Glessner for thirty years, latterly in the region of Kirkuk.

The foreign mission enterprise of our church in its latter stages owed much to four men in the homeland, whose devotion and energy sparked the home base churches into increasing efforts to support their brethren in the field: General Secretaries Allen R. Bartholomew (1887-90, 1902-33), Arthur V. Casselman (1933-44), Frederick A. Goetsch (1936-47), and Dobbs F. Ehlman (1947—).

Home Missions

The first few triennial meetings of the General Synod were seemingly much concerned with the transfer of home mission responsibilities from the boards of the synods to that of the General Synod. At the meeting in Lancaster, Pennsylvania, in 1878 it was resolved that "all the home missions of the church should be brought under direct control of the General Synod's board as speedily as possible."

But this end was not accomplished as speedily as contemplated; the synods seemed reluctant to yield control of the missionary work within their bounds. It was not until 1890 that the Ohio Synod and the Pittsburgh Synod complied, and not until 1893 that the Bi-Synodic Board of Eastern Synod and Potomac Synod did so. This centralization of control, though opposed by some, seemed to work for greater effectiveness in the opening of new missions where most needed and in supporting them once they were begun. When the territory concerned became too large, it was divided into departments of administration.

The ministry of A. Carl Whitmer as superintendent of Home Missions from 1886 to 1914 was outstanding. In 1887 he reported the first three church building funds. By 1922 there were 837 of them, totaling $555,500. Most of these funds became loans to churches, which when repaid went to the help of younger and weaker congregations.

"Special Projects" in home missions began in the latter nineteenth century. The General Synod at Baltimore in 1884 directed the board to appoint an immigrant missionary for the harbor of New York City. The Reverend Paul Sommerlatte, succeeded by the Reverend Paul H. Land, served in this capacity, meeting and aiding especially the German immigrants as they came in great numbers into their new homeland and were faced by many problems and dangers.

The board reported to the Eastern Synod in 1890 the beginning of mission work among the Hungarians, and the Synod appropriated $1,000 to help in this work. The first Hungarian minister, Gustave Jurany, was brought from the old country in 1891 to lead a congregation at Cleveland, Ohio. After World War I, about eighty Hungarian congregations, whose ties with the fatherland were severed and whose support from Europe was cut off, came into organic connection with the Reformed Church in the United States under the special sponsorship of the Board of Home Missions (according to the terms of the Tiffin Agreement, 1921). A Hungarian Department was established in the Lancaster institutions with Alexander Toth in charge, and continued from 1922 to 1936 during which time twenty-seven students completed their scholastic training in these institutions. The Board of Home Missions cooperated with college and seminary in this program, which was given up in the days of retrenchment during the depression.

Charles E. Schaeffer was elected General Secretary of the Board of Home Missions in 1908 and served until 1941, both making home mission history through this long period and recording and interpreting it in books like *The Task of American Protestantism* (1932) and *Beside All Waters* (1937).

A project that linked the home and foreign mission enterprises for almost a half century was the work among the Japanese Americans on the West Coast. The Reverend J. Mori opened the first Reformed mission in San Francisco in 1910, to which several others in California were added. The beginning of the war with Japan in 1941 scattered the members of these mission churches, and work was carried on by the Reverend Carl W. Nugent and others in the concentration camps in other parts of the West.

It was the Board of Home Missions that was particularly involved in the ambitious program of the Interchurch World Movement. With the virtual collapse of that laudable but ill-fated enterprise, as a result of reaction and recession in American church life, many mission churches and their pastors underwent a period of great hardship. The Board of Home Missions itself was hard pressed to maintain solvency, due to the many obligations it had incurred in its advance program. This serious situation for a while threatened the 1934 merger. It reflects great credit on the church as a whole, and especially on the home mission pastors and officials, that very few churches were closed, that the debts have been steadily reduced, and that new and better safeguarded advances in home missions have been made.

The First World War and After

The last period of the history of the Reformed Church in the United States may be regarded as lying between the outbreak of World War I and the Evangelical and Reformed merger of 1934. As for the war itself, it can hardly be doubted that the German origin of the denomination kept it from the fanatical anti-Germanism displayed by some groups of American churchmen, for example, in the exclamations of Newell Dwight Hillis, Billy Sunday, and others, against the allegedly demonic character of "the Hun." For the most part the ministers of our church did not "present arms" in the Ray Abrams sense. Some ministers and congregations of more recent German extraction suffered considerable persecution, due to the popular and sometimes official suspicion of things German. The use of the German language was curtailed or eliminated in a good many churches. So few conscientious objectors appeared among our young men that there was scant provision for giving them such consideration as members of the historic peace churches received from the government.

The Eastern Synod in 1917 adopted a resolution prepared by Theodore F. Herman, professor at Lancaster Seminary and a native of Germany, expressing on the one hand abhorrence of war, and on the other a "firm conviction of the justice and righteousness of the war in which we are engaged." This was probably typical of the attitude of the great majority of the people of the Reformed Church.

The church supplied its share of army and navy chaplains and had a definite part in reconstruction and restoration work for the French and Belgian churches after World War I. During the war and afterward, the National Service Commission, organized January 25, 1918, kept the church in touch with its men in the service through visits to the camps by church leaders, providing the servicemen with literature, and other means.

The utterances of the judicatories leave no doubt as to the support given to the League of Nations and to such proposals as armament limitation (1921) and the outlawry of war (1924). Unfortunately, too many of the rank and file members heeded partisan clamor against the League and thus contributed to the failure of the chief aims of "the war to end war."

One cannot fail to note in reading the minutes of the General Synod and the district synods in this period, a growing interest in the application of Christianity to contemporary problems and conditions, national as well as international. The pioneer leaders of the miscalled "social gospel" (there is only one gospel!) had passed on. Josiah Strong had died in 1916; Washington Gladden and Walter Rauschenbusch in 1918. But the impression of their application of religion to social relationships upon the thought of the Reformed Church seems quite clear. In 1917 the Commission on Social Service was appointed by the General Synod; James M. Mullan gave guidance and direction to it, and teachers like Elijah E. Kresge and Philip Vollmer gave inspiration. Thus "The Social Ideals of the Churches" as formulated by the Federal Council of Churches in 1912 and revised in 1932 were mediated to the people of the Reformed Church.

Resolutions denouncing the Japanese Exclusion Act (1924) and approving the Kellogg-Briand Pact (1928) bear witness to interest in doing away with the causes of war. Support of the prohibition laws and commendation of the Anti-Saloon League are also found in some of the pronouncements of the synods in that era.

Unitive and Ecumenical Activities

Reformed Church leaders were among the first to catch the breezes of interdenominational communication and cooperation. The first General Synod (1863) took to itself—from the synods— the right and responsibility of corresponding with sister churches and named five with whom such correspondence was desired, namely, the Lutheran, Reformed Dutch, New School Presbyterian, Moravian, and the Evangelical Church Union of the West. Efforts to open correspondence with Reformed churches in Germany and Switzerland seem to have failed in the sixties and seventies, but delegates were sent to the Reformed Alliance Holding the Presbyterian System, beginning with 1881.

The nearest the Reformed Church in the United States came to union with another denomination in this period was with the Reformed Protestant Dutch Church (1866), which became the Reformed Church in America (1869). Joint committees met from time to time, leading to a special meeting of the General Synod at Philadelphia, June 4, 1891, at which a proposal for federal union was unanimously carried and then ratified by all but two of the classes. Similar action was taken by the Dutch Reformed, but according to the statement made in the "Digest" of our General Synod (page 136) "when the time came for official promulgation of the action as part of the organic law, such strenuous opposition was made that the authorities of that denomination (Reformed Church in America) concluded to drop the matter."

Contacts and cooperation in Sunday school work, stewardship, promotion, and other fields of common interest with other Protestant churches brought mutual understanding and appreciation that ripened after the turn of the century into a project for a united program of advance. So in 1908 the Federal Council of the Churches of Christ in America was organized with the Reformed Church in the United States as a charter member. This Council and seven other united agencies of Protestantism combined during 1950 in the National Council of Churches. Thus most of the major Protestant bodies in the United States could speak unitedly and wield a growing influence in the moral and religious life of the nation.

As horizons widened and the concept of "the one world" became clearer and more compelling, interest turned more and more toward the world-wide nature of the holy Catholic Church. The Edinburgh Missionary Conference of 1910 ushered in a new era, and before long the word ecumenical was being widely used. Interfaith and international groups on "Faith and Order" and "Life and Work" became increasingly active. In the ecumenical movement the outstanding leader of the Reformed Church in the United States was George W. Richards, for many years president of the Lancaster Seminary and the first president of the Evangelical and Reformed Church. In many respects, he carried on the work of James I. Good in keeping the American church in touch with the life and needs of their brethren in Europe. The ecumenical career of Dr. Richards was climaxed by the important part he played in the First Assembly of the World Council of Churches at Amsterdam in 1948. The untimely death of Nevin C. Harner in 1951 deprived the American church of one of its most able leaders both in his special field of Christian education and in that of ecumenical activity.

The End of an Era

The last fifteen years of the Reformed Church in the United States before her union with the Evangelical Synod of North America to constitute the Evangelical and Reformed Church may be characterized by three words, representing three phases of her situation: advance, reaction, and challenge. World War I had ended in victory for the nation. The crisis had called forth the united effort of the various and often conflicting elements in the population. Idealism was riding high, as were hopes for peace, justice, and righteousness within the nation and among the nations. Leaders of the American churches, who had learned some of the first lessons of working together, were determined to take advantage of this spirit of unity and willingness to sacrifice. The war just past had not affected America greatly. It was regarded generally as a temporary obstacle that had been over-come and a test that had been met. Now the wheels of progress could roll on like the caissons on Europe's battlefields.

Out of this optimism and idealism the churches, singly and cooperatively, launched their movements of advance. That of the Reformed Church was the Forward Movement, initiated at the special meeting of the General Synod at Altoona, Pennsylvania in March, 1919. It projected advance on every front of the church's enterprise: spiritual, educational, and missionary. Four major interests were included in the Forward Movement: (1) enlargement of missionary activities, both foreign and home; (2) strengthening of the twelve educational institutions; (3) stronger support and conservation of the ministry; and (4) development of publications and Sunday school work. While its financial goal was not fully reached, an unprecedented amount, $6,400,000, was subscribed; the approach of the depression years thwarted the full realization of that amount, but the boards and institutions received $4,821,559, including the results of a co-operative campaign of the educational institutions.

The Interchurch World Movement, in which the Reformed Church cooperated with most of the major Protestant commu-nions, extended the united effort to "overcome the overlooking and overlapping" that had obtained in American Protestantism. Surveys were made, new mission points established, and new buildings and other facilities provided for churches faced with special opportunities. Though many of the objectives were at-tained and great progress achieved in benevolent giving, the reaction that so often follows great national efforts was not long in coming. The urge to "normalcy" on the political scene and the isolationism that triumphed over Wilsonian plans for a League of Nations as an instrument of peace, had their counterparts in the moral and religious fields. Ruthless individualism, organized selfishness, and widespread worship of the gods of amusement and pleasure soon brought a period of disillusionment and cynicism that in turn ushered in the years of depression and near-panic. All this carried the churches into retrenchment and left them with heavy debts that took years to pay.

In theology the liberalism that had ruled much American thought in the early years of the century became rather widely discredited. An increasing number of American church leaders responded to the voices of neo-orthodoxy from across the waters. They began to deprecate what man can do in improving conditions, at least in relying on such a delusion as automatic progress. This meant some reaction also from the stress on "social Christianity." Men began to consider evil conditions as the judgment of God on man's sinful pride rather than as something man should campaign to eliminate. Another trend of this period was a greater concern about liturgy, sometimes seen even in some of the descendants of the Old Reformed party. A revival of interest in the Mercersburg movement, particularly in its liturgical and ecumenical aspects, has also developed in recent years.

The Reformed Church in the United States, prior to the merger of 1934, consisted of six synods: Eastern, Potomac, Pittsburgh, Ohio, Midwest, and Northwest. The first three, those east of the Ohio-Pennsylvania line, have been the subject of this chapter. Constituting what has sometimes been known as "The Reformed Church in the East," these three according to the statistical tables for the year 1934, accounted for 31 out of the 58 classes; 794 out of the 1,332 ministers; 1,069 out of the 1,675 congregations; and 241,591 out of the 348,189 members of the entire communion.

So out of a period of recession and reaction, the Reformed Church in the United States moved into organic union with a sister denomination of largely Lutheran background and heritage and of kindred attitudes and aims.

JACOB C. LEONARD

JAMES I. GOOD

JACOB PISTER

JOHN ZIMMERMANN

DAVID B. SCHNEDER

ALLEN R. BARTHOLOMEW

JACOB GASS

PAUL A. MENZEL

5

The Winning of the West

THIS SECTION deals with the westward expansion of the Reformed Church into twenty-one states west of Pennsylvania and three Canadian provinces. It involves the founding and operation of two theological seminaries, three colleges, and several academies. It is the story of growth of the Ohio Classis into five synods. The publishing house in Cleveland, the Fort Wayne Children's Home, the Winnebago mission in Wisconsin, work among the Germans from Russia, ministerial relief, church building funds, home missions, and many other church activities are all a part of "the winning of the West."

Carl Sandburg, the famous poet and biographer of Lincoln, referred to the American pioneers as "Wayshewers." "Their lessons," he said, "are worth our seeing and remembering. They ought not to be forgotten." The occasion for his remarks was the conveyance of Old Wade House State Park as a gift from the Kohler Foundation, Inc., to the State Historical Society of Wisconsin.

Old Wade House, one of the first stagecoach inns in Wisconsin, is a typical example of pioneer courage and enterprise. Located midway between Sheboygan and Fond du Lac on what was first an Indian trail, then a rough plank road, and now a paved highway, it was a popular stopping place for weary travelers. Here August Winter may have stopped on his missionary tours with his famous "Missions-Schimmel," the white horse that the Sheboygan Classis had provided for him—forerunner of the modern car allowance for ministers. Sylvanus Wade from Massachusetts and his wife from Pennsylvania had come west to Joliet, Illinois. In the spring of 1844, they with their nine children arrived in a covered wagon at what is now the village of Greenbush. Here Wade House and other buildings were erected. These buildings have now been completely restored under the inspired guidance of Mrs. Herbert Kohler. The importance of this costly restoration is not merely that tourists now have another interesting show place to visit; rather, it is the fact that we in the West are beginning to value more fully the spirit and enterprise of the "Wayshewers," or, as termed by the Germans, the *Bahnbrecher*.

Prepare Ye the Way of the Lord

The growing interest in pioneer life should be fully shared by the church. The pioneers did not realize that they were building a great nation, nor did the early missionaries plan great denominational structures. They were concerned with immediate problems, and were too modest to record their deeds. It always seems to require the passing of a century, and two or three generations, before interest in the past develops. This was true in the East, where the second century produced such history-minded leaders as Philip Schaff, John W. Nevin, Henry Harbaugh, and D. Y. Heisler; and more recently, James I. Good, William John Hinke, George W. Richards, Charles E. Schaeffer, and others. The organization of the State Historical Society of Wisconsin in 1863 was the result of this new interest in early history. It is hoped that the West, which is now in its second century, will produce leadership that will show the greatness of

our American heritage and the rock from which we are hewn—
especially now that as a United Church we can go back to
Plymouth Rock.

In the Wilderness

At the beginning of the last century what is now Ohio and
Indiana was known, with good reason, as "the western wilderness." There were deep forests where the bear and wolf and
wildcat roamed and the Indian threatened. Roads followed the
line of least resistance and were frequently impassable. Into this
wilderness came German Reformed people from Pennsylvania,
Maryland, and New York. They were a solid, hard-working people who faced the hardships of pioneer life with resolute courage.
They brought with them their Bibles, the Heidelberg Catechism,
and their hymnals. They also brought their Pennsylvania German language, their sense of humor, and their simple piety. But
they also brought some of the eastern religious problems and
tensions, such as New Measurism with its "mourners' bench,"
and the liturgical issue. These immigrants from the East were
soon joined and quickly outnumbered by those who came directly
from Germany and Switzerland.

The first Reformed ministers to serve these scattered groups
in Ohio were John Peter Mahnenschmidt, Henry Sonnendecker,
and Benjamin Faust. Church services were held wherever an
empty space could be found: in log cabins, barns, town halls, and
vacant jails, or, weather permitting, under spreading oak trees.
These missionaries keenly felt the need to provide religious instruction for the children, who grew up, to quote Sonnendecker,
"wild and uncultivated as the country itself."

The Ohio Classis

The Ohio Classis was organized in 1819 at Lancaster, Ohio.
The total recorded membership was about 1,800, divided into
fifty congregations and served by five ministers. The reasons for

this were clear and urgent. Contact with the mother Synod in the East was difficult, and important problems had to be solved locally. Theodore P. Bolliger, in the *History of St. John's Classis*, relates an experience of Benjamin Faust, which illustrates the general poverty, the difficulty of attending the synod meetings, and the hardship and danger of travel. In 1822, while traveling through the mountains to attend Synod at Harrisburg, Pennsylvania, he fell seriously ill. His money was soon gone and he had to borrow thirty dollars to get back home. The following year the Synod gave him permission to retain the offerings that the congregations were required to take each year for synod expenses and apply these offerings to his debt. After four years the amount of these offerings finally reached the thirty dollar mark.

The Ohio Synod

On June 12, 1824, the Classis met in the courthouse in New Philadelphia and there reorganized itself into a synod, at the same time declaring itself independent of the mother Synod. The name of the Synod was the High German Evangelical Reformed Synod of Ohio. This radical action, however, was not taken in bitter rebellion against the eastern Synod; rather, it rested on purely practical considerations. The following reasons were given: refusal of the eastern Synod to permit the Classis to ordain candidates to the ministry; and the time and cost of attending synod meetings. Then, too, the spirit of independence and self-reliance was characteristic of the frontier. In fact, the reason for this action was not unlike that of the earlier declaration of independence from the church in Holland. The new synod accepted the constitution of the eastern Synod, its doctrinal standards and liturgical forms and usages, without modifications. The relations between the synods were cordial and cooperative.

At the time of the organization of the Ohio Synod, the membership had grown to 2,500. There were eleven ministers who served seventy congregations.

Pioneer Hardships

The westward expansion of American life was not a process of natural growth. It was a hard-fought battle of conquest with many casualties. Mothers died during childbirth for want of proper care. Children's diseases, especially typhoid fever, too often proved fatal. One reads of the great epidemic of smallpox that spread throughout the West and the heroic ministry rendered by faithful pastors who, following the example of Ulrich Zwingli, visited the sick, buried the dead, and comforted the people. The real soldiers in this war of conquest were the women, who kept house under most primitive conditions. In small log houses, with or without wooden floors, and with only the simplest housekeeping utilities, they fed and clothed and nursed their growing families.

The hardships of pioneer life were repeated with only slight changes as the frontier moved westward. In Indiana conditions were aggravated by vast swamps that bred malaria and ague. Roads were particularly treacherous because of stumps and mudholes. Several incidents are reported where traveling ministers were given mud baths, without regard to their high calling. Peter Herbruck, on his way from Toledo to Defiance, had such an experience. The wagon upset and he was thrown into a deep mudhole with the wagon on top of him. "When I crawled out," he reported later, "looking like a mud turtle, my companions had a good laugh." A similar incident happened to a group on the way to classis meeting. Shortly before arriving at their destination, they upset with the usual muddy results. That night the president preached the opening sermon dressed in a borrowed overcoat.

In Wisconsin and parts of Illinois and Minnesota, conditions were like those of Ohio and eastern Pennsylvania. Primeval forests, rivers and lakes, a rigorous but healthy climate, and cheap land attracted the stream of German immigration in the middle of the century.

Conditions in the prairie states were much different. The Reverend J. J. Janett, licensed to preach but not yet ordained, was sent to western Iowa in 1869 "to find work and bread" among the scattered homesteaders. In Volume 12 of the *Jugendbibliothek* he published the story of his experiences and described conditions on the prairie. Here the pioneers were spared the backbreaking task of clearing the land of sturdy trees. Instead of log cabins they built sod houses. Square pieces of sod were cut from the prairie and laid on top of each other until the walls were high enough; a few sticks were placed across the walls and covered with a thick layer of hay or straw. Most cabins had no floors because of the lack of wood. There was little or no furniture. A bed consisted of a pile of straw covered with a blanket. Filth prevailed everywhere. Endless swarms of mosquitoes attacked man and beast. Land was free for the homesteader, on condition that he stay five years and make a few modest improvements annually. Yet, with all these inducements, many of the settlers around Storm Lake abandoned their homesteads after a year or two. The loneliness on the prairie was too much for them, especially during the enforced idleness of a long, hard winter. To get a little fuel and a few groceries meant a slow trip to town, usually a two-day journey. Distances were great, even between neighbors, making social contacts difficult. Sickness was common and deaths occurred frequently. Yet homesteaders kept coming. In an incredibly short time, Iowa was transformed into the leading agricultural state, "where the tall corn grows."

Conditions in Kansas, Nebraska, and the Dakotas were much like those of Iowa, with the additional hazard of crop failures caused by hot winds and sandstorms. The pioneers, wherever they happened to be, were confronted by physical hardships that gravely tested their courage and endurance. By successfully dealing with life on the frontier they not only laid the foundation of American prosperity, but, what is more important, they created the American character. The church, through her ministry, had a vital part in this achievement.

Religious Problems

More difficult than the physical hardships were the spiritual problems that severely tried the wisdom and patience of the church on the frontier. Among these were the lack of well-trained ministers, the language and the temperance questions, the liturgical controversy, and the New Measures movement. The last named, already described in an earlier chapter, proved especially divisive and destructive, with its noisy revival meetings and prayer meetings in which men and women prayed aloud at the same time. The mourner's bench and other radical methods fostered a shallow church life and a spiritual conceit that divided congregations and checked their development.

The religious climate of Ohio in the 1840's was favorable to every radical movement. The frontier always welcomed excitement, and religion with its emotional appeal easily led to grave excesses. A degenerated type of Methodism, with its camp meetings, was popular, as was also "Oberlinism," an extreme type of New England legalistic puritanism. All this, together with the superficial training of some "homemade" ministers and the recently won freedom from eastern discipline, made a perfect setting for irresponsible extremes.

The new measure men were especially aggressive in the Canton area. They invaded congregations in the absence of the regular pastor and organized opposition groups of "converted

Christians." The spiritual pride engendered expressed itself in a reference people made to their old pastor: "Before this we were in a state of blindness and irreligion, but now we are enlightened, converted, regenerated, and saved. Our former pastor was never converted." This reminds one of a stanza in a revival hymnal of that time:

> Once I was blind, I could not see
> The Calvinist deceived me.

One might regard new measurism as a petty local squabble, but that would overlook the fact that in the East it had resulted in a vigorous theological investigation of the nature of the church, known as the Mercersburg theology. Moreover, in the West it resulted in another division within the Ohio Synod by the creation of the so-called Herbruck Synod. And, shed of its objectionable extremes, its influence is discernible in the subsequent development of the Ohio Synod and the Central Synod, occupying the same territory. It is evident then that we have to do here with perennial aspects of Christian faith and experience. Such issues were sterile orthodoxy and dead formalism, on the one hand, and on the other, unrestrained emotionalism, which claimed possession and control of the Holy Spirit according to a fixed formula. The church has learned that there are varieties of experiences and gifts, and that the Holy Spirit is not limited to man's plans—nor is the word of God heard only in the thunder of Sinai, but also in the still small voice.

The Herbruck Synod

During the period following the declaration of independence of the Ohio Synod in 1824, the number of organized congregations increased rapidly. There was much confusion and overlapping among the classes, whose territorial limits were ill defined. Congregations passed from one group to another, determined by their attitude toward the controversial questions of the time. Thus birds of a feather tended to flock together. The bitterness between the conservative Reformed and the new measure enthusiasts was increased by a decision of Synod in 1844 that permitted the organization of English congregations within the bounds of German congregations. This unwise action, though rescinded two years later, led to another declaration of independence.

In 1846 the Columbiana Classis separated from the Ohio Synod, taking the name of the German Synod of the High German Reformed Church of Ohio and Adjacent States. The new Synod expressed its regret that separation had been made necessary by the excesses of the new measure men. The following reasons were given for their action: "departure from the ancient usages, doctrines, and symbols of the Reformed Church, and the introduction of the mourner's bench and its accompaniments; the invasion of our congregations by the new measure men, whereby peace has been destroyed, and faction and hate engendered." They declared their firm adherence to the Bible, the Heidelberg Catechism, the doctrines and usages and symbols of the Reformed Church. They also adopted the constitution of the Ohio Synod and declared: "We are prepared at any moment to unite with the Ohio Synod again, as soon as the causes of our complaints have been removed, the evils done away with, and the transgressors punished."

The Herbruck Synod, so called because Peter Herbruck was the leader of the conservative group, evidently had a sobering effect on the old Ohio Synod. The complaints against new measure excesses now received attention and evoked stern action. The conservative group was strengthened by the arrival of a number of well-trained ministers from the East. After eight years of separation, the Herbruck Synod rejoined the old Ohio Synod.

Indiana

The church in Indiana was a natural extension and an organic part of the church in Ohio. The physical characteristics have already been noted. The religious problems were less turbulent, possibly because the first leaders here were well grounded in Reformed theology and were men of sound judgment. The first Reformed minister to visit the scattered settlements of northern Indiana was Peter Herbruck, who reached Huntington, then a village of about eighteen houses, in the summer of 1840. The following is from his report of the journey:

> I looked up some of my former parishioners. In the second home the father greeted me with tears, saying that the mother had been buried four weeks before, but no minister had been available to conduct a service. So I conducted a funeral service in a schoolhouse before a reverent congregation. In Huntington also I preached and conducted another funeral service. In Miami County I preached several times, conducted the Lord's Supper and baptized the children. No Reformed minister had ever visited the community before. On the return trip, traveling through a dense forest, I suddenly came upon a little log cabin in a clearing. A woman was standing at a washtub before the door. Suddenly she cried out: "Isn't your name Herbruck?" On receiving my answer she wept, and said: "How glad I am to see you again! How often I have desired to hear you preach again." I found that I had confirmed her in one of my congregations.

The incidents here related show conditions that were typical on the front line of the church as it moved from Pennsylvania to Ohio, Indiana, Illinois, Wisconsin, and beyond the Mississippi. But even more significant, they reveal the continuity of the life of the church in its westward expansion. The section visited by Peter Herbruck has since become a stronghold of the church. Strong churches have developed in Fort Wayne, Decatur, Huntington, Magley, Vera Cruz, Berne, and Bluffton—to name only a few. Less than thirty years after Herbruck's first visit, at the organization of the Northwest Synod in Fort

Wayne, there were two classes in Indiana with seventy-six congregations.

It is not possible even to list the ministers whose sacrificial service has made this growth possible. However, the life and work of Peter Vitz may well serve as representative of the many others. He came to America from Germany in 1854 with his wife and two children. One of the children was buried at sea. Mrs. Vitz became seriously ill just before landing, and died four months later near Manitowoc, Wisconsin. That same year Peter Vitz, with his five-year-old son, went to Tiffin, Ohio to enter the seminary. In 1856 he was ordained and sent into the wilderness, eighteen miles south of Fort Wayne.

Thus began a quiet, unassuming, but immensely fruitful, ministry over a period of fifty years. The hardships and sacrifices were nobly shared by his second wife. In his first field of labor he organized three flourishing churches: Magley, Decatur, and St. Lucas in Adams County. In 1861 Vitz went to Huntington, where he served ten years. He then went to Lafayette and Newville, and after a brief period in Wisconsin, was called out of retirement to go to Delphos, Ohio where he served the little church for twelve years. His influence was multiplied greatly through his children. Five of his sons became active pastors in the Reformed Church, and three daughters, ministers' wives. Nearly all of these served churches in the territory where their father pioneered.

Reformed Colonies

In general the immigrants arrived in families or small groups. Often the father came alone and the family followed later. There were, however, at least three cases where they came as integrated groups to establish themselves as colonies, much like the Pilgrims of old: New Knoxville, New Glarus, and Town Herman.

NEW KNOXVILLE, OHIO

The ancestral history of the church at New Knoxville reaches
back far beyond the Pilgrim fathers, even beyond the Reformation. The church at Ladbergen, Westphalia, Germany, from
whence these settlers came, celebrated in 1950 the one thou-
sandth anniversary of its founding. The New Knoxville colonists
were a part of the one and one-half million Germans who settled
in the West in the decades after 1830. The description of these
people by Carl C. Taylor of the United States Department of
Agriculture fits New Knoxville and every other German settlement. He observes: "They were educated, thrifty, hard-working
farmers who had left their country to seek political freedom
and economic opportunity. They contributed more than any
other group to a stable agriculture." Arriving in Cincinnati after
the usual hardships on the long journey, they seem to have
divided into two groups. Some went on to Missouri, where they
became active in Evangelical churches; the others found employment on the Miami-Erie canal, then under construction.

Among those so employed at twenty-five cents a day was a
young man, F. H. W. Kuckhermann. Because of his education
and ability he became the schoolmaster. One of the important
textbooks used in the school was the Heidelberg Catechism
along with the Bible. Regular prayer meetings and worship
services were often conducted by the schoolmaster. Like another schoolmaster, John Philip Boehm, in Pennsylvania, Kuckhermann was ordained. From 1844 to 1890 he served the church
faithfully. By his sound biblical preaching and teaching he laid
the solid foundation for a church that has been publicly ac-
claimed by the *Christian Century* (February 22, 1950) as one
of the greatest Protestant churches in America. His twenty-five
years in quiet retirement were a partriarchal benediction upon
his successors.

What led the *Christian Century* to call New Knoxville a "colony of heaven" was the number of ministers and missionaries who came from this church. By 1958 the number of ordained ministers had passed the fifty mark, and the number of ministers' wives, twenty-five. Nearly all of these were graduates of Mission House Seminary in Wisconsin, as were also five of the pastors of this church. They have served as ministers in all parts of the church, as teachers in colleges and seminaries, and as religious workers in Canada and Japan. These sons and daughters have drawn the mother church into vigorous participation in the wider work of the denomination.

NEW GLARUS, WISCONSIN

The Swiss Reformed Church of New Glarus may claim to be the oldest Reformed church in Wisconsin. The church was an integral part of the colony, though the first pastor, Wilhelm Streissguth, did not arrive until 1849. The New Glarus colony was unique in the history of immigration. The Canton of Glarus is one of the most rugged, wildest and most mountainous in Switzerland. The land fit for cultivation was extremely limited, while the population increased steadily. The resultant poverty called for remedial action.

In true democratic fashion, public meetings were held to discuss emigration as a solution. Opinions were divided between those who clung to the old motto: *Bleibe im Land und naehre dich redlich,* and those who proposed their own motto: *Bleibet im Land und fresset einander.* An emigration society was formed and two emissaries were sent to America to find a suitable location for a colony. The experiences of these men, who, like the spies sent out by Moses, or even more like Abraham, who went to a land that the Lord would show him, include too many facts to record here. So, also, does the tragic, heart-breaking story of the 193 who left Glarus in April, 1845 and finally arrived at their destination on August 15 of that year. Their number had shrunk to 108, as some had found employment along the way.

The New Glarus church remained in close contact with the Reformed church in Glarus, using their hymnal, liturgy, catechism, and many customs. The first pastor was sent and supported by the mother church. Later ministers of the Northwest Synod served them. While the church supported the work of the Synod, it was not until 1918, under the leadership of the Reverend G. D. Elliker, that the congregation officially joined the Reformed Church in the United States.

The population of the community increased rapidly from within and through a steady stream of immigrants from old Glarus and other Swiss cantons. The second, third, and fourth generations have spread in all directions, making Green County and beyond a veritable New Switzerland. The expansion of the Evangelical and Reformed Church has kept pace with this growth, as this list of churches shows: Belleville, Paoli, Madison, Monroe, Monticello, Town Washington, Verona, and Mount Vernon. In 1959 the combined membership of this group was 4,534.

TOWN HERMAN, SHEBOYGAN COUNTY, WISCONSIN

On May 4, 1847 a group of 112 emigrants boarded the sailing ship, *Agnes von Bremen,* to come to America. Their reasons for this venture were similar to those of the Swiss colony two years earlier, except that their poverty was less extreme. They came from northern Germany, from the principality of Lippe. The claim that they were escaping religious persecution seems to be overdrawn. It is true, however, that rationalism was widespread, and the Heidelberg Catechism had been replaced by a *Leitfaden* (textbook) for instruction in public schools. No doubt, the Reformed group was longing for religion free from state control, as promised in America.

Conditions on the illegally overcrowded *Agnes* were terrible. During the eight weeks thirteen bodies were buried at sea, among these three of the colonists. Because the ship was overloaded they were landed at Quebec instead of New York. Their destination was Iowa, but when they arrived by water route in Milwaukee, the land agents persuaded them to take up land in Wisconsin. The result was that nearly all of the group followed their leader, Friedrich Reineking, and on July 25, nearly three months after they boarded the *Agnes*, they settled in Town Herman.

The hardships suffered there were especially severe in the winter of 1848-49. They were completely snowed in. Food for man and beast was scarce and contact with neighbors difficult. But through all their hardships on sea and land, and now in the wilderness, they were sustained by their trust in God. While the formal organization of a congregation under the name Immanuel did not occur until 1848, the colonists had always lived and worshiped and prayed together as a part of the church of Christ. The first contact with the Reformed Church was through the Reverend A. Burky, who visited the colony and informed them of the existence of a Reformed Church in the United States. Shortly after this, the Reverend C. Pluess began to supply the church more or less regularly for several years. He was followed by the Reverend J. J. Bossard. Immanuel Church, better known as the Mission House Church, was destined to become the cradle of the Mission House.

The Church in Wisconsin

From 1850 to 1852 the catalog of the Seminary at Mercersburg, Pennsylvania listed among its eighteen students ten who came from Germany and Switzerland in answer to the Macedonian call that stressed the spiritual destitution of the Germans on the western frontier. They were preparing themselves for pioneer work under the able instruction of Professors Philip Schaff and John W. Nevin. From that trained group of young, consecrated men came the leaders of the church in the West, especially Wisconsin. Among them also were the founders of the Mission House. This is another illustration of the unity and continuity of the life of the church in its westward expansion. The seminary in the East thus furnished the leaders for the West.

In 1853 the Reverend H. A. Muehlmeier organized Zion Church in Sheboygan. The Reverend H. A. Winter began work in Milwaukee in the same year. In 1854 Dr. Bossard was called from Fort Wayne to become the first regular pastor of Immanuel Church, and J. T. Kluge, after ordination, became the first pastor of Ebenezer Church in Manitowoc County.

On August 17, 1854, duly authorized by the Ohio Synod, these four ministers and elders Herman Helming and Christian Stoelting met in Immanuel Church and organized the Sheboygan Classis, with Bossard as president; Muehlmeier, secretary; and Stoelting, treasurer. One of the first acts of the new Classis was the appointment of a mission committee, which through its zeal soon became a "Mission House committee." This leads us to the broader question of theological education in the West.

Theological Education

The urgent need for more pastors to serve the scattered groups of settlers was one of the most frustrating problems on the frontier. This was especially serious when the one and one-half million German immigrants came between 1830 and 1860 and settled largely in the Middle West. Various attempts were made to meet this need. The pastors extended their service as far as possible. When the Ohio Classis was organized in 1819, the five ministers were serving fifty congregations. The Ohio Synod, five years later, numbered eleven ministers for seventy congregations. When the Northwest Synod was organized in Fort Wayne, Indiana, in 1867, only five out of fifty-two congregations had full-time pastors to serve them. All others were organized in charges of from two to five congregations. In the Sheboygan Classis, the congregations granted their ministers frequent leave of absence to visit vacant churches or to help organize new congregations. Thus the available ministerial manpower was used to the limit.

Another way to relieve the shortage of ministers was by private instruction. Candidates for the ministry prepared themselves for the examination under the direction of a pastor—something like "reading law" in a lawyer's office to become a lawyer. Some very worthy and effective men entered the service of the church in this way. To substantiate this one need only mention such prominent pioneers as Peter Herbruck, F. H. W. Kuckhermann, and J. J. Brecht. But these had the advantage of a sound general education. On the other hand, the inadequacy and even the dangers of this method were quite apparent. In Ohio the new measure men were able to reinforce themselves in this quick and easy way. Also, it opened the door for men who lacked not only intellectual and theological fitness, but, what was worse, moral and spiritual qualifications. As a result, frequent disciplinary action became necessary. The records of one classis report the expulsion of seven unworthy ministers within two decades.

The shortage of ministers was constantly brought to the attention of the church in the East by urgent appeals to send more laborers into ripe harvests. Mission societies and mission houses in Germany and Switzerland were also urged to send help. The response was often disappointing and sometimes led to misunderstandings. It is understandable that the church in the

East, busy with pressing local needs, did not share the enthusiasm of the church on the frontier. A few candidates were sent from Europe, but the rapid increase in the number of churches more than offset any help from outside. It became increasingly evident that the only possible answer to this problem was the establishment of theological seminaries. This was equally true in Pennsylvania, Ohio, and Wisconsin.

HEIDELBERG SEMINARY

An attempt to establish a theological seminary in Ohio was made in 1838, when the Reverend John G. Buettner was installed as the first professor in Canton. His salary was $250 a year, if he provided the lecture room—otherwise, $230. The courses offered by Buettner were evidently too difficult for the two students. One left after three weeks and the other, after the first year; whereupon the professor went back to Germany. Further efforts to provide theological training were made at Columbus in 1846 and at Carlton some time later.

Heidelberg College was established in Tiffin in 1850. From the beginning the chief purpose of the college was to provide classical and theological training for candidates for the ministry. This institution met a real need—149 students were enrolled the first year. The college with its theological section maintained for some years a strong German department, which graduated a number of effective German ministers for Ohio and the West.

In 1908 the seminary united with the Ursinus School of Theology and continued as Central Seminary at Dayton, Ohio until it merged with Eden Seminary at Webster Groves, Missouri in 1934. Meanwhile, Heidelberg College continues its high-class training for life and for Christian service. There is not a seminary in our church that does not have Heidelberg graduates in its student body.

THE MISSION HOUSE

The reason for founding the Mission House was the need for locally trained men to serve the newly organized churches. This need was especially urgent in Wisconsin for two reasons. First, this was the time when German immigration was at its peak, and Wisconsin, Iowa, and Minnesota attracted the bulk of the newcomers. Second, the pastors and churches of the Sheboygan Classis were mission-minded. These pastors came to America as missionaries, stopping over at Mercersburg only to prepare for their missionary task. None of them had any thought of coming here to teach in a school. It was only when it became clear that their missionary task could not be fulfilled except by multiplying themselves through a mission institute that they accepted this as God's will.

To understand the beginning of the Mission House, one must know something of the men who were destined (predestined, as they believed) to found this institution. They were the same men who organized the Sheboygan Classis: Muehlmeier, Bossard, Winter, and Kluge. They were remarkable for their oneness of purpose, as well as for their differences of personality by which they complemented each other. Herman J. Ruetenik, the editor of the *Evangelist*, after a visit in Wisconsin, mentioned "the gentle meekness of Muehlmeier, the great learning of Bossard, the well-considered thoroughness of Kluge, the fatherly benevolence of Brecht, all illuminated by the fiery zeal of Winter." H. A. Muehlmeier was elected "housefather," and later, "inspector." These terms, as well as the name "Mission House," were borrowed from similar institutions in Europe. Muehlmeier served as the head of the school until his death in 1907. By his modesty, coupled with dignity, he won friends and supporters throughout the church. He and his gracious wife were true house parents to the growing family.

If Muehlmeier was the administrator, J. J. Bossard was the outstanding teacher and scholar. Born in Switzerland in 1818, he was educated in Basel, where he earned a double university doctorate in philology and philosophy. After several years of teaching and further studies in ancient languages, he, too, heard the Macedonian call and decided to become a missionary to the Germans in America. Accordingly, he entered Mercersburg Seminary in 1847, where he both studied and taught under the guidance of another learned Swiss, Philip Schaff. The two became life-long friends. (Schaff visited his friend at the Mission House some years later.) In 1848 Bossard was ordained and began his ministry in Fort Wayne. He preached in German and English, and also frequently visited a French-Swiss group at Vera Cruz, preaching for them in French.

His outstanding ability as a teacher is gratefully acknowledged by one of his students, J. J. Schlicher, who became professor of Ancient Languages at the University of Wisconsin, and who wrote a history of the Mission House for the *Wisconsin Magazine of History*. When Bossard's son, Guido, later a professor at Dubuque Seminary, was a student in Europe, his father corresponded with him in Greek. He complained one day: *"Der Junge macht mir immer noch Fehler."*

The Reverend H. A. Winter, like Muehlmeier and the settlers in Town Herman, came from Lippe-Detmold. After graduation from Mercersburg he went to Upper Sandusky, Ohio where he privately prepared J. J. Brecht for ordination. By his fiery zeal and his untiring efforts he probably did more than any other man to recruit ministers and organize congregations for the church in Wisconsin. Jerome Arpke in *Das Lipper Settlement* credits Winter with influencing nine men to enter the ministry. His success in locating and organizing new fields is equally astounding. It was his custom to organize, build a church, and sometimes, as in Saron near the Mission House, a parsonage also, and then to move on to new conquests. Altogether he listed seventeen congregations as the result of his efforts.

Winter's part in the development of the Mission House also deserves full recognition. He was never a part of the administration or the faculty; such routine duties would have been irksome to his restless spirit. But he was a great promoter and field man. Even before definite steps to establish a school in the West were taken, Winter kept the idea alive in the church through correspondence and articles in the *Evangelist*. While in Upper Sandusky he had come in close contact with Heidelberg College in Tiffin. In an article published in 1860 entitled *"Gedanken über das Missionshaus,"* he described in glowing terms the results of Heidelberg, which was then ten years old. "Ten years ago," he said, "the Tiffin Classis scarcely existed. Now it is the second largest in the West. In the territory around Tiffin, where even the name of our church was unknown, we now have flourishing charges. Think of the many churches in Seneca, Crawford, Wyandot, Sandusky, and adjoining counties, which, almost without exception, owe their existence to Tiffin." Thus Heidelberg furnished the pattern and inspiration for the Mission House. What Winter saw in Ohio repeated itself in Wisconsin around the Mission House.

It is difficult to fix an exact date for the beginning of the Mission House. A definite decision of the Classis to proceed with plans was made in 1860. However, the first building was erected in 1862. This is the year which has been accepted as a basis for anniversary celebrations. Various locations had been under consideration, but because the teachers lived nearby and Immanuel Church seemed to represent the Reformed tradition, the school was located in Town Herman. Several attempts were made to relocate in order to escape isolation and establish contact with broader cultures. Today this problem no longer exists, due to Henry Ford and the state highway department.

The development of the Mission House into an academy, college, and seminary was a gradual process. The sole purpose for many years was to train ministers and teachers for the church. Yet almost from the beginning it was necessary to give some instruction in preseminary courses, especially in classical languages. As the enrollment grew, additional teachers were secured. The gradual development is well illustrated in the reports to the Synod. In 1879 the Mission House Board reported: "According to the judgment of an attorney, to whom we submitted our charter, we have the right to raise the Pre-Seminary (*Vorschule*) to a college to be known as College of the Missionhouse." In the same year Central Synod, which now became joint owner, resolved "to permit the faculty to add two more classes to the preparatory school; and to raise it as soon as possible to a college." In 1880 the Mission House Board reported: "We now have three divisions, academy, college, and seminary. To supervise the instruction and lighten the load of the housefather, your board has elected Dr. J. Bossard as president of the seminary and Professor H. Kurtz as president of the college." During the years, the following men have headed the Mission House: H. A. Muehlmeier (1862-1907), Ernst A. Hofer (1908-20), A. E. Dahlmann (1920-23), John M. G. Darms (1923-28), Paul Grosshuesch (1931-49), Arthur M. Krueger (1951—); Josias Friedli served as acting president on two occasions.

Several important changes were made in 1956. The plan to separate the college and the seminary was put into effect. (The academy had been discontinued.) Both schools continued their work on the old campus with the understanding that the seminary would seek a new location. The Reverend Arthur M. Krueger continued as acting president of both schools until 1957 when he was elected president of the college. In the same year the name was changed to Lakeland College and the constitution and charter were ratified by the General Synod; the seminary retained the name of Mission House. Steps were also taken at this time to erect a new women's dormitory that has since been completed. (The institution had become coeducational in 1931.) That these changes proved beneficial is shown by the increase in enrollment from 138 in 1952 to 343 in 1960.

The separation of the seminary from the college at once demanded an aggressive program of advance. Dr. Krueger served as acting president of the seminary until 1959 when the Reverend Louis H. Gunneman became acting head. In 1960 the Reverend Ruben H. Huenemann was elected president and Dr. Gunnemann continued as dean. The relocation problem found a happy solution in a proposed merger with a Congregational Christian seminary, the Yankton (South Dakota) School of Theology. The location of this new theological seminary of the United Church of Christ will be in the St. Paul-Minneapolis area. This location seems especially promising as the gateway to the great Northwest where the church has a mission field that calls for well-trained pastors.

The Synod of the Northwest

The organization of the Synod of the Northwest involved an important change in the structure of the western church. It relieved the tension over the language question and gave the German churches a new sense of strength and responsibility. The organization had been duly authorized by the General Synod, at the request of the Ohio Synod and the classes involved. This peaceful adjustment was one of the fruits of the General Synod which had been organized in 1863.

The first meeting of the new Synod was held in St. John's Church at Fort Wayne, Indiana in 1867. It included the following classes: St. Joseph, Indiana, Sheboygan, Heidelberg, and Erie. The last two, located in Ohio, joined with the understanding that they with other German classes would later organize a

German synod in their state. The hope of the two groups was realized when the Central Synod was organized in 1881 at Galion, Ohio, including St. John's, Erie, Heidelberg, and Cincinnati classes.

At the first meeting of the Synod of the Northwest a number of important decisions were made: The Synod continued to share in the administration and support of Heidelberg Seminary and its German department. It accepted the offer of the Sheboygan Classis to transfer ownership and control of the Mission House to the Synod, and elected a board of trustees. H. J. Ruetenik was appointed to prepare a statement concerning ways of increasing the participation of churches and especially of elders at synod meetings. This statement appears in the first minutes. A paper on the liturgical question by H. J. Klein and Professor H. Kurtz was ordered for the next meeting. The statistical summary showed: 83 ministers, 162 congregations, 8,660 members, 997 baptisms, 544 confirmed, 20 excommunicated, and benevolent contributions totaling $3,334.06. The hopeful aspects of these figures probably lies in the baptisms, confirmation, and benevolences.

Through the continued westward expansion new classes were organized in Iowa, the Dakotas, Minnesota, Nebraska and as far west as the Pacific Coast, and north in Canada. Also, new synods came into being: Central Synod, as already stated, and later Southwest Synod.

With the German Synod in the East there were now four predominantly German synods. At one time it was proposed that these synods should organize a German General Synod to better promote their common interests. Fortunately, the idea did not take hold, because the churches were rapidly becoming at least bilingual and also because satisfactory ways of cooperation were found in joint ownership of institutions and activities. We now turn to some of these activities.

Central Publishing House

We may be too much inclined today to regard the publishing interests of the church simply as a business enterprise. With our overabundance of reading matter we can scarcely understand what the Bible, Schaff's *Gesangbuch,* and perhaps a copy of the *Evangelist* meant in the lonely log cabin in the forest or the sod house on the lonely prairie. How could the pastor teach without Zahn's *Biblische Geschichten* and the Heidelberg Catechism?

All these and many other needed supplies were available only through the publishing house. *Die Kirchenzeitung* and the *Christian World* were welcome visitors in Christian homes. They edified their readers, stimulated interest in the work of the church, and created an invisible fellowship of readers. It is clear that the publishing house had a big part in the growth of the church in the West.

As early as 1856 H. J. Ruetenik published a monthly German paper called the *Evangelist,* as a private enterprise. When in 1860 he was called to the First Reformed Church in Cleveland, he took the paper with him. Four years later he turned it over to a newly formed *Buchverein,* which continued under various names, later becoming the Central Publishing House. However, Dr. Ruetenik remained the leading spirit in the enterprise throughout his life.

Perhaps there was no man who had a wider and deeper influence on the formative life of the church in the West. He was the guiding spirit in evangelism through the printed page; he promoted the Mission House through his pastorate at Immanuel Church, 1870-73, and through his paper. He was the founder and main teacher of Calvin College in Cleveland, which prepared a goodly number of men for successful service in the Christian ministry.

Home Missions

Following the formation of the General Synod in 1863, an attempt was made to bring all home mission work under one board. This did not prove satisfactory, due to unique local conditions. In the East a tri-synodic, later a bi-synodic board, was constituted. In the West the Northwest Synod promptly constituted a Board of Home Missions and a separate Board of Church Erection. These two boards operated continuously in the vast territory west of Pennsylvania and in western Canada. As new synods were organized they joined these boards by sharing in the management and support.

The two boards, while separate legal bodies, were in reality one in their work, meeting together and taking joint action where building funds were involved. In 1909 the two boards elected G. D. Elliker as general secretary to serve both boards. This dual secretaryship proved so satisfactory that it was continued by electing Josias Friedli in 1915 and Theodore P. Bolliger in 1919 to this position.

Since the winning of the West was essentially a home mission project, it was natural that home missions should be a chief concern of synods and congregations. We are grateful for the more than three hundred congregations nurtured by these boards and for the more than $100,000 invested in churches and parsonages—and repaid practically in full. Yet, knowing the field and the unlimited opportunities, we are humbled by the thought of what might have been done!

The Board of Church Erection was unique in its own organization. Almost from the beginning it had the same president— C. F. Kriete of Louisville, Kentucky. During all these years, he never missed a board or executive meeting—and he never lost his temper. Through the process of mergers the work of home missions has now been absorbed, first by the General Synod

Board, and then by the Board of National Missions of the Evangelical and Reformed Church, to which the Department of the Northwest transferred its assets, without liabilities.

The Winnebago Indian Mission

The Winnebago Indian Mission at Black River Falls, Wisconsin was a project of the Sheboygan Classis. How did this classis, so occupied with caring for the spiritual needs of the German settlers, and so busy with its new seminary, become interested in a mission that promised only continued sacrifice, without adding to the strength of the church? It happened this way: It was the custom of the teachers at the Mission House to use their Sundays not to rest, but to preach in neighboring vacant churches. Thus Professor H. Kurtz, one Sunday, walked twelve miles north to serve a small settlement. On the way back he was caught in a snowstorm. Completely exhausted, he sat down to rest and fell asleep. Had not a kind Providence intervened, he would have been one of many storm victims. Some passing Indians discovered him. They recognized him as "one of the good men who live in the big white house." An old Indian chief described the Mission House thus: "Heap big white house, plenty good men, much eat, much money, much tobacco." The Indians brought Kurtz safely home and, no doubt, were given some of the good things mentioned.

From here on, Dr. Kurtz became an ardent advocate of Indian missions. Gradually the fire of his enthusiasm spread to others. In 1876 the Classis decided: "As soon as we have the money and find a missionary we will send him to the Indians who live nearest us." A year later the Classis recognized "the solemn duty to bring the gospel to the heathen living in our land." Congregations were asked to indicate their interest by donations. The response was heartening. Even more encouraging was the fact that the Reverend Jacob Hauser, a returned missionary from India, was willing to be sent to find a definite location. He found that the Winnebagos on the Black River near the falls were the most neglected tribe in Wisconsin.

On December 20, 1878 Hauser visited the settlement for the first time, wondering if they would receive him. The Indians were understandably cautious in dealing with the paleface visitor. Mistreated by a series of thirteen treaties, forced to move five times west of the Mississippi, then, drifting back to Wisconsin to find only the wasteland along the Black River available to them, they were in no mood to trust anyone. They talked it over among themselves. Three days later, Chief Black Hawk gave the answer: "The words you have spoken are good. We also believe in *Maura* [Earthmaker]. We love our children. It will make us glad to see them well taught. We are glad you have come." A week later the school was opened in the little log schoolhouse that they had built. They, like some modern institutions, failed to realize that it takes more than buildings to make a school. But now they had a teacher sent from God.

The origin of this mission has been given in some detail in the hope that the hand of God may be clearly seen in this work. The story of the subsequent development can here be only a list of successive steps in the ongoing life of the mission. Mrs. Hauser, the first of four missionary wives who spent their lives in hard faithful service for the Indians, died in 1882. Two years later the Reverend Jacob Stucki became Hauser's assistant and soon after, his successor. The name Stucki has become synonymous with Winnebago Indian missions. Including the wives and even the children, the Stuckis have given their lives unstintingly to this work. It meant teaching, preaching, feeding, clothing, and nursing the sick. It meant learning the language and translating parts of the Bible into Winnebago. The greatest test of faith was that it took twenty years before the first converts were won. It was a great day when David Decorah, John Stacy and his wife, Martha, and King of Thunder were baptized and became the nucleus of a growing Indian church.

In 1917 the Classis transferred the mission to the western Board of Home Missions. The war had opened opportunities of employment to the Indians, usually at considerable distance. The result was that the children were too far away to attend the mission school. When Mrs. Big Soldier in 1917 asked the Stuckis to take her two children into their home, because her husband was working in La Crosse, it was the beginning of a boarding school. Others were taken into the missionary's home, and every other available space was used to house some forty children. The result of this was the Winnebago Indian School at Neillsville. It was made possible by the generous gifts of the Woman's Missionary Society. This school has widely affected the life of the tribe in every way. Out of it have come ministers, teachers, nurses, and above all, men and women whose lives bear witness to the power of the gospel.

When the boarding school was established, the missionary's son, Benjamin, was challenged to become the superintendent. He accepted on a temporary basis. After forty years, he is still serving "temporarily." Since his father's death in 1930, "Mr. Ben," as he is familiarly called by his friends, heads the Indian work of the denomination, under the Board of National Missions. The school has become a benevolent institution of the church. Its director is the Reverend Jacob Grether. The Reverend Mitchell Whiterabbit is pastor of the Indian church at Black River Falls. The situations change, but the needs remain. The problem is to adjust methods and plans to meet new and wider opportunities of service to the Indian Americans.

PART TWO

The Evangelical Synod of North America

LANCASTER THEOLOGICAL SEMINARY

EDEN THEOLOGICAL SEMINARY

MISSION HOUSE
THEOLOGICAL SEMINARY

H. RICHARD NEIHBUR

GEORGE W. RICHARDS

JAMES E. WAGNER

LOUIS W. GOEBEL

6

European Background—Evangelical

IT WOULD BE understandable if modern Americans assumed that the German immigrants who settled in the Midwest in 1840 came with approximately the same background as the Germans who had settled in Pennsylvania a century or more earlier. But this is hardly the case. The nineteenth-century German immigrant coming into Illinois, Missouri, or Iowa bore the indelible stamp of certain conditions and developments that made his beginning in America quite different.

For one thing, the nineteenth-century immigrant was a man who bore the scars of the Napoleonic Wars. The generation that lived after the defeat of Napoleon in 1814 faced difficult circumstances, resembling the conditions in our own South following the Civil War. But in spite of starvation and destruction, certain things were beginning to improve. Some of the old split conditions of German life were being overcome. Instead of over three hundred separate political units involved in what we call "Germany" before Napoleon's day, there were now thirty-eight German states. But these provinces formed no national unit until the unification of Germany was achieved under Bismarck in 1871. Thus the German had little sense of national identity.

The Hessian was quite likely to regard the Prussian or the Wuerttemberger as a man from a different world.

Religiously the German reflected a background that was also quite parochial. Though there were two main types of Protestantism in Germany—Lutheran and Reformed—the German brought with him that particular type of worship and religious instruction which he knew in his own small province. What was called "Lutheran" in Wuerttemberg might be quite different from that which was given the same name in Saxony or Hanover. These hundreds of political units also defined as many church administrations. There was no "German" church nor even a "Lutheran" or "Reformed" church. Each province, often as small as an American county, had its own church administration that was tied to the province, much as our school systems come under state supervision. Thus when the Saxon Lutheran met Protestants from Wuerttemberg or Prussia, he was not certain what he ought to think of them. They had used different hymnals and catechisms, and their forms of worship always varied to some degree. The world considered them all Germans; yet they were not sure that they belonged together politically or religiously.

Before and after the age of Napoleon there had been some attempts to create order out of the jumble of German ecclesiastical life. In Prussia, King Frederick William III (1797-1840) took action which gave expression to tendencies that had been noticeable for some time. In 1817 the Evangelical Church, the Church of the Prussian Union, was set up in his kingdom. This date was chosen with some forethought, for it was the three hundredth anniversary of the beginning of Luther's Reformation. In every such act in which a government is involved, men ask whether the action was primarily political or religious. It must be remembered that Luther and all of the Reformers worked in close relation to contemporary rulers. On the European scene there were no church administrations that were not affiliated with governments. They could not imagine a separation of church and state.

To be sure, Frederick William was a resolute monarch, with a paternalistic attitude toward the church in his domain. But he espoused many badly needed changes, such as the abolition of serfdom and alleviation of the troubled condition of the Jews. In a manner that surely would seem highhanded in a modern democracy, he simply ordered such changes as he deemed wise. Thus he decreed that the Lutheran and Reformed elements in his kingdom were to work together as one union. For generations many of his subjects had been asking the question, "Why don't the churches get together?" William announced that the Protestants of his realm would work together as a united church body to be called the "Evangelical Church." It is not to be wondered at that many unwilling spirits regarded the king's order as governmental interference. It was surely governmental action in matters of church administration, but it differed little from countless other involvements of governments in church affairs in Europe, many of which have continued to our own time.

Although this Church of the Prussian Union has been labeled a pawn of the state by dissenting Lutherans, it must be remembered that it did express a desire on the part of many for a union of Protestant forces. The King of Prussia had not undertaken a change against the wishes of the majority of his subjects. For more than two centuries many German churchmen had wrestled with the issue of unity among Protestants. The term evangelical was one that both Lutheran and Reformed could adopt, and often did. Other German provinces proceeded to set up similar united church administrations, believing that the things which Lutheran and Reformed hold in common are so basic that it is possible to carry out the functions of congregational life unitedly.

There was vigorous opposition to the establishment of the union in Prussia when it was realized that this was more than just an arrangement to be adopted in one province. At this time Westphalia, Baden, and other Rhine provinces adopted the same principle. As early as 1818 it was introduced in the Bavarian Palatinate and in 1827 in Dessau. Yet a prominent preacher of Kiel, Klaus Harms, inveighed equally against "rationalism and unionism."

When the king had a common book of worship published in 1830 there was renewed opposition. The introduction of this book was marked by a union communion service in Berlin, according to the new rite in which bread was broken (instead of wafers) and the phrase *Unser Vater* was used in the Lord's Prayer rather than *Vater Unser*, which has exactly the same meaning. Many of those claiming to defend Lutheran liturgy against corruption rebelled against the use of this order of worship. Dissenters were accused of insubordination by government officials. Nonconformity gave rise to separation, and thus a separated Lutheranism went into action. (We must remember that many of the Lutherans had entered into the union. Those who would not enter the union came to be called "Old Lutherans.")

In 1836 seven Lutheran pastors were imprisoned. Naturally they were hailed as martyrs. Fines were levied by the police for harboring rebels and for taking part in Lutheran meetings. Thus a movement which should have promoted fellowship and understanding was associated in the minds of the ultra-Lutherans with suppression and persecution. Naturally some of them thought of leaving the country. Under the leadership of Martin Stephan, plans were made to come to the United States. This was the nucleus of the later Missouri Lutheran denomination. In 1839 these so-called Saxon Lutherans arrived in St. Louis. A similar group came to the Buffalo area and were later absorbed into the Ohio Lutheran Synod.

From this time on many of the Germans who came to America associated their religious background with strife. The fact that church union attempts had been related to governmental pressure simply increased the tendency among some to emphasize confessional differences, as if separatism were a sign of freedom. Many assumed that separatism must be right because they had suffered for it. Even the slightest variation of heritage or custom was condemned as false. To some the thought that a Lutheran German from Saxony and a Reformed German from Hesse might have fellowship at the Lord's Table was unthinkable. Men must be segregated according to detailed beliefs. Lutherans are Lutheran, and Reformed are Reformed, and never the twain shall meet—except in controversy. And the Evangelicals were those who were attempting what was impossible and wrong, to mix the two.

Yet we should not leave the impression that everything worked on the side of separatism. Powerful forces of unification were also at work—forces that were more convincing than the pressure of the state. Many of the Germans migrating to America had had some contact with the various missionary societies that were springing up without governmental encouragement or ecclesiastical promotion. And not every part of Germany was as doctrinaire as Saxony or as authoritarian as Prussia.

Effects of the Pietist Movement

The religious movement known as Pietism had long been giving new life and a more conciliatory spirit to German Christianity. Great personalities like Philipp Jakob Spener, August Hermann Francke, and Nicholas Zinzendorf had convinced many

Germans that faith is more than the possession of pure doctrine, however defined. The strong emotional flavor of Pietism was ridiculed both by wooden orthodoxy and by secular rationalism. John Frederick Oberlin (1740-1826) had many of the features of Pietism, namely, a warm spirit, readiness to serve men as children of God, and an irenic attitude to others.

It is not to be imagined that the warm spirit of the Pietists was coupled with an indifference or opposition to education. In fact, many of the most noted theologians of the eighteenth century were of this persuasion, and the Pietists influenced many who would not be considered as belonging to their company, Friedrich Schleiermacher, for example. Under the leadership of men like Johann Neander, August Tholuck, and Johann Beck a biblical and experiential theology had developed that supplied a dignified scholarly polemic against the tirades of current rationalism. Elements of revivalism began to penetrate both Lutheran and Reformed, and there was a resurgence of hymn writing and religious poetry in Germany. (The Wesleys learned much from these Pietists.)

As the Pietists carried on their work in Wuerttemberg, regardless of sectarian and doctrinaire emphases, questions of ecclesiastical organization never became vital, since Lutheran and Reformed of that region traditionally emphasized points of agreement and worked for positive goals. But in time numerous interconfessional Bible, missionary, and tract societies arose in many parts of Germany, with the avowed purpose of stemming the tide of rationalism. About fifty such societies had arisen in Wuerttemberg by 1800. A direct product of this kind of interchurch work was the founding of the Basel and the Barmen missionary societies, destined in later years to send many missionaries to America.

Though located on Swiss soil, the famous Basel Bible Society, organized in 1804, became the center for the German Pietist missionary movement. The Evangelical Missionary Society of Basel was founded in 1815 (several years before the Prussian Union) and with pietistic fervor began to oppose the narrow confessional separations of that time. The catholicity of Basel was manifested in its close cooperation with the London Missionary Society and the Church Missionary Society. The latter represented the evangelical wing of the Church of England. During the period when Anglican bishops refused to ordain candidates of the London Missionary Society, this organization looked to Germany and Switzerland for its missionaries. Basel was not concerned about the creedal subscriptions or denominational affiliations of her graduates. She refused to differentiate between Lutheran and Reformed, deeming the adjective evangelical of the highest importance.

The unionism of Basel was not of the bureaucratic, Prussian type, but was rather, according to her director, Christian Blumhardt, based on the apostolic method of missions that did not recognize the distinction between Lutheran and Reformed. And this stand won many loyal supporters throughout Germany. Pious Wuerttembergers especially founded societies auxiliary to Basel, the most significant being the one at Stuttgart. The extent to which Germany supported this Swiss society is seen in the fact that of the 200 graduates prior to 1840, 101 came from Wuerttemberg, 56 from the rest of Germany, 29 from Switzerland, and 12 from other lands.

But Basel was not the only society of this type. The Rhine Missionary Society, often called the Barmen Society, was founded in 1828 through a merger of several groups auxiliary to Basel. Under the auspices of the London Missionary Society it sent missionaries to Africa, where its work in Capetown soon became self-sustaining. Thus we see that many Christians in Germany and Switzerland worked together in spite of the creedal fences that others considered serious enough to make fellowship impossible.

So the time came when a desire for fellowship began to have an effect upon their conception of ecclesiastical organization. A large number of Lutheran and Reformed leaders were asking why a union should not take place. Outstanding intellectual leaders like Schleiermacher in Berlin had been advocating it. Both Reformed and Lutheran branches were drawn closer to each other in their common battle against rationalism. Thus when King Frederick William III tried his hand at creating a union among the churches it was not altogether without a deeper spiritual and experimental preparation.

Effects of the Rationalist Movement

We must also turn our attention briefly to another stream of life that was very influential in Germany at this time, designated by the rather indefinite label of "rationalism." This term is usually employed to include both serious criticism of orthodoxy on the part of leading contemporary scholars and a frivolous and irresponsible attitude toward things religious. These two uses of the word rationalism are of course miles apart. A serious criticism of traditional religious thought could only be for the good if it were carried out with sincere motives. The new historical and linguistic study of the Bible, though at first so disturbing to uncritical minds, finally paved the way to a greatly improved understanding of the Bible. In spite of the heat and the shouting, a purifying influence came with the rethinking of convictions and a closer examination of the Bible and its background.

But the man on the street heard self-styled "rationalists" claiming the authority of reason whenever they hammered away at their devout neighbors. Men proudly maintained that they were "rationalists" because they were against all established religion and against local preachers in particular. They would not concede that a Christian might desire to serve as an ambassador of Christ out of gratitude to God. In their minds every preacher was necessarily a man who sought to enrich himself by fleecing innocent victims and imposing on them the shackles of priestly authority. Very often resentment against the injustices of an old society and against political tyranny in Europe took the form of bitterness against the church here in America. And the immigrant from Germany might well think that it was his privilege to scoff at the clergy here because he could not show disrespect to a man who had the position of an "official" in the homeland.

Germans of the educated classes who migrated to America were most proud of their educational heritage. Many of them did not realize that when they compared their own training in Germany to the culture available in frontier communities they were making unfair comparisons. Few of them knew anything about the older educational institutions of the East. Some of these Germans had been given a thorough grounding in Latin and Greek, and were nicknamed "Latin farmers." In a settlement begun in 1832 near Washington, Missouri they exhibited a rather negative attitude toward religion. Nearby, at St. Charles and Marthasville, colonies of educated Wuerttembergers showed a higher regard for religious matters.

At various locations in southern Illinois, near Belleville, groups of educated Germans could be found as early as 1832. In 1836 the Library Society was founded in this so-called "Latin Settlement." Some of these men had left Germany in the wake of collapsing revolutionary hopes. They had not seen any results of their revolutionary activities in the fatherland, whether in 1830 or in 1848. Their "rationalism" gave them little to live by, and they were contemptuous toward both rigid orthodoxy and the warmer Pietism of the Christianity exemplified by the missionaries from institutions like Basel and Barmen. Often they organized their debating societies and singing groups, and occasionally tried to establish a church that they called a "rational" fellowship. Sometimes an educated, freethinking leader would establish himself as minister, going through the motions of religious form, baptizing the children of such immigrants in the name of Liberty, Fraternity, and Equality.

If such men happened to take the name of "Evangelical" for want of another label, it was because they did not know how else to describe themselves. They knew that they were neither Lutheran nor Reformed. What the term evangelical ought to mean did not cause them much concern. At times they might use terms like "United Protestant" or "Free Protestant." But such names did not endure for long when men could not produce their own leadership. This kind of rationalism was sterile in its motives, mainly a revolt against conditions prevailing in another part of the world. In time most of these groups were supplanted by people who expected something more positive and creative of a religious fellowship.

And so we must not be astonished to see the German immigrant of the nineteenth century groping his way in the new world. Just as the immigrant of other times wanted to leave certain things behind, so did this man, though it is not easy to emancipate a man from his heritage, even when desirable. The German could at times be described in terms of three possible attitudes, often mixed in the same person or perhaps giving rise to various groupings. He might be a very stubborn man, trying to preserve what he had been taught, in danger of insisting that what he thought was right and all others were wrong. Or he might be overwhelmed by feelings that were comforting and uplifting, and which made him grateful for the grace of God. All Protestants have such a heritage, though it can often be mechanized by the patterns of wooden orthodoxy. Then again, this immigrant might trust in the abilities of his own mind more than in the power or willingness of God to make himself known to man.

Most of the time this settler was too absorbed in the task of making a place for himself to worry about details of his world-view. In time he was emancipated from the tendency to rebel against what used to be. He came to discover a church that could be very different in many ways from the state churches of Europe. Whether he remained apart in a group speaking his mother tongue, or took his place in what he called a "Yankee" fellowship, he found a spiritual home in the House of God, which is more than any nationality or culture or tongue.

7

Frontier Beginnings

A MIGHTY FLOOD of German immigration swept into the West during the years between 1830 and 1866. Many of the immigrants came along the Ohio and settled in sprouting towns like Cincinnati, Louisville, and Evansville. Others took a northern route via the Erie Canal to Buffalo, thence westward along the Great Lakes. Still others landed at New Orleans and came up the Mississippi to St. Louis and to the towns and farmlands in the valley of the Missouri River.

From 1830 to 1845 the average annual emigration from Germany rose to about 40,000. America was the self-chosen haven for most of those who wanted to leave the depressed economy and the authoritarian political life of the fatherland. There was also widespread resentment toward the ecclesiastical paternalism of the German provincial governments. In most provinces there was strict control over rites of baptism, confirmation, marriage, and burial. The clergy were regarded as state officials. Both Pietists and secular rebels longed for freedom. America was a land of hope for those who would escape the regimentation and official conservatism of the state churches.

But who could minister to the religious needs of these many thousands of immigrants? Many leaders of older American denominations showed concern about them but could do little because of language barriers. For some generations at least, these German newcomers must use their mother tongue. The churches of the German provinces were territorially limited. A state church has no missionary outreach, no facilities for working outside its own borders. Much as individual pastors in Germany might want to help former parishioners, there was little that could be done through official channels.

Not even the older German-background denominations in the eastern part of our country succeeded in making important contacts with these immigrants to the West. Various Lutheran synods were strong in Pennsylvania, for example; but the Germans who went to Missouri, Illinois, or Iowa found these older denominations "foreign" to them. The Reformed immigrants did not feel closely bound to the older Reformed groups in Pennsylvania, though there was some contact. It seemed that the new settlers must shape their own religious fellowship at first, leaving for the future the question of how they were to be related to Christians who had come to America in other days.

Though the established church bodies in Europe could do little to help the immigrant, the voluntary missionary societies could and did help. If these societies seemed weak, they did have certain resources that were needed to face the problems of the frontier church. They had a deep concern for people. They inspired workers to seek out the people who needed the ministrations of the church. They were original and resourceful enough to fashion the tools and methods that the situation demanded. So the greatest assistance came from the missionary societies, both European and American.

In order to understand how a beginning could be made among Germans in the Midwest, let us look at one of the earliest examples of missionary activity, one that became significant for the development of the *Kirchenverein,* the Church Society of the

West. Our example is not taken from the St. Louis area, for that will be described later, but from a "fringe" area as far as the history of the Society is concerned.

The village of Ann Arbor, Michigan was first settled in 1825, the year of the completion of the Erie Canal. Between 1830 and 1855, 5,000 Wuerttembergers from South Germany had settled in Washtenaw County—more people than the entire population of Detroit at that time. A number of the Germans in Ann Arbor became concerned about the religious future of their children. A Presbyterian church had been built in 1829, but in spite of the friendliness of the Presbyterian pastor to the Germans, he could not minister to them. One of the Germans, Jonathan Mann, was a relative of Pastor E. Josenhans in Basel, Switzerland, a member of the executive committee of the Basel Missionary Society. Mann offered to write to his kinsman to see if the Basel Society could help them. He wrote that they needed a virile young pastor to work among the two hundred or more Germans who were interested in forming a congregation.

Friedrich Schmid the Missionary

The Basel Missionary Society reported that a young pastor would be sent in the person of Friedrich Schmid of Waldorf, not far from Stuttgart, the same area from which so many of these immigrants had come. What is significant about this appointment is that Schmid, who came to America in 1833, was the first missionary among 288 Basel Mission Seminary men who were to serve in America in the century to follow. Of this number 158 served churches of the Evangelical Synod. The Reformed Church in the United States received eighteen of them. There are certain areas of the Midwest, like Detroit, Ann Arbor, and St. Louis, where later developments seemed to grow mainly out of the labors of early workers sent to America by the Barmen, Berlin, and Bremen missionary societies. Because these were voluntary groups, not directly related to the state churches, they could act freely. Basel was especially anxious to unite Lutheran and Reformed people, thus expressing the continental meaning of the term evangelical.

What was built on the labors of Friedrich Schmid is indicative of what came, in greater or smaller degree, from the labors of many another missionary sent over by the missionary societies. Schmid established more than twenty congregations during his ministry of over forty years. Throughout all these years Ann Arbor remained his home base, yet he sowed the seed of church development among the Germans in an area reaching from Saginaw in the north to Monroe in the south, a distance of 119 miles, and from Detroit in the east to Lansing in the west, 84 miles. This area is almost as large as the land of Palestine. Later many other congregations grew out of the mother churches that he planted at strategic points.

The missionary pastors did not as a rule represent any one denomination. The fact is that most of the German congregations in the Midwest had no denominational affiliation at first. The older denominations of the East seemed too far away and often impressed the immigrants as being "Yankee" churches. Schmid, for example, did not know what to do about affiliating with a denomination. For a brief time he was a member of one of the better known and recently formed Lutheran synods, but soon stepped out because of what he termed their "doctrinal strife" and their "stiff and strict forms and ceremonies." As long as he lived Schmid kept most of his churches together in a loose federation that he called the "Michigan Synod." Later these churches chose to affiliate with various denominations in the Midwest, namely, Ohio Lutheran, Wisconsin Lutheran, Missouri Lutheran, and the Evangelical Synod.

We have a significant expression of the spirit and method of Schmid and of most of the Basel missionaries in a letter he wrote to Basel in 1851:

I for my part would like to remain faithful to the true teachings of our forefathers and to the beliefs of the Evangelical Church in which I enjoy the peace and blessing of the Lord. For nearly eighteen years I have served in numerous congregations here with the holy Word and sacrament, in which there are Lutheran and Reformed from the homeland, yet I have never had to experience the slightest criticism on the part of the Reformed because of my teachings or creed. As far as church practices are concerned, I maintain everything according to the Wuerttemberg church, except that from early times we did not have communion wafers. If the divine truth is proclaimed in a godly and powerful manner, and the pastor lives in the strength of the gospel, then the truth-loving and truth-seeking people of both confessions can get along together through the strength of the Word, and this will occur too without any attempt to force a union. For that reason there are, I think, many in the congregations here whose parents were Reformed, but I am not certain; I do not inquire about it, for they are happy and united with and through the proclaimed Word of the cross and the holy sacraments. As far as the rigid Old Lutherans are concerned, with whom I have come in contact without learning to know them, I respect their sound teachings, but these people are mostly lacking in living faith, and for that reason there is so little love and so much harshness toward others. This rigid ceremony and this strong condemnation of others are terrible things to me. I find no good fruit here, and despite the fact that a great deal is said about church, church life and activity suffer. I could not join such a synod out of conviction.

What determined the later denominational affiliation of most of these churches was the question of the procurement of pastors. The denomination that supplied a local parish with a pastor usually made headway in gaining that parish as a member congregation. That is why the question of enlisting pastors from Europe or of training them here in America became so important. The Germans were not especially adept at working with lay forces as were the Methodists and Baptists, nor did

German laymen place much confidence in uneducated men. Although this tended to give them a high standard of education for their ministry, if they had ministers at all, it also caused them to lose out in many places simply because no trained ministers were available.

Old Traditions and a New World

What kind of religious attitudes and characteristics prevailed among these German immigrants of the second third of the eighteenth century? It is well to note the main factors in order to understand the conflicts that went on among them. For one thing, they came from a state church or established church background. This meant, for the most part, that the laymen had no experience in managing the affairs of a parish. There had been officials who took care of all that. Voluntary giving to support the church was new to them. A system of taxation left no need for them to decide what to give. (Only the independent missionary societies and benevolent institutions depended upon freewill gifts.) But here in America they must learn to administer congregations and support them without any help or pressure from the state.

Other important features of American life were freedom to worship or not to worship and the absence of any established church. Therefore most men would try to continue the type of worship familiar to them. Friedrich Schmid tried to conduct worship along the rather simple and free pattern of the Wuerttemberg church with which he was familiar. Saxon missionaries tended to give more weight to liturgy and creedalism as exemplified in Missouri Lutheranism. Many of the seeds of diverse American denominationalism had their origin in regional differences in Europe. In America any group was free to perpetuate its own kind.

People who have lived under an established church, whether Protestant, Roman Catholic, or Greek Orthodox, are apt to exhibit some resentment against the church. Many of the immigrants who reached our shores were driven by rebellion against an old pattern in which the church was a part. They wanted to leave all authoritarianism behind. They would acknowledge no bosses, whether kings or bishops. When a minister appeared in a community there would always be some "emancipated" Germans to ridicule him. Many of the vaunted "rationalists" among the immigrants hurled their spite against European authoritarianism upon the frontier church, imagining that these preachers were trying to perpetuate the old life in Europe.

Actually it was not European officialdom of any sort that sent missionaries to work among the immigrants in America, but a very different type of leadership. These pietist missionaries did not have any reason to defend the established churches of Europe. They, too, had often been regarded as rebels or outsiders by the officials. But they came to America with a deep concern for souls, which drove them to do something about the religious needs of the settlers. The Pietists were just as eager to find freedom for their convictions as the rationalists, though their convictions differed greatly. The rationalists looked upon man as the measure of all things, and placed complete confidence in the power of human reason. Pietists believed that men are the creatures of God, dependent upon him, and standing in need of redemption and of a guidance that is higher than human wisdom.

Some German settlements witnessed a prolonged battle between the freethinking rationalists and churchgoing Christians. The rationalists liked to claim all credit for science, culture, and education—thus trying to give an antichurch bias to various social and cultural activities. They claimed that enlightened men could find in the lodge, the singing society, and the club everything worthwhile that the church had to offer, without the poison of clericalism. Thus to be churchless meant to be emancipated. So the rationalists went to war against priestly tyrants and an ecclesiastical censorship that did not exist in America.

The immigrant had to choose among many voices. It was not an easy transition from the officialdom of Europe with its rigid organization and impressive cathedrals to the informality and confusion of the West. Occasionally a shouting revivalist would come by, but few Germans were impressed by the illiteracy and the uprootedness of frontier revivalism. But they could see that their children were growing up in near illiteracy, and with little religious guidance except that which the home might furnish. And the home is rather helpless without a functioning church, especially when the community as such is not ministering to spiritual needs in terms of any meaningful heritage. When a *bona fide* pastor appeared he was sure to be welcomed by some who knew their needs.

Such a pastor would usually try to reach many people in widely scattered settlements. The Lutheran Synod of Ohio reported that in 1837 and 1838 twenty pastors were serving no less than 195 congregations. The American Home Missionary Society report estimates that of 400 German ministers in the United States 250 were Lutheran and 150 Reformed. Yet most of these men could be found in the settled and developed areas.

We have already mentioned the existence of interconfessional missionary societies in Germany and in Switzerland. These societies not only trained many of the early German pastors who worked in the West, but also gave them that missionary perspective which the established churches so often lacked. But there were also creative contributions from American soil.

In 1826 the American Home Missionary Society was formed, and in 1830 it merged with the Domestic Mission Society of Connecticut. A deep concern was felt by many religious leaders in the East over the possible conversion of German immigrants to Roman Catholicism. A group of zealous leaders of Hartford, including Thomas Gallaudet and Richard Bigelow, organized a society long known by the initials L.U.P.O.S. to block the growing power of Rome in America. The initials were later found to mean "Looking Upward, Pressing Onward Society." After Gallaudet made an extensive tour of the West, he insisted to his friends that something had to be done.

More Missionaries from Basel

On December 2, 1835 the executive committee of the Basel Missionary Society considered an appeal from the L.U.P.O.S. on behalf of the German population in the "Mississippi Valley and West Connecticut." The American society offered to support financially any German missionaries whom Basel might send. As a result the two oldest students, Joseph A. Rieger and George Wendelin Wall, were ordained and commissioned to America. Joseph Rieger (1811-69) came of Roman Catholic parentage, but was converted to Protestantism at the age of seventeen, entering the Basel Mission Seminary at twenty-one. George Wall (1811-67) was a native of pietistic Wuerttemberg, as was the first Basel missionary to America, Friedrich Schmid. With these two came another graduate, Johann Gottlieb Schwabe, who was to assist Schmid in Detroit.

On May 31, 1836 the Basel delegation reached New York. Then for three and one half months Rieger and Wall remained in Hartford as the guests of Connecticut friends. This period was invaluable for them in improving their English and acquainting them with certain leading American churchmen. In New

York they had met several men who had been prominent in the establishment of Union Theological Seminary, and who represented a conciliatory attitude in the theology of that time. They also met Calvin Stowe of Lane Seminary. Rieger was much attracted to George Burgess, later Episcopal Bishop of Maine. At Hartford they were visited by Horace Bushnell, and made many other contacts. From the beginning these pioneers were to see that Christianity is far greater than any denomination, and they welcomed contacts with others just as Basel had lively contacts with the London Missionary Society.

On October 17, 1836 the missionaries left Hartford and passed through Philadelphia, Gettysburg, Cincinnati, and Louisville, visiting men whose names had been given them by the Home Missionary Society. They had agreed to work in extended areas at first, not looking for local parishes immediately. About a month later they arrived in St. Louis. Wall soon found himself engrossed in caring for a congregation known as the "German Protestant Evangelical Church of the Holy Ghost." This group was scattered throughout the city, which at this time contained several thousand Germans. Services were being held in the buildings loaned by Methodist and Presbyterian churches.

Soon a campaign was begun to raise funds for a German church. It was to be 42 by 60 feet in size and to cost $8,000. The self-styled rationalists of St. Louis were violently opposed to the erection of this church, but by August of 1840 the first German church of the city was dedicated and called the "German Protestant Church in St. Louis." The communion service on the following Sunday was attended by about 500 persons. Wall was a man of pronounced pietist leanings while many of the members were called "ultra liberal," a prophecy of difficulties to be overcome.

Rieger began his work across the river in Illinois as an itinerant preacher. For nine months he worked in the vicinity of Alton.

In August of 1837 he moved to Beardstown, Illinois. Here he taught school and preached in many nearby settlements, not fearing to preach in English when asked. In 1838 he visited Fort Madison, Iowa, offering "the first sermon and the first communion service among the Germans in the territory." In his diary he says, "We had only corn bread, and a common tin cup as chalice, but the people were glad and did not harp on externalities." His roving commission during this period did not lead to permanent organizations, though churches were founded at many of these points later. In 1839 he decided to visit Germany. On his way east he visited Schmid at Ann Arbor. Here he gave his horse to his friend and continued by boat and train to Hartford.

In 1840 Rieger returned to America with a bride, and his Hartford friends assured him of their support as long as it would be required. He now intended to take a permanent pastorate. He returned from Germany just too late to take part in the founding of the *Kirchenverein des Westens* (Church Society of the West), but he later took an active part in it. There were now four Basel graduates in the St. Louis area—George Wall, Joseph Rieger, Johann Jacob Riess, and Johannes Gerber. Kindred spirits were also found in several men from the Barmen Missionary Society and a remarkably able free-lance pastor named Hermann Garlichs, who worked in the backwoods at Femme Osage and St. Charles, Missouri. These men were eager to do something that went beyond the perpetuation of the sectarianism so rife at that time.

The German element in east-central Missouri and southwestern Illinois was increasing rapidly. The population of St. Louis increased from 16,419 in 1840 to 77,860 in 1850, of which latter number 22,340 were born in Germany. Small congregations had arisen among these immigrants, but few people thought of their churches as needing any wider connections. In Ger-

was returning from Germany with his bride, and might have arrived in time had he not been delayed by an accident that befell his wife in crossing a bridge in Ohio.

The meeting had been called for Wednesday, October 14. In the course of the deliberations, lasting several days, a total of twenty-four resolutions were adopted, covering a wide range of subjects. These were not designed as a constitution, but they paved the way for future developments. It was agreed not to organize a synod at this time, though some kind of association was needed. At the suggestion of Garlichs, who had heretofore worked as a pioneering individual, those present constituted themselves *Der Deutsche Evangelische Kirchenverein des Westens*, the German Evangelical Church Society of the West. (The term *Verein* was variously translated in contemporary documents as "society," "synod," "association," "conference," or "union.") Every effort was made to avoid a rigid institutional organization and to eliminate the bureaucratic features usually associated with synodical bodies. Thus the nucleus of the denomination later known as the Evangelical Synod came into existence as a simple pastoral conference.

Membership was to consist of ordained pastors, lay delegates, and advisory members. Congregations were urged to send lay delegates who would also be entitled to vote. Thus the parity of laity and clergy would be established. No effort was made at this time to induce individual churches to join the Society. To ward off any suspicion that this might be the beginning of a bureaucratic synod, it was explicitly stated that neither the external nor the internal affairs of local congregations could be made the business of the Society.

Since only ordained pastors were eligible to full membership, the one hope for growth lay in the arrival of ordained pastors from Germany or in the admission of candidates of theology. America had become attractive to some theological students who, having passed their theological examinations in Germany, left for America before being ordained. Confronted by the danger of admitting unworthy persons, the Society decreed that all such applicants were to be closely examined with reference to their characters, no mention being made of their theological position. Only in emergencies and with the consent of the president was the examining committee empowered to authorize an ordination between conferences. The raising of barriers against questionable characters was extremely necessary in the unsettled conditions of the West. The confessional statement consisted of only sixteen words. Any uncertainty as to the meaning of the term evangelical was removed by the simple assurance that the church here subscribed to the symbolic writings of "our Evangelical mother church in Germany."

The nonsectarian and irenic spirit prevailing at this meeting found expression in the decision to cooperate wholeheartedly with such benevolent societies as were laboring for the advancement of the kingdom of God. This referred not only to German organizations. The American Tract Society had assisted Riess, Rieger, and Wall. The L.U.P.O.S. had granted Rieger an appropriation of $200. These men also received active assistance from the American Bible Society and the American Home Missionary Society.

"To meet the needs of our youth," the problem of procuring a catechism was also considered. A committee composed of Wall, Garlichs, and Nollau was appointed to prepare the draft of a catechism to be presented to the Society. Members of the Society, in the performance of official duties, were encouraged to appear in the customary vestments used in the "Evangelical mother church." Another committee was appointed to prepare the prospectus of a book of worship to be presented at the next meeting. Thus another move toward independence from the German mother church was made.

The conference of the following year (May 3, 1841) that convened at Friedens Church near St. Charles was the formal constitutional assembly of the *Kirchenverein*. Only Daubert, Heyer, Garlichs, and Wall were present. Riess and Nollau were in Germany; Riess in quest of a wife and Nollau preparing to enter the African mission of the Barmen Society. At this meeting it was stipulated that, if the number of lay delegates at a conference was not equal to that of the clergy, parity should be established by drafting the necessary number from the congregation entertaining the conference—a studied attempt to allay any suspicion concerning the synodical designs of this "pastoral clique." In the doctrinal paragraph, subscription to the symbolical books was made secondary to acknowledgment of the Old and New Testaments as the sole criterion of faith, in the exposition of which the consensus of the symbolical books of the Lutheran and Reformed churches was to be the norm.

The founding of the *Kirchenverein* caused a sensation in the ranks of the rationalists. They asserted that the principles for which they had fought in Germany and the purpose for which they had come to America were threatened. They had successfully repelled the threatened invasion of the Pennsylvania synods only to find that from their own soil a similar "obscurantist institution" was rearing its head. All plans of the Society were described in the *Anzeiger des Westens,* the German newspaper, in terms of "priestly conspiracy" and "synodical conclave" of the "synodical lords." They were especially enraged at Garlichs who had worked so successfully in a settlement containing many of these "enlightened" anticlerics. Character assassination was attempted several times against pastors who took part in the Society. In St. Louis, Wall was attacked by many, and finally in 1843 he resigned and organized another church in northern St. Louis, which was destined to become a bulwark of the *Kirchenverein*. But all of these attacks of the rationalists were so crude and bitter that eventually such opponents were disgraced by their own manners.

News of the formation of the *Kirchenverein* also aroused apprehension among some of the Lutheran synods of that time. The purpose of this association, to effect a union of Lutheran and Reformed churches, was considered impossible. One new group, called the "Evangelical Lutheran Society of the West," in which Garlichs and Heyer had previously held membership, was offended when these men asked for honorable dismissal: "That the Lutheran and German Reformed churches in the United States will ever be united we have not the slightest reason to hope. Their peculiar relations are such as to confirm the belief that they will maintain their distinctive characters." The Lutheran Synod of Ohio counseled the members of the *Kirchenverein* to unite with either the Lutheran or the Reformed Church.

Yet a profound conviction dominated some of the Germans of the West that the future belonged to them. They were not drawn toward the elaborate synodical organizations of the eastern Lutheran groups. And even more important, they did not regard the split between Lutherans and Reformed as a justified separation. A higher unity could be found in Christ, a unity in which Christians of varied opinions could live and work.

This ideal seemed to be mocked by the smallness of the fellowship that espoused it. Only eight men had come into the group, and within a few years several of these members seemed to be lost to them. Nollau went to Africa as a missionary, yet returned later and was readmitted in 1851. Heyer joined the Presbyterians after a vicious character attack was made upon him by the rationalists. Garlichs returned to Germany for a time, planning to return to Missouri later, but he accepted a call to a German Evangelical church in Brooklyn, New York where he worked for eighteen years. He took an active part in the American Tract Society and served as adviser to newly arrived German missionaries bound for the West. Thus at the end of the first decade of activity by its members, only three of the charter members remained: Wall, Rieger, and Riess.

In the year 1846 the tide began to turn. The year before, several more ordained men had arrived, and now Johann Jung and Jacob Knauss from Basel were received into membership. Then came William Frederick Binner from the University of Breslau and Adolph H. Baltzer from the Universities of Berlin and Halle. These two came through the agency of the Bremen Society. They visited briefly with Richard Bigelow in the East. Another university man was Friedrich Birkner from Erlangen. Others also came, so that when the Society was ten years old it included twenty-five pastors. They were all German from abroad, directly or indirectly products of German pietism, and sympathetic with the doctrinal breadth of the Evangelical Church in Germany. The majority came through the agency of one of the missionary societies—12 from Basel, 3 from Barmen, and 6 from Bremen. Four were "self-educated" or had received private theological instruction after their arrival in America. Common to all of these early pastors on the frontier was a passionate concern for building, not a Lutheran or Reformed or Evangelical Zion, but a kingdom of God.

It is impossible to give attention to any local congregations of this period, yet it should be noted that when the first decade of the *Kirchenverein* came to a close in 1850 there were twenty-seven main congregations and various other preaching places. Fourteen of them were located in Missouri, with others in Illinois, Indiana, and Iowa, and one in New Orleans. At the same time, various other congregations not affiliated with the Society had already been organized, but they worked as "free churches" with no definite association with others until later. We shall see that similar associations of churches developed in other parts, notably around Chicago and in western New York State. Later they merged with the Society to form a functioning denomination.

Church Work in Pioneer Communities

Perhaps a further word should be added concerning the general conditions under which this work was done. It is difficult for men of our generation to imagine the ridicule that could be heaped upon pastors and churches in these German communities. The "Forty-eighters," claiming to be apostles of freedom, often denounced religion as an impediment to the welfare of humanity. In Cincinnati, for example, societies of "free Germans" agitated for the abrogation of Sunday laws, Thanksgiving Day, and prayers in Congress and for the removal of all religious literature from school property. In St. Louis a German newspaper uttered the mock prayer: "Lord, do not meddle with us, we will take care of ourselves." No tricks were too crude if they interfered with the work of the churches. Thus drunken parties might gather near the churches to interfere with services. One pastor found a beer keg in the pulpit on Sunday morning, and attached to it was a derisive note. A pastor was told, concerning attendance at communion: "We can drink our wine at the tavern, and don't need the Lord's Supper."

Sometimes opposition took more concrete forms. Pastors were attacked in their homes. At Marthasville, under cover of darkness, vandals wrecked the newly begun church building. The scoffers in a community might suddenly appear at meetings, pretending to be members in order to prevent the election of a pastor. But when there was not overt opposition there was often a naive confidence in the sufficiency of "good morals." Some of the Germans of this time were prone to suppose that churchgoing was permissible for those who could not live de-cent lives without it. One man expressed it so: "In our country thieves, murderers, and such people have to do repentance, but we are Christians by birth, baptism, and confirmation." Many congregations continued the German custom of admitting to church membership anyone having reached the confirmation age of thirteen or fourteen, regardless of spiritual qualifications. Thus many churches had a group of nominal Christians who lacked essential spiritual devotion. This explains why certain American groups become quite insistent on a definite spiritual experience as a prerequisite to church membership.

This also explains why August Rauschenbusch, a very devoted and efficient worker, became dissatisfied with the loose standards prevailing among the immigrant churches. He had come from the Rhineland and was commissioned by the Langenberg Society, which had sent many preachers to America. At first he worked with the American Tract Society. Coming to St. Louis in 1846, he soon worked with Wall and Riess of the *Kirchenverein*. Later, without becoming narrowly sectarian, he accepted Baptist views and so worked as a German Baptist minister, beginning about 1855. His illustrious son, Walter Rauschenbusch, later taught at the Baptist Seminary at Rochester, New York. August Rauschenbusch kept contact with the Evangelical pastors in Missouri, enlisting their aid in the work of the American Bible Society.

The continued presence of fraudulent or irreligious "pastors" constituted an embarrassing problem for those who were genuinely concerned about religion. Local groups were often willing to employ any literate man who claimed to be a preacher and who was a ready talker. Thus an unscrupulous impostor could have a high time as pastor of a group of free Germans who wanted a man that did not interfere with their habits. Careful Christians thus came to rely more and more upon a pastor's relation to one of the known missionary societies. After *Der Friedensbote* was established as the official journal of the

Society in 1850, one frequently found notices warning unsuspecting congregations about certain characters. Yet there were always voices who protested against their loss of local "freedom" when cooperative safeguards were suggested to prevent the employment of bogus pastors.

The economic status of pastors was of course very uncertain. They were dependent on the economic ability of their people and did not expect anything better, but often they suffered more than their people because Germans were not accustomed to the voluntary support of churches. Most of their living quarters were exceedingly primitive. Many of the men could not have avoided embracing other occupations and thus diminishing their parish work, if they had not received assistance from the Home Missionary Society. Such grants were made on condition that the local church raise at least one half of the total. From 1841 to 1861 not less than twenty-one members of the *Kirchenverein* received help from the Home Missionary Society. All told, between $7,000 and $8,000 was appropriated during this period.

Pioneer conditions of insufficient religious education, along with gross materialism, made some of the German-born pastors lean more heavily in the direction of evangelistic methods than would have been the case in the homeland. Yet they usually refused to count conversions as many were apt to do. Typical of the German attitude was that of Birkner: "Seven families have begun a new course of life—but I should not like to think myself more sharp-sighted than Elijah, who knew nothing of the 7,000 in Israel who had not bowed their knees to Baal."

One can say that these men were deeply concerned about individual souls. Many a pastor risked life and limb in order to ride to the home of some parishioner, or even a stranger, to be with him in a time of trouble. It was expected that every home should be visited by the pastor, who made inquiries concerning the conducting of the family altar. Some laymen of course resented the questions the pastor might ask concerning religious practices in the home.

Throughout the first decade, as we have noted, the *Kirchenverein* was essentially a society of pastors serving congregations that they had organized according to local needs. Before the Society existed a large number of separate, so-called "Evangelical" churches had come into being, many of them exceedingly loose and antisynodical. Thus the term evangelical might be used by some who were anything but evangelical in the view of the Society. Some rationalistic churches preferred to be known simply as "Protestant." Even conservative churches insisted upon freedom of action and refused to surrender their freedom to pastors or organizations. The election of a pastor occurred by majority vote in an open congregational meeting where, after a number of candidates had preached at least one "trial sermon," their respective merits were officiously discussed.

Church membership needed to be more clearly defined, for the lack of religious training often made it possible for people of the most lax standards to regard themselves as members in good standing. Binner reported that in Wisconsin some farmers "sold" their church membership along with the farm. When such untrained church members were elected to offices in the parish, it was all the more difficult for sincere members to uphold spiritual goals.

An important heritage from Germany, which the pastors could usually maintain, was the practice of catechetical instruction in preparation for confirmation. At first pastors used any one of several catechisms that were being used in various areas in Germany, usually of the union type, uniting elements of Luther's Smaller Catechism with parts of the Heidelberg Catechism of the Reformed Church. In 1847 the *Kirchenverein* published its own catechism containing 219 questions and answers supported by a number of Bible verses. The main parts of the catechism dealt with the Decalogue and the Apostles' Creed (in which scriptural teaching was expounded concerning God and his attributes, followed by an exposition of the three articles of the Apostles' Creed). Then came a section on prayer, including the Lord's Prayer; one on the sacrament of Baptism and a final one concerning the Lord's Supper.

Thus the Society succeeded in providing for the Evangelical Church in America what the Union Church in Germany had not achieved, namely, a union catechism. The new catechism was welcomed as a standard textbook that would help to foster unity of heart and mind. But this was no unchangeable doctrinal formulation. Nor was it too practical for general school purposes, especially because of its cumbersome language. Later it was simplified and improved.

At first many churches had parochial schools, so the Sunday school movement did not attract much attention. In 1867 it became necessary to publish a children's paper (German), which shows that Sunday schools had become more common than the records seem to indicate. Later most of the parochial schools were abandoned, largely for the reason that the danger of segregating children from community at large seemed to outweigh the benefits to be derived.

Emphasis on an Educated Ministry

It was natural that German immigrants should hope to have German-trained ministers as their leaders, but there were never enough pastors on hand to meet the need. Often it was found that men who were prepared according to European academic standards were not ready to face the new conditions that awaited them in America. Yet the Germans did not abandon their tradition of an educated ministry. Some of them argued that there was no other way than to import pastors from across the sea. How could native sons be prepared for the ministry among Germans when there were no institutions adequate to the task? The churches were not strong enough to establish training schools, and without such schools the church could not grow. It seemed like a vicious circle.

In 1845 the Society appointed a committee, composed of Riess, Wall, and Nollau, to assist in every possible way young men desiring to enter the ministry. Not much came of this gesture except that a few men were being trained in the homes of older ministers, but in a June, 1848 session, attended by only six of the fourteen members, the subject of a school for pastors was discussed officially for the first time. It was pointed out that nothing could be done without the support of all the congregations in the adjacent territory. So a detailed plan for a seminary was sent to congregations in Missouri, Illinois, Iowa, and Indiana with the request that they elect delegates to a special conference to convene at St. Peter's Church, St. Louis. The lay response was disappointing, for only two churches other than the host church were represented; but a resolution was passed indicating that a seminary should be established "to educate teachers and preachers for the Evangelical Church of America."

Where should it be located? Economic advantages led to the selection of an idyllic site in Warren County, Missouri, on the Femme Osage Creek, midway between the villages of Femme Osage and Marthasville, the latter being the name adopted for the seminary. It was argued that escape from the wicked urban environment to nature's solitude was necessary for the training of God's ambassadors. A notable visitor from Germany named H. Krummacher stated that the location of the school in the forest reminded him of the Norbert Monastery in the valley of Prémontré in France. The cornerstone was laid on

July 4, 1849. A business manager, called a "steward," and one professor were elected. Before the building was completed a class of six students was being instructed by William Binner, the professor.

This seminary was the most ambitious project ever undertaken by the *Kirchenverein*, and even with the best of support, the group needed help from the outside. American friends viewed with admiration the determination of this small group to found an educational institution in the West. The Presbyterian Synod of Missouri sent a substantial donation. The Society for the Promotion of Collegiate and Theological Education for the West sent an appropriation of $500 after two representatives inspected the school. More was sent later. Again, Richard Bigelow of New York, the generous benefactor of the *Kirchenverein*, made a series of gifts to the school.

Help was also received from Germany. King Frederick William IV of Prussia sent fifty German *Taler*. In 1852 Wall attended the fifth Evangelical Church Diet at Bremen and brought the needs of the school to the attention of German friends. More than 2,000 books were received for the seminary library. Wall appealed to the king for permission to gather an offering for the school among the churches of Germany. This was held up when an inquiry through the German consul at St. Louis brought back the consul's opinion that the seminary was a disreputable backwoods school conducted by questionable characters. The prejudiced report seemed to doom any hope of further support in Germany, but after conferences with church leaders Wall was able to establish confidence in the cause. Inquiries were directed to Philip Schaff at Mercersburg and to Samuel Schmucker at Gettysburg. The replies were so favorable that the king authorized the collection in 1854 on condition that the funds derived be kept in the control of German church leaders. A sum equivalent to about $10,000 was received in the course of several years. For some time the interest was sent to the school annually, but since the early part of the twentieth century the fund has been used for training German pastors going to scattered German settlements in various parts of the world.

The Marthasville Seminary opened in 1850 with an enrollment of eight students. It seems that all were of German birth. An interdenominational spirit was imparted by the presence of one Methodist and one Mennonite student. In the second year three students were sent by the Church Society of Ohio, later to merge with the *Kirchenverein*. The school year extended from July to June, with four weeks of vacation following the annual synod meeting. At first the course of study was to extend over two years, but the class of 1856 was held over for an additional year, thus establishing a three-year course. In 1865 the period was extended to five years, for many of the first students had little, if any, preparatory training.

There were two professors, assisted by the business manager who taught some preparatory courses. When Friedrich Birkner resigned as professor to return to Germany, the head of the Basel Seminary was persuaded to send Andreas Irion to be installed as "second professor." Irion was a man who possessed all of the virtues of German Pietism, together with an impressive ability as an educator. For several years the affairs of the seminary seemed to be going as smoothly as could be expected. Then in 1857 William Binner resigned as head professor. Irion was advanced to this position. Adolph Baltzer was brought in as a professor of equal rank with Irion; he served until he became president of the Society in 1866. Thus the initial difficulties were overcome. Irion gave the school good theological guidance and Baltzer contributed wise and brilliant administrative ability.

In this period scores of colleges were established on the western frontier, and it should not be surprising that the Society also attempted, in vain, to develop a college in Missouri. The college idea had always been associated with the founding of the seminary; in fact, the need of it as a preparatory school for the seminary was urgent. In 1854 the decision was made to erect a college building on the seminary grounds. During that same year the Missouri Pacific Railroad came to Washington, Missouri which was only six miles away. The cornerstone of the school was laid in November, 1855, but the school was not opened until April, 1858. A four-year course of instruction was to be imparted in German and English. One of the teachers was Horace Elijah Boardman, later pastor of the first Congregational church at Fort Dodge, Iowa.

In its second year the college enrolled eighteen students, fifteen of whom were Germans. The highest attendance ever reached was twenty-seven. The death blow to the college came during the Civil War; parents refused to send their sons to this guerilla-infested region along the Missouri. When only five boys appeared for the second semester in 1862, it seemed useless to continue. It is interesting to note that of the eighty-five colleges in Missouri, seventy-seven collapsed during the Civil War. It took about five years to clean up the debt that remained on the ill-fated college and on the seminary. Thus the small fellowship failed in this one attempt, though the seminary was to become the center of a much larger fellowship. Indeed, it can be said that in the century to come no other institution proved to be so central to the whole life of the Evangelical Synod as the seminary that had its beginnings at Marthasville.

As the church association began to grow, it was inevitable that members were drawn into the support of various missionary and benevolent projects. Many of the churches were themselves indebted to the initial help given by American and European

FRONTIER BEGINNINGS • 185

agencies. It was natural that pastors would try to obtain offerings for the mission societies that had commissioned them. Of the 156 members of the *Kirchenverein* joining between 1840 and 1866, fifty are definitely known to have come from the mission schools at Basel and Barmen. These men were not merely alumni of the schools in question, for they often reported back to the "mother house" and wanted to support the work carried on by their schoolmates. Thus Friedrich Schmid in Michigan sent many a gift to Basel, both personal gifts and offerings from his congregations. There was little question for most of these early pastors that they should share in the work of foreign missions by supporting those mission societies with which they had been associated. Thus it took many years before the question of establishing a foreign mission field became meaningful for the Society.

For Churchly Care of the Sick

A mission to the Indians in our own land came up for discussion at various times, but no practicable plans developed. Nearly every growing parish in the Midwest became involved in what we can call church extension. Congregations, founded a century or so ago, sometimes gave birth to a half dozen other churches when there were sufficient people and leaders to warrant it. But soon it was necessary to do other benevolent work. Sickness and accidents often took a terrible toll from the hardworking immigrants. Parishes sometimes tried to set up societies to give aid to widows and orphans, but it was found that a local group could hardly muster the strength to give adequate help in times of tragedy.

As early as 1853 the feasibility of establishing a deaconess hospital in St. Louis, with its four strong churches, had been discussed. Dr. W. A. Passavant's hospital in Pittsburgh, the pioneer German-American deaconess hospital inspired by Fliedner's institution at Kaiserswerth (1836), was admired as a model for such an enterprise. The work actually got under way in St. Louis when Mrs. Wilhelmina Meier, the widow of a former janitor of St. Peter's Church, discovered among some newly arrived German immigrants a friendless orphan girl stricken with typhoid, whose parents had died on their way to this country. Mrs. Meier nursed the girl back to health. This revealed to Nollau and to others the need of providing a hospital where patients would have both physical and spiritual care. Donations were received, and a building was rented.

In Nollau's first report the acceptance of Passavant's principle indicated that no distinction of creed, race, nationality, or color would be made in the acceptance or treatment of patients. At the end of a year twenty-four beds were available. During the last half of 1858 about two hundred patients had to be rejected for lack of space. The Saxon Lutherans also established a hospital at the same time, designed mainly for sick fellow believers; all but one of the fifteen patients received were Lutherans. The broad policy of the Evangelical hospital gained wide support from various organizations in the community. The new hospital opened its doors in March, 1861 under the name of "The Good Samaritan Hospital." With the coming of the Civil War there was much to do. For a time the government took over the entire hospital to care for the wounded after the capture of Camp Jackson.

Especially insistent in demands on Christian love was the plight of children orphaned through cholera epidemics and other perils of frontier life. Appeals were often made to German pastors when children were in danger of falling into the hands of unscrupulous persons. Nollau was again the initiator. He took a number of children into his own home and when the need grew he appealed to laymen to help, for the parsonage at St. Peter's was too small. In 1859, before the new hospital was completed, a house was rented to shelter orphaned children. By 1860 there were 22 children. Orphan "societies" were organized among the parochial school children with monthly dues of 3 to 5 cents. In 1863, where they were 53 orphans, the building was devastated by fire. The children were then housed in the hospital.

Another cholera epidemic in 1866 emphasized the need for better facilities. The hospital was moved nine miles west of the city to a 65-acre estate on the St. Charles Road, which is still the home of this institution. In time many other such homes and hospitals were to be established in various parts of our land.

"Messenger of Peace"

Another important creation of the *Kirchenverein* of this period was a journal that continued until December, 1958. No association of Christians can be imagined without an organ through which to express itself. The eastern synods, both Lutheran and Reformed, were amply supplied with English and German papers, many of which were being used by members of the Society. The American Tract Society published papers that were widely used in the fellowship, but as far back as 1843 the need was voiced for a periodical belonging to the Society.

An appeal was directed to Basel in the hope that funds might be granted for the purchase of a printing press. In 1849 the matter of a periodical was taken up again. Binner, the seminary professor, was elected editor, to be assisted by Baltzer. In January, 1850 the first issue appeared.

The publication bore the name *Friedensbote*, the "Messenger of Peace." On the title page appeared Ephesians 4:3: "Eager to maintain the unity of the Spirit in the bond of peace," which came to be adopted as the motto of the church. The leading editorial in the first issue emphasized the keynote of peace and pleaded for an understanding of the peaceful mission of this publication.

The *Friedensbote* and the seminary had been founded in the same year; together they had their origin and together they flourished. They had common leadership, for the editor of the journal was also head of the seminary. This continued when Irion became successor to Binner in 1857. For two and one-half years the *Friedensbote* was published in St. Louis, where the business affairs were in the hands of Wall. In the first year the project made a profit of $64.90, which evidently prompted the seminary directorate to recommend the purchase of a press. It was about this time that Bigelow donated the sum of $500 for the reduction of the seminary debt. With the announcement of this gift came the news that the seminary had its own press, valued at $300, the gift of the same benefactor. To provide adequate accommodations for the press, Bigelow had added $500 for the erection of a printing shop. A building was erected, the first floor of which contained a dining room for the seminary. The printing press was located on the second floor with quarters for the printer and his apprentice.

In 1858 the paper appeared semimonthly at an annual subscription rate of 50 cents. It tried consistently to avoid theological controversy. At one time the existence of the press was threatened by men who submitted something it would not print.

The printer often received job-printing assignments from the people of the neighborhood. The printing of a bill of sale was rejected because slaves were listed among the articles of merchandise. Threats of reducing the establishment to ashes were made by the enraged slaveholders.

The *Kirchenverein* was forced to travel a most difficult road in the early years of its growth. With few exceptions the leaders were the spiritual sons of continental missionary societies. The pietistic traditions of these societies were sometimes upheld to the disparagement of the cultural values espoused by the rationalists. This put the leaders of the church in the dangerous position of retreating from contemporary learning. Fortune played into the hands of this little group when a number of university graduates arrived who could stand as representatives of the best pietistic tradition and also as men of academic integrity. Though the two types never clashed on vital issues so as to divide the Society into an "old" and a "new" school, they constantly represented two distinct cultural and religious points of view.

Financial dependence of many German churches in the West upon assistance from friends in the East served to acquaint the German pioneers with the real spirit of American Christianity. Discovering an affinity between the rigors of American Puritanism and the ascetic tendencies of German Pietism, *Kirchenverein* pastors often followed the customs and practices prevailing in Presbyterian and Congregational churches. A man like Rieger, for example, learned English very quickly and used the language much more readily than others of lesser stature, because he was thrown into intimate contact with some of the most ardent missionary leaders of the East.

8

Western Consolidation

WHEN THE GENERAL CONFERENCE of 1866 changed the name of the *Kirchenverein* to "Synod," it made no difference in the character of the *Verein*, which had to all intents and purposes been a synod. A synod was ordinarily stricter in its requirements for membership and exercised wider authority than a *Verein*. The change of name was, for all that, something more than just a recognition of the *status quo*. It was a rededication to the work which the founders of the *Verein* had begun; it was also the acceptance of new responsibilities, commensurate with a generation's increase of strength. Awareness of these new responsibilities led also to the unprecedented action of the General Conference in electing Adolph H. Baltzer as full-time president.

The choice of Adolph Baltzer for the enlarged office of president was a fortunate one, for, as Hugo Kamphausen says, "he was a born leader and churchman. What others often lacked, the sense of law and order, of the subordination of the individual and the importance of a firm organization, he possessed in a high degree. Without him the *Kirchenverein*, which became the Evangelical Synod, would hardly have been given the durable framework it needed to withstand the many disruptive forces that threatened it."[1] For fourteen years, from his election in 1866 to his death on January 28, 1880, he dominated no less than he represented the Synod. His administration set a pattern of interests and activities that we can follow with some modifications through the next fifty years.

The first test of the full-time presidency came in the General Conference of 1868, held in Indianapolis at Zion Church. This conference was itself marked by an innovation that was being put to the test. It was the first "delegate" conference to meet under the revised statutes of 1866. All previous general conferences had been made up of the full membership of the *Kirchenverein*. This had been both desirable and feasible while the membership and the territorial spread of the *Kirchenverein* were smaller, but it had now become expensive and burdensome. Under the revised statutes the General Conference was made up of delegates elected by the districts (three in 1868), according to the ratio of one clerical delegate for every six pastors and one lay delegate for every six member churches.

The three districts were represented by the following number of pastors and laymen, respectively: Eastern, 8 and 7; Middle, 8 and 3; Northern, 5 and 2. The Conference had a total of 21 pastors and 12 lay delegates, and 3 officers, the Reverend Adolph H. Baltzer, president; the Reverend Louis E. Nollau, secretary; and the Reverend Ernst E. Roos, treasurer.

President Baltzer struck the keynote of the conference in his sermon at the opening session. For his text he had chosen 1 Corinthians 15: 58—"Therefore, my beloved brethren, be ye stedfast, unmoveable, always abounding in the work of the Lord, forasmuch as ye know that your labour is not in vain in the Lord."

---

[1] From *Geschichte des religiösen Lebens in der Deutschen Evangelischen Synode,* p. 37.

What must we do to be always increasing (abounding) in the work of the Lord?

First, we must remember that we have been called to the work of the Lord. Now the Lord requires diverse gifts for manifold tasks in his vineyard, but one spirit pervading all: the spirit of faithfulness, of obedience, of discipline. So it is of the greatest importance for us servants of the Lord to note well what share in his work we have been specially called to do. Our Synod would accomplish little if, even with the best intentions and the utmost zeal for God's kingdom, we should lose sight of the fact that right now our first duty is toward the German Evangelical people of this country and the oncoming stream of German Evangelical immigrants, to provide them with the Word and the sacraments and to offer them the ministration of the Evangelical Church. Should we permit any other purpose, no matter how worthy in itself and serviceable in general to God's kingdom, to divert us from our appointed task, the Synod could scarcely increase in the work of the Lord.

Secondly, in order to increase in the work of the Lord, our text exhorts us to remain stedfast, unmoveable in faith, on the firm foundation of the Lord's work. This firm foundation is the fact of salvation: "God was in Christ, reconciling the world unto himself." On our standard is inscribed the truth: "Christ alone! Faith alone! The Bible alone!" Against attacks by mockery, disdain, or foolish prattle about the claims of reason, we are not in danger of yielding an inch of ground. But when this truth is seemingly granted by some, while equating it with or subjecting it to the priority of one or another set of confessional statements, or insisting on adherence to some particular church and acceptance of its doctrine, or on this or that special means of grace, by which alone faith and godly life can come to birth, or perhaps on some particular type of organization or order of worship, then it behooves us to stand firm and unmoveable, for then we are in danger; then the pharisee in each of us, with his confidence in outward works, is likely to show himself.

But, finally, are we perhaps engaged in a hopeless task? Are we pouring water in a sieve? Is all our prayer, faith, witness, and struggle in vain? Has it no future? The answer of our text is the promise that "in the Lord, your labour is not in vain." Our labor, rightly done, is the Lord's work, and therefore cannot be vain, empty, useless, or unblessed. No matter if in individual congregations things go wrong, the ways of the world take over and undo the faithful labor of the pastor and elders, still the work that was done in the Lord has not been in vain; the seed that was strewn will bear eternal fruit. Synods may endure for a while, perform their task and pass away; denominations may be swept away; some of the great churches of Christendom may collapse and yield their domain to godlessness—yet whatever of their work was done in the name of the Lord and in his spirit will remain and bear eternal fruit.

It would be difficult to find anywhere plainer statements than we have in this sermon of the special mission and the distinctive doctrine and position of the Evangelical Synod. Taken together, they were the guiding principles in every important decision during the remaining years of the nineteenth century—the German era.

When the conference had been organized for business Baltzer delivered his report for the past biennium. He had spent fully half of the time during that period away from home in fulfillment of one of the duties laid upon him when he took office, namely, to visit as many churches having membership in the Synod as his time and strength would allow. Beginning in November, 1866, he had traveled thousands of miles (impressive figures in those days) by railroad and steamboat, on horse and on foot, going far beyond his instructions in visiting not only the eighty churches having membership in the Synod, but also nearly all of the additional one hundred congregations served by the Synod. Usually on his visit to a church there would be a service of worship at which the pastor gave a short sermon and Baltzer delivered a somewhat longer address. After the service there was always a meeting with the church council, at which there was sure to be a fruitful exchange of ideas and information. With justifiable satisfaction Baltzer noted that the collections taken up at these church services amounted to more than a thousand dollars, and that the expense connected with the visitations had been less than half of that amount.

This was the first and last time the president of the Synod undertook a general visitation. The report of 1868, written by Baltzer while the impressions he had received were still fresh, is a unique survey of churches and church life in town and country. Its dominant note is thankfulness to God.

A Survey of the Church

There had been an increase of nearly 20 per cent in the number of both pastors and churches, and a considerable increase in church membership within the past two years. An equal cause for thankfulness was the fact that the material welfare of the congregations had shown notable improvement. Referring to the effects of the Civil War (only three years past) Baltzer remarked: "Only a few of our congregations have been hit by the tragic consequences of the late war, and these but lightly, so that they were able to recover quickly." Almost everywhere the Lord had blessed the industry of the German farmers with bountiful crops, which they had been able to sell at high prices. The value of their property had increased. Astonishing changes had taken place in the German settlements (especially in the West) within a period of ten years.

Fields and meadows, houses, barns, stables, fruit orchards, and vineyards speak plainly of the rapidly increased prosperity of the owners. The little log cabin rural churches are rapidly disappearing, in fact they have become a rarity; their place is taken by more spacious and appropriate frame or stone churches. In the cities also, though in a lesser degree, there is evidence of improving economic conditions, although in the nature of the case, our city churches will generally lag behind the country churches, so far as worldly goods and possessions are concerned. The membership of the city church is too fluctuating, consisting, as it does, mainly of propertyless day laborers and artisans. Yet evidence of prosperity is not lacking in the cities, as shown by a number of large and costly church buildings, and quite respectable schools and parsonages. Bells peal out from many church towers; some churches have magnificent organs; and there are few so poor as not to have a melodeon. Congregations are making a real effort to place pastors and teachers beyond want.

Turning to a consideration of the moral and spiritual well-being of the congregations, Baltzer found every reason to thank God for the evidence he had seen of genuine spiritual life.

Church attendance appears to be good in general, and where it falls off, the reason is likely to be that the minister is relying too much on his natural gift for speaking instead of preparing his sermons by study and prayer. Communion services are held almost everywhere at least four times a year (oftener in the larger congregations), and most church members partake of communion at least once a year. But this is not really satisfactory, and the fault lies in part with the pastors, who fail to stress the value and the blessings of the Lord's Supper. With respect to discipline and order, there seems to be steady improvement. Exclusion from the Lord's Supper and expulsion from the congregation occur relatively seldom. The exercise of stricter discipline is a problem which still awaits solution. It cannot be imposed from without; it must come from within as the outgrowth of faithful acceptance of the gospel and devout submission to the Word of God. The constitutions of most congregations offer the pastor, the church council, and the congregation sufficient authority for the exercise of Christian discipline, which, however, can be used with wholesome effect only when the spirit of discipline (der Geist der Zucht) has taken hold of the congregation.

In the election of the church council, the congregations have generally shown sound judgment. The choice usually falls on older, reputable, comparatively influential men whose conduct does credit to their Christianity. One seldom finds on the council either the pharisaical type or that other sanctimonious type (sonderliche Heiligen), who want to put the uniform of the ideas they wear on everybody else. Where (as in most of the congregations) the members of the council do not consider themselves chosen primarily to be overseers of the pastor (or even regard him as the congregation's hired man), where the pastor does not try to lord it over the council but, regarding himself as a fellow member shows the council due honor and respect, the blessings of such an administration will flow through the whole congregation and beyond it.

President Baltzer then came to what he called a very special object of concern for the Synod as a whole and for each of its constituent congregations—the education of the children.

There is no question that over a large area of our Synod there is to be found an eager desire for the establishment and maintenance of parochial schools, so essential to the life and progress of our congregations. But the regrettable fact remains that a good many churches fall far short of the effort which can fairly be expected of them. Not a few churches not only have no school, they even lack the desire to have one. While it is true that often great obstacles stand in the way of organizing church schools, it is certain that these obstacles could in many cases be overcome by sincere effort on the part of pastor, church council, and congregation.

We frequently hear complaints about what is happening to our young people after confirmation—how frivolous they are, often defiant of restraint, paying little heed to religion. There is less of this sort of thing, for obvious reasons, among rural congregations, least of all among those which have the benefit of a good parochial school. It is a painful fact that so little is being done or can be done under the circumstances in this area of our responsibility as a church. We should leave untried no method that has been found helpful in dealing with the problem—such as organizing a young men's society under competent leadership, providing good reading matter, and bringing the witness of God's Word to bear on the ideal of Christian family life, especially in Sunday school and in regular services of worship for the youth of the church.

The picture that he presented was not that of pioneer churches on the frontier. In the country were prosperous farming communities, founded a generation earlier by German immigrants, who had established a way of life that was not to change greatly for another forty or fifty years. Their language was German. German was not only the language of their worship, but the mother tongue, usually a dialect that was their everyday speech. Even where the children attended a district school they were likely to play ball at recess and break out into their dialect, mixed with a little English: "*Schmeiss der Ball mit all der Schpeed wo du hoscht!*" With German the language of daily intercourse in a community whose contacts with the outside world were only casual, it was not too difficult for the pastor to teach the children to read German in a Saturday morning school so that they were able to read the German Bible and hymnbook and to study the catechism in German. The second generation continued German quite naturally as the language of the home and the community, and so it went on until the relative self-containment of the rural communities came to an end about the time of World War I. For the church there was no important language problem in the rural areas until the war came, and then it was usually a matter of gradual transition from German to English.

In the cities the Germans, like all other European groups, tended to settle in compact and frequently extensive areas where German was kept alive, not only in the churches but also in stores and offices until past the turn of the century and in many cases until 1917. It did not commonly remain the language of the home and daily intercourse, however, beyond the first generation. The children of the immigrants learned to speak and read German either at home or in school. They might attend a parochial school or the church's Saturday school where German would be taught, or, in a good many cities, have the optional privilege of attending a half-hour class in German every day in the public school from the fourth grade through the eighth. They used German when they attended Sunday schools, confirmation instruction classes, services of worship, and the *Jugendverein* (Young People's Society). But sooner or later they spoke English among themselves, and when they married and had families English was the language of their homes. It became necessary to introduce English into the Sunday school for their children—in some churches even before 1890—then to give catechetical instruction in English, to use English in the young people's societies, and to introduce English services of worship. So these churchmen were moved by their own changing needs to use the language of their new homeland.

Synod Presidents, Full-Time and Part-Time

We have quoted Baltzer's report extensively because it was written by a master with an eye to just such details as make vivid history for posterity. But when, for instance, Baltzer painted a glowing picture of the prosperity of the farming communities and of the cities he had visited, he was not writing for posterity; he was reminding his hearers that the congregations of the Evangelical Synod had both cause and means for showing their gratitude to God by giving generously to the work of the kingdom. This was not merely a report, but a program of action that might determine whether Baltzer would remain full-time president. Although he had been elected almost unanimously for an indeterminate period only two years earlier, considerable opposition had developed, not so much toward Baltzer personally as toward the institution of the full-time presidency.

The chief objection was that the Synod could not afford to pay the salary of a full-time president. These were hard times; the Synod was running into debt, it was said, with every treasury empty. Congregations were said to be withholding contributions because they were opposed to the full-time presidency; there was no need for it, since most of the time-consuming task of visiting all the pastors and the churches could and should be done by the district presidents. The money spent on the office of a full-time president should be used where it would do more good in the work of the kingdom.

In defense of the full-time presidency it was pointed out that the Evangelical Church was still in the adolescent stage in this country and therefore required all the more a firm organization like that which the older Lutheran and Reformed synods already possessed. A motion to abolish the full-time presidency was defeated by a fairly close vote (20 to 14), and Baltzer remained in office. He was not only confirmed in his office as president;

he was also elected to fill the vacant editorship of *Der Friedens-bote*, a part-time job, with the understanding that this was to be one of his duties as president.

In the course of the next year (1869), he added to the burden of his office by taking over the management of the publishing business, after the death of his friend and associate Louis E. Nollau. Nollau, a tireless worker like Baltzer, had been secretary of the Evangelical Synod and manager of its publishing business besides being the administrator of the Good Samaritan Hospital and the German Protestant Orphans Home at St. Louis, pioneer Evangelical charities that he had founded.

At the next General Conference, in Louisville, Kentucky, Baltzer surprised the assembly by offering his resignation. He felt he did not have the support of the majority. A long debate ensued that was ended by the decision not to accept the resignation. However, several important changes were made with regard to the presidency. It was decided by a large majority that the Synod should return to the former practice of electing the president for the period extending from one general conference to the next, the incumbent being eligible for re-election. A proposal to the effect that the president must be the pastor of a congregation was rejected, but another, fixing the salary of the president at $500 a year, was accepted. Now the conference, having declined to accept Baltzer's resignation, could not ask him to continue in office at a quarter of his former salary, nor was this intended. It was arranged to pay him an additional $700 a year as editor of *Der Friedensbote* and to leave the management of the publishing business in his hands with a commission of 10 per cent. The income from all three sources could be expected to amount to about the same as his former salary of $2,000.

Baltzer asked for time to consider (just as in 1866 he had taken time to consider before accepting the full-time presidency). Two things were clear: (1) The great majority of the

Synod was opposed to an indefinite term of office for the president. (2) On the other hand, the Synod had expressed confidence in Baltzer's leadership and wanted him to continue in office, in spite of differences of opinion.

To Baltzer all that really mattered was that he had the confidence of the Synod and the opportunity to serve it. He accepted the presidency under the new setup. He was re-elected in 1872, 1874, and 1877 (the General Conference then meeting every three years) without serious opposition. His unexpected death in January, 1880, at the age of sixty-three, may have proved that the combination of offices he held was too heavy a burden. His duties as president were undertaken by the vice-president, Karl Siebenpfeiffer of Rochester, New York. However, the new president, pastor of a large congregation (Salem Church), was unable to take Baltzer's place as editor of *Der Friedensbote* and as manager of the publishing business.

When the General Conference met at St. Louis (St. John's Church) in September, 1880, Siebenpfeiffer, presiding, laid before the assembly a number of overtures from district conferences concerning the office of president of the Synod. It appeared from these that most synod members were opposed to both the full-time presidency and the indeterminate tenure. They did not take to the idea of having "a bishop." A motion to the effect that the president of the Synod could and should serve a congregation was carried by a vote of 52 to 12. This motion made no provision for a salary, so various proposals were offered, but none of them were acceptable. It was finally resolved that "the president shall receive an honorarium of an amount to be determined later." Siebenpfeiffer, who had just completed Baltzer's term, was elected president. Due to the breaking down of his health under the strain of serving both the Synod and his large congregation, he resigned the presidency in 1882. The vice-president, John Zimmermann, pastor of Zion

Church, Burlington, Iowa took over the presidency and was elected to the office by the General Conference of 1883 in St. Louis, Missouri (St. Peter's Church). Zimmermann served the Synod for eighteen years as president—longer than any other incumbent. He declined re-election in 1901 when he reached the age of seventy-five.

In his very first report (1883) as president, Zimmermann told the General Conference that its constitutional administrative agencies were wholly inadequate both on the district and the synod level. "It should be possible," he said, "for the district president to make periodic visits to every pastor and congregation. It could be done by giving him an assistant—an upperclass seminary student, for instance—during the summer half year." As for the synod presidency (in which he was filling out Siebenpfeiffer's unexpired term), he remarked that the question whether the next president should serve a congregation, along with the office, "deserves the most serious consideration of the Synod."

President Zimmermann had the support of the First District (later divided into the New York and Atlantic districts) with strong congregations and influential pastors in Baltimore, Buffalo, and Rochester. This district had advocated a return to the full-time presidency in an overture to the General Conference. When the question came before the General Conference, however, that body, "while recognizing that the combination of the synod presidency with an active pastorate presents great difficulties," took the amazingly lighthearted view that "most of these difficulties will disappear if the president will take advantage of the liberty which the constitution of the Synod gives him to send written reports to districts whose conferences he does not find time to attend," and therefore voted to make no change in the office of the president.

By 1889, however, when the Synod numbered 643 ministers

(as against 427 in 1883) who, according to Zimmermann's report, served 100,000 families, the General Conference recognized the fact that it was impossible for the president to fulfill his statutory duties adequately while also serving a church. It voted, therefore, that henceforth the president should no longer serve a church and fixed his salary at $2,000 a year. It also recommended that the president be given indeterminate tenure of office and requested the districts to express their opinions by the time of the next General Conference. The General Conference of 1892 voted to make no change, that is to say, the president was to serve full time for a salary of $2,000, and his term of office would be from one general conference to the next.

The General Conference of 1898 swung back in the other direction by voting to make the presidency an honorary office with stipend *(ein besoldetes Ehrenamt)*, the stipend being $500 annually besides expenses. It was continued as such by President Jacob Pister from 1901 to 1909. In the latter year, Pister, in his report to the General Conference, frankly avowed his conviction that it was not possible for the president of the Synod to fulfill the manifold duties of his office while serving a church as pastor. Pister had just recovered from a serious illness, brought on mainly by overwork, which had incapacitated him for months and required him still to depute a large part of his work to an assistant. Moved by esteem and appreciation for the president and concern for his health, the General Conference voted that the president should not serve a church during the next quadrennium and that he should receive a salary of $2,000 a year.

The Evangelical Synod of the West had never been the only formal organization of Evangelical pastors and congregations in the United States. The United Evangelical Synod of the Northwest included strong rural and urban churches in southern

Michigan and northern Illinois, and possessed outstanding leaders in men like the Reverend K. W. F. Haas of Detroit and the Reverend Joseph Hartmann of Chicago. The United Evangelical Synod of the East had some large churches in Buffalo and Rochester, New York, and numerous rural churches stretching from western New York to northeastern Ohio. As the names indicate, these two synods were identical in doctrine and polity with the Synod of the West. Like it, they had been formed by young ministers coming from Germany and Switzerland to serve the German-speaking Evangelical people settling in the United States. It was inevitable that they should one day unite. Various plans for union had been discussed from time to time since 1851.

Union of the Synods

At last, fresh approaches, begun in 1871, led in 1872 to the formal union of the three synods at the General Conference of the Synod of the West in Quincy, Illinois. Since the Synod of the Northwest had been the first to make overtures and draw up terms of union with the Synod of the West, it was given first place in the ceremony of admission to the Synod of the West that consummated the union. The terms of agreement could scarcely have been simpler:

(1) The United Evangelical Synod of the Northwest becomes the fourth district of the Evangelical Synod of the West.

(2) The Evangelical Synod of the Northwest accepts the statutes of the Evangelical Synod of the West in place of its former constitution.

(3) Directly upon the accomplishment of the union of the two synods, the Evangelical Synod of the Northwest agrees to turn over to the Synod of the West its seminary in Elmhurst as common property on condition that an institute for theological training shall be continued on it, and that the Synod of the West assumes the debt resting on it.

(4) Should the union of the two synods, contrary to expectations, not take place, the Evangelical Synod of the Northwest is willing

to sell the entire seminary property to the Evangelical Synod of the West at cost.

(5) The complete ratification of this agreement must take place before the end of the year 1872.

Following the formal admission of the Synod of the Northwest as the Fourth District (continuing under its own name at first), the Synod of the East was admitted on the basis of points (1) and (2) as the Northeast District.

The figures below show the relative strength of each of the three synods before the union, and of the enlarged Synod of the West after the union:

Before Union	Pastors	Affiliated and Non-affiliated Congregations
Synod of the West	194	219
Synod of the Northwest	56	82
Synod of the East	33	36
After Union	283	337

The union was so logical and so clearly advantageous to the aims of all three synods that one wonders why it had not been brought about earlier. In 1858 a plan for a federative (not an organic) union had actually been considered at a meeting held in Cincinnati by the parent bodies of the three groups that were united in 1872, namely, the *Kirchenverein des Westens*, the Evangelical *Kirchenverein* of Ohio, and the German United Evangelical Synod of North America, which had called the meeting. The *Kirchenverein* of the West was favorable to the federative plan. In the course of discussions that inevitably stretched from conference to conference, the federative plan came to appear unworkable. At the same time, the two *Kirchenvereine* (of the West and in Ohio) were drawn so closely together that the Ohio *Verein* united as a body with the *Kirchenverein* of the West by joining its eastern district at the conference of 1857 in Evansville. They added only nine pastors to the numerical strength of the larger body, but among these nine were Philipp Goebel and Albert Schory; and Ohio was opened up to the Synod of the West.

On the other hand, the German United Evangelical Synod of North America, which had initiated the plans for a union of all Evangelical synods, was torn by internal dissensions as a result of which two new synods appeared while the parent synod dropped out of the picture. In 1858 the ten pastors of the Eastern District (from Buffalo and other towns, the most prominent being Karl Siebenpfeiffer) resigned because of what they regarded as the domineering attitude of the officers (one of them, the Reverend Joseph Hartmann of St. Paul's Church, Chicago) and formed a new synod with a name that was later shortened to the German United Evangelical Synod of the East. The very next year, 1859, twelve pastors from the Western District under the leadership of Joseph Hartmann quit what was left of the German United Evangelical Synod of North America, in protest against its rationalism, and organized the German United Evangelical Synod of the Northwest.

The plan for a union of the Evangelical synods received a setback in consequence of these developments; but this was undoubtedly salutary. Within a few years good feeling was restored between the two new synods, and both established cordial relations with the *Kirchenverein* of the West. In God's providential design, it was the Synod of the West that he had been preparing for leadership in the union of Evangelical churches in America.

What led to renewed, and this time fruitful, discussions of union in 1871 between representatives of the Synod of the West and of the Synod of the Northwest was the conviction, gained by the experience of twenty years, that by uniting their forces in the common task of serving the German Evangelical people in the United States, they could accomplish far more than the sum of their separate efforts. There was need for money to put preachers in promising mission fields, especially the fast-growing cities of the West, and to provide sustained financial support for them until they could get churches started. Lack of this sustained support had compelled the Synod of the West, as President Baltzer pointed out in his report of 1868, to give up promising beginnings in Iowa, Nebraska, and Minnesota.

Schools of the Church

But it was not only money that was needed; men were needed, and these were to be had only by training them. Though most of the Synod's pastors were born in Germany, most of them were trained at Marthasville. The Synod of the West had its well-established theological seminary at Marthasville; it was this, above all, that had drawn the small but earnest *Kirchenverein* of Ohio into union with the *Kirchenverein* of the West. But Marthasville had only two professors; it ought really to have had a third—as Baltzer had pointed out in his report.

Since 1866 the Synod of the West also had a teachers' seminary which had that very year (1871) been moved from Cincinnati to Evansville, where it was combined with a proseminary intended to prepare students for the theological seminary. President Baltzer had expressed the conviction that a third institution was desirable, if not indeed necessary—a college of liberal arts (though he did not call it that) where young men would be prepared for the professional schools of medicine, law, or other vocations, or might simply acquire a general education. Baltzer was all the more favorably disposed toward the idea of a college because he had been head of the short-lived Missouri College, established on the campus of the Marthasville Seminary in 1858 and closed in 1862 on account of the Civil War.

The Synod of the Northwest had a theological seminary also. The Melanchthon Seminary, as it was called, had been started with private support by Joseph Hartmann of Chicago and taken over in 1865 by the Synod of the Northwest. It was housed at that time in a rented building in the town of Lake Zurich, Illinois, thirty miles or so northwest of Chicago. By 1869 it had ten students and two professors (William Binner, who had been the first inspector of the Marthasville Seminary, and E. Keuchen). The Seminary Board now acquired a plot of thirty acres, with a large frame house on it, in Elmhurst, Illinois, sixteen miles west of Chicago, and moved the seminary there. However, the seminary did not flourish as expected. No new students applied for admission, and by the summer of 1871 all had completed their studies. This was the situation when the president (Adolph Baltzer) and the Seminary Board of the Synod of the West met by invitation the president (K. W. F. Haas of Detroit) and the Seminary Board of the Synod of the Northwest in the historic conference of August 29-31, 1871 in the Melanchthon Seminary, at which were drawn up the terms of agreement for the union of the two synods.

It was fitting that this meeting should have been held in Melanchthon Seminary because, as we have indicated, the common need of training men for the ministry among the German Evangelical people of the United States was the most effective single motive for the immediate union of the separate Evangelical synods. How large a part the educational problem played in bringing about the union is shown by the terms of agreement.

One of the most gratifying and significant results of the union of 1872 was the rapid growth of the proseminary (Elmhurst College) and the impressive development of Eden Seminary. We have already noticed that the Synod had decided to close the teachers' seminary in Cincinnati and to replace it with a proseminary at Evansville, Indiana, which was to prepare young men for the theological seminary, but was also to include a division for teacher-training.

The need for such a proseminary had been felt from the beginning of the theological seminary. There were able, consecrated young men who wanted to study theology but had not had the necessary education. One year, of nine who applied for admission, only three could write. Where was a farmer's son (or, for that matter, many a preacher's son) to get anything beyond a district or parochial school education?

The seminary undertook to remedy the deficiency by setting up preparatory classes within its own walls. President (or to give him the title he carried, Inspector) Andreas Irion in his report for 1870, lists among the subjects taught (besides dogmatics, exegesis, homiletics, and other theological disciplines) Greek, Latin, German, English, general history, geography, and arithmetic. Most of these subjects were taught by one or two young men who were appointed to the staff for a year or two, or by the more advanced students. That it was a real preparatory course is shown by the fact that of 9 students admitted in 1855, only 3 were graduated and ordained in 1858; 3 in 1860; while 3 others dropped out. Its thoroughness and efficiency is proved by the fact that it produced the fifth president (the last with the title of inspector) of the theological seminary, Louis F. Haeberle (1879-1902), and the second president of the proseminary (Elmhurst College), Philipp F. Meusch (1875-80).

It is to the credit of the *Kirchenverein* that in spite of the acute need of preachers, its officers insisted on an acceptable minimum standard of education before ordination. Since there were not enough aspirants for the ministry from within the *Kirchenverein*, it had to depend on the mission societies and mission institutes of Germany and Switzerland, either for ordained men or for young men willing to come to the United States and study at Marthasville for the ministry. It was even suggested that the *Kirchenverein* should establish a proseminary in Germany. The General Conference of 1870 rejected this idea in favor of establishing a proseminary at Evansville, Indiana, as we have already noticed, with a division for teacher-training.

Nothing was said at this time about admitting students not intending to become either preachers or teachers; Baltzer and other leaders still thought in terms of a separate liberal arts college. The curriculum of the proseminary after a few years, however, was so nearly identical in substance with that of a good academy, that there was no reason for limiting the institution to pretheological or teacher-training students except, at times, lack of space.

There were 23 students in the teachers' seminary at Cincinnati when it was closed in October, 1870. When the Proseminary opened at Evansville in January, 1871 with 15 students, 8 were prospective teachers, but only a few of them had been at Cincinnati. The number of teacher-training students rose gradually at Elmhurst to 29 in 1883, only to drop to 17 in 1886. There was a sudden rise in 1889 to 30, and in 1892 it even went to 43, then faded away to 6 in 1900. In 1915 the teachers' course was given up.

Probably it must be admitted that the Evangelical Synod never had a clearly defined policy for parochial schools. There was almost complete unanimity of opinion among pastors, down to the end of the eighties, that every congregation should, if at all possible, establish a full-time school with at least one trained teacher. However, there was a shortage of teachers, which led more than a few churches to engage men who proved utterly unsuited for the place. An attempt had been made to meet the need of teachers by setting up a special course for teachers at the Marthasville Seminary, but this was unsatisfactory.

A separate teachers' seminary was indicated. Ernst Roos of Zion Church, Cincinnati was so concerned that he offered to establish such a seminary in a building he would erect alongside his church. The offer was accepted provisionally. President

Baltzer and others doubted the wisdom of trying to combine the administration of a seminary and a church.

The seminary opened its doors on May 23, 1867, to twelve students, a most encouraging beginning, and the number was to double during the year, while contributions of money poured in from all parts of the Synod. Five students were graduated in October, 1868; new students were admitted to replace them.

The General Conference of that year, pleased with the progress of the new institution, voted to continue the seminary in Cincinnati for the time being, but appointed a committee that was directed to present recommendations for a permanent location at the next General Conference (1870). The institution had been so far a good deal of a family affair, with Pastor and Mrs. Roos as housefather and housemother, and Roos doing a good deal of the teaching with the assistance of part-time instructors.

The increased enrollment in 1869 (twenty-three), and the larger variety of subjects taught necessitated the appointment of a second teacher. The man chosen, the Reverend Frederick Weygold, a son-in-law and former associate of J. H. Wichern of the famous *Rauhe Haus* in Hamburg, proved himself an unusually competent teacher.

The growth and progress of the teachers' seminary was gratifying, but a number of incidents that had created tensions between the Board of Directors, on the one hand, and Roos and his congregation, on the other, led the General Conference of 1870 to vote for the removal of the seminary from Cincinnati and its reopening as a proseminary.

The Proseminary at Evansville

With regard to the location of the proseminary, the General Conference stipulated that it must not be tied in with a congregation, and that neither the head nor any of the teachers of the institution should be pastors of churches. The committee, appointed in 1868 to make recommendations on a suitable site, reported to the General Conference of 1870 that it had carefully considered sites offered in St. Charles, Missouri; Freeport, Illinois; Evansville, Indiana; and St. Louis County, Missouri. The choice of the Conference fell on Evansville.

In selecting Evansville it was the original intention to buy the former Marine Hospital, built on a site along the Ohio River, which could be bought for $15,000. Since it had cost $75,000 to build, this looked like a bargain. However, the cost of remodeling appeared prohibitive, and there was the added fear of Ohio River floods. The choice fell, therefore, on a large dwelling surrounded by extensive grounds that could be rented for a year with the option of buying. The Reverend Carl F. Kranz of Mishawaka, Indiana was chosen to head the new institution.

On Monday, January 17, 1871 the proseminary was opened with an initial enrollment of nine students (later increased to fifteen), in the presence of the pastors and many members of the churches of the area. One of the pastors (Gottlieb Mueller) presented what he called a sponsor's gift (*Patengeschenk*) of $200 on behalf of the church at Bethlehem, Indiana. H. Feldwisch, the delegate of Zion Church, Cincinnati, which had sponsored and now lost the teachers' seminary, signalized the good will of his church by pledging a gift of $100. So the new institution made an auspicious beginning.

During the summer of 1871, however, a meeting took place at Elmhurst, Illinois between representatives of the synods of the West and of the Northwest, in the course of which it was decided that Melanchthon Seminary would be closed and the proseminary moved to Elmhurst. A college (strictly speaking, an academy) was to replace the institution in Evansville which had failed.

The Beginnings of Elmhurst

On December 6, 1871 the proseminary was reopened in the former Melanchthon Seminary building at Elmhurst with fourteen students. This building, a spacious frame dwelling, was made to do for the fourteen students who came with the institution from Evansville and for half a dozen who came a month later. Inspector Kranz, however, could not go on alone with the incredible load he had been carrying as sole teacher of twenty boys of various ages, aptitudes, and degrees of preparation, besides being responsible for the whole household of this boarding school. So Weygold, who had proved his competence at the teachers' seminary in Cincinnati, was called as the second professor. "He was a great teacher," said a former pupil, "and an object of admiration for us on account of his universal knowledge."

In June, 1872 the proseminary sent forth its first two graduates, John H. Dinkmeier and W. F. Gieselmann, both taking positions as parochial school teachers. They had completed a three-year course begun in Cincinnati, continued in Evansville, and finished at Elmhurst. Dinkmeier later entered the ministry, as did a considerable number of other former teachers.

When the General Conference met at Quincy, Illinois in July, 1872, the Conference at which the union of the synods of the Northwest and the East with the Synod of the West was ratified, the proseminary at Elmhurst took up a good deal of its attention. Enrollment had risen from 14 in December, 1871 to 31 in July, 1872, more than doubling in six months. More room was needed. The General Conference approved the erection of a new building at a cost not to exceed $12,000 and ordered a house collection in all congregations during September and October to pay for it. The instructions for this collection stated that each pastor would be permitted (was actually required) to select a brother minister to assist him in taking up the collection in his congregation. The officers of the General Conference were directed to prepare a short statement of the needs of the Synod's educational institutions and to have a sufficient quantity printed to supply each pastor with enough copies for his congregation. In order not to impair the success of this collection, pastors and churches were requested to permit no other collections to be taken before this one.

The new building had been begun promptly and completed for dedication on June 23, 1873. It was a plain brick structure, about 40 x 60 feet, two stories in height with a high basement and an attic, and relieved the congestion at Elmhurst for a few years. The number of students at the time of dedication was 34 and the faculty consisted of 3: Kranz, Weygold, and a teacher of English. Before the next year (1874) was over, both President Kranz and Professor Weygold resigned their posts at Elmhurst to return to the pastorate. They had done their work well and laid a solid foundation on which their successors could build. The new head of the school, the Reverend Philipp F. Meusch, proved himself ideally fitted to meet the problems of the rapidly expanding institution. By June, 1876 the enrollment had increased to the point where it was necessary to transfer the class of 1877 to the theological seminary a year ahead of its time in order to make room for new students.

The General Conference of 1877 therefore approved the construction of a second new building at Elmhurst, to cost $12,000, and voted another house collection to pay for it. The new building, known now as "Old Main," cost nearly twice as much as had been allowed, but was worth it. For the first time the Evangelical Synod had a building which, it was felt, would stand comparison with any buildings erected by other denominations. The building was dedicated on October 31, 1878, with the appropriate reading of Romans 5 and the singing of *"Ein'*

Feste Burg." It seems appropriate also that the chairman of the Seminary Board, who delivered the dedicatory address, was Karl Siebenpfeiffer of Rochester, New York, a leader of the former Synod of the East.

"Since we have room at the proseminary, teachers and students are enjoying their new quarters." So reads, in translation, the report of the Board about Elmhurst to the General Conference of 1880, which informs us also that the enrollment stood at 120 and the faculty now numbered seven. For further details, the report refers the reader to the catalog that appeared for the first time in 1878.

The satisfaction concerning the achievements at Elmhurst is mingled, however, with deep regret over the death of the man to whom, more than to any other one person, so much of the credit for this progress was due. President Meusch died on July 28, 1880 at the early age of forty-four. One of his successors, Daniel Irion, who had served under him as a teacher, said of him: "He was a man of unaffected piety and deep moral earnestness. He knew how to gain the intellectual respect of his pupils, while they knew that the care of their souls was his great concern. That was the secret of his popularity." The student body honored the president's memory by naming their general association the Meusch Society.

Another teacher who left a lasting memory among his students was William K. Sauerbier, a graduate of Heidelberg College, who taught English from 1875 to 1879. He died in a train collision not far from Elmhurst.

As successor of Meusch at Elmhurst, the Seminary Board chose the Reverend Johann Peter Goebel of Alhambra, Illinois. Goebel could not bring himself to accept the call, however, until it came as a mandate from the General Conference in the form of an election by a large majority—the only time such an election took place. During the interim between the death of Meusch in July and the arrival of Goebel in November, Professor G. von Luternau was acting head of the school. Goebel remained in office until 1887, when he accepted a call to the church at Peotone, Illinois. Genuine piety and conscientious performance of duty were the outstanding characteristics by which he was remembered. A perusal of his reports shows him to have been a keen analyst of trends, ahead of most of his contemporaries in advocating more emphasis on the development of the institution not only as a proseminary but also as a college.

Religious Education

While there was no language problem as such for the Evangelical Synod before the end of the eighties, there was always the problem of religious education. This was met in a respectable number of churches by the establishment of parochial schools where a qualified teacher taught about the same subjects as were taught in the public schools, some subjects in German and some in English, besides religious instruction. Some of the larger city churches had flourishing schools, employing several teachers. The first appears to have been St. Peter's Church in St. Louis, which in 1846 engaged Wilhelm A. H. Saeger, a trained teacher who, remaining at this post until 1884, promoted the highest spiritual ideals in the educational development of the day. But most of the schools were one-room affairs.

There was hardly a congregation so small or so poor that it did not have either a schoolhouse or a schoolroom attached to church or parsonage. Where there was no other teacher, the pastor took it on himself to teach boys and girls to read German at least well enough to be able to study their catechism and to read the Bible and the church hymns. It could be done on Saturday mornings, for instance, with tolerable results if parents would spare their children from work at home.

Fairly reliable statistics about the congregations of the Synod of the West are available from 1854 on. In 1854 when 37 pastors served 49 congregations, there were 20 parochial schools and 17 Sunday schools—the latter with an enrollment of 1,141. In 1869, when 145 pastors were serving 190 congregations, there were 85 parochial schools (no enrollment given) and 54 Sunday schools with an enrollment of 4,854.

In the previous year (1868) the General Conference had authorized the publication of a German Primer (*Fibel*) and First Reader. In two years 2,094 primers and 1,344 first readers were sold. Encouraged by this success, a second and eventually a third reader were published in addition to other textbooks. The primer was selling at an average of 4,000 copies a year by 1877, and close to 6,000 a year by 1883. It was used not only in the weekday or Saturday schools, but also in some Sunday schools.

The Sunday schools of these and earlier days often bore little resemblance to those of the present day. They were quite commonly held in the afternoon, and might last longer than an hour because the children were not only taught Bible lessons, but there were classes in German reading for those who needed them. In 1872 the number of Sunday schools for the first time exceeded the number of parochial schools. There were (in the now united three synods) 282 pastors serving 337 churches. The number of Sunday schools was 139 with an enrollment of 11,957; the number of parochial schools was 145 with no enrollment given, but perhaps 8,000. Five years later (1877) we find 324 pastors, 440 congregations, and 235 Sunday schools with an enrollment of 22,728 as compared with 193 parochial schools (but only 96 professional teachers) with an enrollment of 11,224. The Sunday schools continued to gain massively while the parochial schools recorded slight gains. In 1883 there were 428 pastors, 557 congregations, and 412 Sunday schools with an enrollment of 41,588 while 266 parochial schools (with only 110 full-time teachers) had an enrollment of 12,513.

The General Conference took occasional notice of Sunday schools in connection with the activities of its publishing business. So in 1870 and 1872 there were proposals for the Synod to acquire the publication rights for the *Christliche Kinderzeitung* (Christian Children's Paper), commonly used in Evangelical Sunday schools and privately published (since 1866) by the Reverend C. Witte. (It was finally taken over by the Synod in 1886.) In 1874 the General Conference approved the publication of what became one of the most widely used and useful books, *Biblische Geschichten* (*Bible Stories*, in the later English translation). Before lesson quarterlies came into common use this book of Bible stories was the standard textbook of the Sunday school. In the same year the proposal was made to take over either of two privately published German Sunday school hymnals, but it was 1882 before the Synod published its *Liederbuch für Sonntagschulen*. The book was very popular and had an enormous sale for some forty years. The tunes included chorales, folk song melodies, and spiritual *Lieder*, but no "gospel hymn" tunes, according to Armin Haeussler in his *Story of Our Hymns*.

There is one item that we must not omit from the list of standard supplies for Sunday schools between 1866 and 1883. The Publication Committee reported in 1883: "Since the stock of Sunday school cards published by the late President Baltzer has been exhausted, we are now offering an attractive new card at only fifty cents a package." Some years ago, the most interesting exhibits at the seventy-fifth anniversary of an Evangelical church were, next to photographs, copies of those old parochial and Sunday school books and papers, and the cards that were punched every Sunday you were there.

Organizational Changes

What were the visible effects of the union of the three Evangelical synods? For one thing, it became necessary to redistrict the greatly enlarged body. The General Conference of 1872 had made a temporary arrangement by admitting the Synod of the Northwest as the Northwestern District, and the Synod of the East as the Northeastern District. Since these overlapped the three districts of the Synod of the West, it was obviously desirable to make a compact regrouping of districts. A committee was appointed, consisting of one member from each of the five districts, with instructions to submit a plan for redistricting the Synod to each of the next year's district conferences, so that these could report their approval or make alternate recommendations to the General Conference of 1874. The committee presented a plan for setting up seven numbered district conferences, which plan was accepted by the General Conference of 1874. This Conference also accepted the proposal to hold its meetings every three years.

It is interesting to note that the General Conference of 1874, in setting up the seven new districts, directed each district to start a new minute book and to deposit the old ones, along with any other historical material, in the archives to be established at the theological seminary.

The division into seven districts stood until 1883 when an eighth district was created by dividing the first. In 1886 the Synod was divided into eleven districts that were named after states. At the same time the Synod passed a resolution empowering the president to sanction any changes proposed by a district if he deemed them beneficial. This privilege was used from time to time to increase the number of districts, eventully by 1933 to twenty, besides the India Mission District.

Church Publications

A result that could be expected from the union of the synods was a considerable increase in the circulation of *Der Friedens-bote*, the official organ of the Synod of the West. (The *Union* and the *Hausfreund*, published by the Synods of the East and the Northwest, had been discontinued; the *Hausfreund* had been burned out by the great Chicago fire of 1871.) The circulation of *Der Friedensbote* (one dollar a year, biweekly), went up from 4,912 in 1870 to 6,500 in 1872, to 7,600 in 1873, and to 7,900 in 1874. In the year of its twenty-fifth anniversary, 1875, the circulation reached 8,000 and stayed there until 1878, when it started to climb slowly at the rate of about 200 a year until it reached 8,651 in 1880.

The twenty-fifth anniversary of *Der Friedensbote* gave rise to expressions of gratitude to God and warm appreciation for the services that the editors had rendered, as well as attention to the question of what to do to win more readers. The goal was: "Every family a subscriber." The Reverend Reinhard Wobus, who took over the work of the managing editor after President Baltzer's death in January, 1880 published figures that showed the over-all average for the whole Synod to be 26 per cent—one family of subscribers in four. The little seventh district, Western Missouri, showed a surprising 49 per cent—every other family a subscriber. Hardly less impressive was the showing of the fourth district (eastern Missouri and southern Illinois) with 43 per cent of a much larger constituency.

It would be hard to overrate the importance of *Der Friedensbote* to the Evangelical Synod. To the ministers, as well as to many of the lay members, it was a house organ. To it they looked for changed addresses, obituaries, and all official notices. For many subscribers, especially in rural areas, it was the only good reading matter that entered their homes regularly. That was one reason general conferences often took time for long discussions as to what should go into *Der Friedensbote*—how much space for edification, how much for information (the biweekly, later weekly, summaries of news of the world were among the best to be found anywhere), and how much for entertainment (a serial story and a popular puzzle corner). Editors of *Der Friedensbote* since 1880 have been F. H. Rudolph John (1880-98), William T. Jungk (1898-1922), and Otto Press (1922-58).

Not the least of the benefits of *Der Friedensbote* was its annual net profit, which was divided between the educational institutions and home missions. The profits seem to have averaged about $800 a year between 1868 and 1873; then they rose steadily as subscriptions increased, from $1,165 in 1874 to an estimated $4,000 in 1880.

In this connection we should mention also the *Evangelischer Kalender*, the German almanac that first appeared in 1872 and became at once a household favorite. An edition of 8,000 was sold out the first year in a short time, and the demand increased steadily, usually keeping pace with the circulation of *Der Friedensbote*. The *Kalender* was always prepared by the editor of *Der Friedensbote*. It served a threefold purpose: (1) supplying a complete yearly calendar, with every Sunday and every feast day of the church named in its place, besides naming the birthdays of famous people (especially German and American) and of notable men in the history of the Evangelical Synod; (2) listing all pastors and teachers in the Evangelical Synod, besides giving other information; (3) providing good reading matter for entertainment, information, and inspiration.

Still another product of the union was the decision made by the General Conference in 1872 to publish a journal of theology. The first number appeared under the title of *Theologische Zeitschrift* in January, 1873, with the Reverend Johann Bank as editor. From 1877 to 1898 it was, except for a few numbers, edited successively by Professors Karl Emil Otto and Carl Kunzmann, and by President W. Becker of the theological seminary. During most of this time it included a department of pedagogy for parochial school teachers. In 1898 it underwent a change of name to *Theological Magazine*, along with other changes intended to broaden its usefulness to pastors. Louis J. Haas was the editor from 1898 to 1917, and Hugo Kamphausen from 1917 to 1933. After 1921 more and more of its articles were written in English. The *Theological Magazine* was discontinued in 1933, on the eve of the merger of the Evangelical Synod with the Reformed Church.

9

Growth and Outreach

IT IS TIME to turn our attention now to the theological seminary. When Adolph Baltzer left his professorship there to become president of the Synod, his place was filled by appointing the Reverend Frederick Kauffmann. Two recent graduates, G. von Luternau and N. Severing, assisted the two professors (Andreas Irion and Kauffmann) by teaching the preparatory classes. Even so, it was recognized that there was need of a third professor to reduce the load of the other two and to enrich the curriculum. The Reverend Louis F. Haeberle, who later became president, was offered the position but declined. The Reverend Karl Emil Otto was therefore elected and accepted the position. When he arrived at Marthasville at the end of July, 1870, Professor Irion had just died after a sudden illness.

Andreas Irion

The death of Andreas Irion in his forty-seventh year was an all but irreparable loss to the Synod. "He could have done great things had he lived longer," says Hugo Kamphausen, who devotes a dozen pages to Irion's work and influence in his *Geschichte des religiösen Lebens in der Deutschen Evangelischen*

Synode. "Andreas Irion's task," he continues, "was like that of Philip Schaff within a narrower framework. Death prevented him from completing the systematic exposition of his theology, but we have the essentials of it in his *Explanation of the Small Evangelical Cathechism.* His position was thoroughly evangelical, neither narrowly confessional nor modernistic."

For the Evangelical Synod, it was providential that it was a man like Irion who guided the theological thinking of the seminary during its formative years, for he illustrated perfectly in his own thinking what was meant by the union position. At the point of the most obvious difference between Lutheran and Reformed, the doctrine of the Lord's Supper, Irion was Lutheran (*massivlutherisch,* according to Kamphausen) in his personal conviction. True to the union standpoint, however, he respected the Reformed position, and never represented his private opinion, which he took no pains to conceal, as the union consensus. "He taught our ministers to think," comments Kamphausen, "while at the same time making them aware that believing means living, and not holding opinions."

Karl Emil Otto

Irion's successor was the Reverend Johann Bank, who resigned after little more than a year on account of poor health. The popular young Otto was then chosen, in 1873, to head the seminary. He had already established himself as Irion's successor in influence as a theological teacher, though in a wholly different manner and spirit. Irion had been magnificent in his exposition of the deep thought content of biblical conceptions. His temper was mystic and speculative; his strength lay in systematic theology. Otto's strength lay in exegesis. He knew Latin, Greek, Hebrew; he had learned the results of the historicocritical methods at the University of Halle, where he came under the influence of August Tholuck, Julius Mueller, and Herman Hupfeld.

Karl Emil Otto's career was to reveal the influence of all three of these men to such a degree that what is said of their theological position could be said of him. In his scientific work as an exegete, he follows Hupfeld, whose *Commentary on the Psalms* displays a profoundly devout attitude, along with a complete independence of the exegetical and isagogic tradition. He gives the impression of downright honesty. It was this independence that brought a charge of heretical doctrines against Hupfeld in 1865 from theologians of the Hengstenberg School. From this charge he successfully cleared himself, the entire theological faculty joining Tholuck and Mueller in bearing testimony to Hupfeld's sufficient orthodoxy. In the same year Otto came to the United States, undoubtedly rejoicing in the vindication of his teacher, little guessing that he too would find himself one day a respected teacher charged with the teaching of certain unbiblical doctrines.

In 1865 Otto was sent by the Berlin Society to the United States under an agreement to serve the Wisconsin Lutheran Synod for five years. He came in the same spirit that moved thousands upon thousands of student volunteers to enlist for Christian service. Otto had completed his theological studies and spent several years—the usual lot of a candidate for the ministry —at tutoring and teaching. In September, 1864 he had attended the *Kirchentag* at Altenburg. There he heard two preachers from the United States setting forth the need of adequately trained theologians in America. One was speaking in behalf of the Wisconsin Lutheran Synod; the other, the Reverend George Wall of St. Louis, was speaking in behalf of the Evangelical Synod. Otto volunteered to go to America. The Berlin Society, which undertook to pay his expenses, had an agreement with the Wisconsin Synod. So in 1865 Otto came to Milwaukee and there received his assignment. It was a parish in Dodge County, consisting of three small congregations—two Lutheran and one Reformed.

Though happy in his work, Otto was not too happy in his relations with the Synod. The Wisconsin Synod originally represented a milder Lutheranism that, for instance, made it possible to set up such a parish as Otto was serving. But this milder Lutheranism was giving way to a rigid confessionalism like that of the Missouri Synod. At the conference of 1866 in Fond du Lac, Otto, declaring that he represented the union standpoint, requested and was given honorable dismissal.

Meanwhile Otto had attracted the attention of the Reverend Louis von Ragué, one of the home mission pioneers of the Evangelical Synod, who was working in Wisconsin at this time. Ragué induced Otto, who was about his own age, to join him on a trip to St. Louis and Marthasville. Favorably impressed, Otto accepted a charge that was offered him at Columbia, Illinois and was admitted in 1867 to the Evangelical Synod. The Berlin Society approved the change that Otto had made, broke off relations with the Wisconsin Synod, and thereafter cooperated with the Evangelical Synod.

In 1870, Otto, still at Columbia, completed the five years' service in America that had been stipulated in his agreement with the Berlin Society. He was planning to return to Germany when there came to him the offer of a professorship at Marthasville. He accepted, made good, and in less than three years, at the age of thirty-eight, found himself at the head of the institution—a man of consequence, whose opinions were sought and heard with respect.

The *Theologische Zeitschrift*, which was started in January, 1873, with Bank as editor, gave Otto an opportunity to reach a wider audience. In the March, 1873 issue appeared the first of three installments of an article on "The Exegesis of Romans 5: 12-19." This dealt with the dogmatic determinations concerning the origins of sin and its consequences. The subject is one on which an original thinker like Otto might easily make a statement open to challenge. Otto himself said, years later, that his motive in publishing these articles was to acquaint members of the Synod with the kind of teaching he was offering his students.

After the appearance of two installments, he waited a year and then, at the urgent request of readers, published the third. He had no reason to suppose that there were any serious objections to his teaching. As for his students, they counted the hours spent in Otto's classes as among the most treasured in their lives, according to the recollections of Daniel Irion, who was one of them. In 1877 Otto was chosen editor of the *Theologische Zeitschrift*—another mark, one would think, of complete confidence in him.

In 1879, however, Otto's great popularity and prestige were really the remote cause of the most serious disciplinary trouble in the whole history of the seminary. The students struck against the other professor (there were only two at this time) because, in their opinion, he did not come up to Otto's standard. The outcome was that Otto's colleague resigned his professorship and Otto resigned the presidency while remaining as professor.

Louis F. Haeberle, the unanimous choice of the Board for president, took up, in 1879, the office that he filled with grace, humility, and distinction until his retirement in 1902. Under his tactful, but none the less firm, administration, the seminary settled down to its normal quiet way.

New trouble broke out for Otto, however, when his teaching was assailed in a letter directed to the Seminary Board by Bank. What Bank did was to dig up Otto's articles of 1873 and 1874 in the *Theologische Zeitschrift* on sin as the wages of death, on original sin, and on atonement and justification, as evidence that Otto held and taught unbiblical doctrines. In a formal letter to the Seminary Board, Bank and his like-minded friends demanded an investigation of Otto's teaching.

The Board took up the question at its meeting in the spring of

1880. On request, Otto submitted to the Board his lecture notes on dogmatics, which the Board studied in detail, especially with reference to his teaching on the meaning of Christ's death for atonement; on the death of man; on the miracles of Christ, particularly the stilling of the tempest; and on the sacrifice of Isaac. The outcome was set forth by the Board in two resolutions:

> (1) The Seminary Board has convinced itself that the doubts raised about Professor Otto's teaching have no basis in fact, and that therefore his further continuance at the seminary must be desired by the Board;
>
> (2) That Professor Otto shall be requested to forget what has happened and on the basis of strengthened confidence to continue his work with good cheer and courage.

The chairman of the Board was Karl Siebenpfeiffer of Rochester, New York, president of the Synod since Baltzer's death in January. It looked as if Otto would come out of this affair stronger than ever. But Otto himself ended all possibility of remaining in the professorship when he published a series of four articles on a study of the temptation story (Genesis 3) in the *Theologische Zeitschrift* from May to August, 1880. The first installment must almost certainly have been in the hands of the printer before the Seminary Board met near the end of April. That made no difference to Otto, to whom it was an intolerable thought that he should submit anything he wrote to the imprimatur of any higher authority than his conscience.

The articles created a sensation. "They were," says Hugo Kamphausen, editor of the *Theological Magazine* from 1917 to 1933, "beyond any question superior in thoroughness, originality, and clearness to any others ever published in this periodical in the fields of exegesis or biblical theology, and inferior to nothing produced by German theologians." At the beginning of his study, Otto reviewed the different types of exegesis—allegorical, literal, dogmatical, and theosophical—which had been employed in the interpretation of the story of the temptation in the Garden of Eden, rejecting them all for convincing reasons. There remained the symbolic explanation, which he held to be the only one that would stand up. Certain aspects of the story clearly ruled out the literal interpretation as too grossly anthropomorphic. As Otto said later in defense of his position, "You have in this story the kernel of truth, which is that sin is grave disobedience to God; and the shell, which is the tree, the serpent, and the conversations."

The matter came before the General Conference in September. The committee appointed to deal with the question declared its finding that Otto had deviated from the doctrinal standpoint of the Synod and demanded that Otto should promise to adhere to the doctrinal position of the Synod in the future. Otto defended himself with dignity, insisting that he stood on the basic confession of the church and accepted the unconditional authority of the Scriptures, but felt that the teacher must be allowed a certain latitude in interpretation. He was asking for the recognition not of the "liberal," but of the "neological" (modern) method of scriptural study. The General Conference, moreover, was not competent to decide such questions, he held, but a committee of real experts should deal with it, and he should be given full freedom to defend himself.

The General Conference declared, by a vote of 47 to 9, that it "must decidedly repudiate any neological method of teaching and explanation of the Scriptures, and insist firmly that in our seminary the Christian doctrine is presented in the manner of the positive believing direction, as it is done in the Evangelical Church of Germany."

Otto thereupon resigned his professorship as well as his membership in the Synod. The Reverend Carl Kunzmann was appointed professor at the seminary in his place. Otto returned to the Synod, after about a year's absence, to serve as pastor of a church. In 1890 he was called, amid general good will, to the proseminary at Elmhurst as professor of Ancient Languages and other subjects. Retiring from teaching in 1904, he returned to Columbia, Illinois, where he died in 1916 at the age of nearly eighty.

What Otto asked for himself in 1880—complete liberty (under his own conscience) in the scientific interpretation of scripture— was something which, as Kamphausen comments, "no other American denomination except the Unitarian would have tolerated from its professors."

Eden in St. Louis

Ever since the union of 1872, there had been a growing demand for the removal of the too secluded theological seminary from Marthasville, Missouri. The erection of the fine main building at Elmhurst in 1878 intensified the demand for a new building for the theological seminary in a new location. The Seminary Board contented itself with remarking that while there was much to be said for removing the seminary to a more favorable location, the Board did not care, under the present circumstances, to recommend an undertaking that would involve the assumption of a considerable debt.

From the floor of the General Conference of 1880, however, voices rose to call for action. Some suggested moving the theological seminary to Elmhurst and setting up a teachers' seminary somewhere else. It was also reported that the city of Washington, Missouri had offered to raise the money to buy a site in its midst. This led to the motion, which was carried, that the Seminary Board be authorized to consider all offers for a new site and, if a suitable one was found, to take steps concurrently with the officers of the Synod and the district presidents to effect the removal of the theological seminary.

The site selected by the Board was a tract of about nineteen acres, not far from the Evangelical Orphans Home on the St. Charles Road, some seven miles from the courthouse of St. Louis. The nearest railroad station was a stop on the Wabash Railroad called "Eden," so that became the name of the seminary. The site was paid for by the churches of St. Louis. The architect's plan for the new building called for an estimated $30,000. A circular letter, describing these plans and their cost, was sent to every pastor and every church, with the request to take steps at the district conferences to raise the necessary money. Every district having approved the plans, the Board appointed a building committee consisting of three laymen, four pastors, and the president of the seminary. Then the Board, going over the plans once more, came to the conclusion that they had one serious defect: they did not allow for the certain growth of the seminary. Would it not be better to build big enough right away so that it would not be necessary to build again for many years? Guided by this consideration and relying on the help of God, the committee accepted plans for a much larger building.

Ground was broken in the fall of 1882, and the cornerstone was laid in April, 1883. The completed building was dedicated on Sunday, October 28 (Reformation Day), 1883. This was as close as they could come to the four hundredth anniversary of Luther's birthday on November 10, 1483.

In spite of rain all morning and mud all over the site, a great throng was present for the ceremony. The members of the General Conference meeting in St. Louis were also in attendance. Many of them had come with mixed feelings. During the sessions of the Conference they had learned that the new building had cost, not the $30,000 that had been approved, but, excluding the cost of the site, about three times that amount—$86,700. So there had been, quite naturally, a good deal of indignant expostulation against what was characterized as "inexcusable disregard of instructions." When the critics had inspected the building, however, and pondered the motives of the building committee, they accepted the accomplished fact. It took years to pay the debt, but by 1889 it had been reduced to $24,925.

There never has been any further question that the Seminary Board acted wisely in building for a rapid expansion. Marthasville closed with an enrollment of 45; Eden began with 70 and mounted to 100 between 1884 and 1886. Then there was a gradual but continuous yearly decline to a low of 54 in 1896-97. By 1900, the fiftieth anniversary, it had risen again to 77. Between 1906 and 1913 the seminary was able to maintain an average enrollment of 68.

Most of the students entering Eden from 1883 to 1933 came from Elmhurst College. From 1883 to about 1913, there was a steadily declining number of students born and prepared in Germany. Wherever they came from, there were never quite enough to supply the demand for ministers. The faculty in 1883 consisted of President (Inspector) Louis F. Haeberle, Carl Kunzmann, and W. Becker. Kunzmann resigned in 1886 on account of poor health and his place was taken by F. H. Rudolph John. (In fact, they exchanged places, Kunzmann becoming John's successor as pastor in Edwardsville, Illinois.) John retired in 1889, and was succeeded by the Reverend K. Pirscher, who came highly recommended from Germany. When Pirscher left in 1894 the vacancy was filled by the Reverend Albert Muecke, the second alumnus on the faculty, President Haeberle having been the first. Haeberle insisted on retiring in 1902, after twenty-three years of fruitful labor. Becker was appointed president in his place, and the Reverend A. Grabowski was appointed professor. In 1904 Muecke returned to the active pastorate, and the Reverend W. Bauer was called from Rochester, New York to become professor. In 1911 Grabowski resigned his position, and the Reverend G. Braendli was called to the faculty. In the same year, F. S. Saeger began his work as director of music and instructor in German and English hymnody. All of these men taught in German as their predecessors had done from the time of the founding of Marthasville in 1850.

The Use of English

The necessity of training men to officiate and preach in English had been recognized from the beginning, but as wholly subsidiary to German. There was a great difference of opinion, moreover, among the pioneers of the seminary as to the importance of English. Joseph A. Rieger, chairman of the Board until his death in 1869, would have had every seminarian able to preach in English. He was able to do it himself, and he saw not merely the necessity, but also the advantage of a German pastor being able to preach as well as officiate at baptisms, weddings, and funerals, in English. Rieger, however, was the exception and not the rule. Rather elementary English was taught at Marthasville by student assistants, nearly every year, so that the German-born student, who knew no English and had little chance to hear any in the world-forsaken Marthasville, might not be absolutely unable to read or understand it. In 1870 English on the elementary level became a part of the curriculum at Marthasville.

From 1890 on, English was taught by competent men, and taught on a much more advanced level, as practical theology or homiletics. Most of the instructors were ministers, appointed as assistant professors on a part-time basis. The last, and the longest in service, was the Reverend F. W. Nolte, 1899-1908.

In September, 1908 the first full professorship in English was given to the Reverend Samuel D. Press, an Elmhurst-Eden alumnus, who had spent several years in the study of theology in Germany and now came from a successful pastorate in Houston, Texas. The distinction of being the first professor to teach the English language full time was the opportunity for Press to make history at Eden Seminary, first as professor, and after June, 1919 as president of the seminary.

Home Missions

The story of home missions (or, to use the present designation, national missions) in the Evangelical Synod properly began when the Synod, *out of its own means,* systematically sent preachers out among unchurched settlements of German Evangelical people in rural areas or in cities, and supported them until the congregations were able to support themselves.

In 1854, at the request of the *Kirchenverein,* Pastor Theodor Hermann Dresel of Burlington, Iowa spent four months, mostly in the saddle, looking over the German settlements of Iowa. He reported that, in spite of initial difficulties and discouragement, the interior of the state could become a scene of blessed labor for the Synod. The Conference of 1855 thereupon elected the Reverend Karl Hoffmeister of California, Missouri, as traveling preacher with a salary of $250 a year. His home base was German Creek, in Washington, Iowa. It turned out that there was no home available, so the officers of the *Kirchenverein* asked Hoffmeister to go to Princeton, Illinois (sixty miles from the Iowa line) where a pastor was wanted, and use it as a base for circuit riding in Iowa.

The General Conference held in June, 1859, at Louisville, was unable to do anything about home missions because there were no ministers to spare; it was not even possible to fill all the vacancies in the existing churches. An important step was taken, none the less, when this conference set up the Treasury of the Evangelical Church Association *(Kirchenverein)* of the West for Home Missions. The administration of funds was entrusted to the officers of the *Verein;* and to these officers the districts were instructed to direct their requests for financial aid or for preachers.

The report of the General Conference of 1864 states: "Traveling preaching is to be resumed, and the officers are instructed to look about for a suitable man." This was ten years after the tentative efforts of Dresel and Hoffmeister. But the report of the General Conference of 1866 informs us that on account of various obstacles it had not been possible to do anything about "traveling preaching." The officers were able, however, to report that new outposts had been established in three rapidly growing cities under these pastors: Karl Hoffmeister at Council Bluffs, Iowa; Heinrich Kirchhoff at St. Joseph, Missouri; and J. Christoph Feil at Kansas City, Missouri.

Representative Home Missionaries

We get an idea of the difficulties under which these men labored from a letter written by J. Christoph Feil, a Basel man, who had completed his studies at Marthasville and been ordained in 1860, in the same class with Louis F. Haeberle, Johann Peter Goebel, Heinrich Buchmueller, and Heinrich Kirchhoff:

> With instructions to do missionary work for our Evangelical Church in the West, it was by God's leading that I arrived in Kansas City last September. [This was written in August, 1866.] At that time there were very few here who showed any interest in the church. Often there were only three or four men at the service of worship. Everywhere there was nothing but hate for anything that had even a tinge of religion. Good-natured ridicule was the reward I got from most people for what they called my vain and hopeless work. But, thank the Lord, things have changed. People can see that my results are turning out different from what they expected. It is still a hard fight. There are mighty foes to overcome. But the Lord stands by us. We have had to hold our services now here, now there, now at this hour, now at another. We had no church and have none now. The want of a church can only hurt our cause. We are now better off, so far as regularity of time and place is concerned, but our meeting place is too unsuitable. You see, we are conducting our services of worship in our house. Under these circumstances the desire arose for a church of our own, but most of our people thought it's quite impossible, the most we can hope to raise is $300 or $400. But at last we took courage and decided to risk it and see what we could raise by pledges toward building a church. And behold, the Lord shamed our little faith; we raised

over $1,200. But though that is a considerable sum, it is not nearly enough yet, for we shall have to spend at least $500 for a suitable building place. We are not thinking of a large and splendid church, but it ought not to look quite like a mere hut either. Our success has not been brilliant, but it is there for any one to see. Interest in the church has grown and will, we hope, increase. In order that we may not be delayed but encouraged in our difficult mission work, I request every Christian who prays from his heart "Thy kingdom come," to remember us with a contribution to the First German Evangelical Church here in Kansas City. Our fast-growing city has about 14,000 inhabitants and two thirds of them are German. There is no German church here as yet, but we have three breweries and almost countless saloons.

While Feil's work in Kansas City was rewarded by success, President Baltzer reports in 1868 that attempts to establish churches in Omaha, Council Bluffs, and other cities with a large German population, had to be given up for lack of money to keep men in the field:

The work is peculiarly difficult, to be sure, because the estrangement of German immigrants from God and the church is nowhere so great as in our fast-growing frontier cities—yet all these difficulties and drawbacks are not so great that they could not be overcome, with the help of God, by a program of sustained financial support. So long as the Synod has to content itself with the present inadequate financial resources, we shall be compelled to do without traveling preachers. If the Synod believes that we dare not longer neglect this missionary work among our fellow Germans, which is peculiarly our very own task, then we must see to it that more abundant financial means are kept flowing into the home mission treasury.

A remarkable home missionary whose labors in the field extended over nearly fifty years, from 1864 to 1910, was the Reverend Louis von Ragué. An alumnus of the Barmen Mission House, he had volunteered for foreign missions but accepted as God's will an assignment for service in the United States. His first charge was in Town Rhine, Sheboygan County, Wisconsin where he arrived at the end of 1864. Emil Otto came to Milwaukee a few months after this. Reference has already been made to the trip they took together to St. Louis and Marthasville.

Working from Town Rhine as his home base, Ragué gathered congregations and built churches at Town Russell, Onion River, Town Eleven, and other places. Called to Milwaukee, he became the pastor of the first Evangelical congregation in Milwaukee—Friedens Church, founded in 1869. The congregation grew so rapidly that it would have kept most ordinary men busy, but Ragué possessed a restless energy that constantly sought new outlets. While in Milwaukee, he was instrumental in founding churches in Butler, Franklin, Portage, Fond du Lac, and Wauwatosa.

So unusual had been the success of Ragué in founding new churches, that he was asked in 1871 by the Northern District, of which he was a member, to go to the Twin Cities of St. Paul and Minneapolis to organize congregations. He had been asked to take a leave of absence from his church in Milwaukee for three months. When the three months were up, he was prevailed upon to stay in St. Paul to assure the successful continuance of the work begun there. As usual, he would not confine himself to a single project or two, but organized congregations at Lake Elmo, Cottage Grove, Osseo, and New Schwanden. Not every congregation organized by Ragué and other mission workers became the sole charge of a pastor; there would not have been half enough ministers. Most of the congregations shared the services of a pastor with another church—sometimes two or three. Eventually, however, a great many became sole charges.

Ragué even began work in Duluth, a mere 160 miles north of St. Paul. The work there was carried on by a young pastor named J. Lueder, who was to begin, a few years later, a long and honorable career as professor at Elmhurst. There is a story about Lueder's pastorate in Duluth that came to the mind of the writer while reading John Flucke's interesting account of the life of

Ragué in his *Evangelical Pioneers*. Ragué was evidently a man of infinite resources, who might have made a fortune in business. Whether it was an organ, a parsonage, or a new church that was needed, he knew how to get it. While in Germany on a visit in 1869, he procured two large church bells for the new church in Town Rhine (we are not told how).

Lueder also wanted a bell for the new church in Duluth, so he asked perhaps the most unlikely person one could think of—and obtained what he wanted. This was in 1872. He addressed a personal request to the German Emperor, the old Kaiser Wilhelm I, setting forth the need and the prospects for the kind of work he was doing in ministering to the spiritual needs of Germans in the faraway northwestern country. A church was soon to be built. The reader can follow in his own imagination the eyes of the Kaiser's secretary as he read the eloquent plea for the simple gift of metal to cast a bell whose tones would be, as it were, a voice from over the water summoning the people to worship God in the manner of their fathers. The kindly old emperor was touched by the request of this earnest young preacher, and in due time there arrived in Duluth, to the happy amazement of everybody, the shipment of bell metal that was to be cast for the Duluth church's bell.

Gifts of this sort, some of them amounting to thousands of dollars, cannot have been too uncommon. The records of St. John's Evangelical Church at Naperville, which celebrated its centennial in 1957, show that on several occasions Adolph Hammerschmidt, one of the founders of the church, wrote to relatives and friends in Germany and in Switzerland when the church could not meet the cost of certain necessary improvements and received more than they had asked for (over $1,000 in one case).

It was as pastor of St. John's Church in Naperville (at the opposite corner of DuPage County from Elmhurst) that Louis von Ragué closed one of the most productive careers in the history of home missions in the Evangelical Synod. We left him, in our story, at St. Paul and Duluth. We must add Ellsworth and Oak Grove, Wisconsin to the list of churches he founded while at St. Paul.

After ten strenuous years of home mission work, Ragué, on the advice of another restless worker, President Adolph Baltzer, became pastor of an established church, first at Hoyleton, Illinois, then in New Orleans, and finally in Quincy, Illinois as successor to Simon Kuhlenhoelter in one of the largest congregations in the Evangelical Synod. He demonstrated by his successful administration of these old and large congregations that, while it does take special qualities to be a successful mission worker, the same men can have the qualities also that are needed in big churches.

Again, as if to prove that a veteran of nearly thirty years service can still do great things, Ragué accepted in 1893 the invitation of the South Illinois District to establish a congregation in Belleville, Illinois. Within two months he had organized Christ Church, and its fine building was dedicated a year later. Even after he had retired, he returned to the field in 1903 to start Calvary (now Kloeckner Memorial) Church in the Austin section of Chicago and, in 1906, Gethsemane Church in the northwestern part of Chicago.

Home Mission Administration and Support

In the hope of stimulating more interest in home missions and in order to use increased means more effectively, the General Conference of 1870 voted to create a *Board fuer Innere Mission*. The fact that the English word board was chosen instead of a German equivalent probably means that the members of the Synod were familiar with the operation of boards among the English-language churches and meant to have one like them. The first members of the Board were Pastors Wilhelm Kampmeier of the Northern District, Philipp Goebel and Friedrich

Pfeiffer of the Middle District, and Ernst Roos of the Eastern District. Its instructions included the following points:

(1) The board is authorized and required to secure the funds necessary for sending out and paying the salaries of traveling preachers, and where necessary for the support, from time to time, of the congregations which they have called into existence. These funds are to be raised through:
  (a) A regular annual offering which the churches associated with the Synod will be asked to contribute
  (b) Acceptance of voluntary contributions, gifts, legacies, etc.
  (c) The contribution of one dollar a year from each pastor of the Synod, and the profits of *Der Friedensbote*.
(2) The mission board is to be represented at the annual examination of the candidates for ordination at the seminary by one of its members who will submit to the president of the Synod the names of men who seem to be most suitable for home mission work.
(3) The board is to keep in touch with the district presidents so that the latter may bring to the attention of the board promising fields for home mission work and pastors who are willing and fitted to become traveling preachers.

The next General Conference in 1872 (the union conference) abolished the Board of Home Missions and returned to the districts the responsibility for home mission work within their boundaries. The common home mission treasury was retained, however, under the care of the Synod treasurer. Each district was required to draw up a budget for home mission work at its annual conference and submit the budget to the president of the Synod, who, being informed by the treasurer of the funds available, would determine the appropriation for each district accordingly. The treasury was assured of one dependable source of income when the General Conference voted to divide the net profit of *Der Friedensbote* between home missions and the educational institutions. To meet the responsibility for the pursuit of home mission work now returned to them, the districts found it advisable to set up separate home mission committees. The four officers of the General Conference constituted the central committee for home missions with nothing to do (as President Baltzer remarked) except to pay out to the district committees the money they asked for, if there was any money.

Home Mission Fields

The creation of district committees undoubtedly helped to stimulate interest in home missions. There was a notable increase in contributions from 1877 on. About this time also, the leaders of the Synod began to look around farther for new fields. There was apparently a promising opening in Chattanooga, Tennessee, which, however, came to an end in 1878, when the young minister, G. H. Brenner, died of yellow fever contracted while nursing members of his congregation who had been stricken with it. The same fate befell the first of our ministers to serve a church in New Orleans, A. Bathe. He was succeeded by Julius Kramer, and it was not long before two other churches in New Orleans were served by members of the Evangelical Synod. (Serving old established churches is not, however, home mission work by definition.) Through the efforts of the three Evangelical pastors, and particularly of A. H. Becker, three more Evangelical churches were founded in New Orleans.

The General Conference of 1880 directed its attention toward Texas and also toward California and Oregon, besides the central states. Texas was known to have several German settlements, some of them established before Texas was admitted to the Union, and to be attracting a considerable number of German immigrants. The Evangelical Synod, however, was not represented in Texas. The nearest district responsible for any home missionary work there was the fourth (centering in St. Louis and including eastern Missouri and southern Illinois). The district home mission committee, looking about for the right man to send to Texas, recognized him in F. Werning of Berger, Mis-

souri, and succeeded in winning him for the difficult work that
might await a traveling preacher in Texas.

Werning came to Waco in October, 1881, and had a small congregation already organized by Christmas. In the fall of 1882
this congregation (Zion) was able to dedicate its new home, the
first Evangelical church in Texas. Werning, while serving this
church as pastor, found time also to preach and organize congregations in Fort Worth, Temple, Bartlett, West (in Washington County), and Houston. The Board of Home Missions sent
excellently qualified reinforcements to Werning (a policy they
were not always able to follow). Within five years, the Evangelical Synod had 9 preachers ministering to 11 organized congregations, and 4 preaching stations in Texas. By 1889 Werning
could report, as president of the Texas District, that in 12 counties there were 14 pastors serving 21 congregations, of which nine
were self-supporting and two more would be within a year.

The General Conferences of 1883 and 1886 reveal an increasing
realization of the challenge of home missions. "It is the sacred
duty of our Synod," declared President John Zimmermann. "It
is only when we begin to acknowledge our responsibility, look
over the field, and start to work, that we realize how great is
the task that home missions presents to us. There are seven million Germans in the United States. If we divided them up in
congregations of five hundred souls each, we should have 14,000
German congregations. How many have we actually?"

"Where should we carry on home missions?" he then asked.
"Wherever our fellow countrymen live. If some hundred to five
hundred families live close together in a large city, then we ought
first to set up our tents among them. Was not that the apostolic
order, to begin first of all in the larger cities? In general, our
Synod has acted on that maxim; but too often we have come into
a community about ten years too late."

The president might have added that within the three years

from 1880-83 the flood of German immigration had reached the highest annual average on record with nearly 200,000 people arriving from Germany each year. It had taken all the German denominations by surprise, for the average annual immigration during the years 1876-80 had only been about 42,000.

The larger cities received a greater share of the Synod's mission work during the rest of the eighties. In Buffalo, New York three new churches were founded as mission enterprises with exemplary support from the older churches and their pastors. They were Trinity, Bethany, and Bethlehem. In Chicago, during the eighties, new churches were being built at an average of one a year, including Immanuel, Bethlehem, Trinity, St. Nicolai, Friedens, St. Luke, Zion (Auburn Park), Ebenezer, and St. Mark's. (Some of these have since merged with others.)

The increase in the number of churches was most conspicuous in Chicago because no other city attracted so large a number of German immigrants. It would take us too long to attempt to enumerate all the churches founded in the other large cities, in smaller cities and villages, and out in the country. The Synod received an increase in the number of its churches, from time to time, also, when hitherto independent churches (belonging to no synod) were drawn into affiliation with the Synod after electing a member of the Synod as pastor.

While the eighties saw much home mission activity in the cities, the rural areas were by no means neglected unduly. As the Synod had lifted its eyes to "faraway Texas," so it turned its attention also to the Far West and Northwest. One of the finest products of home mission work was the successful establishment of colonies through the efforts of a society for colonization. The first of these colonies was New Salem, North Dakota, founded in 1883; the second was Hebron, North Dakota, founded in 1885. The first pastors to minister to the colonists were H. Gyr and R. Kruger. They were followed by A. Debus in Hebron and A.

Schuenhutz in New Salem. It was the hope, expressed by President Zimmermann, that these two churches would become the bases for numerous traveling preachers going out among the settlers along the line of the Northern Pacific Railroad. The first church in Colorado was Salem in Denver, organized by the Reverend A. H. J. Bierbaum of Holstein, Missouri in July, 1884. The first regular pastor was J. G. Muller, who began his work in the fall of 1884. At the same time, E. J. Hosto started his work as traveling preacher for the Seventh District (western Missouri) in the colony of Whitmore (Shasta County). The Reverend G. Niebuhr, fresh from the seminary, arrived in San Francisco in 1885, and through hard work and patience succeeded in getting St. John's Church started. In 1886 the first Evangelical church in Los Angeles was founded by the Reverend Paul Branke.

Home mission work seems to have been peculiarly difficult in California, and not merely because the Evangelical Synod had arrived late on the scene. But in spite of discouraging failures in several places, there were enough pastors and churches in California by 1894 to justify organizing them as the Pacific District. The new district was represented for the first time at a General Conference in 1898 by its president, the Reverend J. G. Mangold. There is no official report from the district, but the Board of Home Missions reports that ten churches received a total of $2,665.25 during the preceding three years, an average of less than $90.00 a year for each of these churches. Averages, however, are likely to be misleading. Two of the churches received only $25.00 and $44.00, one year; two others received totals of $880 and $637.50.

In comparison with the sums allotted for the triennium to other districts, Pacific (receiving $3,180) and Atlantic (receiving $3,025) stand in the median position between Northern Illinois ($4,933) and Pennsylvania ($578).

The total spent on home missions between 1895 and 1898 amounted to $48,123, not counting the deficit of $5,985 left over from 1894, which was made up. The total income was $54,311, of which $30,258 came from contributions, and $22,417 from the profits of Eden Publishing House.

The conviction had been growing for some time that the home mission work had become too large an enterprise for the elementary administrative organization set up in 1872. The General Conference of 1898 declared home mission work not merely one of its chief responsibilities, but the indispensable requirement for the continued existence and growth of the Synod. It voted to create a board of home missions, similar to the Board of Foreign Missions, to consist of five members from five different districts. The ministers elected to this Board were K. W. F. Haas of Detroit, L. Kohlmann of East St. Louis, F. A. Reller of Evansville, John Baltzer of St. Louis, and W. Hattendorf of Chicago. The new Board was disappointed with the income of its first three years, which fell below that of the previous triennium. In 1901 the General Conference approved the appointment of a secretary for home missions. It was not until January, 1903 that the Reverend F. H. Freund took over this position.

The Colorado Mission District, organized in 1902, included Colorado, Utah, and eastern Idaho. The Reverend G. A. Schmidt was an indefatigable pioneer in this district. Utah, overwhelmingly Mormon as it was, did have scattered groups of Evangelical people. The only way to get a congregation going, however, was to build a church. The Board of Home Missions agreed to do this in Ogden where there was the best chance to build up a congregation, if the young people's societies would undertake to raise the money needed to build a church. The *Jugendbund* (Young People's League) agreed to do this, and the Mission Board called the Reverend Ph. Tester, who began work in July, 1909. The church, paid for by the young people, was dedicated in the spring of 1912. In 1909 work was begun also in Payette, Idaho and this (unlike the Utah missions) has endured—to this day, the only Evangelical and Reformed church in Idaho.

In 1909, also, the work in Washington had progressed to the point where a mission district could be organized with Freund (who had given up the post of Home Mission Secretary) as president. The Washington Mission District included Washington, Oregon, and western Idaho. The first church in this district was St. Paul's in Seattle, organized in October, 1903 by the Reverend A. Leutwein. In June, 1904 Home Mission Secretary Freund was able to organize St. Paul's in Portland, Oregon with forty men; the Reverend J. Hergert became the first pastor. In October, 1904 the Reverend E. J. Fleer began work in Spokane and organized First Evangelical Church there on New Year's Day, 1905. New congregations were organized in 1906 in Everett and Seattle.

In 1910 the long-neglected field of Montana was entered by the Reverends R. Maurer and Stelzig, joined later by the Reverend J. Kisselmann. It was hard work, which in the end left no permanent traces except two prosperous churches in Billings and Hardin. Home mission work is like that; its success simply cannot be measured merely by permanent churches established.

For many years the Board of Home Missions tried to carry on work in Manitoba, Alberta, and Saskatchewan, Canada. It was known that Evangelical farmers had moved from Minnesota and the Dakotas to the rich Canadian wheat fields. It was not among them, however, but among the German-Russians in Winnipeg that the Synod began its work between 1905 and 1909. Two small congregations were started in Winnipeg, first served by the Reverends E. G. Albert and F. Fischer who also served some small congregations out in the country. In 1917 the Winnipeg churches were being served by Pastors Winger, father and son; the Reverend J. Newmann was serving another small parish.

The German-Russians

One of the most challenging opportunities that came to the Board of Home Missions for many years was presented by the German-Russians in Colorado. These German-Russians were the descendants of German colonists who had settled at the urgent invitation of the Empress Catherine (the Great) and later rulers, along the lower stretches of the Volga. They came to Russia with the guarantee that they could retain their language, their religion, and their customs. The pact was kept for more than a hundred years, but under Nicholas II a policy of Russification ignored these special rights of the Germans in Russia. So they came in large numbers to the United States. In Colorado many turned to the sugar beet industry.

Wherever they settled they formed groups determined to preserve their religious faith and, insofar as possible, also their language. Among all the German denominations in the United States, they found the Evangelical Synod more like themselves in doctrine and practice.

Several congregations were organized among them, the largest at Fort Collins. Then it became clear that the German-Russians were likely to keep coming in even greater numbers. The Reverend G. A. Schmidt, president of the Colorado District, submitted an eight-point plan, the chief feature of which was that it proposed to establish, under the auspices of the Board of Home Missions an academy to train young men from among the German-Russians themselves as preachers and lay workers. The plan was welcomed by the German-Russians.

The academy was opened in November, 1914 at Fort Collins under the leadership of the Reverend J. Jans with nine students; in February there were eleven. The academy was in trouble from the start, however, through no fault or lack of good will on anybody's part. Most of the students were married men who had to support as many as five or six children. There was not money enough to subsidize the families, nor could any man earn enough while studying. A further and fatal difficulty was that the coming of the war in August, 1914 had cut off all immigration. In May, 1916 the Seminary Board took over the academy and decided before long to close it. The academy had not existed wholly in vain however. Five of its students were ordained; one entered Eden Seminary; and two others hoped to study for the ministry.

Foreign Missions

"No other German church body in the United States," claims Professor Albert Muecke, "save the Moravian Church, has done so much from the beginning for foreign missions as has the Evangelical Synod." This early concern for missions among the heathen reflected the influence of the missionary institutes (Basel and Barmen) where the founders of the *Kirchenverein* had been trained for a service from which they had been diverted by the imperative need of preachers among the German settlers in the United States.

Only a year after George Wall founded the German Evangelical Congregation in St. Louis (1843), a mission society existed among its members. In 1848 this society, encouraged by the formation of other societies among *Kirchenverein* churches, requested Basel Mission House to send one of its graduates to St. Louis to start a mission among the Indians of the West. Basel responded to this appeal by commissioning newly ordained Theodor Hermann Dresel for this service.

Dresel arrived in St. Louis before the end of the year, only to learn that the expected support for the Indian mission had not materialized. He accepted a call to the church in Burlington, Iowa and in time became one of the leading figures of the Evangelical Synod.

Although the *Kirchenverein* had proved itself unable to support a mission field of its own, interest in missions did not abate. The three St. Louis churches celebrated a union mission festival in October, 1849 at which the two mission societies reported contributions amounting to nearly $400 during the past year, besides sacrificial gifts of jewelry. This missionary interest was not confined to the St. Louis area. The Ohio Synod published a little paper called the *Missionsbote* which was incorporated in 1852 with *Der Friedensbote.* The Synod of the Northwest encouraged union mission services among the churches in cities like Detroit and Chicago, and urged the churches to contribute to the support of mission houses like Basel and St. Chrischona in Switzerland.

In the Synod of the West the contributions to the mission houses of Basel and Barmen took so large a share of all benevolent giving that President Baltzer was impelled to plead, in the report of 1870, that congregations which had contributed $5,000 to foreign missions should realize the need of doing better than an average $7,000 to $8,000 a year for their own theological and teacher seminaries.

An Independent Field?

When the several synods had united, the first task was to strengthen their educational institutions and home missions. Interest in foreign missions, however, did not slacken. In 1880 the fourth district (Missouri and southern Illinois) recorded its conviction, after an address by the Reverend C. Bechtold, that the Evangelical Synod had the right and the duty to take on the responsibility of a mission field of its own as soon as God opened the way, and called upon the next General Conference to appoint a standing committee to take the initial steps. The General Conference took no action except to refer the question back to the districts.

The question was not simply: Are you in favor of supporting foreign missions? A great many of the most ardently mission-minded pastors and lay members of the Evangelical Synod were opposed to taking over an independent mission field because they believed that more good could be done by supporting the established mission fields of Basel, Barmen, and other German societies. Moreover, they held that the Evangelical Synod had a moral obligation to continue the support of these German societies, to whose help the Synod owed its existence. A lively debate ensued between proponents and opponents of an independent mission. The proponents, led by Bechtold, and Kunzmann of the theological seminary, organized a society and presented their arguments in an illustrated paper called *Der Missionar*. The opponents, led by the Reverends Johann Balthasar Jud, A. Klein, and F. Buesser, presented their side in a paper that they called *Evangelischer Missionsfreund*.

Beginnings in India

The question was settled with unexpected promptness at the General Conference of 1883. Among the missionary societies that had received some support from members of the Evangelical Synod (including the very active participation of Dresel, at this time in Brooklyn, New York) was the German Evangelical Mission Society in the United States. In spite of the name, this society had no official connection with the German Evangelical Synod of North America. Organized in 1865 by an interdenominational group of German churches, including German and Dutch Reformed, Lutheran, Moravian, Presbyterian, and Evangelical, it had been conducting a promising work since 1868 in the Central Provinces of India. The Society was now offering to turn over this field to the Evangelical Synod because the opportunities were greater than their own limited resources could meet.

The offer was prayerfully considered by a committee of nine, including two laymen and seven of the most respected leaders of the Evangelical Synod. At the end of its deliberation, the committee appeared before the General Conference with this eloquent declaration:

> As strongly as your committee was convinced (with only one dissenting voice), at the beginning of our discussions, that *now* was not yet the time for the Synod to take over a mission field of its own, so little are we now able, after the discussions we have had, to advise against taking this step.
>
> Three reasons in particular impel your committee to recommend immediate action in this matter:
>
> (1) The movement within the Synod for a mission of our own has grown in spite of all objections and opposition to a force which can no longer be ignored.
>
> (2) Acceptance of the flourishing mission offered to us in a densely populated area of India occupied by no other society will save us the costly experiments invariably connected with the opening of a new mission field.
>
> (3) The inescapable question whether the successful completion of the new seminary building in spite of our doubts and hesitations is not God's way of telling us that in addition to our work among our own German fellow countrymen he wants to entrust a wider and more comprehensive responsibility to us.
>
> Since your committee sees in this matter the sign of God's will for which we have been waiting for years, the committee hereby moves that the Synod take over as soon as possible the mission field offered to it by the German Evangelical Mission Society.

It was a solemn and historic occasion for the Evangelical Synod when, after a long and thorough discussion, the eighty-eight members of the General Conference (fifty-six pastors and thirty-two laymen) were ready to vote. "God wills it!" was the overpowering conviction that swept through the assembly as the delegates voted, with but one dissenting voice, to take over the proffered India mission field. The formal transfer was completed in May, 1884. The mission property which the Synod now took over included:

> (1) The station of Bisrampur, established in 1868 by the Reverend Oscar Lohr on a tract of 1,926 acres of wasteland, bought from the government on the advice of a British official. Here were

the headquarters of the mission, with a church built in 1873, at the center of a steadily expanding village, the industries of which were directed by Julius Lohr, son of the missionary.

(2) The station at Raipur (largest city in Chhattisgarh), under the direction of the Reverend Andrew Stoll since 1879, with a home for the missionary and a small church.

What the advocates of a mission field "of our own" had hoped for came to pass in greatly increased interest and contributions. Veteran missionary Lohr had for years been pleading for help in carrying on the evangelistic work beyond the mission stations. In July, 1885 the first two new missionaries, the Reverends Th. Tanner and John Jost, were commissioned at a service in St. Peter's Church, St. Louis, which contributed $1,000 toward their traveling expenses. Jost remained in the work until his retirement in 1915. Tanner had to leave the field in 1889 on account of illness in the family. He was replaced by August Hagenstein, a pastor in Texas, who became an almost legendary figure among the natives as *Sadhu* (the saint) Hagenstein. The Reverend Karl W. Nottrott, commissioned in 1892, began the work among the lepers for which Chandkuri station (established in 1886 by Stoll and taken over in 1888 by Jost) has become world famous. In 1893 the Reverend Jacob Gass began a lifetime work in Raipur, which made his name known to all friends of the Indian mission.

No additional missionaries were sent to India until 1908. One reason was that India was visited by terrible famines in 1897 and 1898, and an even more disastrous one in 1900. In those times it was better to send money than men. A second reason was that the missionaries were developing assistants (catechists) and teachers among the natives.

10

The Postwar Era

IN THE TWO PREVIOUS CHAPTERS we have tried to present a picture of the Evangelical Synod of the West in 1868 as President Baltzer's report reveals it to us, to trace the threads of the union of 1872 and its effect on the progress of educational institutions, to come to grips with the problem of administration (the full-time presidency, the Synod, and the districts) and with the doctrinal stand of the church (Andreas Irion and Emil Otto), and finally to follow its home mission activity and its foreign mission enterprise. So we have come nearly fifty years from 1866 to 1914 with but one important omission—the story of Elmhurst.

Elmhurst College

We left the story of the proseminary (Elmhurst College) at the year 1887, when Johann Peter Goebel resigned the president's office. The Board did not look far for his successor. They chose the pastor of St. Peter's Church in Elmhurst, Daniel Irion, who became the fourth president in September, 1887. A graduate of the class of 1874, he was the first alumnus to hold the office, and he was also the first president who had had previous experience in the institution as a teacher. The eldest son of the late Andreas

Irion, Marthasville's great theologian, he never suffered by comparison because he achieved greatness in his own way on a different level. He remained at the head of the school until 1919, when he felt that the times called for a younger man as president. In accepting his resignation the Board requested Dr. Irion (one of the first men to receive the honorary degree of Doctor of Divinity from Eden Seminary) to remain on the faculty as professor of Ancient Languages. He taught his last classes in Greek in the school year 1927-28.

The thirty-two years covered by his administration have often been called the "Irion era." It is an appropriate designation because the period shows a remarkable continuity of everyday life, custom, and tradition among students, faculty, and "help," and in the relations of all three to the community. During the whole of these thirty-two years, the "old man" (really a title of respect that the students transferred to him from his predecessor almost from the start) made the rounds of the dormitory floors of Old Main and other buildings every morning after the five-thirty rising bell; met practically every student and all teachers every day; conducted or attended morning and evening devotions; looked after sick boys or boys in trouble; attended to dozens of requests during office hours and kept track, in a little black book, of everything anybody did or wanted. He was a really remarkable administrator; he had to be, for there was an absolute minimum of hired help, and he had to see to it that the students did the work assigned to them. But he was above all a great teacher whose lessons on the Bible stories, the catechism, and the New Testament in Greek left a lasting impression on his students. What he said of his predecessors was no less true of himself: he won the intellectual respect of his students and held an incalculable spiritual influence over them.

The characteristic of the Irion era was stability. This does not mean that there was no progress. The progress was essentially a steady improvement without any radical change in the curriculum at any one time. About 1901 the curriculum of the proseminary was accredited by the University of Illinois for admission to the university with advanced credit in German, Latin, and Greek. Up to 1911, the proseminary usually maintained a preparatory class for boys, who, though fourteen years old and confirmed, had not completed eight grades in the grammar school. When this preparatory class was given up, the requirements for graduation were advanced a year beyond high school requirements. Meanwhile, Elmhurst graduates were beginning to demand the expansion of the curriculum to make the proseminary a liberal arts college that would justify its name as Elmhurst College.

The enrollment increased gradually to a point where it could no longer be said, "We have room enough." One way to provide more space was suggested and seriously considered—the removal of the teacher-training department to Hoyleton, Illinois, where a large frame building was offered along with other inducements in 1889. In the end, the Seminary Board decided to keep the teacher-training department at Elmhurst. President Irion thereupon declared that it would be necessary to construct a new unit. So the building, the main function of which ever since has been to serve as the dining hall, was planned and completed in time to celebrate the twenty-fifth anniversary of the college in 1896. It occupies the site of the original Melanchthon Seminary building that had continued in use, mainly for professors' apartments. The original building was removed in sections, which were set up and rebuilt on Alexander Boulevard, where they still house four professors' families.

The next addition to the campus was Irion Hall, built in 1911, when the proseminary was forty years old. It was named in honor of Irion, who was completing his twenty-fifth year as president in 1912, when the building was dedicated. The new Irion

Hall was, first of all, a dormitory—the first modern dormitory on the campus. It contained also an apartment for the president and (as an extension, forming a T-shaped building) an attractive chapel beneath which was a gymnasium.

In response to the overwhelming sentiment in favor of developing Elmhurst as a four-year liberal arts college, the General Conference of 1917 directed the Seminary Board to take the steps necessary at least to give the proseminary the rank of a junior college. Irion, being wholly in favor of the development, felt that a younger man should take over the new responsibility and in the spring of 1919 he submitted his resignation as president. It was accepted with regret and understanding. An era had come to a close.

During the thirty-two years while Irion was president, the faculty was gradually increased from six to eight, including the president. In all that time, these five to seven places were filled by only eighteen different persons. In 1887 the faculty included J. Lueder, H. Brodt, C. J. Albert, G. A. Ebmeyer, and J. C. Rahn. Lueder, a favorite teacher of history, remained in service until 1910, when he was succeeded by the Reverend H. Arlt. Brodt, the master pedagogue who trained the parochial school teachers, retired in 1918 with no direct successor. Albert, best known for the teachers' agency he founded, was succeeded in 1892 as professor of English by G. A. Sorrick, a Heidelberg College graduate, who won high regard among his students for his learning and his competence as a teacher. Later he turned from English to mathematics and physics. Ebmeyer, a notable Germanist, quit teaching to take up journalism. His successor was Emil Otto, formerly of the theological seminary, who was venerated at Elmhurst, also, as a great scholar and thinker. In 1890 Carl Bauer began his long and brilliant career as a scholar of almost encyclopedic knowledge. C. C. Stanger, coming in 1896 to succeed Rahn as professor of music, completed fifty years of service on the faculty in 1946, when he was head of the department of Romance languages. Others who taught during the latter years of the Irion era were: J. J. Wilkinson, H. L. Breitenbach, Paul N. Crusius, and John E. Schmale—all teachers of English—and Emil Hansen, professor of Greek.

The man chosen to succeed Irion was the Reverend Herman J. Schick of Evansville, Indiana. Under his administration the institution was reorganized as Elmhurst Academy and Junior College. The transition was comparatively simple. There had been a five-year curriculum since 1911, the last of which was essentially a year of college work. Eight students of the class of 1919 elected to remain at Elmhurst for another year and receive the first diplomas of the Junior College in 1920. In 1923 it was announced that the college would definitely offer a third and a fourth year to complete the requirements for the A.B. degree. Three young men had the courage to stay on and receive the first A.B. degrees given by Elmhurst College.

The Synod had understood that it was not enough to add courses and professors to make a college. New buildings were needed. The library, erected by the Evangelical (young people's) League as a memorial to the young men of the Evangelical Synod who had died in the service of their country during World War I, was followed by South Hall, a new dormitory.

It was also necessary to expand the faculty. Excellent people had served—many of them, however, for only a short time. A college needs stability. The men and one woman who gave the college this stability are, besides those already mentioned as members of the faculty under Irion: Theophil W. Mueller (first dean of the college), Homer H. Helmick, Karl Henning Carlson, Harvey De Bruine, C. C. Arends, Genevieve Staudt (now dean of students), and Oliver M. Langhorst. All these have served twenty-five years or more.

President Schick did not remain in office long enough to bestow the first degrees on the graduates of 1925. He resigned in 1924 to become pastor of Immanuel Church in Chicago. Dr. Schick had accomplished a great deal in a difficult period of transition.

For his successor the Board chose H. Richard Niebuhr, a graduate of Elmhurst and Eden, who had just won the highest honors in theology at Yale Divinity School. A better choice could not have been made. Niebuhr immediately won the hearts of all students without effort, and the complete confidence of faculty and Board, as well as (not the least important) that of the officers of the Synod. With a clear vision and a sure instinct, he charted the course of the college for the immediate as well as the more distant future. Within three years, however, he resigned his post at Elmhurst College to take up more congenial work at Eden Seminary, from where he went, a few years later, to the Yale Divinity School. Niebuhr gained for his faculty and students a priceless legacy when he won the Board to a more realistic, that is to say, a more generous conception of the cost of keeping a good college going. A much improved salary scale was introduced, and also, for the first time, adequate budgets for the library and laboratories.

The Board, not prepared to choose a successor for Niebuhr at once, placed the administration of the college in the hands of a committee consisting of Mueller, Helmick, and Crusius. Taking time to be sure, they selected the Reverend Timothy Lehmann of Columbus, Ohio as the new president. Lehmann set earnestly to work, after a careful study of the situation, to bring to realization the things Elmhurst College needed. One was a system of sabbatical leaves, which, carried over a number of years, resulted in improving the scholarly resources of members of the faculty. Another was the expansion of the curriculum, which was one of the factors that led to the accreditation of Elmhurst College by the North Central Association in 1934. Not, perhaps, as something absolutely needed, but desirable for Elmhurst and the Synod, was the admission of women to the college in 1930. All this, accomplished within six years, was glory enough for any administration. Mention should be made also of the completion of the new gymnasium in Lehmann's first year, 1928.

Eden at Webster Groves

Eden Seminary seemed to be set for a clear course in 1919 with W. Becker as president, W. Bauer and F. Mayer as the German faculty, and Samuel D. Press, Carl Edward Schneider, and H. Richard Niebuhr as the English faculty. The death of Dr. Becker in 1919 was mourned as a real loss to the cause of theological thinking in the Synod. Press was the logical choice to succeed Becker.

The outstanding achievement of the next few years was the removal of the seminary from the no longer desirable location at Wellston to the handsome group of buildings erected on the beautiful campus in the attractive St. Louis suburb of Webster Groves, Missouri. The total cost ran to a million dollars with only $200,000 in the treasury. $400,000 came in as contributions; an equal sum came readily from the sale of bonds, and there was every reason to trust that this sum would be redeemed in a few years by further gifts.

In 1925 there were six full-time teachers and one part-time teacher on the faculty. In 1929 there were eight full-time professors and three part-time instructors. Philip Vollmer had reached the age of retirement, and F. Mayer had resigned to accept a call to his former church in Freedom, Michigan. Niebuhr had returned to the Eden faculty after a leave of absence begun in 1922, which included three years as president of Elmhurst College, and was assigned to the newly created department of history and philosophy of religion. John Biegeleisen was taking over the New Testament department, in which the Reverend M.

Manrodt had been serving for three years. The Reverend Werner Petersmann had been engaged in 1928 to teach in the department of historical theology. The Reverend H. H. Lohans, pastor of the Webster Groves Evangelical Church, was giving half time to teaching several courses in practical theology. Harold A. Pflug and Elmer J. F. Arndt, younger members of the faculty, were both to be on leave of absence for further study at Yale University. From the report of Press, it was clear that the faculty was at this time genuinely concerned with what seemed to be the real need of the day: functionalizing the courses of study in order to deal realistically with the social and economic turmoil. During 1933 world history was in a critical condition.

From German to English

The coming of World War I accelerated a process that had been going on within the Synod for more than a generation—the change from the German language to the English. This is commonly but not accurately called Americanization. The German-speaking founders of the Synod and all their successors correctly insisted that, though they used the German language, they and their church were American.

As early as 1874 the General Conference adopted a motion to include in the pocket edition of the book of worship, English as well as German formularies for baptisms, both regular and sick communion services, weddings, and burial services. In 1877 the Reverend P. J. Andres submitted to President Adolph Baltzer a translation of the catechism into English, which he was certain would be useful to ministers in the case of young people who were unable to read German. It is worth noticing that pastors like Henkel (Syracuse, New York) were in favor of publishing such a translation because there were a good many children in eastern communities who were not conversant with German.

By 1886 President John Zimmermann deplored "the fact that

we are losing a good many young people, for whom the German churches are not fashionable enough." In 1889 the president of the Indiana District reported that the number of parochial schools was constantly declining, despite considerable sacrifices made to keep them going. The result was the estrangement of a large part of our German-American youth. "The only thing that remains to be done," he said, "is to train our seminarians to preach in English and to get our catechism published in English as soon as possible."

The first notice of the English catechism appeared in 1892. The number sold was only 290 against 26,468 of the German catechisms. Three years later 1,820 English catechisms were sold. Zimmermann warned against premature, unnecessary resort to English but insisted that an English professorship must be established before long at Eden. In 1898 the new hymnal in English of the Evangelical Church was rapidly nearing completion, and competent critics declared that it would be a first-rate book.

In 1901 the president of the Indiana District, the Reverend F. Hohmann, wrote: "Particularly in the cities we have been working a long time for the English churches. An English Lutheran minister once said to me, 'You German brethren are doing my hardest work, you educate my best members.'" All the eastern district presidents agreed that there were very few churches left which did not demand English services.

It was high time, therefore, that the Synod should authorize the publication of an English-language counterpart to the *Friedensbote*, the *Messenger of Peace*, to appear monthly beginning in January, 1902. The Reverend A. H. Becker was appointed editor with the Reverends C. G. Haas and W. H. Schild as associate editors. Becker soon resigned, and Haas became editor. The first year's subscriptions totaled 786; the second, 1,530; the fourth, 1,998. The report to the General Conference of 1909 was submitted (in German) by the Reverend Julius H. Horstmann, who had become editor. The circulation had increased by 70 per cent. Horstmann proposed the publication of the *Evangelical Year Book*, which made its first appearance in 1910.

In 1913 the General Conference approved the change of name from *Messenger of Peace* to *Evangelical Herald*, and authorized its publication weekly. The circulation was disappointing, actually dropping from 5,377 in March, 1914, to 4,879 in March, 1917. By 1921, however, it had risen to 8,233. In 1931 it reached a maximum of 12,465, from which it fell off during the depression.

We must content ourselves, because of lack of space, with only a few further instances of the change from German to English. In the minutes of the General Conference of 1913 appeared the first official use of English—an appendix on "Evangelical Brotherhood History and Constitution." The second occurred in 1917— "Report on the State of the Evangelical Brotherhood."

In 1921 English translations (or versions) of all resolutions of the General Conference were given after the German originals. English was used more extensively in the minutes of 1925, and after that (in 1927, 1929, and 1933) exclusively.

The appearance of *Christian Hymns*, edited by Henry Katterjohn in 1908; of the new *Evangelical Hymnal*, edited by David Bruening in 1917; and of the *Elmhurst Hymnal* edited by a committee with Paul N. Crusius as chairman in 1921; was accompanied in each case by the express desire to preserve as much as possible of the German heritage of hymns and tunes. All three of them carry translations of German hymns into English by Julius H. Horstmann, Rudolph A. John, J. Christian Hansen, and others. These men, notably Horstmann, editor of the *Evangelical Herald*, have done an incalculable service in making it possible to carry over the messages of stirring hymns like "The Work Is Thine, O Christ, Our Lord" from German into English.

A generation earlier, Walter Rauschenbusch and others were making it possible for the German-speaking people in the United

States to share the spirit of the popular gospel hymns. Some of the translations were not good, but in the case of at least one hymn, "Brightly Beams Our Father's Mercy," Rauschenbusch produced a German translation that is immeasurably superior to the English original.

The wonder is that it was possible to keep the young people's work continuing in German as long as it did. The work had been conducted, on a local level only, by the organization of various types of young people's societies. Christian Endeavor societies, conducted in German, were introduced not later than the nineties. They had an ardent advocate in the Reverend G. Berner of Buffalo, who published a German paper for them, and also a hymnal with many of the translations from the English that we have mentioned. These societies either disappeared or shifted to the use of the English language.

Youth Work

The General Conference in 1901 authorized the district- and synod-wide organization of young people's societies under the name of the *Jugendbund*.

The organization of the *Jugendbund* was effected on September 18, 1902. The Reverend Henry Katterjohn, president, made effective use of statistics in his report to the General Conference of 1909. "During the past quadrennium alone," he wrote, "50,842 young people were confirmed but the *Jugendbund* has a membership of only 30,892."

The *Jugendbund*, though never reaching the goal set for it, increased in membership and in directed activity. Regional groups took over certain responsibilities. In 1913 the Ann Arbor group undertook to pay the salary of Missionary Frederick A. Goetsch; Ohio supported a medical mission in India; Cincinnati gave $500 for the new building at Elmhurst.

In 1913 the name of the *Jugendbund* was changed to the Evangelical League. The first report in English was submitted to the General Conference of 1921. Paul G. Moritz, president, reported $38,927 raised for the Memorial Library of Elmhurst College. In that year, General Conference brought the League, along with the Brotherhood and the Women's Union, into the Evangelical Federated Activities, with the Reverend H. L. Streich as executive secretary. The next General Conference (1925) accepted the recommendation that the League enter into joint relationship with the Board of Religious Education to establish a young people's office. This plan proved very satisfactory under the new executive secretary, the Reverend O. P. Schroerluke. The College Student Department was maintaining contact with 1,800 students in over one hundred colleges. Among special projects were a book fund for Eden Seminary and a student chapel and center at the University of Missouri.

The Evangelical Brotherhood

The Evangelical Brotherhood was organized in 1913 at the General Conference in Louisville. The initiative was given by the district federations of Indiana and Ohio, which existed prior to the national organization. Good progress was made in organizing local brotherhoods and federations by the efforts of the officers. But a full-time executive secretary was needed. The General Conference of 1921 met this need part of the way by federating the activities of the Brotherhood, the Evangelical League, and the Women's Union under H. L. Streich as executive secretary. From then on, the Brotherhood grew in number of local societies from 279 in 1921 to 496 in 1933.

The activities of the Brotherhood included the sponsoring of men's retreats, celebrating Evangelical Day and similar occasions, calling for denominational loyalty, carrying on boys' work, supporting theological students at Elmhurst and Eden, encouraging family devotions, and assisting "undershepherd service." The most ambitious project was to pay for the purchase of a splendid piece of property conveniently located in St. Louis—a 26-room mansion on a lot, 185 x 280 feet, intended to house the executive offices of the Synod and therefore called Synod House.

The report of the Brotherhood for 1933 included this item: "We gladly call attention to the recently organized Reformed Churchmen's League. . . . We eagerly look forward to closer relations with the Churchmen's League, pending our proposed merger."

The Women's Union

Although they were the most numerous and most active of all societies in the Evangelical Synod, the women's societies (known by various names) were the last to organize on a synod-wide basis. A committee was appointed in 1919 to work out plans for the first convention, which was held at the Price Hill Church, Cincinnati in June, 1921.

This convention, attended by about 260 representatives, adopted a constitution and elected officers, whose installation was deferred until after the General Conference had approved the organization.

The growth of the Women's Union was phenomenal. No other organization within the Synod ever grew so rapidly. In 1921 only Cincinnati, St. Louis, and Evansville had city-wide unions, and only the New York District had a federation. In 1933 there were 43 local federations, 11 district unions, and 1,429 societies with a membership of 78,739. The gifts of the Union to designated causes within the Synod amounted to $150,621.73 between 1929 and 1933. The projects for 1934 were the Synod Pension Fund, the training of nurses and evangelists in Honduras, and the support of an Ozark worker.

The last convention reported, at Detroit in 1929, was attended by about two thousand delegates and visitors. It was the largest convention ever held by any group in the Evangelical Synod.

Home Missions

Home mission work received a new impulse when the Reverend W. L. Bretz, treasurer of the Board, accepted the office of Executive Secretary for Home Missions in 1919. New interest was created in the problems of home missions and their fundamental importance was better recognized through a number of mission institutes. The great problems were still lack of available men and lack of money necessary to build chapels or small churches.

The frontiers were still, as before, the Rocky Mountain states, the Pacific Coast, and the South.

A new source of help for the struggling mission churches was found in the activity of "big brother" churches that took the little mission brothers under their wings.

Impressive evidence of progress is obtained by a comparison of amounts spent on home mission work between 1917 and 1927:

1917	$41,018.98	1924	$83,061.49
1918	44,698.42	1925	87,842.21
1919	69,535.20	1926	117,106.07
1922	81,373.02	1927	119,085.69

Bretz resigned in February, 1931, and was succeeded by the Reverend John Jacob Braun. The office was moved to the synodical headquarters in Eden Publishing House, St. Louis. This made contacts easier with the Church Extension Fund Board, which was involved continually with the problems of home mission churches.

Valuable work has been done since 1919 by field superintendents, working in cooperation with the executive secretary. In the mission districts the president was field superintendent. Both Dr. Braun and the Reverend Charles Enders did invaluable work in organizing churches; Enders in the Detroit area and Braun in Chicago.

Special Home Mission Projects

THE SEAMEN'S MISSION

The Immigrant and Seamen's Mission continued to be a special work, regarded as well worthwhile. Since World War I, to be sure, Baltimore had ceased to be a port of entrance for immigrants. The mission could, therefore, no longer serve immigrants directly. It found a field of work, however, among the crews of German freighters and, through regular visits to the Marine Hospital, made contacts with seamen of all countries. The Reverend F. A. Giese was in charge of the work of the Immigrant and Seamen's Mission after the death of the Reverend Otto Apitz in October, 1918.

CAROLINE MISSION

In an underprivileged area in St. Louis, not far from the publishing house, Eden Seminary students surveyed the neighborhood's great needs and started a Sunday school, boys' and girls' clubs, and other features of what was once known as a "settlement." This was the beginning of the Caroline Mission, named for Mrs. Caroline Schultz, whose two sons gave the house that became the first permanent unit of the enterprise. Here a wide and varied service has been rendered to people of different races whose great common need included the nourishment of both body and soul. Here the principles of the social application of Christianity have been expressed and implemented in continued day-and-night service.

THE OZARKS

A special work that belongs with peculiar appropriateness to the Evangelical Synod is the work in the Ozarks. The Ozarks were almost completely neglected by other denominations when the Reverend Paul A. Wobus began to look over the territory in the first half of the 1920's. In October, 1925 he began to hold services once a month at Lesterville, but was unable to follow up the work himself. The result was that a small sectarian group took over.

A year later, better success attended the work at Stone Hill. The Evangelical Women's Union offered to raise $3,000 for a resident worker, and the Board of Home Missions voted to place a resident pastor in the Ozarks. In October, 1927 Louise Backer and Laura Gillman came to work at Bunker. Miss Backer died in 1929, and Miss Gillman left to study at Oakwood.

Meanwhile, Zenith F. Young, a veteran home mission worker in the Ozarks, had begun his resident ministry at Bunker. As a result of his work, community churches were organized at Bunker (November, 1928) and at Bixby (June, 1929). The Shannondale Ozark Center was established at Gladden, Missouri with the aid of $1,500 in special gifts. The Reverend Vincent W. Bucher has served there as pastor and director for more than a quarter of a century.

BILOXI, MISSISSIPPI

In Biloxi the Reverend Oscar Nussmann, assisted by Mrs. William F. McDonnell, began work among the people living in the Back Bay region under unspeakably unsanitary conditions. Their main effort was to educate the people to healthier standards of living and to train them in the way of Christian character. When, after four years of devoted effort, Nussmann left Biloxi, in 1933, and the Reverend Fred J. Mehrtens was placed temporarily in charge, money was still badly needed for a building program.

MADELINE ISLAND

Another project at the other end of the country is Madeline Island, near the Wisconsin shore of Lake Superior. It is a rather nice summer resort, which calls for one kind of service, and the year-round home of some four hundred islanders with no church of their own. The Women's Union felt it well worth their efforts to contribute toward a new parsonage on the island.

Church Extension

Closely associated with the work of the home missionary is the Church Extension Fund, founded in 1889 for the purpose of making loans available at low rates of interest to churches in need of such assistance. In the quadrennium ending with 1933, the Fund had loaned $224,548.92, while it conducted its business at an amazingly low cost of about $800 a year.

Sunday Schools

In 1892 the General Conference called upon the districts to encourage the organization of Sunday school associations that might later unite to form a general association. Three years later the Synod resolved to name a Sunday school committee, which consisted of the Reverends S. Kruse, H. Rahn, and M. Schroedel. This committee, reporting in 1897, recommended the appointment of a Sunday school committee in each district. The Synod continued to stress the importance of systematic training for Sunday school teachers. The General Conference of 1913 combined the hitherto separate school (parochial school) and Sunday school boards.

On May 15, 1915 the Reverend Theodore Mayer became the General Secretary of the Board of Religious Education, with an office in Eden Publishing House. The amount of work that he set in motion and kept under control was enormous.

His first objective was what the General Conference had already emphasized—teacher training. Particular efforts were made to introduce Mrs. Emma K. Bomhard's excellent manual, *Apt to Teach,* and to secure subscriptions for *The Evangelical*

Teacher. The greatest success attended the opening of the Elmhurst Summer Training School in 1914. The school continued to meet annually at Elmhurst, becoming so popular eventually that it was impossible to take care of all students in one session. Similar schools were organized at Waveland, Mississippi; Camp Rose, California; and other places.

The first School of Methods was conducted in Buffalo in the winter of 1916. The enrollment was 475. Similar schools were planned in other large cities.

The first National Sunday School Convention, held in conjunction with the Evangelical League in the summer of 1916 in Cleveland, was attended by 1,881. The second was held in Chicago in 1919 and was also well attended.

A beautiful lake-front property on Lake Erie was acquired at Dunkirk, New York, and gradually developed into an attractive park with meeting halls, dining hall, and cabins, suitable for summer schools, retreats, camps, and the like.

Mayer, who had blazed a pioneer's trail in this work, beginning in 1921, was succeeded by the Reverend C. J. Keppel who, like his predecessor, gave all that he had to what he felt was the greatest responsibility in the world—the task of religious education. He, in turn, was succeeded by his brother Alvin, who combined the practical training and special knowledge of a successful schoolman with consecrated devotion to the work of religious education.

Foreign Missions

In 1904 the retirement of the founder of our India mission, the venerable Oscar Lohr, may be said to mark the beginning of a new stage of foreign mission enterprise in the Evangelical Synod. In that year, the Reverend E. Schmidt, secretary of the mission board, made a lengthy visitation that gave the Board a better insight into many problems and resulted in more effective cooperation. A mission to reach the secluded Indian wives had been opened at Raipur in 1900, and Chandkuri Leper Hospital had been founded by the Reverend Karl W. Nottrott in 1897. W. H. P. Anderson continued the work among the lepers. Schools were established wherever possible, at first only on the grade school level, but they set a new standard of efficiency for India. The educational policy of the mission looked beyond the most elementary needs, however, toward the training of native teachers and preachers. In 1898 Jacob Gass founded the theological school at Raipur, which has produced a small but devoted group of ordained men and numerous catechists and teachers. The first men ordained (in 1920) were the Reverends Ramnath Bajpai, P. Gottlieb, and Yishu Prakash. In 1911 Dr. Gass opened St. Paul's High School in Raipur, to which has been added Salem Girls' School, also in Raipur. New stations were opened at Mahasamund in 1907 and at Sakti in 1909.

World War I caused a temporary setback in the operations of the mission, since no new missionaries were permitted to enter India. It was just after the war, before the restrictions on India had been lifted, that the attention of the Board was directed to a new field—Honduras. After careful investigation, the Board concluded that it was God's will that the Synod should take over this work. The Reverend H. A. Dewald, an experienced missionary, was the first to be sent, in 1920. He was followed, the next year, by the Reverend and Mrs. Harold N. Auler, Sr. and Anna D. Bechtold. They began their work in San Pedro Sula, and were soon followed by others. In 1924 there were ten people working in our Honduras mission and twenty-nine in India. As in India, the founding of schools was the most important activity of the Honduras mission at the start, but always the missionaries kept looking for new opportunities to set up preaching missions.

In 1923 Timothy Lehmann, long an active member of the Board, made the second visitation to India. Schmidt, who had been mission secretary for nearly a quarter of a century, had resigned and his place was taken by the Reverend Paul A. Menzel of Washington, D. C.

A seventh station in India was opened in 1923 at Khariar. In 1924 a Bible training school for women was opened by Mrs. Helen Enslin Sueger and Mrs. Almeta Twente. It is worth noting also that the budget for missions was rising to meet the new opportunities.

In the four years ending in 1925, $443,508.29 was spent on India and Honduras. In the next four years, the amount was $585,151.79. To this must be added a considerable sum that came by voluntary gifts. Both in India and Honduras there are school buildings, clinics, hospitals, dormitories, and other buildings, erected as memorials by American friends of the mission.

In 1929 the first medical station was founded at Tilda in our India mission—the beginning of our expanding service of mercy. In 1933 there were in service in India ten ordained men, two physicians, three nurses and 17 other ladies, including the wives of missionaries, who commonly assumed special responsibilities— a total of 32. To this would have to be added more than 200 native catechists and teachers. In Honduras there were twelve missionaries preaching, teaching, and conducting two boarding schools and a valuable health service.

Pension and Relief

In the 1850's provisions for the widows of pastors of the *Kirchenverein* were made on the basis of contributions (assessments) from the ministers. One such plan was the Five Dollar Plan, each member paying an assessment of five dollars upon the death of a member pastor. This was continued on a voluntary basis. In 1874 the General Conference created a fund for "invalid" pastors, that is, for pastors incapacitated for holding regular positions, and in 1883 a fund for the support of widows and orphans. In 1910 all provisions for pension and relief were combined in the Pension and Relief Fund. A contribution of five dollars every three months by the minister or teacher who was a member, entitled him to a retirement pension at age seventy or after forty-three years of service, or relief when necessary, and provision for his widow and children. Disability pension was granted according to the number of years of membership in the fund, which was augmented by contributions from the Synod and by gifts.

Benevolent Institutions

Benevolent institutions and works were an important form of Christian service which the denomination had wisely left to local and district initiative. The Conference in 1901 deemed it wise, however, in view of the spread of the deaconess movement, to appoint a committee to draw up plans for the coordination of deaconess work and other charities with the purpose of giving recognition and encouragement to the work. The committee recommended that the Deaconess Hospital in St. Louis should be recognized as the mother-house of the Evangelical diaconate (others were later given equal status), and that the Board for Benevolent Institutions should be created. This board reported regularly to the General Conference the information it was able to gather from deaconess hospitals, children's homes, homes for the aged, and similar institutions, but little progress seems to have been made toward effective coordination. In 1921 the Board for Christian Service replaced the older board; four years later it had succeeded in organizing a Federation of Evangelical Charities, and, in cooperation with the Seminary Board and other agencies, had founded Oakwood Institute in Cincinnati as a training school for Christian workers. The training school was opened in 1923 under the presidency of the Reverend F. C. Kuether; by 1929 seventeen students had qualified for the diploma, given at the end of a three-year course. The depression, however, reduced the enrollment as well as the demand for graduates trained in church work, and the school was closed in 1933.

Christianity and Social Problems

Practical Christianity, which had hitherto expressed itself mainly through individual or institutional concern for the poor, the sick, the orphans, and the aged, found a new outlet in the early 1900's. At the General Conference of 1917 the newly created Commission for National Welfare, headed by the Reverends J. G. Stilli, J. Goebel, and F. Weber, reported that it had brought Professor Walter Rauschenbusch to Eden Seminary for a lecture on social issues; published pertinent articles in the *Evangelical Herald*; and contributed articles to the *Evangelical Teacher* (the official church school teachers' manual) on the social application of the church school lessons. It received the approval of the General Conference, which suggested that the name be changed to Commission on Christianity and Social Problems. The commission urged in 1925 the adoption of a declaration in favor of the outlawry of war and of the "Social Ideals of the Churches" as enunciated by the Federal Council of Churches. In 1933 it proposed an earnest study of the question whether it would be wise to repeal the Prohibition Amendment.

We began this survey of the Evangelical Synod from 1866 to 1934 with Adolph Baltzer as president up to his death in 1880. His successors were: Karl Siebenpfeiffer (1880-82), John Zimmermann (1882-1901), Jacob Pister (1901-14), John Baltzer (1914-29), C. W. Locher (1929-34), Paul Press (1934). It is worth noting that the first four had served as vice-president before becoming president. The nineteen years during which Zimmermann was president were marked by a growth in which the Synod more than doubled in number of pastors, churches, and members. During most of the 1880's the Synod was still using only the German language, but after 1889 the use of English increased steadily.

In the thirteen years (1901-14) while Pister was president, new trends were strongly in evidence. English gained further recognition in 1901, when the English Literary Committee was added to the list of standing committees. Its first members were: Dr. J. U. Schneider, the Reverend C. G. Haas, and the Reverend Theophil W. Mueller. It was at this time also that the publication of the *Messenger of Peace* was authorized. In 1905 Pister announced in his report to the General Conference that he had appointed the Reverend H. Noehren as the Synod's representative on the executive committee to plan for the first meeting of the National Federation of Churches and Christian Workers. The General Conference approved this action and appointed the Reverends H. Noehren, John Baltzer, Th. F. Bode, Paul A. Menzel, and W. Schaefer as the Synod's representatives at the first meeting of the National Federation of Churches and Christian Workers, to be held in New York on November 15, 1905. The Evangelical Synod thereby became one of the charter members of the Federal Council of Churches of Christ in America.

When Pister died (of a broken heart, many said) not long after the outbreak of World War I, he was succeeded by John Baltzer, one of the three minister sons of Adolph Baltzer. John Baltzer, a product of the Evangelical Synod, born in Missouri and educated at Elmhurst and Eden, had already won recognition as eminent preacher, able administrator, and dynamic leader. With firmness and tact he steered the course of the Synod through the most difficult years in its history, the years 1917 to 1919, when the United States was in the war. "There were many days," he said later, "when only the grace of God and our Lord's guidance kept us from being crushed to the wall. We lived through it. We prayed through it. We labored through it. Thanks be to the Lord."

The General Conference of 1917 appointed a War Welfare Commission to minister to the spiritual and material needs of 25,000 Evangelical young men in the armed services. The Reverend Reinhold Niebuhr and others rendered notable service in this work. After the war, President Baltzer and the Reverend Henry Bode (treasurer of the Synod) took the lead in organizing synod-wide assistance for victims of the war in Germany.

Two actions taken by the General Conference during John Baltzer's period in office may be understood as typical of the new outlook and outreach of the postwar years. In 1925 the General Conference, on the recommendation of the Commission on Christianity and Social Problems, adopted a resolution in favor of outlawing war, drawn up originally by a group including Sherwood Eddy, Kirby Page, John Haynes Holmes, F. Ernest Johnson, Bishop Paul Jones, Reinhold Niebuhr, and Charles Clayton Morrison.

In 1927 the General Conference, at a special meeting held at Chicago (St. Paul's Church), dropped the word German from the name of the Evangelical Synod of North America.

President Baltzer retired in 1929. His report to the General Conference was his apologia and his valediction. "Since 1921," he says, "the keel of our synodical ship steered straight forward in a course that was necessary for her to take. Her leaders realized that, if we would continue as a church, our course must now steer forward unconcerned as to language or lineage. We knew . . . it must be our duty to hold the growing generation that knew little or nothing about the German language, the German heritage of our parents and our own. . . . And today, for the first time in the history of the Evangelical Synod of North America, the president of the Synod reads his report to the General Conference in the language of the country."

PART THREE

The Evangelical and Reformed Church

11

Journey into Union

How DID THESE TWO CHURCHES, the Evangelical Synod and the Reformed Church, each having independently arrived at denominational maturity, effect such contacts that within a period of five years they agreed to surrender their separate existences to emerge as a new denomination? The story reads like the reunion of two lost brothers who, having left their father's house and established their separate homes in a foreign land, in almost casual manner discover their common heritage and are reunited in the old family fellowship. Various factors, historical and geographical, had kept them apart. As German immigrant churches in widely separated areas they had become engrossed in the task of maintaining their peculiar ecumenical tradition, as gradually each grew into full denominational stature.

The union commitments of both the Reformed Church and the Evangelical Synod in 1929 occurred in the midst of the ecumenical movement of the first half of the century—midway between the World Missionary Conference at Edinburgh in 1910 and the founding of the World Council of Churches at Amsterdam in 1948. Edinburgh was followed by the Stockholm Conference on Life and Work (1925), the World Conference on

Faith and Order at Lausanne (1927), and the Jerusalem Conference (1928)—all prophetically witnessing to a deeper conception of the unitive nature of the Christian church and to its further relevance in the relations of Christian denominations to each other. Nor was this a vain witness in the midst of a total of ninety-one plans of union and reunion advanced between 1907 and 1952.

On the American scene this witness became manifest in such movements as those of the Federal Council of Churches of Christ founded in 1908 and the Interchurch World Movement of North America begun in 1918, as well as in the united advances in the fields of Christian stewardship, Christian education, and home and foreign missions. These movements and advances challenged American churches to practical cooperation, and in all these our two churches participated.

Both churches, in the midst of denominational consolidation but striving to maintain their unitive traditions, had reached a decisive stage toward the end of the first quarter of the twentieth century. How would they respond to the ecumenical urgencies of the new day?

The denominational trend of the Evangelical Synod had been accompanied by a reluctance to abandon landmarks dear to the fathers. Indeed, it was not until 1925 that the president's report to the Evangelical Synod was first read in English. Yet both young and old were loyally committed to the union principle which in the past had been honored more by pious affirmation than by practical enactments. A new day was dawning, heralded by the rise of a younger and more vocal generation less fearful than its fathers that the Americanization of the church would involve a loss of its Evangelical tradition. Thus, in considering a change of name (1925) in which the word German would be dropped, overtures from various districts proposed such variations as The Church of the Evangelical Union in America or

The United Evangelical Church in America. One district was pledged to "any name which would clearly express the union position." In more venturesome spirit the General Conference of 1925 admonished its officers to "enter into negotiations with kindred communions, looking toward organic union."

The enthusiastic reports of Samuel D. Press, President of Eden Theological Seminary, and John Baltzer, President General of the Evangelical Synod, on their visit to Stockholm sharpened the ecumenical focus and brought expressions from various districts that the "ecumenical spirit should move from mere statements of principle to their realization." The Southern District overtured the General Conference of 1927 "to approach some other communion which in their opinion is nearest us in doctrine and polity." Indiana was looking toward cooperation through federation and eventual union with some other denomination, and North Illinois expressed the desire "to realize the coveted unity in the spirit for which our church has ever stood."

Responding to the challenge of such union interest, President Baltzer in 1927 proclaimed, as a guiding principle to be observed: "Not the personality of Luther nor that of Calvin, but only the personality of Christ—and 'he liveth'—may, can, and will give to all the basis of union in spirit." The full story of these developments, which cannot be told here, would be incomplete without reference to the stirring editorial utterances of Julius H. Horstmann in the *Evangelical Herald*. Dr. Horstmann summarized, as it were, his previous arguments with the plea that in view of the historical position of the Synod it was "becoming necessary to propose some practical project in this [union] direction if it would not lay itself open to the charge of insincerity."

In the meantime, events were moving toward practical realization. Unofficial meetings of Evangelical and Reformed pastors were being held in such widely separated areas as Baltimore,

Maryland (1927) and Appleton, Wisconsin (1928). On various occasions leading churchmen of both denominations were brought into contact with each other. Philip Vollmer and George W. Richards were particularly active in these relations —the latter delivering a series of addresses at the district conferences of 1928.

It was no unwelcome event when President Baltzer announced at the Conference of 1929 that he had appointed a Commission on Closer Relations with Other Church Bodies: H. Richard Niebuhr, chairman; Julius H. Horstmann, F. Frankenfeld, Louis W. Goebel, John Baltzer; together with three laymen: J. C. Fischer, W. F. Hazlebeck, and John W. Mueller. The commission had entered into union negotiations with the Reformed Church in the United States and the United Brethren in Christ. Indeed, it had moved with such dispatch that a merger with these churches seemed assured. A tripartite Plan of Union had been submitted to the districts, all of which, "true to the principles which the founders laid down when they sought to bridge the divisions between the branches of the church of Christ," had welcomed the step taken by the commission. The almost unanimous acceptance of the union resolutions, which provided for the detailed enactment of the union, was greeted with such "enthusiastic applause as veteran members of the Synod said they had never before heard in that body." "After the applause," continued the official report of the proceedings, "the delegates rose and fervently sang the Doxology."

The Reformed Church had similarly experienced a renewed commitment to its ecumenical heritage. There was hardly a period in its history, as we have seen, in which it had not demonstrated its ecumenical tradition by union conversations with some other denomination. The discussions with the Evangelical Synod climaxed an illustrious train of such negotiations. The Reformed Commission on Closer Union consisted of: Drs.

George W. Richards, Charles E. Miller, A. E. Dahlmann, Jacob C. Leonard, and Allen R. Bartholomew; with Messrs. E. L. Coblentz, D. J. Snyder, Reuben J. Butz, and E. H. Marcus as lay members.

In the midst of the ecumenical stirrings of the day, the Reformed Church, like the Evangelical Synod, was engaged in establishing a new constitutional order. In the course of these deliberations the denominational consciousness was being challenged by wider conceptions of the church. It was contended that the traditional idea of the church as an institution "for the maintenance of truth and order" was derived from the controversial period of the Reformation, whereas, essentially, the church is directed toward the establishment of the kingdom of God on earth. It is therefore not, in the first place, an objective institution, but a fellowship of believers in Christ, where the emphasis is "upon individuals, persons, men, women, and children, who are moved by the Spirit of Christ." Whereas the Evangelical Synod was committed to the Augsburg Confession and the Lutheran and Heidelberg Catechisms, the Reformed Church had identified itself with exclusive subscription to the Heidelberg Catechism as the authoritative means to insure the maintenance of truth and order. It was now urged that a wider noninstitutional conception of the church would be in accord with "those things which are vital" and related more directly to the ideals of the kingdom.

A Plan of Union Emerges

With emphases such as these the way was broadened for the union movement. In 1926 the Reformed Commission on Closer Union reported overtures from the Philadelphia Classis and the Classis of North Carolina looking toward union with the Presbyterian Church in the United States of America and the Reformed Church in America. More general petitions for promoting church union and for effecting a closer union with the Presbyterian family of churches had also been revived. However, since neither the Presbyterian Church nor the Reformed Church in America was prepared to begin negotiations, the Commission on Closer Relations and Church Union under the chairmanship of George W. Richards began to confer with the United Brethren in Christ. The attendance at the meetings of representatives of the Evangelical Church (a union in 1922 of the United Evangelical Church and the Evangelical Association), which had been in contact with the United Brethren, made it appear for a moment as though the prospective union would be enlarged. But the representatives of the Evangelical Church—which later merged with the United Brethren—were not ready at this stage to continue discussions and withdrew from the negotiations.

It was at this point (July, 1928) that the representatives of the commission on union appointed by Baltzer began to participate in the deliberations of the already existing joint commissions of the Reformed Church and the United Brethren. In arduous and loyal cooperation this three-fold Joint Committee prepared a Plan of Union which was referred for consideration and action to the supreme judicatories of the three churches, all three of which convened in 1929. Hopes ran high that a new church under the name of The United Church in America would emerge. The Reformed Church was particularly hopeful for reunion with the United Brethren, since the differences which caused their division in the early 1800's had long since been overcome.

Although the United Brethren acted favorably upon the plan as containing initial steps for the ultimate union, insuperable difficulties prevented their further participation in the discussions. The plan was also approved by the General Synod of the Reformed Church, and the classes were invited to offer suggestions and amendments; but it did not elicit the enthusiastic response that marked its reception by the Evangelical Synod. There still prevailed the hope that the United Brethren, the Reformed Church in America, and the Presbyterian Church in the United States of America could be included. Indeed, a brief interruption of negotiations with the Evangelical Synod occurred in order to permit a final effort to effect relations with the other bodies. When this did not materialize, negotiations with the Evangelical Synod were reopened (February, 1932) and, by the time the two bodies met again (the Reformed Church in 1932 and the Evangelical Synod in 1933), a final plan of union had been formally and unanimously approved by the joint commissions. The plan maintained that "each denomination exists not for itself but as an agency for the advancement of the kingdom of God" and that in the proposed union "the essential principles of the Christian faith and life, common to all, would not only be conserved but would also be more effectually applied" toward that end.

In the history of church unions and as a study in ecumenics this Plan of Union is a unique document. Its brief preamble and twelve short articles are as significant for what is omitted as for what is said. Could the premise of Christian union have been stated more succinctly than it was in the preamble: "Under the conviction that they are in agreement on the essential doctrines of the Christian faith and on the ideals of the Christian life as contained in the Old and New Testaments and as defined in their respective standards of doctrine, [the two churches] do hereby declare their desire to be united in one body." The premise subordinated institutional interests to the affirmations of faith, since a faith strong enough to call for union would find the way to overcome the forms that divide. The sister churches of the Protestant Reformation had long been divided by doctrinal differences in the interpretation and espousal of their common heritage. Without defining or establishing a consensus of beliefs or the extent of agreement or disagreement, a unity in spirit was affirmed as a sufficient basis for the steps now to be ventured. The Plan of Union thus lost the aspects of a contractual merger and was thrown into the area of faith.

The ensuing twelve articles were designed to provide an operational basis to bridge the gap between the prevailing forms and usages and the new emerging structure to be more closely defined in the forthcoming constitution. The document avoided any semblance of constitutional suggestions as to how the supreme judicatory and the various boards and agencies of the two churches were to be reorganized, and how or even whether their respective rights and privileges were to be preserved. Similarly the plan did not presume to establish a statement of fundamental beliefs, but merely acknowledged and accepted "the historical confessions of the two churches as the doctrinal basis of union." Furthermore, the custom of each congregation prior to the union was not to be abrogated, and assurance was granted that there should be no interference with the freedom of worship which was being enjoyed by the negotiating churches. There was no mistaking the manner in which the union plan was accepted as a means to provide for the continued functioning of each church during the interim period when new forms would be devised in which united devotion to the cause of the kingdom could freely express itself.

Approved by unanimous vote of the Reformed Synod of 1932, the Plan of Union, according to Reformed procedure, was sent to the classes for their approval. By the time that the Evangelical Synod met in 1933 the necessary majority of the fifty-eight classes had declared their approval, so that, since more than the requisite number of districts had also expressed their approval, the way was clear for the final consummation of the union at the historic meeting in Cleveland on the night of June 26, 1934.

The Historic Day

On the morning of that eventful day, the two denominations concluded their individual historical existences in final conference sessions—the Reformed Church in the Eighth Reformed Church and the Evangelical Synod in Zion's Church, several blocks away. A prophetic spirit—not without nostalgic undertones and a mixture of holy longings, joyful anticipations, perplexity and fear—hovered over both assemblages. The spiritual tone for these meetings was set by a final admonition: "It is obvious that the proposed union can be consummated only on the basis of mutual confidence and an abiding faith in the guidance of the Spirit of the living God." "If our action today," reported President Paul Press of the Evangelical Synod, "shall be in accord with the will of God, we will not be chiefly interested in the mechanics of the merger. We must not be concerned about technical difficulties which may disturb us. God forbid that we should stoop to means and methods to gain an advantage. Principally, we enter into a spiritual union with the Reformed Church, and if our approach is made on the basis of the spiritual implications of the merger we need not become agitated about possible technical difficulties. As we have been guided by the Spirit of God in the development of the negotiations, so will we be directed by the same Spirit into the correct organizational adjustments which will become necessary."

Echoing this attitude, F. William Leich, in a sermon preached on Ephesians 5: 25-27 in the Reformed assemblage, warned: "Christianity has ever been in danger of hardening about organization, polity, buildings, rituals, dogmas. . . . To free ourselves from such bondage or to maintain the freedom we have achieved requires more than ordinary courage . . . and a more sacrificial spirit than a comfortable age produces." Quoting Forsyth he continued, " 'The great issue within Christianity is not between systems and doxies, but a battle for the holy as the one all-inclusive gift of Christ.' " True union, Leich seems to say, is built on faith and is an act of faith, "which means more than mere intellectual assent, more than a certain knowledge. It denotes a practical positive relation and attitude of genuine self-committal to a divine person, which the Heidelberg Catechism describes as a hearty trust."

The concluding act of the Reformed Church, before it passed out of existence as a corporate body, occurred when the members of Synod, gathering in the afternoon at the chancel of the Pilgrim Congregational Church (almost as an omen of a future development), united in confessing their faith through the Apostles' Creed, praying the Lord's Prayer, and singing the Doxology. From this service of worship the members of the Reformed fellowship proceeded to the joint meeting that followed.

At seven o'clock on the evening of this day, the delegates of the two conferences—65 ministers and an equal number of laymen representing 21 districts of the Evangelical Synod, and 120 ministers and 93 elders representing 56 of the 58 classes of the Reformed Church—came from opposite directions to meet at the door of Zion's Evangelical Church. Then in pairs they entered the sanctuary where in joint session and by joint resolution they declared that the union of the churches had been duly effected. The presidents of the churches and the chairmen of the committees on union, Paul Press and Louis W. Goebel for the Evangelical Synod and Henry J. Christman and George W. Richards for the Reformed Church, led the uniting processions and presided over the final formal enactments. As if testifying that what had transpired was more than the fulfillment of a purely historical event, delegates, representatives, and friends of the uniting churches together partook of the Lord's Supper with ministers of both churches distributing the elements. Two streams of faith, long divided by obstacles set by man, had converged in the birth of a new denomination—the Evangelical and Reformed Church.

Perhaps no one outside the immediate circle of the new church interpreted the profound meaning of this union for American Protestantism as a whole so well as Samuel M. Cavert, General Secretary of the Federal Council of Churches of Christ, who, in a tribute to the union, testified:

> This union . . . has a far-reaching significance that transcends that of . . . other unions of the twentieth century. . . . The two uniting churches *have entered upon it in such a spirit of complete mutual trust and respect that you have not had to define all the formal terms of agreement in advance.* You have been willing to *unite,* and to work out the details of union afterwards in your united fellowship. You have become a single church without having drafted your constitution, without having set up a new doctrinal formula, without having decided how your various agencies are to be combined. You have not allowed any minor point of organization or of definition to obscure your unity of spirit and faith, or to become a barrier in your advance to a new expression of that unity. Your decision to *unite* and to trust to the future for the working out of the implications of the union sets a new precedent in the history of American churches.

The Christian Century commented: "If the spirit which animated this union should become contagious and sweep across the world we should witness a vast crumbling of denominational walls."

Descending from the mountaintop experience of this union service the first General Synod of the new church convened the following morning to elect for its first president, George W. Richards, the stalwart proponent of many union movements in his day, and for its vice-president, Louis W. Goebel, a no less ardent advocate of the union cause as exemplified in the Evangelical tradition. A more significant action, however, was the adoption of a number of carefully prepared resolutions which implemented the Plan of Union and paved the way for the further organic integration of a united program, and the appointment of an executive committee to promote the work of the church and to expedite the correlation and unification of the hitherto separate agencies and activities.

Reconciliation and Agreement

Thus was inaugurated a "reconstruction period"—in many respects the most critical years in the history of this church. The final constitution was not formally adopted until 1938; the intervening years witnessed the decline of loyalties to abiding traditions, destined to be reborn in a greater loyalty and a more dynamic witness to the Lord of the church. As a venture in faith each denomination, with many an individual, was confronted by the task of renewing a venerable historical tradition in terms of a more precious spiritual heritage. With new insights of the Spirit, denominational traditions succumbed to the transcending ecumenical witness of the kingdom so that the concept of church *merger* was supplanted by that of an organic union.

As a study in ecumenics the fashioning of a denominational constitution may belong to the less inspiring aspects of church union, for constitutions are not made in heaven. With much experience behind him, Richards could testify: "The church may make a constitution, but a constitution does not make a church." The first constitutional draft appeared in December, 1935; the lively discussions carried on throughout the church and recorded in the church papers and a mass of documents revolved mainly, and at times critically, around the questions of organization, doctrine, and worship.

Quite early in the union negotiations attention had been directed to widely differing types of organization and polity. Could the centralization in the Evangelical Synod be reconciled with the freedom amongst the Reformed, where boards were to a large degree autonomous in their own fields? The fear of a rising ecclesiastical hierarchy, denying traditional democratic customs, practices, and usages, was nurtured by comments in a Swiss Reformed paper that the union was effected "solely on the ground of practical considerations without previous clarification of the fundamental questions of doctrine and organic law." The proposed government of the church was opposed as being "not presbyterian, but hierarchical to the core," as setting up "a Congregational-Episcopal system," or as having been "borrowed from the Methodist Episcopal form of government." Such voices continued until 1938 and led Richards at one time to warn against "the dampening of ardor in Synod and Classes regarding the union." Undaunted, however, the hard-working Committee on Constitution continued its labors to weave together the strands of freedom and authority, and finally evolved a plan of government, described as essentially presbyterian but functionally congregational.

A second tension that required conciliation was grounded in differing emphases on liturgical and nonliturgical practices in worship. Although again challenging the leaders to a basic rethinking of the significance of historically derived forms— the wide variety of usages and practices prevailing in the congregations of each denomination "as formal in some as in Anglicanism and as free in others as among the Baptists"— the question of worship never became a serious subject of controversy. Indeed, one of the first acts of the Executive Committee was to authorize the preparation of a common hymnal and a common book of worship so that from the beginning the two groups would be able to sing and pray together—again a more spiritually conceived ecumenical procedure than to theologize and argue oneself into the unity of the Body of Christ.

The article on doctrine, accepting "the historical confessions of the two churches as the doctrinal basis of union," occasioned more incisive discussion. Obviously a statement was required in which the heritage of both churches would be more precisely expressed. A new formulation, in the nature of the case, would involve variation if not deviation from the prevailing forms in such a way as to raise questions of correct interpretation of the faith held by the fathers—and all this despite the fact that both bodies stood solidly together within the non-confessionalistic stream of the Protestant movement. A small group of dissentients, it should be added, were disturbed by the prospect of combining in one document a common acceptance of both Calvinistic and Lutheran standards of belief. From a perspective where the integrity of the Christian faith was premised on doctrinal purity, the question of reformulation presented formidable difficulties.

Let us note how some of these issues came to discussion with respect to the doctrinal paragraph in the constitutional draft of 1935, which stated: "The Scriptures of the Old and the New Testaments are recognized as the Word of God and the ultimate rule of Christian faith and practice. The doctrinal standards of the constituent churches are accepted as interpretive statements of the essential truth of evangelical (Protestant) Christianity as taught in the Holy Scriptures. In these statements of faith, ministers and members are allowed liberty of conscience whose final norm is the Word of God." Since the statement underwent various changes until it reached its present form, the discussion that ensued is a matter of historical interest as indicating how creedal loyalty was both respected and transcended. The genius of the Evangelical and Reformed Church is revealed by the manner in which its doctrinal position came to be formulated.

There were those who resented the relegation of the Heidelberg Catechism to a mere "footnote," designed purely to show the historical background of the two churches. The canonicity and inspiration of the Old and New Testaments as objective norms of Christian faith, it was contended, needed to be more precisely safeguarded. A more radical voice, as indicated above, emanated from a strict Calvinist minority, which had consistently opposed the union and now objected to the acceptance of Lutheran standards on an equal basis with the Reformed.

The more ecumenical view which prevailed was that "Christian life and salvation do not depend on our accepting a certain interpretation (Lutheran or Reformed) of the Scriptures." Indeed, historically, were not both churches essentially committed to a consensual acceptance of Lutheran and Reformed standards with liberty of interpretation according to the norms of Holy Scripture! This had made it possible, it was pointed out, for pastors of both churches, in common devotion to the essentials of the gospel, to teach the truths of salvation—one according to the Lutheran tradition, another according to the Reformed interpretation, and still another through reference exclusively to the Word of God. Even if a church might find it difficult to abandon its historical traditions, these heritages of the past would be most nobly preserved, not in the form of dogma, institutions, or forms of worship, but in spirit and in life and in the hearts and minds of a faithful community. The heritage of both churches was founded in a common Protestant tradition, established not in dogmatically formulated doctrine, polity, or ethical demands, but in the comprehension of the church as the fellowship of those who, committed to God in the Lord Jesus Christ, live by his mercy and power.

Thus both the Reformed Church (in its derivation from the "union" Church of the Palatinate) and the Evangelical Synod (in its derivation from the Church of the Evangelical Union) moved toward a new union in which Luther's Catechism, the Heidelberg Catechism, and the Augsburg Confession were "accepted as authoritative interpretations of the essential truth taught in the Holy Scriptures." Throughout, the sovereignty of the Word was maintained over the authority of the confessions, which were subject to the believers' interpretation "in accordance with the liberty of conscience inherent in the gospel." Although some of the quoted formulations are of a later day (the first revision occurred in 1942) their cast is presaged in the doctrinal statement embodied in the constitution, adopted by the General Synod in 1936 and referred to the districts and classes for approval or rejection. The adoption of the constitution was a slow process, affording the spectacle of a denomination functioning for a period of six years without constitution or bylaws. When, after wide freedom of discussion, it was approved by the lower judicatories, the constitution was formally adopted by the General Synod of the united church at Columbus, Ohio, in 1938, not becoming completely effective, however, until so declared in 1940 by the Synod at Lancaster, Pennsylvania.

Pending its final adoption, the consolidation of the national boards and agencies proceeded unabated. In 1934 Central Theological Seminary of the Reformed Church at Dayton, Ohio united with Eden Theological Seminary of the Evangelical Synod at Webster Groves, Missouri. The yearbooks of both churches were published jointly the same year. The united church was further strengthened, in 1936, by the consolidation of *The Evangelical Herald* (E), *The Reformed Church Messenger* (R), and *The Christian World* (R) into *The Messenger,* and the union of *Die Kirchenzeitung* (R) with *Der Friedensbote* (E)— unions which were happily described as "a practical form of the communion of saints."

This process of reconstruction, without finesse of reservation here and concession there, proceeded sometimes with adoption of new names and sometimes with combinations of existing names. Thus the Woman's Missionary Society (R) and the Evangelical Women's Union (E) became the Women's Guild. The Board of Home Missions and the Board of Foreign Missions were transformed respectively into the Board of National Missions and the Board of International Missions. The Board of Pensions and Relief (E) united with the Board of Ministerial Relief (R) to become the Board of Pensions and Relief.

When, therefore, after interminable and arduous labor, a more stately denominational structure had been created to provide for the functioning of the new denomination, there was general rejoicing that the united church was now formally constituted to carry on anew its ancient witness. Consistent with the spiritual nature of the union from the time of its inception, the prior question still persisted—whether any church or denomination assuming to represent the spirit of Christ is created by the skills, and is dependent upon the ingenuities, of man for the fulfillment of its mission. "Without the Christlike spirit," came the prophetic word from Richards, "no constitution will ever be effective; with that spirit one will need only a minimum of law for the administration of the affairs of the fellowship of men and women."

12

The New Witness—1940 to 1959

THE EVANGELICAL AND REFORMED CHURCH be-
came a fully established legal entity during the first business
session of the General Synod of 1940. It was the fourth General
Synod of this new church, and at that first session on Thursday,
June 20, President Goebel formally declared "the Constitution
and Bylaws . . . as adopted at the General Synod of Columbus,
Ohio, June, 1938, in effect as the basic law of the church; and . . .
further . . . that it supersedes in all respects the instrument under
which we have hitherto conducted the affairs of the Evangelical
and Reformed Church, that is, The Plan of Union."

Before that morning session recessed the Reverend Paul M.
Schroeder was authorized to go to Albany, New York to repre-
sent the church in proceedings toward legal incorporation under
the laws of the State of New York. Dr. Schroeder returned on
Saturday bearing the Certificate of Incorporation, which is dated
June 21, 1940.

It was a historically significant year for three constituencies
now united in the new church, and the General Synod of 1938
had anticipated this by authorizing appointment of a committee
on anniversaries. The observances were held in October, 1940,
marking the two hundred and fifteenth anniversary of the be-

ginnings of the former Reformed Church in the United States, the one hundredth anniversary of the beginnings of the former Evangelical Synod of North America, and the fiftieth anniversary of work among Hungarian Reformed people who had immigrated to this country.

Preserving thus a grateful remembrance of its European heritage, the Evangelical and Reformed Church, at last adequately equipped organizationally with Constitution, Bylaws, and a Certificate of Incorporation, moved forward to develop its faith and life and work in a process which President Goebel, with characteristic prescience, at that General Synod asserted would require "the necessity of a constant re-study of the whole diversified program of the church."

The following years were to be marked by institutional flexibility and by a dynamic responsiveness on the part of the church to a growing sense, not only of its own internal needs, but also of the needs of a world which was already being engulfed in catastrophic war and the processes of an equally catastrophic social upheaval made more so by its world-wide reach and its seemingly interminable projection. The new church, to justify its validity as a church of the Reformation tradition, had to demonstrate that it was not only a Reformed but also a reforming church, responding to the ever-changing needs of man and to the never-changing imperatives of the church's Lord.

Measurable Growth

There are *more* things, and more *important* things, which are not told by statistics than *are* told by them; but what statistics do tell is most easily told and is a good point of departure for evaluating the larger, deeper picture of an institution's development. Within these limitations, and as far as they will allow the story to be told, the following statistical data are offered. First is the year-by-year record of communicant membership and of giving for missions and benevolences at home and abroad and for the cause of wartime and postwar relief and rehabilitation.

Year	Membership	Apportionment	World Service
1940	655,366	$ 853,027	$ 44,139
1941	662,953	958,755	59,309
1942	665,920	1,057,163	142,321
1943	675,958	1,214,610	205,757
1944	689,780	1,320,130	282,711
1945	695,971	1,658,217	664,055
1946	708,282	1,724,695	1,195,398
1947	714,583	1,773,850	693,193
1948	718,635	2,008,438	840,164
1949	726,361	2,044,856	880,188
1950	735,941	2,080,869	594,668
1951	743,070	2,593,141	479,771
1952	752,144	2,675,857	492,145
1953	761,842	2,766,226	596,172
1954	774,277	3,354,580	633,075
1955	784,270	3,450,810	653,059
1956	794,047	3,557,600	749,046
1957	800,961	4,447,170	691,052
1958	807,280	4,511,545	686,050
1959	810,007	4,558,361	692,618

There has been substantial growth in communicant membership. In the period 1940-59 the population of the United States grew from 131,000,000 to 178,000,000—an increase of 36 per cent. During the same period the communicant membership of the Evangelical and Reformed Church increased 23.6 per cent. At first glance that would seem to indicate that the increase in communicant membership did not keep up with the increase in population, that, in other words, we were not holding our own.

It should be noted, however, that 90 per cent of Evangelical and Reformed churches and communicant membership is to be found in these thirteen states: New York, New Jersey, Pennsylvania, Ohio, Michigan, Indiana, Illinois, Iowa, Wisconsin, Minnesota, Nebraska, Kansas, and Missouri; that is, east of the Rocky Mountains to the New York-Connecticut line and north of the Mason-Dixon Line, the Ohio River and westward. The greatest gains in national population have been registered in Florida, Arizona, Nevada, and the west coast states. For the one census period 1940-50 the population gain in the thirteen states where almost all Evangelical and Reformed strength lies averaged only 9.5 per cent, while the communicant membership of Evangelical and Reformed churches in those states increased 12.3 per cent. Moreover, since communicant membership in the Evangelical and Reformed Church rarely includes those under thirteen years of age, usually beginning a year or two beyond that, the full impact of the biggest factor in national population increase—the "postwar babies"—will begin to be felt only in the early 1960's. It is evident that the church grew substantially in numbers since 1940.

An even more significant statistical picture will be found in a comparison of the budgets adopted by the General Synods of 1940 and 1959. Figures for 1959 are amplified by listing the Guaranteed Advances (paying schedule) for 1960 in the case of the educational institutions.

1940	Budget Items	1959
$504,200	International Missions	$1,100,000
442,818	National Missions	970,000
3,000	National Missions Building Fund	485,000
161,321	Pensions and Relief	735,000
94,650	Christian Education and Publication	360,000
42,183	Eden Theological Seminary	121,500
15,350	Lancaster Theological Seminary	98,300
60,000 {	Mission House Theological Seminary	45,000
	Lakeland College	49,225
76,000	Elmhurst College	80,916
25,000	Heidelberg College	62,206
15,000	Cedar Crest College	45,375

13,926	Catawba College	56,916
....	Ursinus College	50,916
....	Franklin and Marshall College	50,916
....	Hood College	47,416
....	Massanutten Academy	19,250
....	Mercersburg Academy	23,760
5,500	Churchmen's Brotherhood	8,000
*3,300	Women's Guild	2,000
5,000	Evangelism	48,500
5,000	Christian Social Action	65,000
8,000	Evangelical Synod Interest	....
50,000	Debt Liquidation	....
....	Stewardship	29,000
....	Higher Education (administration)	5,000
....	Church and Ministry	66,000
....	Health and Welfare Services	20,000
....	Historical Society	7,500
....	Subsidy—Full-time Synod Presidents	75,000
....	Synod Travel Equalization	5,500
**..........	Student Loans	90,000
....	Department of United Promotion	127,000
....	Bureau of Audio Visuals	80,000
....	Church Union Fund	130,000
....	Church Paper Subsidies and Board of Business Management (administration)	120,000
....	National Council of Churches	18,500
....	World Council of Churches	14,500
....	Alliance of Reformed Churches	3,800
....	Chaplains' Pensions	5,500
....	Ecumenical Travel Fund	15,000
....	Contingent Fund	50,000
***79,028	Administration Fund	175,000
	Add adjustments in Guaranteed Advances to Colleges and Academies	63,104
$1,609,276	1940 TOTAL BUDGETS 1959	$5,625,300

NOTES: *This amount in 1940 was divided, $1,800 to the Evangelical Women's Union, $1,500 to the Women's Guild. **In the early part of this period aid to students for full-time church-related vocations was provided directly by the synods. ***The

Administration Fund in the 1940 budget included not only provision for salaries of general officers of the church and their office expenses but also the relatively minor expenditures at that time for promotion, for meetings of such agencies as the Commission on Higher Education and Commission on Benevolent Institutions, and for contributions to ecumenical and confessional organizations.

A discerning reader could infer a substantial and significant part of the history of these two decades in a comparison of the budgets adopted in 1940 and 1959.

Mission in Higher Education

One inference would be that the church had come clear in recognizing and accepting the field of higher education as an integral part of the Christian mission. In 1940 the General Synod budgeted approximately $87,000 annually toward operating expenses of its three theological seminaries. In 1959 it budgeted $264,800 for this purpose, and at the same time authorized the United Seminary Appeal for 1960-61 aimed at securing an additional fund of $2,000,000 "for the undergirding of the theological seminaries," primarily for capital purposes, building, and endowment.

In 1940 the General Synod budgeted approximately $160,000 for five colleges. In 1959 it budgeted, for its eight colleges and two academies, $550,000 on which, in accord with a new formula approved at the same time, the General Council adopted a Guaranteed Advance for 1960 in the amount of $486,896. Three colleges—Ursinus, Franklin and Marshall, and Hood—were first included in the budget for 1943. The two academies, Massanutten and Mercersburg, received their first subsidies in 1945. More than ordinary significance surely attaches to the fact that in 1959 the General Synod allocated to its educational institutions a total budget item second only to the items approved for International and National Missions.

Aside from provision for institutions of higher education, there are eighteen items specified in the budget of 1959 which are not mentioned in the budget of 1940. Some of the concerns represented by these items were included, in very modest amounts to be sure, in the Administration Fund for 1940—expenses for promotion and contributions to ecumenical and confessional organizations being examples of this. Others, such as stewardship and benevolent institutions (health and welfare services), twenty years ago were carried on by agencies in which administrative responsibilities were borne by their chairmen or secretaries, usually pastors, who devoted to such causes as much time as their interest in them impelled and as they could "steal" from their parish duties.

Wheels Within Wheels

The 1940 text of the Constitution and Bylaws provided for three program boards—National Missions, International Missions, and Christian Education and Publication; and three boards dealing with financial aspects of the church's life—Pensions and Relief, Investments, and Business Management. Collateral provisions were made for the boards of the theological seminaries ("shall be determined by their respective charters"), and for the board of Elmhurst College. Four commissions were provided for —Evangelism, Christian Social Action, Higher Education, and Benevolent Institutions (now renamed Health and Welfare Services); and two auxiliary organizations — the Churchmen's Brotherhood and the Women's Guild. But to the provisions then made for boards, commissions, and auxiliary organizations, in each category was added the phrase—as if the good sense of the church anticipated what would happen—"and such others as may be created by the General Synod."

The General Synod did not belie that anticipation, for, as the years moved along, the expansion of administrative organization developed in a variety of ways. Some of the agencies operated for years as best they could with the volunteer leadership of pastors, college and theological seminary professors, and others serving as chairmen and secretaries. Not to this day have the Board of Business Management and the Board of Investments had even part-time paid administration.

The Commission on Evangelism and the Commission on Christian Social Action did not inaugurate full-time executive secretarial offices until 1945. The Commission on Benevolent Institutions offered little more than the opportunity once a year for the heads of such institutions to meet and exchange experiences and ideas until the General Synod of 1959, recognizing the increase in number of such institutions (from 35 in 1940 to 51 in 1958) and the church's responsibility "for cooperating with other agencies operating in the field of social welfare," renamed the agency as the Commission on Health and Welfare Services and authorized establishment of a full-time administrative office. The office opened in February, 1960.

The promotion of education in Christian stewardship and commitment to its practice was assigned from 1939 on to a committee headed by a pastor and the Secretary of the Church, but in 1950 a Commission on Stewardship was established. It functioned under part-time leadership until 1958 when a full-time executive secretary was installed.

During the triennium 1950-53 a Committee on Vital Christian Living had been at work, in consultation with existing agencies, charged to "concern itself with vitalizing the spiritual life of our membership by any and all means relevant to existing needs." One of its recommendations was "that a denominational department of the ministry be set up." Meanwhile, the Study Committee authorized by the General Synod of 1950, which proved to be the most decisive influence on the life and structure of the church since the Constitution and Bylaws were adopted, recommended that a Commission on Church and Ministry be established with responsibility for pastoral relations, life enlistment, administration of loans to students preparing for church-related vocations, in-service training of pastors, religion and health, social and parish workers, and correlation of the work of synodical committees on church and ministry (formerly known as Boards of Examiners). The General Synod of 1953 adopted this recommendation, assigning also to the new commission the responsibilities previously carried by the Committee on Chaplains. The new commission did not succeed in finding a full-time executive until 1956.

THROUGH WAR AND ITS AFTERMATH

The Constitution and Bylaws went into effect ten months after Hitler's armies marched into Poland, and less than eighteen months before the disaster at Pearl Harbor plunged the United States into the widening catastrophe of World War II. It was a word of compassion which later took on the cast of foreknowledge when President Goebel in his report to the General Synod of 1940 said, "I would ask this General Synod to concern itself very earnestly with the necessity of establishing an agency through which it may systematically gather funds, and enlist the services of our people in every possible manner, so that they may help provide for the needs of the victims of this war, whether they be those who have remained in their homelands destitute, or whether they be homeless refugees in foreign lands, or on our own shores." Appropriately, it was an item in the recommendations of the committee on the report of the Commission on Christian Social Action which, adopted by the General Synod, authorized the establishment of the War Emergency Relief Commission.

Relief was soon seen to be not the only wartime concern of the church; when the General Synod met two years later it heard reports from the Committee on Army and Navy Chaplains, the Christian Committee for Camp Communities, the Bureau for Men in Service, the War Emergency Relief Commission, and, from the Commission on Christian Social Action, a report on counsel and aid being given conscientious objectors to military training and service. Most of these concerns were later concentrated in the Commission on World Service when it was established in 1953 "to render ministries of mercy in areas of need," its responsibilities to "include, but not be limited to, interchurch aid, defense services, and disaster relief"; or in the new Commission on Church and Ministry.

After President Goebel had focused the General Synod's attention on world-wide suffering as a summons to the church's ministry, and the Synod had acted to set up the machinery through which the church's response could be enlisted, Dr. George W. Richards supported the move by remarks reported as follows in the *Lancaster* (Pennsylvania) *Intelligencer Journal* of June 25, 1940:

> It seems to me that the time has come when it is urgent business for this General Synod to ask every congregation to give not less than $10 and as much as they can raise for war sufferers. We need to do more than send fine resolutions. We must send bread, clothing, and medicine, and the only way we can do that is to give our money to buy them.
>
> Yesterday [referring to the Synod sermon he preached Sunday in St. Paul's Church] I said that the churches should appeal to our government to take the four billions which they propose to spend for defense each year for the next five years, and send it in the form of real help to the suffering people of China. It may have sounded like a foolish proposal, but I am convinced that if it were ventured by our government it would simply overwhelm the peoples of the lands to which such large help came.
>
> But if we were to ask our government to do such a thing, and before we would think of asking it, we ought to underwrite our request by ourselves collecting in the coming year not less than

$100,000 for the same purpose. That's the kind of pacifism for which I stand, and that's the kind of militarism in which I should like to engage what energy and years remain to me.

The suggestion of $100,000 for war relief in addition to the regular missions and benevolence budget of the General Synod seemed to many of the 1940 delegates a staggering proposal. The record of the twenty years following, however, is ample evidence of the depth to which the tragedy of wartime suffering and postwar disease, hunger, and homelessness captured the compassion and generosity of Evangelical and Reformed people. During that period, while contributing more than $48,000,000 to the regular missions and benevolence budget, they gave almost $12,000,000 more (so far as the record shows) for World Service causes.

TELLING THE STORY—ENLISTING THE RESPONSE

One of the anomalies of the period, when a strengthened and expanding program was made possible by steady increase in the giving of Evangelical and Reformed people, is that the very agency charged with promoting the program and support of it, functioned for twelve years (1941-53) before the General Synod got around to incorporating formal provision for it in the Constitution and Bylaws. That agency is the Department of United Promotion. By the promotional materials it prepared, the annual conferences it sponsored for the chairmen of synodical Kingdom Service committees, and by the strategy of its field workers in their patient, plodding, congregation-by-congregation consultations to interpret the denominational program as the local church's instrument and opportunity for fulfilling the Great Commission, this agency, undergirded by the work of the Committee (now Commission) on Stewardship and by the program agencies as they told their own stories and enlisted widening support thereof, gave the local churches, pastors and lay people, the information, the stimulus, and the guidance toward intelligent and devoted participation in these two decades of mission and service at home and abroad.

A new arm to the Department's work was assured when the General Synod of 1953 authorized the establishment of full-time synod presidencies and provided a basic subsidy toward support of each such office because the full-time synod president, in addition to his regular administrative duties, was expected to "direct, supervise and promote the work of the church within the synod."

Twenty-five of the thirty-three regional synods had established the full-time office within five years after the authorization was voted. It should be noted that the church will never fully know how much it owed to those men who in the earlier years added to their pastoral labors the exacting burdens of synod administration and those who in eight smaller synods must still do this. With the advent of the full-time synod presidency, the synod presidents have assumed a widening influence in the life of the church. Pastors and churches now have counsel and guidance close at hand and readily available. In their annual conference the synod presidents, part-time as well as full-time, concern themselves not only with technical administrative problems but with a continuing evaluation of the denominational program and the machinery and methods by which it is being carried forward. They exercise a growing function as advisers to the officers of the church and to the General Council. As the boards and commissions and auxiliary organizations learn better how to cooperate with them and make use of them, the synod presidents are coming to fulfill what the Study Committee of 1950-53 had conceived, and at the same time have served to stabilize denominational procedures within the synods to the end that all things should get done "decently and in order."

A lay delegate coming to synod or General Synod for the first time is likely to be overwhelmed as he hears references to six boards, eight commissions, three auxiliary organizations, at least two major standing committees (Liturgics, and Theological Education), and, in addition, to the Department of United Promotion and the General Council as well as to the synod and General Synod themselves. Just as likely, the delegate's pastor may have had his moments when he too was overwhelmed by the mail received from many of these agencies, and frustrated in his attempts to introduce into the local church's program all the causes, projects, and appeals emanating from St. Louis, Cleveland, and Philadelphia, where denominational offices are located. More than a few times protests have been voiced at the multiplicity of denominational agencies, and some of those who protested resorted to the first chapter of Ezekiel for what they felt was the appropriate phrase, "wheels within wheels."

The Spirit in the Wheels

Two responses are suggested by Evangelical and Reformed experience through these two decades. First, that if the church had not had this or that agency it would have had to create one, as indeed it did in several instances, simply because one area of life after another registers its claim on the church's witness and service.

The second response, which the encouraging record of the period will verify, is that those who quote the first chapter of Ezekiel should read the whole chapter and quote it more fully: "Their appearance and their work was as it were a wheel within a wheel. And when the living creatures went, the wheels went beside them. Whithersoever the spirit was to go, they went; thither was the spirit to go: and the wheels were lifted up beside them; for the spirit of the living creature was in the wheels."

That vision has had an encouraging measure of fulfillment in the life of the Evangelical and Reformed Church during these two decades. Or, to borrow from another scripture (1 Chronicles 14:15), if there was a multiplying of the branches of the structural tree of denominational life, the church had reason to think that it heard "the sound of marching in the tree-tops" with that sound's reassuring impetus to "go out to battle, for God is gone out before thee to smite the host."

The increase in giving and in communicant membership has already been referred to.

Committees on Hymnal and on Book of Worship had been organized by early 1936. Two years later the General Synod authorized publication of *The Hymnal* which became available in 1941. The *Book of Worship* required more time, some of the orders having been tested by provisional use, and the book was finally approved by the General Synod of 1942.

CHURCHES AT HOME

First glance at the number of churches in the United States would not seem to support an encouraging inference. The statistical tables for December 31, 1939 recorded a total of 2,861 congregations. There were only 2,753 listed as of the end of 1959. An evaluation of such statistics must, to begin with, take account of the inevitable process of stabilizing and reconciling statistical procedures after two communions whose practices had varied have been brought together. It is thus certain that tabulations after twenty years are more accurate than at the beginning. During this period, moreover, a reappraisal of church locations and of home missions strategy had to reckon with several factors in the changing social scene. Quick and easy transportation meant that two or three churches four or five miles apart, fully warranted in the horse-and-buggy days, could merge, and in some cases have done so. In addition, the country's changing economic picture, affecting many rural areas as well as once busy industrial centers, has resulted in "ghost" churches as well as "ghost" towns and rural communities, and the inevitable closing of churches in many such places.

On the other hand, since 1940 the Board of National Missions has aided in organizing approximately two hundred new home missions churches in residential areas which have developed from coast to coast. Many of these churches have become, in little more than a decade, strong and still growing centers of Christian witness in a time when evangelization has been doubly difficult because, with families moving frequently from one place to another, the churches, as one expert has put it, have been engaged in "evangelizing a procession."

WIDENING HORIZONS

The story of missions overseas is even more encouraging. When the union was signalized in 1934, the Reformed Church in the United States had mission interests in Japan, China, and on a small scale in Iraq. The Evangelical Synod of North America was at work in India and Honduras. No one on earth could anticipate then that a quarter-century later China would be closed to missionaries, Iraq almost completely so, and operations in India becoming increasingly difficult. Looking back, it is as if God had anticipated these developments and, not only to counterbalance their effects on the missionary zeal and outreach of the Evangelical and Reformed Church but also to widen the horizons of its people, was preparing to open new doors to them.

In 1945 the Reverend and Mrs. Paul H. Streich opened the United Andean Indian Mission at Picalqui, Ecuador, where the Evangelical and Reformed Church has carried the main burden in cooperation with the Evangelical United Brethren Church and the northern and southern Presbyterian Churches. Early the next year, in response to the joint appeal of the Scottish Mission (Church of Scotland), the Paris Mission Society (Reformed Church of France), and the Evangelical (Ewe) Presbyterian

Church of Togoland, the Reverend and Mrs. Eugene E. Grau began their work in what is now the Trans-Volta Territory of Ghana, and by 1960 the largest corps of Evangelical and Reformed missionaries overseas was at work in this part of western Africa. And, as 1960 opened, the Reverend and Mrs. Myles H. Walburn were poised in Hong Kong ready to sail to begin their work in Indonesia on the staff of Makassar Theological Seminary. Evangelical and Reformed people are probably only beginning to comprehend how truly during this period God has been "enlarging the place of their tent, stretching out the curtain of their habitations, lengthening their cords and strengthening their stakes," using the agencies of the church as instruments to this end.

WITNESS TO THE SOCIAL ORDER

No agency of the church had more difficulty in establishing its place in the confidence and support of the membership as a whole than had the Commission on Christian Social Action. It is clear that from the beginning the church was convinced that it must have such an agency. It is just as clear that the Commission had to win its way against not only a simple inertia but also a reluctance to concede the prophetic imperative which is at least as old as the days of the prophet Amos. However, the staff now numbering three, including an ordained Negro as Associate Secretary for Race Relations, and the Commission composed of ministers and lay men and women, have persisted steadfastly in their assignment until after twenty years, while many may disagree with what the Commission says on a specific issue, few if any of the ministers and lay members would now contend that any area of social life is exempt from Christian scrutiny or the claims and judgments of God.

As the years have moved on, the Commission has led the church in considering such issues as war, armaments, conscientious objectors, treatment of aliens in wartime, racial discrimination and inequality, civil liberties, marriage and divorce, juvenile delinquency, the liquor problem, vice and crime, Christian citizenship, the Christian family as a social group and as influenced by social conditions, international relations, pastors' salaries, federal aid to public education, labor-management relations, interfaith marriage, clergy participation in Social Security, immigration policy, religion and public education, the United Nations, technical assistance and economic aid to underdeveloped areas of the world, and the responsible use of nuclear energy. One senses that by the end of this double-decade the church was clear in understanding that if Christians, even against their own will or desire, were not moved with concern about such issues and to action according to the best insights they could achieve, they would by their default leave such issues to be decided by individuals and groups with interests less or other than Christian.

LEARNING AND TEACHING

All the while, advances in Christian education were undergirding the life of the church, providing leadership training and curricular materials by which Evangelical and Reformed children, young people, and adults might "grow in the grace and knowledge of our Lord and Savior Jesus Christ." The summer camp and conference program, which had had promising antecedents in both the Evangelical Synod of North America and the Reformed Church in the United States, grew steadily until by 1960 it was anticipated that 15,000 would be enrolled in a total of 167 camping periods for various age groups and for families. Of 45 camp and conference locations throughout the United States, 13 are owned by the church, the 32 others being rented for varying periods.

The General Synod of 1953 authorized a Voluntary Service

Program which got under way two years later. A Training Center was erected near Pottstown, Pennsylvania, which provides facilities not only for this program but for occasional small conference groups. The voluntary service program is open to any who have finished high school or are at least eighteen years old, who can satisfy minimal aptitude and physical requirements, and who wish to devote at least one year to full-time volunteer service for Christ and the church. Enrollees undergo two months' training at the Center and are then assigned for a minimum of ten months' service in homes for aged or children or retarded persons, city missions and social agencies, and other church institutions serving in health, welfare, or home mission fields. In the first five years of the program's operation a total of seventy persons have been enrolled. A program for training of older adults is being planned for those who wish to enter various forms of lay service which have developed in recent years.

Preparation for confirmation and communicant membership was greatly strengthened by the publication of two volumes with which the name of the late Nevin C. Harner is associated. The confirmation class manual *My Confirmation*, first published in 1942 and revised in 1954, reflected the union of 1934 in its helpful cross references to both the Heidelberg Catechism and the Evangelical Catechism. Twenty printings have been made in a total issue of 210,661 copies. The substance of its contents was determined by theologians, pastors, and workers in Christian education, with Dr. Harner assigned to reduce it to a text of literary unity. His own volume, *I Believe—A Christian Faith for Youth*, was published in 1950, and has gone through twenty-seven printings totaling 425,360 copies. Included in that total were 212,527 copies in editions bearing the imprint of the Methodist Church for use in that denomination's youth program. *I Believe* has found considerable use in doctrinal classes for adults as well as for young people, and has been published in translations including Portuguese, Japanese, South Korean, and Thai. The first edition of *My Confirmation* was adapted for use in Congregational Christian churches and published in 1954 by the Pilgrim Press under the title *My Church.*

The latest of these efforts to provide aid to Evangelical and Reformed people in understanding the faith commonly held among them was the publication in 1959 of a volume, *The Faith We Proclaim*, to which the present *History* is intended to be a companion volume. The substance of *The Faith We Proclaim* was developed in a series of consultations by the Theological Committee of the Evangelical and Reformed Church, and its writing then committed to a member of that committee, Dr. Elmer J. F. Arndt, who meanwhile, by happy coincidence, had become chairman of the Commission to Prepare a Statement of Faith for the United Church of Christ.

Like every communion in American Protestantism, the Evangelical and Reformed Church has had a vast educational enterprise centered in the Sunday church school. Enrollment for 1940 was reported as totaling 509,662, and then for four successive years suffered steady decline to a low of 414,382 in 1944. From then on, with the exception of 1948, enrollment steadily increased year by year until it reached 532,388 in 1956. Slight declines were reported the next three years to 518,931 for 1959.

To provide classroom materials and teaching aids in order that these half-million and more might "sit at the feet of Jesus and learn of him," the Board of Christian Education and Publication devoted itself steadfastly to the task of developing an adequate curriculum. The long-standing International Uniform Lesson Series was passing into disuse generally, partly because its structure did not encourage adoption of currently accepted pedagogical method, partly because it did not recognize the total experience of pupil and teacher in classroom, church, family, and community as being included in "the curriculum of religious education," partly because the objectives of Christian education were coming to be seen as involving much more than knowledge of the Bible, central and important as that knowledge surely is.

From 1941 to 1947 the Board published jointly with the Board of Christian Education of the (northern) Presbyterian Church in the U. S. A. a curriculum which was known in its Evangelical and Reformed edition as the Bible-Life Series. In 1948 a new three-way curriculum project was inaugurated, the religious education agency of the Congregational Christian Churches joining with those of the Presbyterian and the Evangelical and Reformed Churches to produce what in United Church of Christ constituencies has been familiar as the Church and Home Series. By 1960 more than two thirds of the church schools of the Evangelical and Reformed Church were regularly using at least some of these materials. Meanwhile, religious educators of both constituencies of the United Church of Christ, enlisting the aid of many pastors, lay leaders, theologians, and specialists in education, anticipating consummation of the establishment of the United Church of Christ, have been at work for a decade or more, developing the United Church Curriculum, the first units of which, nursery class materials, were ready for use in the fall of 1960, the whole to be available by the fall of 1963.

THE CHURCH PAPER

Not only primary in the education and inspiration of a Christian communion but also a good barometer of the intensity of the devotion of its people is the denominational journal, the "church paper." Following the union of 1934 the two German-language papers, *Die Kirchenzeitung* (Reformed) and *Der Friedensbote* (Evangelical), were combined and published under the latter name until the end of 1958, when a declining subscription list and the retirement of its long-time editor precipitated the decision to discontinue publication. The *Reformatusok Lapja*, ministering to a Hungarian-language constituency, reported a subscription list of approximately 4,000 in 1959.

The major publications in English, *The Evangelical Herald* and the *Reformed Church Messenger*, were merged soon after the Evangelical and Reformed Church was established, and the paper was published thereafter under the name of *The Messenger*. To the General Synod of 1940 it was reported that on February 1 of that year there were 17,830 subscribers. This journal had a steady, indeed remarkable, growth so that by October, 1958, when publication was begun jointly with *Advance* (Congregational Christian) under the name of *United Church Herald*, more than 100,000 copies were being published of each issue of *The Messenger*. Within the first year of publication of *United Church Herald* the St. Louis edition (Evangelical and Reformed subscription list) was being published in 110,000 copies. The church paper had thus become in twenty years a familiar visitor in a substantial proportion of Evangelical and Reformed homes.

The Ordained Ministry

In a statistical reflection of the ordained ministry during these two decades, it should be noted that even at the end of the period 85 per cent of each year's candidates for ordination had received their professional training in the denomination's three theological seminaries—Eden, at Webster Groves, Missouri; Lancaster, at Lancaster, Pennsylvania; and Mission House, at Plymouth, Wisconsin. Total enrollment in these schools had exactly doubled, 144 in 1940, 288 in 1959. Eden had expanded from 63 to 151, Lancaster from 56 to 110, Mission House only slightly from 25 to 27 although an enrollment of 36 was in prospect for the fall of 1960. Regarding the latter school, by spring of 1960 there was considerable assurance that, as one of the first fruits of the establishment of the United Church of Christ, Mission House would merge with the Yankton School of Theology, Yankton, South Dakota, and the merged school relocate in the Minneapolis-St. Paul area as a theological seminary of the United Church of Christ to serve especially the new church's constituency in the great Northwest.

During the twenty years under consideration in this chapter a total of 1,277 young men *and women* were ordained to the Christian ministry, the first young woman, a graduate of Lancaster Seminary, having been ordained in 1948. (It might be noted in passing that the General Synod elected its first woman Moderator in 1959—Frances Kapitzky.)

A study of the yearly ordination figures moves one to draw an imaginary line between 1951 and 1952. In the twelve years before that line, 1940-51, the number of ordinations (615) averaged 51 per year. In the eight years following, ordinations totaled 662, an average of 83 each year. This increase followed a pattern common among all the churches following World War II but without doubt one factor in it was the work of the Committee on Life Enlistment and its projection in the intensified program under the Commission on Church and Ministry.

The ordained ministry was further augmented during these twenty years by more than 300 ministers of other denominations who were granted Privilege of Call looking toward their reception into the ministry of the Evangelical and Reformed Church. An examination of their applications reveals some encouraging implications as to the way the Evangelical and Reformed Church has been looked upon by those outside it. In listing their motives for wanting to enter the Evangelical and Reformed ministry, these applicants have noted the desire to get into a communion with an adequate program of Christian education, freedom from what they felt to be the arbitrary constraints of an appointive ministry, possibility of the use of liturgical forms of worship without jeopardy to freedom in worship, and most frequently cited, especially by applicants from smaller, more sectarian groups, to get into a communion fully identified with the ecumenical movement and spirit.

Through the procedures of ordination and of Privilege of Call, the church has continued to sustain the historic tradition of an educated ministry with its minimum standard of the four-year college and three-year theological school disciplines.

THE PASTOR'S KEEP

The place of the ordained ministry in the life of the church is certainly reflected in the increasingly generous provisions the churches have made for their pastors. The purchase or construction of new parsonages has kept pace with the postwar construction of new churches or additions to older ones. Supplementary provisions for associate or assistant pastors, secretarial assistance, longer vacations, in-service training and postgraduate study, reimbursement for pastoral use of an automobile, and other "perquisites," have marked these years.

Improvement in pastors' salaries and pensions has been steady throughout the period, and, for the improvement of the former as corollary to improvement in the latter, the church's ordained ministry is largely indebted to the persistent leadership of the Reverend Silas P. Bittner, who has been secretary-treasurer of the Board of Pensions and Relief since February, 1943. As he went from synod to synod each year, and in his presentations before the General Synod, his plea for better pensions had coupled with it always a plea for better salaries. Meanwhile, devout laymen with an appreciation of the declining value of the dollar and aware of the corresponding increase in wages, salaries, and the so-called "fringe benefits" in what business and industry were doing for their employees, supported Dr. Bittner's plea. The outcome is one of the brightest phases of the history of this twenty-year period.

THE PENSION FUNDS

When the pension funds of the two uniting constituencies, the so-called "old funds," were brought into the custody of the new Board of Pensions and Relief, the maximum pension in the former Evangelical Synod was $350 per year; in the former Reformed Church, $250 per year. Efforts were immediately initiated to persuade the General Synod to make better provision for members of the old funds. First positive response was made by the General Synod of 1947, raising the maximum to $500. Successive General Synods raised the maximum still further, to $720 (1950), to $900 (1953), to $1,200 (1956), the "maximum" being available to a member retiring after 43 years of service, and the new benefits graded downward to the point where a member of either old fund retiring with only one to five years of service is now eligible to a pension of $686.

Meanwhile, effective January 1, 1941, the new Ministers' Retirement Annuity Fund, established that year on an actuarial basis, required the minister to contribute annually three per cent of his salary, the charge to contribute annually the equivalent of five per cent of the pastor's salary. The charge's proportion was later increased to eight per cent, and in more recent years, after ministers became eligible for federal social security pensions requiring at first their payment annually of three per cent on a maximum of $4,200 of income, the charge was encouraged to contribute annually the equivalent of 11 per cent of the salary to the pastor's account in the Ministers' Retirement Annuity Fund. In the spring of 1960 it was reported that more than a thousand pastoral charges were making the 11 per cent contribution.

The Ministers' Retirement Annuity Fund, established January 1, 1941, with "no assets, capital or endowment funds," enrolled 900 ministers and their respective charges in that first year. The General Synod of 1947 ordered that thereafter no synod should confirm a pastoral call unless the minister was a member of the Fund and the charge prepared to contribute the annual minimum to his membership account. Doubtless aided by this pressure from the General Synod, but more largely reflecting the generosity and sense of fairness on the part of responsible lay leaders and the discipline of prudence on the part of the ministers, more than 2,200 ministers are now enrolled in the Ministers' Retirement Annuity Fund. Now, a minister enrolling in the Fund at age twenty-five, married to a wife two years younger than he, and retiring after 40 years of continuous service at an average salary of $4,500, can anticipate a pension of at least $2,297.

THE LABORER'S HIRE

The General Synod of 1940 adopted a recommendation that "$1,200 and house be regarded as the minimum" compensation for a pastor. Seven years later the General Synod was informed that, on the basis of data reported to the Board of Pensions and Relief, 21 per cent of the pastors were receiving salaries of less than $1,800, 55 per cent receiving from $1,800 to $2,499, and 24 per cent receiving $2,500 or more.

The Commission on Christian Social Action was requested to continue the study which it had begun. By 1950 it was reported that 22 synods had already established a minimum salary ranging from $2,000 to $2,500, and the General Synod took action "to establish the principle of a living minimum salary for ministers, for example $3,000 and parsonage, the exact amount of which is to be agreed upon by each local synod," and further study of the matter was provided for. In 1953 the General Synod raised the minimum to $3,600 and enjoined a yearly review by each charge. The recommended minimum was increased to $4,000 in 1956 and the General Synod of 1959 urged that in the annual review of the pastor's salary "consideration be given to years of service (as well as) the increasing cost of living." As a result of this continuous attention, in the twelve years 1947-59 the average salary was almost doubled: 1947, $2,398; 1950, $2,867; 1953, $3,390; 1956, $4,086; 1959, $4,689. In 1960, of 1,809 pastors reporting, 17 had salaries under $3,000. The other 1,792 pastors reported salaries averaging $4,792.

So the work moved forward, in missions at home and abroad, in prophetic witness to the times, in Christian education, and in the ordained ministry and the laity's response thereto. Undergirding it all, usually less susceptible to statistical measurement and report but no less fundamental, was the work of the Churchmen's Brotherhood and the Women's Guild and of the commissions charged with leading the church in evangelism and the deepening of the devotional life, and in the stewardship of all of life.

Change on the Captain's Bridge

The General Synod of 1953 witnessed the retirement of the Reverend Louis W. Goebel as President of the Church and the election of the Reverend James E. Wagner as his successor.

No one who had participated in the church's life from its beginnings in 1934 could fail to discern, looking back, the hand of God in the choosing of the church's first two chief executives. During the first four years, 1934 to 1938, when the Constitution and Bylaws of the new church were being fashioned and the lines of its polity and doctrinal genius being determined, it had the guidance of George W. Richards, theologian, church historian, and ecumenical pioneer. That simple fact was to guarantee that the Evangelical and Reformed Church would be aware of its roots in the mainstream of the Christian tradition and, at the same time, aware also that "the great new fact of our time," the ecumenical movement, was being used of God to summon the churches to move beyond their confessional confines into a fresh realization and fuller implementation of their oneness in Christ.

When the Constitution and Bylaws were adopted in 1938 to be declared in effect in 1940, the responsibilities of the President's office were redirected toward the task of translating the text of the Constitution and Bylaws into day-to-day administrative detail and procedure. At this stage Dr. Richards, in the opinion of one of his most grateful students, would have been lost and frustrated.

Then it was that "there was a man sent from God whose name was Louis." The General Synod of 1938 elected Dr. Goebel as the second President of the Church, first full-time President. He was destined to serve in that office for the next fifteen years; and, if it is true that an institution is only the lengthened shadow of a man, the Evangelical and Reformed Church is the reflection of the genius of Dr. Goebel's leadership through this period when the administrative pattern of church life had to be developed, and precedents had to be established where there had been no precedents to guide. He brought to the office and retained through the years an unusual capacity for detail, nicely balanced by both a sense of humor and an underlying devotional spirit always easily identifiable with the Evangelical heritage of German pietism. A conservative in politics, he constantly insisted on the church's responsibility for social action and concern. Like Dr. Richards a delegate to both the Oxford and Edinburgh conferences of 1937, Dr. Goebel was among those whose leadership brought about the organization of the World (1948) and National (1950) Councils of Churches; and it was this instinct for ecumenicity that doubtless accounts for his ready response to the first approaches from the Congregational Christian Churches toward the possibility of union. Alongside all this, his leadership accounts for the establishment of the Study Committee in 1950, the work of which, submitted to the General Synod of 1953, pulled together the loose ends of administrative procedure and strengthened the structure of the Evangelical and Reformed Church so that he could hand over to his successor a stronger organization of the church's life and an accumulation of sound precedents, both of which were calculated to free the next President of the Church for attention to other concerns which meanwhile had come to the fore.

Self-study and Adjustment

Not that the church—having undergone the major plastic and internal surgery induced by the report of the Study Committee in 1953—settled back in the complacent assumption that full health and wholeness had been achieved. Through the following three years the boards, commissions, and auxiliary organizations of the church, under the guidance of a joint committee composed of three executives and three members of the General Council, engaged in a "self-study" with reference to "the total program of the church in the light of the present opportunities and needs." Some progress was made also in effecting a larger measure of liaison between the Commission on World Service and the Board of International Missions, since it had become apparent that these two agencies *together* represented the overseas, world-wide outreach of the church here at home.

The continuing process of re-appraisal—a true Reformed Church is ever a reforming Church, it has been said—was reflected in the General Synod of 1959 when reports were received from seven study committees which had been at work during the preceding triennium. The areas to which these committees had been assigned were: (1) Facilities and Programs of the Theological Seminaries; (2) The Church's Responsibility in the Care of the Mentally Ill and Mentally Retarded; (3) The Future of the Deaconess Order; (4) The Relationship of Our Hospitals to the Church; (5) A Formula for Allocation of Funds to Institutions of Higher Education (academies and colleges); (6) Proposed Full-time Executive for the Commission on Benevolent Institutions; and (7) the special problems of the Rocky Mountain and Dakota synods.

The formula for allocating funds to the church-related academies and colleges was put into effect in 1960. The Commission on Benevolent Institutions, with its name changed to the Commission on Health and Welfare Services, was given a full-time executive for the first time beginning in 1960 also, and to this Commission has been referred the findings of the second, third, and fourth study committees mentioned above. The special problems of Rocky Mountain and Dakota synods derive in part from the exceedingly small number of churches in each; in part from the great distances involved as, for example, in Dakota Synod where it is roughly fourteen hundred miles between the churches farthest apart; and in part from the inevitable adjustments confronted as a German-speaking constituency moves farther away from its cultural past. These problems have been made a concern of the Department of Town and Country Church of the Board of National Missions, and a full-time "area minister" is now at work giving assistance and counsel to the churches in these two synods.

Theological Renewal

The report of the Committee to Study the Facilities and Programs of the Theological Seminaries not only resulted in several specific actions which will be mentioned later in this chapter, but in doing so reflected a general movement for theological renewal in the life of the church which has been an outstanding mark of the last five or six years. The first intimation of this movement was the 1953 General Synod's instruction to the General Council to establish a Theological Committee. This decision was precipitated by several overtures sent up to the General Synod for which adequate disposition would involve basic theological concerns. These overtures were the new committee's first assignments, and resulting from its work have come a clarification and enhancement of the status of "commissioned workers" in the life of the church, and a statement on "ordination" which clearly enunciates the Reformation's nonsacerdotal concept of the ordained ministry. The statement, approved by the General Synod, reads in part as follows:

> Ordination is the rite by which the church sets apart for the sacred office of the Christian ministry one whom it recognizes as having been called of God, who exhibits the mental, moral, and spiritual qualifications of his calling, and who has completed a satisfactory preparation for and is called by the church to the exercise of the duties and responsibilities of the ministry. This rite does not raise him to a unique spiritual estate, as though it conferred upon him gifts of the Spirit which he did not before possess or which those not ordained cannot possess; but it does entrust him with the privileges and responsibilities of the spiritual office to which God has called him.

The General Synod commended the Committee "for its definitive and excellent work" and encouraged it "to continue its study and discussion of important theological issues for further report to the church." A charter was thus provided for the Committee's continuance and its service as the recognized body of competence in the church's life to which can be referred theological issues of any kind and particularly theological documents from ecumenical and confessional bodies which seek responsible denominational response thereto. The Committee's most recent major contribution to the life of the church was the publication of the doctrinal volume, *The Faith We Proclaim,* under its auspices.

It was probably a chance meeting in a Pullman car and a casual conversation between Dr. Wagner and Dr. Louis H. Gunnemann, dean of Mission House Theological Seminary, that eventually brought about the Tri-Seminary Faculty Conference held for the first time in the summer of 1954. A similar conference has been held every summer since, meeting in turn at Mission House, Eden, and Lancaster. This conference has without doubt done much to develop a "doctrinal viewpoint generally prevailing in the Evangelical and Reformed Church." But it has done more. It has overcome the provincial character that formerly distinguished the three seminaries (and indeed their historic constituencies) from one another. It opened the way for publication of a quarterly magazine, *Theology and Life,* issued first in February, 1958 by Lancaster Seminary, but within a year taken over and sponsored by an editorial board jointly representative of the three seminaries. And the Tri-Seminary Faculty Conference has served as the medium through which the church's theologians have explored together the function of the seminaries in the life of the church and have engaged in a continuous process by which the seminaries have re-examined their own structures and curricula in the light of that function and of the new demands laid upon them by the ecumenical movement.

Counterpart to all this and to something which has been happening in other communions is the development of theological interest among lay members of the church. The first Lay School of Theology was held at Lancaster for a week in the summer of 1959. With enrollment limited to fifty, the response was so general that registrations were closed early in the year and almost a hundred applicants turned away. Two such schools were scheduled for the summer of 1960, one at Lancaster, one at Eden. Not to be outdone by the lay members, the pastors responded with enthusiasm to the first Summer School of Theology held for five weeks at Lancaster in 1959, with 38 enrolled; and a second held at Eden in the summer of 1960 opened with 45 enrolled.

Meanwhile, three specific results have come from the work of the Study Committee on Facilities and Programs of the Theological Seminaries. The General Synod of 1959 greatly increased its allocations to the annual operating budgets of the three seminaries. It authorized what came to be known as the United Seminary Appeal aimed at securing $2,000,000 for the capital undergirding of these schools. And it established a standing Committee on Theological Education with responsibility "to engage in continuing exploration of the purpose and content of theological education in the life of the church, to interpret to the church the needs of the seminaries, and to interpret to the seminaries the concerns and the needs of the church with respect to those who serve it in full-time vocation."

In such readily discernible ways it is evident that the Evangelical and Reformed Church has been sharing in the surge of theological renewal, with its recovery of doctrinal and biblical depth, which has characterized the world-wide Christian community in recent years. Among the leaders who represented our church in this theological development were the Niebuhr brothers (Reinhold and Richard) and Paul Tillich.

In the World-wide Christian Community

At least once a week the devout affirm their awareness of and commitment to the world-wide Christian community. Reflecting the two traditions merged in the union of 1934, the Lord's Day liturgy includes alternate readings so that in reciting the Apostles' Creed churches coming out of the former Reformed Church background declare their belief in "the holy catholic

Church," while those of the former Evangelical Synod background with its strain of Lutheranism say "one holy universal Christian Church." By either wording, by the common use of the most ancient and universal of the ecumenical creeds, Evangelical and Reformed people symbolize their community of mind and heart with "the whole Christian Church throughout all the world."

That faith underlies the receptivity toward and entrance upon a variety of ecumenical outreaches which have marked the church's life throughout these years. One such movement which came to be known as the Conference on Church Union, was launched at a conference held December 14-16, 1949, at Seabury House, Greenwich, Connecticut. This movement was committed from its beginning to a quest for "an organic union, a fellowship and organization of the church which will enable it to act as one body under Jesus Christ who is the Head of the church." The Evangelical and Reformed Church was active in this movement until it ceased operations not long after the 1957 North American Conference on "The Nature of the Unity We Seek" had made it apparent that other approaches to Christian unity were pre-empting the interest of the churches. Not so enthusiastically, but to an extent sufficient to indicate that it did not want to ignore any responsible movement in the field, the Evangelical and Reformed Church kept in touch with the organization commonly identified with the name of E. Stanley Jones and his proposal of a form of "federal union"; but the church seemed to sense that this movement offered little more than was already possible within the Federal (later National) Council of Churches.

The Evangelical and Reformed Church was one of the first to support proposals for the organization of the World and National Councils of Churches, and was represented by full delegations at the founding of each respectively in Amsterdam,

1948, and in Cleveland, 1950. After a decade, it is not inaccurate to say that although the Evangelical and Reformed Church is not among the largest member communions in these ecumenical organizations it is generally acknowledged to be among the first in its financial support and in active participation in the work of both.

Meanwhile, it has maintained its membership in the World Alliance of Reformed and Presbyterian Churches, perpetuating a connection which the former Reformed Church had with this world confessional body almost since the Alliance was formed in 1875. A delegation of six represented the Evangelical and Reformed Church at the eighteenth General Council of the Alliance in São Paulo, Brazil, in the summer of 1959 when the President of the Church was elected one of the vice-presidents of the Alliance. This confessional association of the Evangelical and Reformed Church, and the decision of the United Church of Christ to retain for the immediate future a relationship to both the World Alliance and the International Congregational Council, seem to be especially propitious since formal conversations have now been initiated between representatives of both world confessional bodies to explore their common heritage in the Calvinistic branch of the Reformation and the possibility of closer relations between the two bodies on a world-wide scale, and to make this exploration in light of the wider concerns of their common Christian heritage.

Consonant with the denomination's ecumenical outreach has been the schedule of overseas travel on the part of the President of the Church, seven trips, considerably more than a hundred thousand miles, in the period 1955-60. In addition to representing the church at meetings of the Central Committee of the World Council of Churches and the Executive Committee of the World Alliance, he has visited the denomination's mission interests in Japan, Okinawa, Hong Kong, Honduras, Ecuador,

Ghana, and French Togoland, in conjunction with which journeys he has also visited national Christian leaders in Brazil, Formosa, the Philippines, and the Union of South Africa, as well as in Hungary, most of western Europe, and in the British Isles.

Both as a symbol and as a resource, the Ecumenical Travel Fund is significant as an item only recently incorporated in the denominational budget. The General Council in 1955 set aside from contingent sources a modest sum so designated, and the General Synod of 1956 approved its inclusion as a regular budgetary item in the amount of $15,000 annually. The account is cumulative from year to year to provide for those years when major calls must be made upon it.

It was just such a contingency which prompted establishment of the Ecumenical Travel Fund. For in 1954 the church was represented at three ecumenical gatherings, the Third General Assembly of the National Council of Churches, the Second Assembly of the World Council of Churches, and the Seventeenth General Council of the World Alliance. All three met in the United States but the reimbursement of expenses of delegates, which together placed a considerable strain on the denominational budget when no provision had been made for this contingency, suggested the question, What will happen five or six years from now when the World Alliance and the World Council hold their general assemblies in distant lands? Will the church then be represented by only a token delegation, or will it be prepared to participate fully in those gatherings and in ecumenical activities which were already beginning to expand? The Ecumenical Travel Fund has enabled the church to give a positive response to those questions. At the General Synod of 1956 for the first time, and from the resources of this Fund, fraternal delegates were present from the national churches with which Evangelical and Reformed missionaries were at work in Japan, India, and Togoland; and at the General Synod of

1959 from Honduras, Japan, and the Hong Kong Council of the Church of Christ in China. The church was able to send fraternal delegates to the four hundredth anniversary celebrations of the Reformed Church of France and the Reformed Church of Switzerland, and to the one hundredth anniversary of the Presbyterian Church of Brazil; and was also represented in the fall of 1960 at the four hundredth anniversary of the Church of Scotland.

It is apparent that the Evangelical and Reformed Church has come to realize that such kinds of ecumenical exchange in conference and fellowship, especially where the so-called "younger churches" are involved, are part of the missionary strategy of our times and, in the case of the younger churches, a means of stimulating and enriching the older churches by the less heavily encumbered insights, spirit, and methods of the younger.

The United Church of Christ

The earliest official record in the archives of the Evangelical and Reformed Church bearing on the eventual establishment of the United Church of Christ is to be found in the minutes of the General Council for September, 1941, and January, 1942. For September, 1941, the minutes read simply: "Chairman Richards reported that the Committee on Church Relations has had informal conversations and will have another in about a month with the corresponding commission of the Congregational Christian Churches. These are absolutely informal and reports should not be made regarding them until the meeting of the General Synod."

The minutes for January, 1942, record: "Dr. Richards spoke of the status of the negotiations of our Committee on Church Relations with the Commission on Inter-Church Relations and Christian Unity of the Congregational Christian Churches. The

Committee wishes a decision from the General Council as to whether or not it should publish anything regarding the meetings with the Commission on Inter-Church Relations and Christian Unity of the Congregational Christian Churches. Dr. Richards read a report of the two meetings held thus far, but no action was taken since this whole subject will be considered by the General Synod. The statement he read will be presented to the General Council of the Congregational Christian Churches. *Voted* that this report appear only in the Blue Book of the General Synod."

At the General Synod of 1942 the Committee on Closer Relations with Other Churches reported that two meetings had been held, March 18 and October 13, 1941. Fraternal delegates from the Congregational Christian Churches were present and spoke briefly at the General Synod, and the Committee was "authorized to continue its conversations with the Congregational Christian Churches."

The Committee took its assignment so seriously that by the time the General Synod of 1944 met the second revised text of the Basis of Union had been before the fall 1943 meetings of the synods, and a third and further revised text was presented to the General Synod itself. This year, 1944, both the General Synod of the Evangelical and Reformed Church and the General Council of Congregational Christian Churches approved the "procedure" which the negotiating committees had recommended.

The Basis of Union underwent five further revisions including what proved to be its final text dated January 22, 1947. The following year, at Oberlin, Ohio, the General Council of Congregational Christian Churches, under pressure from a small but determined group opposing the proposed union, adopted a series of "Interpretations" in the approval of which a concurring action of the Evangelical and Reformed Church was requested.

A special meeting of the General Synod was held at Cleveland,

Ohio, April 20-21, 1949, when it was voted (249-41) to approve the Interpretations contingent on the further approval of the synods to which action was thereupon referred. At their spring meetings in the weeks immediately following, 33 of the 34 synods approved the Interpretations, one synod disapproved, and the General Council (E&R) declared the Interpretations adopted.

A uniting General Synod for the proposed United Church was planned for June 26, 1950. But it was not to be held. For in April, 1949, a Congregational Christian church in Brooklyn, New York, instituted injunction proceedings and challenged the right and authority of the General Council (CC) to participate in the establishment of a United Church on the basis provided for in the Basis of Union and Interpretations. This lawsuit and the appeals subsequently involved required almost five years until, on December 3, 1953, the New York State Court of Appeals affirmed a decision of the Appellate Division of the Supreme Court of New York which opened the way for the resumption of union negotiations.

The Congregational Christian General Council of 1952, meeting in Claremont, California, had adopted resolutions including a proposal looking toward "preparation of a draft of a proposed constitution *for the General Synod* of the united fellowship" (italics added). When, then, the 1953 decision of the New York State Court of Appeals was announced, and the President of the Church was asked for a statement to be published in *The Messenger* of December 29, he wrote in part:

> Many questions have been raised among us, further, as to just what is meant by a "constitution for the General Synod of the united fellowship." The fact that the words "General Synod" and "the united fellowship" appear to have been placed, not in apposition, but in complementary relation to each other, has suggested that what the Claremont action contemplated was only a unification of top-level administration of the work being carried on by our two fellowships. The reply made many times to that possibility has

been that the Evangelical and Reformed Church is interested only in merger in the fullest, most real, organic sense—in precisely the sense in which we experienced it ourselves a score of years ago. We want to be "one body," not just "one head," with whomever we join heart and hand.

Negotiations were resumed at a joint meeting of the General Council (E&R) and the Executive Committee (CC) October 12-13, 1954, at which time it was agreed to proceed on the basis of the Basis of Union and Interpretations, with the understanding clarified that Article IV-A anticipated preparation of a "Constitution of the United Church" and not merely a "constitution for the General Synod of the united fellowship."

The negotiations were continued, beset, it is true, by difficulties, by perplexities, always under the shadow of the small but persistent antiunion group within the Congregational Christian fellowship, but each successive meeting of the negotiators found them clearer as to what each meant and what both coveted for the United Church, surer that they were being led by the Holy Spirit, confident and confiding when the time came to set the date and lay the plans for the Uniting General Synod.

The Uniting General Synod was held at Cleveland, Ohio, June 25-27, 1957. In addition to formal declaration of the union, commissions were appointed to prepare a Constitution of the United Church and a Statement of Faith; also a Committee on Methods of Solicitation, Collection, and Disbursement of Missionary, Benevolent, and Administrative Funds; and the Executive Council was established and authorized to set up a committee to begin study of geographical and other factors involved in the realignment and reorganization of associations, conferences, and synods.

Two years later at Oberlin, Ohio, the Second General Synod of the United Church of Christ received and approved "as an excellent working document" a first draft of the proposed Constitution and Bylaws of the United Church of Christ. This draft was referred to the churches, associations, conferences, and synods for study and comment, and provision was made for its revision in the light of comments received and the submission of a revised draft to an adjourned session of the Second General Synod to be held in the summer of 1960.

The same Second General Synod, in an exalted moment which those present are not likely to forget, also approved a Statement of Faith which has enjoyed widening acceptance, commendation, and use not only throughout both constituencies of the United Church but from various parts of the Christian world community. The Second General Synod adopted a "Call to Christian Action in Society" which it is believed will serve as an adequate charter for the United Church's prophetic witness and redemptive service in society. Further steps were taken in outlining the financial structure of the United Church and toward the time when the reorganization of associations, conferences, and synods into associations and conferences of the United Church will take place. Authorizations were voted as a result of which by spring of 1960 a Commission on Worship and a Commission on Christian Unity and Ecumenical Study and Service had been set up and the Long-Range Planning Committee and the Stewardship Council had begun their work.

As was confidently expected the adjourned session of the General Synod of 1959, meeting at Cleveland, Ohio, July 6-8, 1960, unanimously approved, with relatively minor amendments, the proposed Constitution and Bylaws of the United Church of Christ and submitted the same to the Congregational Christian churches and the Evangelical and Reformed synods for vote. If that vote proved adequately favorable in both constituencies —as it was believed by many would be so—it was hoped that the Third General Synod of the United Church, to be held July 3-7, 1961, at Philadelphia, Pennsylvania, would declare the Constitution and Bylaws adopted and in force, and steps could quickly follow toward a unified program on a unified budget in an effectively functioning corporate reality, the United Church of Christ.

So, the Evangelical and Reformed Church, only a quarter-century after it was established in a great venture of faith at Cleveland in 1934, in the spring of 1960 was already well embarked on an even greater venture of faith in establishing the United Church of Christ.

True to Its Past

In all this the Evangelical and Reformed Church and its earlier constituencies which had united to establish it were being truer to their own past than probably most of their ministers and lay members realized.

There are four great names at the Reformation headwaters of the Evangelical and Reformed Church—Luther, Zwingli, Calvin, and Melanchthon. Commenting on the phrase "the holy catholic Church" Luther in his Larger Catechism wrote: "I believe that there is upon earth a holy congregation and communion of pure saints ruled under one Head, Christ, called together by the Holy Spirit in one faith, in the same mind and understanding, furnished with multiple gifts yet one in love and in all respects harmonious, without sects or schisms." Zwingli's view has been summarized as affirming "that those who live in Christ, 'the Head of all believers,' constitute 'the Church or communion of saints, the bride of Christ, the Catholic Church.'"

Calvin, also in commenting on the phrase from the Apostles' Creed, wrote: "Therefore it is called 'catholic' or universal since we are not to think of two or three Churches, lest Christ be divided—which cannot happen. . . . Therefore 'communion of saints' is added . . . because it perfectly expresses the quality of the Church, as if it were said that the saints are gathered to the fellowship of Christ by the rule that whatever benefits God confers upon them they should mutually communicate to one another." And, if Melanchthon is adequately represented by the Augsburg Confession which he wrote, it is there affirmed that "that one Holy Church is to continue for ever. Moreover, the Church is the congregation of saints in which the Gospel is rightly taught and the Sacraments are rightly administered. And unto the true unity of the Church, it is sufficient to agree concerning the doctrine of the Gospel and the administration of the Sacraments."

And in the Evangelical and Reformed tradition, in which "the final norm is the Word of God," beyond the Reformers, important as they are in that tradition, are two others: one who affirmed the "unity of the Spirit in the bond of peace . . . one body and one Spirit . . . one hope . . . one Lord, one faith, one baptism, one God and Father of all, who is above all and through all and in all"; and Another and greater who prayed "for those who are to believe in me . . . that they may all be one . . . that the world may believe that thou hast sent me."

No Evangelical and Reformed biblical scholar has ever interpreted that high-priestly prayer as anticipating the denominational divisions which have marked the church's life these recent centuries. But the Evangelical and Reformed tradition is such that this church believes that any church taking that prayer seriously must ever be at work striving to make real by making visible to the world "our oneness in Christ," translating that oneness which is given of God into that oneness of corporate life and witness which only God's people, by their humble willing to do so, can bring about.

On that belief the Evangelical and Reformed Church rounds out a quarter-century throughout which it has had much to be thankful for, and stands on the threshold of what it firmly believes will be a losing of its life only to find that life more fully in the United Church of Christ.

Statistical Records

THE EVANGELICAL SYNOD—1934

DISTRICTS	PASTORS IN CHARGE OF CHURCH	NOT IN CHARGE OF CHURCH	MEMBERS
1. Atlantic	37	10	12,814
2. California	17	11	1,526
3. Colorado	14	3	2,293
4. Indiana	105	6	33,322
5. Iowa	68	7	12,290
6. Kansas	36	1	3,553
7. Michigan	65	13	20,593
8. Minnesota	73	6	10,761
9. Missouri	110	42	25,195
10. Nebraska	31	2	6,124
11. New York	59	7	21,062
12. North Illinois	57	24	38,340
13. Ohio	71	8	22,644
14. Pacific Northwest	10	2	790
15. Pennsylvania	25	1	6,703
16. Southern	17	4	4,660
17. South Illinois	78	10	20,223
18. Texas	47	—	8,866
19. West Missouri	34	5	7,187
20. Wisconsin	97	6	21,894
21. Canada and Montana (missionary)	8	—	758
TOTALS	1,059	168	281,598

THE REFORMED CHURCH IN THE UNITED STATES—1934

SYNODS CLASSES	MINISTERS	CHARGES	CONGREGATIONS	MEMBERS
Eastern				
1. East Pennsylvania	43	32	62	16,562
2. Lebanon	29	21	42	13,198
3. Philadelphia	59	38	40	11,633
4. Lancaster	56	34	53	13,555
5. East Susquehanna	23	19	55	9,355
6. West Susquehanna	24	19	59	6,660
7. Tohickon	27	22	38	9,803
8. Goshenhoppen	14	14	30	8,314
9. Lehigh	44	35	68	23,003
10. Schuylkill	24	21	38	8,690
11. Wyoming	35	25	43	9,071
12. Reading	32	21	30	15,536
13. Eastern Hungarian	17	13	13	1,375
14. New York	22	15	15	3,532
15. German Philadelphia	15	14	15	4,245
TOTALS	464	343	601	154,532
Ohio				
1. Central Ohio	34	27	41	7,084
2. East Ohio	43	34	55	13,406
3. Northeast Ohio	55	41	47	14,943
4. Northwest Ohio	52	39	46	9,509
5. Southwest Ohio	39	34	39	9,030
6. West Ohio	19	16	27	4,404
7. Lakeside Hungarian	13	13	15	1,250
TOTALS	255	204	270	59,626

THE REFORMED CHURCH IN THE UNITED STATES—1934

SYNODS CLASSES	MINISTERS	CHARGES	CONGREGATIONS	MEMBERS
Northwest				
1. Sheboygan	49	36	42	8,187
2. Milwaukee	26	20	29	5,922
3. Minnesota	17	14	19	3,244
4. Nebraska	11	9	11	940
5. Ursinus	12	12	13	2,042
6. South Dakota	10	9	28	2,034
7. Portland-Oregon	14	9	9	917
8. Manitoba	4	4	8	491
9. Eureka	9	9	26	1,400
10. North Dakota	2	3	13	470
11. Edmonton	3	3	5	490
12. California	11	8	8	662
TOTALS	168	136	211	26,799
Pittsburgh				
1. Westmoreland	28	23	36	8,577
2. Clarion	6	13	28	3,641
3. St. Paul's	10	11	17	3,530
4. Somerset	21	17	38	4,594
5. Allegheny	25	22	25	5,282
6. Central Hungarian	13	18	10	1,162
7. West New York	18	13	13	4,846
TOTALS	121	117	167	31,632
Potomac				
1. Zion's	24	18	36	8,725
2. Maryland	33	26	49	8,903
3. Mercersburg	15	11	19	3,775
4. Virginia	17	15	28	2,953
5. North Carolina	40	28	56	9,726
6. Gettysburg	21	16	33	7,658
7. Carlisle	9	9	18	2,119
8. Juniata	28	22	45	6,459
9. Baltimore-Washington	22	17	17	5,109
TOTALS	209	162	301	55,427

THE REFORMED CHURCH IN THE UNITED STATES—1934

SYNODS CLASSES	MINISTERS	CHARGES	CONGREGATIONS	MEMBERS
Midwest				
1. Fort Wayne	19	20	24	4,915
2. Chicago	15	15	15	2,387
3. Iowa	11	12	14	1,200
4. Lincoln	7	8	8	711
5. Indianapolis	21	14	15	4,443
6. Missouri-Kansas	22	18	21	2,640
7. Kentucky	11	11	15	2,709
8. Zion's Hungarian	9	10	13	1,168
TOTALS	115	108	125	20,173

GRAND TOTALS

Synods: 6 *Classes:* 58	1,332	1,070	1,675	348,189

Bibliography

ALBRIGHT, RAYMOND W. *The Fiftieth Anniversary of the Massanutten Academy,* n.d.

ALDEN, JOSEPH P., AND STIBITZ, GEORGE. *Central Theological Seminary, 1850–1934.* Dayton, Oh., 1957.

APPEL, THEODORE. *The Beginnings of the Theological Seminary.* Philadelphia, 1886.

———. *Life and Work of John Williamson Nevin.* Philadelphia, 1889.

———. *Recollections of College Life.* Reading, Pa., 1866.

ARNDT, ELMER. J. F. *The Faith We Proclaim.* Christian Education Press, 1960.

———, ed. *The Heritage of the Reformation.* New York, 1950.

ARPKE, JEROME. *Das Lipper Settlement.* Milwaukee, 1895.

ATKINS, G., AND FAGLEY, F. *History of American Congregationalism.* Boston, 1942.

BAKER, HELEN E. *The Flags of Dawn,* A Story of the International Missions Enterprise of the Evangelical and Reformed Church. Philadelphia, 1944.

BALTZER, A.C.G. *Recollections of a Missouri-Bred Preacher.* Rio de Janeiro, 1939.

BALTZER, ADOLPH H. *Denkschrift zur 25 jährigen Jubelfeier des Prediger-Seminars.* St. Louis, 1875.

———. *Zur Erinnerung an Pastor E. L. Nollau.* St. Louis, 1869.

BALTZER, HERMANN. *Ein Lebersbild aus der Deutschen Evangelischen Kirche Nord-Amerikas.* St. Louis, 1896.

BEHRENDT, W. *Die Heidenmission der Deutschen Evangelischen Synode von Nord Amerika.* 1901.

BERNER, GOTTFRIED. *Aus der Fremde in die Heimat, Ein Lebensbild des Missionars und Pastor Johannes Huber.* Buffalo, 1904.

BINGHAM, JUNE. *Courage to Change: An Introduction to the Life and Thought of Reinhold Niebuhr.* New York, 1961.

BINKLEY, LUTHER J. *The Mercersburg Théology.* Manheim, Pa., 1953.

BOARD OF HOME MISSIONS. Jubilee addresses on home missions delivered on the occasion of the fortieth anniversary of the Board of Home Missions of the Reformed Church in the U.S. Philadelphia, 1914.

BODE, HENRY. *Builders of Our Foundations.* Webster Groves, Mo., 1940.

BOLLIGER, THEODORE P. "The Westward Expansion of the Reformed Church," *Bulletin*, Theological Seminary of the Reformed Church in the U.S., II (January 1931): 63–103. Lancaster, Pa.

―――. *The Wisconsin Winnebago Indians and the Mission of the Reformed Church*. Cleveland, 1922.

―――, ed. *History of Saint John's Classis*. Cleveland, 1921.

BREADY, GUY P. *The Fathers of the Reformed Church*, Vols. 7–12. Typescript, Historical Society of the Evangelical and Reformed Church. Lancaster, Pa. 1955–56.

―――. *Messenger Index*, Vols. 1–12. Typescript, Historical Society of the Evangelical and Reformed Church. Lancaster, Pa., 1827–1953.

BRICKER, FLORENCE M., ed. *Church and Pastoral Records in the Archives at Lancaster, Pennsylvania*. Lancaster, Pa., 1982.

BRICKER, GEORGE H. *A Brief History of the Mercersburg Movement*. Lancaster, Pa., 1982.

BRUEGGEMANN, WALTER A. *Ethos and Ecumenism: A History of Eden Theological Seminary, 1925–1975*. St. Louis, 1975.

―――. *The Evangelical Catechism Revisited, 1847–1972*. St. Louis, 1972.

BRUENING, DAVID, KOCKRITZ, EWALD, AND HORSTMANN, JULIUS H. *Evangelical Fundamentals*, Part One, "Evangelical Principles and History." St. Louis, 1916.

BUTOSI, JOHN. "The Calvin Synod: Hungarians in the United Church of Christ." In Zikmund, Barbara Brown, ed., *Hidden Histories in the United Church of Christ*, I. New York, 1984, 124–139.

CASSELMAN, ARTHUR V. *The End of the Beginning*. Philadelphia, 1936.

CHADWICK, OWEN. "The Making of a Reforming Prince: Frederick III, Elector Palatinate."

CHRYSTAL, WILLIAM. *A Father's Mantle: The Legacy of Gustav Niebuhr*. New York, 1982.

―――. "Samuel D. Press: Teacher of the Niebuhrs." *Church History* (Dec. 1984): 504–21.

―――, ed. *Young Reinhold Niebuhr: His Early Writings, 1911–1931*. New York, 1982.

CLAPP, J. C., and LEONARD, J. C. *Historic Sketch of the Reformed Church in North Carolina*. Philadelphia, 1908.

CORT, CYRUS, et al. *Digest of Acts and Decisions of the General Synod of the Reformed Church in the United States, 1863–1899*. Philadelphia, 1902.

DAVIS, K. CLAIR. "The Reformed Church of Germany: Calvinists as an Influential Minority."

DAVIS, MARTIN P. *Sadhu Hagenstein, A White Man Among the Brown*. St. Louis, 1930.

DEITZ, PURD E., AND SCHROER, CORNELIA R. *Christianity Makes a Difference.* St. Louis, n.d.

Diaries of the Rev. Michael Schlatter, June 1–December 15, 1746, Journal of the Presbyterian Historical Society, September, 1905.

DIEFENTHALER, JON. "H. Richard Niebuhr: A Fresh Look at His Early Years." *Church History* (June 1983): 172–185.

————. *H. Richard Niebuhr: A Lifetime of Reflections on the Church and the World.* Macon, Ga., 1986.

DIFFENDERFFER, R. R. *The German Exodus to England in 1709.* Lancaster, Pa., 1897.

DIKOVICS, JOHN. *Our Magyar Presbyterians.* New York, 1945.

DIPKO, THOMAS E. "Philip William Otterbein and the United Brethren." In Zikmund, ed., *Hidden Histories,* II, 115–29.

DORNER, J. A. *The Liturgical Conflict in the Reformed Church of North America* (translation). Philadelphia, 1868.

DUBBS, JOSEPH H. *Historic Manual of the Reformed Church.* Lancaster, Pa., 1885.

————. *History of the Reformed Church, German.* (American Church History Series, Vol. 8). New York, 1902.

————. *The Reformed Church in Pennsylvania.* Lancaster, Pa., 1902.

DUNN, DAVID. "The Evangelical and Reformed Church," Chapter 15, *The American Church of the Protestant Heritage,* Vergilius Ferm, ed. New York, 1952.

EISENACH, GEORGE. *A History of the German Congregational Churches in the United States.* Yankton, 1938.

The Evangelical Catechism. New York, 1987.

Festival of the Church: Celebrating the Legacy of the Evangelical Synod of North America. St. Louis, 1978.

Fifty Years of Foreign Missions of the Reformed Church in the United States, 1877–1927. Philadelphia, 1927.

FISHER, SAMUEL R. *History of the Publication Efforts in the Reformed Church.* Philadelphia, 1885.

FLUCKE, JOHN W. *Evangelical Pioneers.* (Brief biographies of Joseph A. Rieger, George W. Wall, Johann J. Riess, Hermann Garlichs, Louis E. Nollau, William Binner, Adolph H. Baltzer, Andreas Irion, Simon Kuhlenhoelter, John J. Schwarz, Louis von Ragué and Oscar Lohr.) St. Louis, 1931.

FOX, RICHARD WIGHTMAN. *Reinhold Niebuhr: A Biography.* New York, 1985.

FRANTZ, JOHN B. "The Awakening of Religion Among the German Settlers in the Middle Colonies." *William and Mary Quarterly* 33 (1976): 310–11.

————. "The Unionistic and Separatistic Movements in the Evangelical and Reformed Church with Particular Reference to These Movements in the Former Reformed Church in the United States." Unpublished S. T. M. diss., School of Theology, Temple University, Philadelphia, 1957.

GARRISON, J. SILOR. *History of the Reformed Church in Virginia, 1714–1940*. Winston-Salem, N.C., 1948.

GEDENKSCHRIFT. *Fiftieth Anniversary of Sheboygan Classis*. Cleveland, 1904.

GELZER, DAVID GEORGE. *Mission to America, Being a History of the Work of the Basel Foreign Missions Society in America*. Ph.D. diss., Yale University, 1952.

Geschichte der Deutschen Synode des Nordwestens, 1867–1917. Cleveland, 1941.

Geschichte des Missionshauses. Cleveland, 1897.

GLATFELTER, CHARLES H. *Pastors and People: German Lutheran and Reformed Churches in the Pennsylvania Field, 1717–1793*. Breinigsville, Pa., 1980.

GOOD, JAMES I. *History of the German Reformed Church, 1729–1792*. Reading, Pa., 1899.

————. *History of the Reformed Church in the Nineteenth Century*. New York, 1911.

————. *History of the Swiss Reformed Church Since the Reformation* Philadelphia, 1913.

————. *Life of Rev. Benjamin Schnieder*. Philadelphia, n.d.

————. *Origin of the Reformed Church in Germany*. Reading, Pa., 1887.

GOSSARD, J. HARVEY. "John Winebrenner: From German Reformed Roots to the Church of God." In Zikmund, ed., *Hidden Histories*, II, 130–48.

GRAMM, CARL H. *Life and Labors of the Reverend J. I. Good*. Webster Groves, Mo., 1944.

GUNNEMANN, LOUIS H. *The Shaping of the United Church of Christ*. New York, 1977.

————. *United and Uniting: The Meaning of an Ecclesial Journey*. New York, 1987.

HAEBERLE, LOUIS. *Festschrift zum Goldenen Jubiläum des Prediger-Seminars*. 1900.

————. *Joseph Rieger, Ein Lebensbild aus der Evangelischen Kirche Nord Amerikas*. St. Louis, 1871.

HAFER, HAROLD F. *Evangelical and Reformed Churches and World War II*. Boyertown, Pa., 1947.

HARBAUGH, HENRY. *The Life of Rev. Michael Schlatter*. Philadelphia, 1857.

HARBAUGH, HENRY, and HEISLER, D. Y. *Fathers of the Reformed Church*. Lancaster, Pa., 1857; Reading, Pa., 1888.

HARRITY, GRANT E. "Events Leading to the Founding of Ursinus College." Unpublished B.D. diss., Lancaster Seminary Library, 1949.

The Heidelberg Catechism with Commentary. Four hundredth anniversary edition. Philadelphia, 1962.

HERRMAN, JOHN. *Lebenserinnerungen von Johann Jakob Schwarz, 1841–1919.* St. Louis, n.d.

HINKE, WILLIAM J. *Life and Letters of the Reverend John Philip Boehm.* Philadelphia, 1916.

———. *Ministers of the German Reformed Congregations in Pennsylvania and Other Colonies in the Eighteenth Century.* Lancaster, Pa., 1951.

———. *Minutes and Letters of the Coetus of Pennsylvania, Acts and Proceedings of the Coetus and Synod, 1791–1816.* Chambersburg, Pa., 1854.

HOEFER, H. *Lebensbild von Simon Kuhlenhölter, 1860–1882.* St. Louis, 1886.

HORSTMANN, JULIUS H. *Evangelical Fundamentals,* Part Two, "Evangelical Fundamentals, Part One, "Evangelical Principles and History."

HORSTMANN, JULIUS H., and WERNECKE, HERBERT H. *Through Four Centuries.* St. Louis, 1938.

HORTON, DOUGLAS. *The United Church of Christ: Its Origins, Organization, and Role in the World Today.* New York, 1962.

IRION, ANDREAS. *Erklärung des Kleinen Evangelischen-Katechismus der deutsch-evangelischen Synode des Westens.* St. Louis, 1870.

JABERG, EUGENE C., et al. *A History of Mission House-Lakeland.* Philadelphia, 1962.

KALASSAY, ALEXANDER. *Az Amerikai Magyar Reformatus Egyesulet Mukodesenek Huszonoteves Tortenete (The Twenty-five Year History of the Activities of the Hungarian Reformed Federation).* Pittsburgh, n.d.

———. *Az Amerikai Magyar Reformatusok Tortenete (History of the Hungarian Reformed People in America).* Pittsburgh, n.d.

———. *Huszonotevi Munka a Jotekonysag Mezejen, 1906–1931 (Twenty-five Years of Benevolent Work).* Pittsburgh, 1934.

KAMPHAUSEN, HUGO. *Geschichte des religiösen Lebens in der Deutschen Evangelischen Synode von Nord Amerika.* St. Louis, 1924.

KAMPHOEFNER, WALTER D. *The Westfalians: From Germany to Missouri.* Princeton, 1987.

KEGLEY, CHARLES W., ed. *Reinhold Niebuhr: His Religious, Social, and Political Thought.* New York, 1984.

Keiling, Hanns Peter. *Die Entstehung der "United Church of Christ" (USA).* Berlin, 1969.

KIEFFER, ELIZABETH CLARKE. *Life of Henry Harbaugh.* Lancaster, Pa., 1945.

KLEIN, FREDERICK S. *The Spiritual and Educational Background of Franklin and Marshall College.* Lancaster, Pa. 1949.

KLEIN, H. M. J. *A Century of Education at Mercersburg, 1836–1936*. Lancaster, Pa. 1936.

———. *History of the Eastern Synod of the Reformed Church in the U.S., 1747–1940*. Lancaster, Pa., 1943.

———. *History of Franklin and Marshall College, 1787–1948*. Lancaster, Pa., 1952.

———. *History of the Phoebe Home*. 1956.

———. "The Library of the Historical Society of the Reformed Church in the U.S." *Bulletin*, Theological Seminary (October 1943).

KNOX, R. BUICK, ed. *Reformation, Conformity, and Dissent*. London, 1977.

KOCKRITZ, EWALD. *Memorial Diamond Jubilee of the Evangelical Synod of North America*. 1915.

KOENIG, ROBERT E. "Our Educational Heritage Through the Evangelical Tradition." *Church School Worker* (Dec. 1966): 19–23.

KOSTYU, FRANK A. *Adventures in Faith and Freedom: A History of the United Church of Christ*. Montclair, N.J., 1979.

LADY, DAVID B. *History of the Pittsburgh Synod*. Greensburg, Pa., 1920.

———. *A History of St. Paul's Orphans' Home of the Reformed Church in the U.S.* Philadelphia, 1917.

LEONARD, JACOB C. *History of the Southern Synod, Evangelical and Reformed Church*. Lexington, N.C., 1940.

LIVENGOOD, FREDERICK G. *Eighteenth-Century Reformed Schools*. Norristown, Pa., 1930.

LUTZ, EARLIN H. "George Warren Richards: His Life and Learning, Work and Witness." Typescript, Historical Society of the Evangelical and Reformed Church, Lancaster, Pa., 1958.

MCKINNEY, WILLIAM, ed. *New Conversations: Toward Theological Self-Understanding in the United Church of Christ*. Spring, 1985, 1–56.

MCMINN, EDWIN. *Life and Times of Henry Antes*. Moorestown, N.J. 1886.

MARKHAM, DON C. "The Reformed Church and the Civil War." Unpublished B.D. diss., Lancaster Theological Seminary Library, 1959.

MAXWELL, JACK MARTIN. *Worship and Reformed Theology: The Liturgical Lessons of Mercersburg*. Pittsburgh, 1976.

MELICK, EDITH MOULTON. *The Evangelical Synod in India*. St. Louis, 1930.

———. *Seed Sowing in Honduras*. St. Louis, 1927.

MENZEL, EMIL W. *I Will Build My Church*. Philadelphia and St. Louis, 1943.

MILLER, DANIEL. *Early History of the Reformed Church in Pennsylvania*. Reading, Pa., 1905.

MILLER, HENRY K. *History of the Japan Mission of the Reformed Church in the United States, 1879–1904*. Philadelphia, 1904.

MOORE, JAIRUS P. *Forty Years in Japan, 1883–1923*. Philadelphia, 1925.

MUECKE, ALBERT. *Geschichte der Deutschen Evangelischen Synode von Nord Amerika. Im Auftrage der Synode zu ihrem 75-jährigen Jubiläum*. St. Louis, 1915.

NEVIN, JOHN H. *The Mystical Presence and Other Writings on the Eucharist*. Thompson, Bard, and Bricker, George H., eds. Philadelphia, 1966.

NICHOLS, JAMES H., ed. *The Mercersburg Theology*. New York, 1966.

———. *Romanticism in American Theology: Nevin and Schaff at Mercersburg*. Chicago, 1961.

NIEBUHR, REINHOLD. "A Landmark in American Religious History." *Messenger* (June 18, 1957): 11–13.

OMWAKE, GEORGE L. *A Survey of the Reformed Church in the United States*. Philadelphia, 1914.

———, ed. *Forward Movement Handbook*. Philadelphia, 1920.

———, ed. *The Great Advance, The Story of the Forward Movement, 1919–1926*. Philadelphia, 1926.

PARSONS, WILLIAM T. *German Reformed Experience in Colonial America*. Philadelphia, 1976.

PAUL, ROBERT S. *Freedom with Order. The Doctrine of the Church in the United Church of Christ*. New York, 1987.

PAYNE, JOHN B. "Philip Schaff: Christian Scholar, Historian and Ecumenist." *Historical Intelligencer* 2 (1982): 17–24.

PRESS, SAMUEL D. "The Church-Union Memoirs of Samuel D. Press." *United Church Herald* (July 1, 1965): 20–22.

———. "Toward a United Church of Christ." *Messenger* (Nov. 29, 1955): 8-11.

RANCK, HENRY H. *The Life of the Reverend Benjamin Bausman*. Philadelphia, 1912.

RAPP, DAVID H. "The Attitude of the Early Reformed Church Fathers Toward Worldly Amusements." *Pennsylvania Folklife* 9 (1958): 40–53.

RASCHE, RUTH W. "The Deaconess Sisters: Pioneer Professional Women." In Zikmund, ed., *Hidden Histories*, I, 95–109.

REID, W. STANFORD, ed. *John Calvin: His Influence in the Western World*. Grand Rapids, 1982, 123–38.

REITER, I. H. "History of the Ohio Synod." *The Reformed Quarterly Review,* 1 (1879): 143–68.

RICHARDS, GEORGE W. "The Genius of the Reformed Church in the U.S. in the Light of Its History." *Theological Magazine* (of the Evangelical Synod of North America), 1933.

———. *History of the Theological Seminary of the Evangelical and Reformed Church at Lancaster, Pennsylvania*. Lancaster, Pa., 1952.

———. *The Synod of the German Reformed Church in the United States of America from 1793 to 1863*. Pamphlet, 1942.

ROYER, HARRY G. "Baptism in the Evangelical and Reformed Tradition." *Prism* (Spring 1986): 40–49.

RUETENIK, HERMAN J. *The Pioneers of the Reformed Church in the United States of North America.* Cleveland, 1901.

SAYRES, ALFRED N. *The Evangelical and Reformed Church* (Church and Home Series). Philadelphia, 1956.

SAYRES, ALFRED N., and STANGER, ROBERT C. *March On with Strength.* Philadelphia, 1953.

SCHAEFFER, CHARLES E. *Beside All Waters, A Study in Home Missions.* Philadelphia, 1937.

———. *Glimpses into Hungarian Life.* Philadelphia, 1923.

———. *Handbook of the Board of Home Missions of the Reformed Church in the United States.* Philadelphia, 1928.

———. *The Man from Oregon—John Gantenbein.* Philadelphia, 1944.

———. *Our Home Mission Work.* Philadelphia, 1914.

———. *A Repairer of the Breach, The Memoirs of Bernard C. Wolff.* Lancaster, Pa., 1949.

SCHAEFFER, CHARLES E., and DEEMS, MERVYN. *Historical Sketches of the Congregational Christian Churches and the Evangelical and Reformed Church.* Philadelphia, 1955.

SCHAFF, DAVID S. *The Life of Philip Schaff.* New York, 1897.

SCHLICHER, J. J. "The Beginning and Early Years of the Mission House" and "The Mission House in the Eighties," reprint of two articles in *The Wisconsin Magazine of History.*

SCHNEIDER, CARL E. *The Genius of the Evangelical Synod of North America.* St. Louis, 1940.

———. *The German Church on the American Frontier, A Study in the Rise of Religion among the Germans of the West.* Based on the history of the *Evangelischer Kirchenverein de Westens,* 1840–1866. St. Louis, 1939.

———. *History of the Theological Seminary of the Evangelical Church.* St. Louis, 1925.

———. "The Origin of the German Evangelical Synod of North America, 1935." Reprint from *Bulletin,* Theological Seminary.

———. *The Place of the Evangelical Synod in American Protestantism.* St. Louis, 1933.

SCHORY, ALBERT. *Geschichte der Deutschen Evangelischen Synode von Nord-Amerika.* St. Charles, Mo., 1889.

SCHROEDEL, M. *Pastor Louis von Ragué, Erinnerungen aus seinem Leben und Wirken.* Hoyleton, Ill., 1912.

SHINN, ROGER. *Unity and Diversity in the United Church of Christ.* Royal Oak, Mi., 1972.

SILLS, HORACE S. "The Union Church: A Case of Lutheran and Reformed Cooperation." In Zikmund, *Hidden Histories,* II, 13–31.

SOUDERS, D. A. *The Magyars in America*. New York, 1922.

SPIKE, ROBERT W. "The United Church of Christ: In Search of a Special Calling." *Christian Century* (Feb. 20, 1963).

SPOTTS, CHARLES D. "Our Reformed Church Educational Heritage." *Church School Worker* (Oct. 1966): 15–17.

STOERKER, FREDERICK. *Know Thy Church,* A General Course in Church History with Special Reference to the Evangelical Synod of North America. St. Louis, n.d.

The Synod of the Northwest, 1917–1940. Cleveland, 1941.

Tercentenary Monument: In Commemoration of the Three Hundredth Year of the Heidelberg Catechism. Chambersburg, Pa., 1863.

THOMPSON, DANIEL BARD. "An Historical Reconstruction of Melanchthonianism and the German Reformed Church Based on Confessional and Liturgical Evidence." Unpublished diss., Columbia University, 1953.

———. *Essays on the Heidelberg Catechism*. Philadelphia, 1963.

TOTH, ALEXANDER, ed. *Jubileumi Evkonyv (Jubilee Book)*. Pittsburgh, 1940.

TROST, THEODORE L., JR. "The Order of Holy Communion of the Evangelical and Reformed Church." *Prism* (Fall 1986): 37–46.

VISSER, DERK, ed. *Controversy and Conciliation: The Reformation and the Palatinate 1559–1583*. Pittsburgh, 1986.

———. *Zacharius Ursinus: The Reluctant Reformer*. New York, 1983.

VRIESEN, H. T. *The Reformed Synod of the Northwest, 1917–1940*. Cleveland, 1941.

WALKER, WILLISTON, ed. *The Creeds and Platforms of Congregationalism*. New York, 1960, 1990.

WATTS, FRANKLIN P. "The Free Synod Movement of the German Reformed Church, 1822–1837." Unpublished diss., Temple University, Philadelphia, 1954.

WEAVER, GLENN. "The German Reformed Church and the Home Mission Movement Before 1863." *Church History* (Dec. 1953): 298–313.

WHITMER, A. CARL. *One Hundred and Fifty Years of Home Missionary Activity, An Outline History of the Home Missionary Work of the Reformed Church in the U.S.* Lancaster, Pa., 1897.

WILLIAMS, E. I. F. *Heidelberg: Democratic Christian College, 1850–1950*. Menasha, Wis., 1952.

WOBUS, PAUL A. *First Fruits, The Glory of God in Ozark Lives*.

WOSSIDLO, C. *Erinnerung an den Ehrw. Hermann Garlichs*. New York, 1865.

YODER, DONALD HERBERT. "Christian Unity in Nineteenth Century America." In Rouse, Ruth, and Neill, Stephen C., eds. *A History of the Ecumenical Movement, 1517–1948*. London, 1954, 247ff.

352 • BIBLIOGRAPHY

YUNDT, THOMAS M. *A History of Bethany Orphans' Home*. Philadelphia, 1907.

ZIEGLER, HOWARD J. B. *Frederick Augustus Rauch: American Hegelian*. Lancaster, Pa., 1953.

ZIKMUND, BARBARA BROWN. "Theology in the United Church of Christ: A Documentary Trail." *Prism* (Fall 1985): 7–25.

———, ed. *Hidden Histories in the United Church of Christ*. 2 vols. New York, 1984, 1987.

ZUCK, LOWELL, H. *European Roots of the United Church of Christ*. Philadelphia, 1976.

———. "Evangelical Pietism and Biblical Criticism: The Story of Karl Emil Otto." In Zikmund, ed., *Hidden Histories*, II, 66–79.

———. *Four Centuries of Evangelism in the United Church of Christ*. New York, 1987.

———. *New-Church Starts: American Backgrounds of the United Church of Christ*. New York, 1982.

———. *Socially Responsible Believers: Puritans, Pietists, and Unionists in the History of the United Church of Christ*. New York, 1986.

Minutes of synods and districts, reports of officers and boards to districts and synods, periodicals published by the Evangelical Synod: *Friedensbote, Messenger of Peace, Herald, Theologische Zeitschrift,* and its successor the *Theological Magazine;* publications of various boards, agencies, and institutions; histories of individual districts and congregations; as well as diaries and correspondence are available in the Eden Archives in the Luhr Library of Eden Theological Seminary, Webster Groves, Missouri.

Here also may be found photostat copies of documents in European archives and of American Home Missionary Society correspondence, etc., pertaining to the Evangelical Synod.

Minutes of synods and classes, copies of the Reformed Church *Messenger, Outlook of Missions, Almanacs* (East and West), *The Year Book, Mercersburg Review, Reformed Quarterly Review, Reformed Church Review, Bulletin* of the Theological Seminary, *Western Missionary, Der Evangelist, The Guardian, Reformed Church Monthly, Der Deutsche Kirchenfreund,* and other periodicals; histories of individual classes and synods; biographies of ministers; anniversary booklets; diaries, memoirs, private papers, and books by Reformed ministers are available in the Archives of the Evangelical and Reformed Historical Society located in Lancaster, Pennsylvania in the Shaff Memorial Library of Lancaster Theological Seminary.

Index of Names and Places

Advance, 316
Africa, 153, 174, 311
Aintab, 104
Albert, C. H., 94
Albert, C. J., 255
Albert, E. G., 245
Albrechtsleute, Die, 62
Albright, Jacob, 62
Allentown Female Seminary (See Cedar Crest College)
Alsace, 5
Alsentz, John George, 42
Altenburg, 224
Alzei, 9
America, 16, 19, 23, 31, 53, 58, 61, 67, 71–72, 75, 83, 103, 112, 125–128, 133–134, 147, 151–152, 155, 158–166, 169, 171–173, 175, 177, 180, 205, 224–225
American Bible Society, 12, 177
American Board of Commissioners for Foreign Missions, 103–104
American Home Missionary Society, 165–167, 172, 178
American Tract Society, 172, 175, 177, 187
Amsterdam, 112, 279, 328
Amsterdam, Classis of, 34–35, 37–38, 51
Andernach, 9
Anderson, W. H. P., 270
Andres, P. J., 259
Anhalt, 14
Anspach, William W., 102
Antes, Heinrich, 34
Anti-Christ, or the Spirit of Sect and Schism, 74
Anti-Saloon League, 110
Anxious Bench, The, 73
Anzeiger des Westens, 173
Apitz, Otto, 266

Apple, Henry Harbaugh, 95
Apple, Joseph Henry 96
Apple, Thomas G., 79, 83, 91–92, 95, 100
Apt to Teach, 268
Arends, C. C., 256
Arizona, 299
Arlt, H., 255
Arndt, Elmer J. F., 259, 314
Arpke, Jerome, 134
Asia Minor, 104
Asperg, 9
Atlantic District, 201, 243
Augsburg, 7
Augsburg, Diet of, 14
Augsburg, League of, 9
Augsburg Confession, 283, 293, 337
Auler, Harold N., Sr., 270
Auler, Mrs. Harold N., Sr., 270
Ault, Mary B. (See Mrs. William E. Hoy)
Aurandt, John Dietrich, 61

Backer, Louise, 267
Baden, 5, 9, 150, 169
Baghdad, 106
Bajpai, Ramnath, 270
Baker, David D., 101
Baltzer, Adolph H., 175, 183, 187, 190–191, 193–195, 198–200, 206–207, 209–210, 217, 219, 222, 227, 235, 238, 240, 248, 252, 259, 273–274
Baltzer, John, 244, 273–275, 281–282, 284
Bank, Johann, 220, 223, 225–226
Barmen, 185
Barmen Mission House, 235, 248
Barmen Missionary Society, 152–153, 156, 161, 168–169, 173, 175, 247, 249
Bartholomew, Allen R., 106, 283
Basel, 5–6, 22, 134, 160, 185

Basel Bible Society, 152
Basel Mission Seminary, 160, 166, 183, 247–248
Basel Missionary Society, 152–153, 156, 160–162, 166–169, 175, 185, 187, 247, 249
Basis of Union, 332–334
Bathe, A., 240
Bauer, Carl, 255
Bauer, W., 231, 258
Bausman, Benjamin, 78, 80, 100
Bavaria, 5, 9, 169
Bayreuth, 5
Beam, J. Albert, 105
Beam, Mrs. J. Albert, 105
Beaver, I. M., 101
Bechtel, John, 35–36
Bechtold, Anna D., 270
Bechtold, C., 248–249
Becker, A. H., 240, 260
Becker, Christian L., 65
Becker, W., 220, 231, 258
Benchoff, Howard Johnston, 97
Berg, 14
Berg, Joseph F., 73, 75
Berlin, 72, 150, 154, 175
Berlin Missionary Society, 161, 224–225
Bern, 6
Berner, G., 262
Beside All Waters, 108
Bethany Orphans Home, 83, 98
Bethlen Home, 98
Bible Stories (See *Biblische Geschichten*)
Bible–Life Series, 315
Biblische Geschichten, 217
Biblische Geschichten (Zahn's), 139
Biegeleisen, John, 258
Bierbaum, A. H. J., 243
Bigelow, Richard, 166, 175, 182, 188
Big Soldier, Mrs. 143
Binner, William Frederick, 175, 179, 182–183, 187–188, 207
Birkner, Friedrich, 175, 178, 183
Bisrampur, 104, 250
Bittern, Silas P., 318–319
Blumer, Abraham, 54
Blumhardt, Christian, 153
Board for Christian Service, 272

Board of Business Management, 300, 302–303
Board of Christian Education and Publication, 100, 299, 302, 314–315
Board of Church Erection, 140
Board of Foreign Missions (E), 244, 269–270, 294
Board of Foreign Missions, (R), 57, 103–104, 294
Board of Home Missions, (E), 238–239, 241, 243–246, 265, 267, 294
Board of Home Missions, (R), 107–108, 140, 294
Board of International Missions, 295, 299, 302, 323
Board of Investments, 302–303
Board of Ministerial Relief, (R), 99, 295
Board of National Missions, 141, 143, 295, 299, 302, 310, 324
Board of Pensions and Relief (E), 295
Board of Pensions and Relief (E & R), 99, 295, 299, 302, 318–320
Board of Publication (R), 77
Board of Religious Education (E), 263, 268
Board of Visitors, 78
Boardman, Horace Elijah, 184
Bode, Henry, 275
Bode, Th. F., 274
Boehm, John Philip, 32–38, 43, 52, 126
Boehringer, Emanuel, 83
Boger, George, 56
Bolliger, Theodore P., 118, 140
Bolman, Frederick deWolfe, Jr., 95
Bomberger, John H. A., 75–76, 83–85, 93, 95–96
Bomhard, Mrs. Emma K., 268
Book of Worship, 85, 309
Bossard, Guido, 134
Bossard, J. J., 129–130, 133–134, 136
Bowman, John C., 92
Braendli, G., 231
Brandenburg, 14
Branke, Paul, 243
Braun, John Jacob, 265
Braun, Theodore C., 101
Brazil, 329, 331
Brecht, J. J., 131, 133–134
Breda, 27

Breisach, 9
Breitenbach, H. L., 256
Bremen, 14, 182
Bremen Missionary Society, 161, 175
Brenner, G. H., 240
Breslau, 175
Bretz, W. L., 265
British Isles, 23, 330
Brodt, H., 255
Bromer, Edward S., 92, 94
Broosa, 104
Brotherhood of Andrew and Philip, 102
Brotherhood of the Evangelical Synod, 103, 263–264
Brown, John, 56
Bruening, David, 261
Brunswick, 21
Bucer, Martin, 13
Buchanan, James, 68, 80
Bucher, John Conrad, 49
Bucher, Vincent W., 267
Buchmueller, Heinrich, 234
Buesser, F., 249
Buettner, John G., 132
Bulletin (Lancaster Seminary), 102
Burgess, George, 167
Burky, A., 129
Bushnell, Horace, 167
Butz, Reuben J., 283

California, 108, 240, 243
  Camp Rose, 269
  Claremont, 333
  Los Angeles, 243
  San Francisco, 108, 243
"Call to Christian Action in Society," 335
Calverts, the, 25
Calvin, John, 11, 52, 74, 86, 281, 336
Calvin College, 139
Camp Mensch Mill, 100
Canada, 127, 138, 140, 245
Capetown, 153
Carlson, Karl Henning, 256
Caroline Mission, 266
Casselman, Arthur V., 106
Catawba College, 94, 300
Catherine the Great, 246
Cavert, Samuel M., 289

Cedar Crest College, 96, 299
Central Hungarian Classis, 90
Central Publishing House, 139
Central Synod, 89, 122, 136, 138
Central Theological Seminary, 88, 94, 132, 294
Certificate of Incorporation, 296–297
Chandkuri, 251
Chandkuri Leper Hospital, 270
Charles II, King, 23
Charles V, Emperor, 7
Charles Phillip, Elector, 16
Chase, Philander, 169
Chhattisgarh, 251
China, 105–106, 305, 310
Christian Century, The, 126–127, 289
Christian Endeavor Societies, 262
Christian Hymns, 261
Christian World, The, 100, 139, 294
Christliche Kinderzeitung (Christian Children's Paper), 217
Christliche Zeitschrift (See *Reformierte Kirchenzeitung*)
Christman, Henry J., 288
Christman, Jacob, 56
Church and Home Series, 315
Church Extension Fund Board, 265, 268
Church Missionary Society, 153
Church of Christ in China, 105
Church of Christ in Japan, 105
Church of England, 153
Church of the Palatinate, 37, 293
Church of the Prussian Union (See Evangelical Church of Germany)
Church people, 4–5, 27, 36, 40
Church Society of Ohio, 183, 204, 206
Church Society of the West (See Evangelical Synod of North America)
Church World Service, 99
Churches of God, 62
Churchmen's Brotherhood, 103, 300, 302, 321
Churchmen's League, 103
Cincinnati Classis, 138
Civil War (U.S.), 69, 77, 79–81, 83, 87–88, 95, 147, 184, 186, 194, 206
Clapp, J. C., 94
Clarion Classis, 64

Classical School (See Marshall College)
Cleves, 14
Coblentz, E. L., 283
Coblentz, Lloyd E., 90
Coetus (R), 32, 37–39, 41–44, 47–48, 50–51, 53, 56, 58, 64, 98
College Student Department, 263
Colorado, 243–244, 246
  Denver, 243
  Fort Collins, 246
Colorado Mission District, 244, 246
Columbiana Classis, 123
Commentary on the Psalms, 224
Commission on Benevolent Institutions, 301–303, 324 (See also Commission on Health and Welfare Services)
Commission on Christian Social Action, 300, 302–305, 311, 320
Commission on Christianity and Social Problems, 273, 275
Commission on Church and Ministry, 300, 304–305, 317
Commission on Evangelism, 300, 302–303
Commission on Health and Welfare Services, 300, 302–303, 324
Commission on Higher Education, 300–302
Commission on Inter-Church Relations and Christian Unity (Congregational Christian), 331–332
Commission on Social Service, 110
Commission on Stewardship, 300, 303, 306
Commission on World Service, 305, 323
Commission to Prepare a Statement of Faith for the United Church of Christ, 314
Committee on Army and Navy Chaplains, 304–305
Committee on Closer Relations with Other Churches, 331–332
Committee on Constitution, 291
Committee on Life Enlistment, 317
Committee on Liturgics, 308
Committee on Theological Education, 308, 327
Committee on Vital Christian Living, 303
Committee to Study Facilities and Programs of the Theological Seminaries, 324, 327
Concord, Formula of, 15
Conference on Church Union, 328

Congregational Association of Massachusetts, 103
Congregational Christian Churches, 315, 323, 331–332, 334
Connecticut, 166
  Greenwich, 328
  Hartford, 166–168
Constitution and Bylaws, 296–297, 302–304, 306, 321–322
Constitution and Bylaws (United Church of Christ), 334–335
Crusius, Paul N., 256–257, 261
Curtis, William F., 96

Dahlmann, A. E., 136, 283
Darms, John M. G., 136
Darmstadt, 5
Daubert, Karl, 169–170, 173
Deaconess Hospital (St. Louis), 272
De Bruine, Harvey, 256
Debus, A., 242
Decorah, David, 143
Delong, Irwin H., 92
Department of United Promotion, 300, 306–308
Dessau, 150
Devitt Sanitarium, 98
Dewald, H. A., 270
Dickinson College, 66
Dinkmeier, John H., 212
"Directory of Worship," 85
Distler, Theodore A., 95
Domestic Mission Society of Connecticut, 166
Dorsius, Peter Henry, 34, 42
Dresel, Theodor Hermann, 233–234, 247, 249
Dubbs, Joseph H., 54, 74, 76, 82
Dutch Reformed Church (See Reformed Church in America)

East, the (U.S.), 83–85, 100, 116–117, 122–123, 130–132, 140, 155, 161, 166, 169, 175, 189
East Pennsylvania Classis, 64, 75
East Susquehanna Classis, Eastern District, 239
Eastern District, 239

Eastern Hungarian Classis, 90
Eastern Synod, 53–55, 57–70, 72–73, 75–87, 89–93, 95–96, 99–100, 103–105, 107, 109, 114, 117, 187, 198
Ebmeyer, G. A., 255
Ecuador, 310, 329
Eddy, Sherwood, 275
Eden Publishing House, 244, 265, 268
Eden Theological Seminary, 132, 207, 229–232, 247, 249, 253, 257–258, 260, 263, 266, 273–274, 281, 294, 299, 316, 326–327
Edinburgh Missionary Conference, 112, 279, 322
Edwards, Jonathan, 60
Ehlman, Dobbs F., 106
Elliker, G. D., 128, 140
Elmhurst College, 207–209, 212–214, 229, 231, 236, 252, 254–258, 262–263, 269, 274, 299, 302
Elmhurst Hymnal, 261
Elmhurst Summer Training School, 269
Emden, 6
Enders, Charles, 265
England, 3, 20, 24, 73
English Literary Committee, 274
Eppenheim, 9
Erie Classis, 137–138
Erlangen, 175
Europe, 3, 8, 13, 18, 52, 73, 82, 91, 107, 112, 132, 134, 149, 155, 157, 159, 162–165, 330
Evangelical and Reformed Church, 3, 85, 90, 96, 102–103, 112, 128, 141, 289, 292, 296–299, 308, 310, 314–317, 321–323, 326–329, 331–333, 336–337
Evangelical Association, 62, 284
Evangelical Catechism, 179–180, 197, 260, 313
Evangelical Church, 284
Evangelical Church of Germany, 148–149, 153, 162, 172, 175, 180, 182, 228, 293
Evangelical Commission on Closer Relations with Other Church Bodies, 282
Evanglical Herald, 101, 261, 273, 281, 294, 316
Evanglical Home, 98
Evangelical Hymnal, 261

Evangelical League, 256, 262–263, 269
Evangelical Lutheran Society of the West, 174
Evangelical Magazine (Helmuth's), 70
Evangelical Orphans Home, 187, 199, 230
Evangelical Pioneers, 237
Evangelical (Ewe) Presbyterian Church of Togoland, 310
Evangelical Synod of North America, 97, 102, 104, 111–112, 159–161, 168–169, 171–185, 187–193, 195–196, 198–213, 215, 217–229, 233–235, 238–250, 252, 256–260, 264, 266, 268–275, 279–283, 285–288, 290, 293–294, 297, 310, 312, 319, 328
Evangelical Synod of the East, 203–204, 212, 214, 218–219
Evangelical Synod of the Northwest, 202–207, 211–212, 218–219, 248
Evangelical Synod of the West (See Evangelical Synod of North America)
Evangelical Teacher, The, 268, 273
Evangelical Union of Prussia, 70
Evangelical United Brethren, 284, 310
Evangelical Year Book, 261
Evangelischer Kalender, 220
Evangelischer Missionsfreund, 249
Evangelist, 133, 135, 139
Explanation of the Small Evangelical Catechism, 223

Fabian, Peter, 4
Faith We Proclaim, The, 314, 326
Fathers of the German Reformed Church in Europe and America, Vol. II, 57
Faust, Benjamin, 117–118
Federal Council of Churches of Christ in America, 110–111, 273–274, 280, 289, 328
Federation of Evangelical Charities, 272
Feil, J. Christoph, 234–235
Feldwisch, H., 211
Ferris, J. M., 104
Fischer, F., 245
Fischer, J. C., 282
Fisher, Charles G., 99
Fisher, Samuel R., 77, 84, 90, 99, 100
Fleer, E. J., 245

Florida, 299
Flucke, John, 236
Formosa, 329
Fort Wayne Children's Home, 115
Forward Movement, 99, 113
France, 7–9, 11, 20, 181, 331
Francke, August Hermann, 151
Franconia, 5
Frankenfeld, F., 282
Frankenthal, 9
Franklin, Benjamin, 5, 49
Franklin and Marshall Academy, 97
Franklin and Marshall College, 68, 90–91,
   95, 97, 300–301
Franklin College, 43, 68, 70, 90, 95
Frantz, Oswin S., 92
Frederick William III, 14–15, 17, 148–150,
   154
Frederick William IV, 182
Freeland Seminary, 84, 95
Freiburg, 10
French and Indian War, 49
French Togoland, 329
Friedensbote, Der, 177, 187–188, 199–200,
   218–220, 239, 248, 260, 274, 294, 315
Friedli, Josias, 136, 140
Fritchey, John Christ, 56
Freund, F. H., 244–245

Gallaudet, Thomas, 166
Garlichs, Hermann, 168–169, 171–174
Gass, Jacob, 251, 270
Gast, Frederick A., 91–92
Gemeinschaftliche Gesangbuch, 70
General Conference of the Evangelical
   Synod, 191, 200, 214, 217, 248, 268, 272
   of 1855, 233
   of 1859, 233
   of 1864, 233
   of 1866, 190, 234
   of 1868, 191, 210, 216
   of 1870, 199, 208, 210–211, 217, 238
   of 1872, 203, 212–213, 217–218, 220,
      239–270, 244
   of 1874, 217–218, 259, 271
   of 1877, 213
   of 1880, 200, 214, 228–229, 240
   of 1883, 201, 230, 241, 249–250

   of 1886, 241
   of 1889, 202
   of 1892, 202, 268
   of 1898, 202, 243
   of 1901, 244, 262, 272
   of 1905, 274
   of 1909, 202, 260, 262
   of 1913, 261, 263, 268
   of 1917, 255, 273, 275
General Conference of the Evangelical
   Synod
   of 1921, 261, 263–264
   of 1925, 263, 275, 281
   of 1927, 275, 281
   of 1929, 275, 282
General Council, 307–308, 323, 325, 330–
   331, 333–334
General Council (Congregational Christian),
   332–333
General Synod of the Evangelical and Reformed Church, 136, 302, 306–308, 318–
   319, 331–332
   of 1934, 289
   of 1936, 294
   of 1938, 294, 296, 309, 322
   of 1940, 294, 296–297, 299, 301, 304–
      306, 316, 320
   of 1942, 304, 309, 332
   of 1944, 332
   of 1947, 319–320
   of 1949, 332
   of 1950, 303, 320
   of 1953, 304, 307, 312, 320–321, 323, 325
   of 1956, 330
   of 1959, 299, 301, 303, 317, 321, 323, 327,
      330, 335
General Synod of the Reformed Church,
   35–36, 81–84, 90–91, 93, 99, 106, 110–
   111, 137, 284, 288
   of 1863, 64, 79, 82, 88, 94, 99, 110
   of 1872, 85, 93
   of 1875, 93
   of 1878, 85, 106
   of 1884, 107
   of 1887, 102
   of 1891, 111
   of 1896, 100
   of 1899, 105

of 1917, 110
of 1919, 113
of 1929, 103
of 1932, 286
General Synod of the United Church of Christ, 333–335
Geneva, 14–15
Georgia
Savannah, 50
Gerber, Johannes, 168
Gerhard, Paul L., 105
Gerhart, Emanuel Vogel, 69, 78, 80, 82, 91–92, 95
German Evangelical Missionary Society in the U.S., 104, 249–250
German Reformed Church (See Reformed Church in the United States)
German Reformed Church Magazine, The, 67
German Reformed Synod of Pennsylvania and Adjacent States, 64–66
German Synod of the East, 59, 89, 138
German Synod of the High German Reformed Church in Ohio and Adjacent States, 123
German Synod of the Northwest, 89
Germany, 5–7, 9, 11, 13, 19, 24, 28, 58, 67–68, 109, 111, 117, 125–126, 128–129, 131–132, 147–148, 151–155, 158–160, 165, 168–169, 171–174, 179, 181–183, 203, 206, 208, 225, 231–232, 237, 242, 275
Gesangbuch 139
Geschichte des religiösen Lebens in der Deutschen Evangelischen Synode, 222
Ghana, 311, 329–330
Giese, F. A., 266
Gieselmann, W. F., 212
Giessen, 68
Giesy, Henry, 56–57
Gillman, Laura, 267
Gladden, Washington, 110
Glarus, 127–128
Glessner, Jefferson C., 106
Glessner, Mrs. Jefferson C., 106
Goebel, Johann Peter, 214–215, 234, 252, 273
Goebel, Louis W., 282, 288–289, 296–297, 304–305, 321–322
Goebel, Philipp, 205, 238
Goetsch, Frederick A., 106, 262
Goetschy, John Henry, 34
Good, James I., 61, 69, 74, 93–94, 112, 116
Good, Jeremiah H., 84
Good Samaritan Hospital, 185–187, 199
Goshenhoppen Classis, 64
Gotha, 21
Gottlieb, P., 270
Grabowski, A., 231
Graffenried, Christopher von, 29–30
Grau, Eugene E., 311
Grau, Mrs. Eugene E., 311
Grether, Jacob, 143
Gring, Ambrose D., 85, 104
Gring, Mrs. Ambrose D., 85, 104
Gros, Daniel, 42
Grosshuesch, Paul, 136
Guardian, The, 101
Gueting, George Adam, 48, 61
Guldin, Samuel, 12, 32, 36
Gunnemann, Louis H., 137, 326
Gyr, H., 242

Haas, C. G., 260, 274
Haas, K. W. F., 203, 207, 244
Haas, Louis J., 221
Hacke, Nicholas P., 57
Haeberle, Louis F., 208, 222, 226, 231, 234
Haeger, John Frederick, 28
Haeger, John Henry, 29–30
Haeussler, Armin, 217
Hagenstein, August, 251
Hall, William W., 95
Halle, 21, 61, 175, 223
Hamburg, 210
Hammerschmidt, Adolph, 237
Hanau, 5
Hanover, 148
Hansen, Emil, 256
Hansen, J. Christian, 261
Hapsburgs, the, 7
Harbaugh, Henry, 57, 78, 80, 82, 91, 101, 116
Harms, Klaus, 150
Harner, Nevin C., 93, 112, 313
Hartman, Edwin Mitman, 97

Hartmann, Joseph, 203, 205, 207
Hattendorf, W., 244
Hauck, Albert, 56
Hauser, Jacob, 104, 142
Hauser, Mrs. Jacob, 142
Hausfreund, 219
Hautz, Anthony, 57
Hazlebeck, W. F., 282
Heidelberg, 6, 9, 13, 16, 21, 33, 68
Heidelberg Catechism, 14–16, 32–33, 39, 48, 54, 70, 72, 76, 82–83, 87–88, 117, 123, 126, 128, 139, 179, 283, 288, 292–293, 313
Heidelberg Classis, 137–138
Heidelberg College, 69, 94–95, 132, 135, 214, 255, 299
Heidelberg League, 100
Heidelberg Seminary, 132, 138
Heisler, D. Y., 116
Helffenstein, Samuel, 59, 65, 79
Helfferich, Donald L., 96
Helfferich, John Henry, 39
Helmick, Homer H., 256–257
Helming, Herman, 130
Helvetic Confession, Second, 12
Helvetic Consensus, 12
Hendel, William, Jr., 61, 65–66
Hendel, William, Sr., 42, 47, 54–55, 65
"Hendel's Hymnbook," 54
Hendricks, Francis, 93
Henkel, the Reverend, 259
Henop, Frederick L., 47
Herborn, 21, 47
Herbruck, Peter, 119, 123–124, 131
Herbruck Synod, 122–123
Hergert, J., 245
Herman, Frederick, 64
Herman, Lebrecht Frederick, 64–65
Herman, Theodore F., 92–93, 109
Hertzler, Henry, 49
Hesse, 151
Hesse-Darmstadt, 5
Hesse-Kassel, 14
Hesshus, Professor, 13–14
Heyer, Philip, 170, 173–174
Heyser, William, 80
Higbee, Elnathan Elisha, 91
Hillegass, Michael, 50

Hinke, William J., 93, 116
Historical Society, 83, 300
History and Genius of the Heidelberg Catechism, The, 74
History of St. John's Classis, 118
History of the Reformed Church in the Nineteenth Century, The, 61
History of the Reformed Church in the United States, The, 74
Hodge, Charles, 74
Hofer, Ernst A., 136
Hoffman Orphanage, George W. and Agnes, 98
Hoffmeister, Karl, 233–234
Hohmann, F., 260
Hoke, Elmer Rhodes, 94
Holland (See The Netherlands)
Holland, Church of, 36, 38–39, 42–43, 51, 53, 64–65, 69, 118
Holland Synod, 37
Holmes, John Haynes, 275
Homewood Church Home, 98
Honduras, 264, 270–271, 310, 329–330
Hong Kong, 311, 329–330
Hood, Mrs. Margaret E. S., 96
Hood College, 96, 300–301
Horstmann, Julius H., 101, 260–261, 281–282
Hosto, E. J., 243
Hoy, William E., 104–105
Hoy, Mrs. William E., 105
Huenemann, Ruben H., 137
Hunan Classis, 105
Hunan Province, 105
Hungarian Reformed Federation of America, 98
Hungary, 330
Hunter, Governor, 28
Huping Christian College, 105
Hymnal, The, 309

I Believe—A Christian Faith for Youth, 313
Idaho, 244–245
  Payette, 245
Illinois, 120, 124, 147, 155, 159, 167–168, 175, 181, 203, 219, 240, 248, 299
  Alhambra, 214
  Alton, 167

Beardstown, 168
Belleville, 155, 238
Centerville, 170
Chicago, 176, 203, 205, 207, 238, 242, 244, 248, 257, 265, 269, 275
Columbia, 225, 229
East St. Louis, 244
Edwardsville, 231
Elmhurst, 202, 207, 211–212, 214, 229, 237, 252
Freeport, 89, 211
Hoyleton, 238, 254
Joliet, 116
Lake Zurich, 207
Naperville, 237
Peotone, 215
Princeton, 233
Quincy, 170, 203, 212, 238
Immigrant and Seamen's Mission, 266
India, 104, 142, 249–251, 262, 270–271, 310, 330
India Mission District, 218
Indiana, 117, 119, 124–125, 175, 181, 263, 199
 Berne, 124
 Bethlehem, 211
 Bluffton, 124
 Decatur, 124–125
 Evansville, 158, 204, 206–207, 209–212, 244, 256, 264
 Fort Wayne, 89, 93, 124–125, 130–131, 134, 137
 Huntington, 124–125
 Indianapolis, 103, 191
 Lafayette, 125
 Magley, 124–125
 Mishawaka, 211
 Newville, 125
 St. Lucas, 125
 Vera Cruz, 124, 134
Indiana Classis, 137
Indiana District, 260, 281
Indonesia, 311
Interchurch World Movement, 108, 113, 280
International Congregational Council, 329
International Uniform Lesson Series, 314
Iowa, 120, 129, 133, 138, 147, 159, 175,
 181, 206, 233, 299
Burlington, 201, 233, 247
Council Bluffs, 234–235
Fort Dodge, 184
Fort Madison, 168
Storm Lake, 120
Washington, 233
Iraq, 106, 310
Ireland, 24
Irenicum, 16
Irion, Andreas, 183, 188, 208, 222–233, 252–253
Irion, Daniel, 214, 226, 252–256
Irvine, William Mann, 97

James II, 23
Jamestown, 4
Janett, J. J., 120
Jans, J., 246
Japan, 85, 92, 104–105, 108, 127, 310, 329–330
Japanese Exclusion Act, 110
Jerusalem Conference, 280
Jesuits, 10, 16
John, F. H. Rudolph, 220, 231
John, Rudolph A., 261
John Frederick (Saxony), 7
Johnson, F. Ernest, 275
Jones, E. Stanley, 328
Jones, Bishop Paul, 275
Josenhans, E., 160
Jost, John, 251
Jud, Johann Balthasar, 249
Jugendbibliothek, 120
Jugendbund (Young People's League), 244, 262
Jugendverein (Young People's Society), 197
Julich, 14
Jung, Johann, 175
Jungk, William T., 220
Jurany, Gustave, 107

Kaiserswerth, 186
Kalassay, Alexander, 98
Kalmes, Peter, 26
Kamphausen, Hugo, 190, 221–223, 227, 229
Kampmeier, Wilhelm, 238

Kansas, 120, 299
Kapitzky, Frances, 317
Katterjohn, Henry, 261–262
Kauffmann, Frederick, 222
Kellogg-Briand Pact, 110
Kelly, William, 105
Kentucky
  Louisville, 89, 158, 167, 199, 233, 263
Kepler, Johann, 20
Keppel, Alvin R., 95, 269
Keppel, C. J., 269
Kern, Michael, 50
Kerschner, J. B., 91
Keuchen, E., 207
Khariar, 271
Kieffer, J. Spangler, 80
Kieffer, M., and Company, 77
Kieffer, Moses, 77
Kiel, 150
King of Thunder, 143
Kirchenrath, 15
Kirchenrathsordnung, 15, 33
Kirchentag, 224
Kirchenverein des Westens (See Evangelical
  Synod of North America)
Kirchenverein of Ohio (See Church Society
  of Ohio)
Kirchenzeitung, Die, 139, 294, 315
Kirchheim, 9
Kirchhoff, Heinrich, 234
Kirkuk, 106
Kisselmann, J., 245
Klebitz, Deacon, 14
Klein, A., 249
Klein, H. J., 138
Klein, H. M. J., 55
Klein, J. H., 84
Kluge, J. T., 130, 133
Knappenberger, J. William, 96
Knauss, Jacob, 175
Koch, Henry, 57
Kocherthal, Joshua von, 19, 28
Kochheim, 9
Kohler, Mrs. Herbert, 116
Kohler Foundation, Inc., 115
Kohlmann, L., 244
Kramer, Julius, 240
Kranz, Carl F., 211–213

Kresge, Elijah E., 110
Kriete, C. F., 140
Krueger, Arthur M., 136–137
Krueznach, 9
Kruger, R., 242
Krummacher, Frederick William, 72
Kruse, S., 268
Kuckhermann, F. H. W., 126, 131
Kuether, F. C., 272
Kuhlenhoelter, Simon, 238
Kunzmann, Carl, 220, 228, 231, 249
Kurhessen, 169
Kurtz, H., 136, 138, 141

Ladbergen, 126
Lakeland College, 136, 299
Lakeside Hungarian Classis, 90
Lampe, William E., 102
Lancaster Classis, 64
Lancaster Theological Seminary, 67, 71, 90,
  94, 102, 109, 112, 299, 316–317, 326–327
Land, Paul H., 107
Landis, Evan M., 93
Langenberg Society, 177
Langhorst, Oliver M., 256
Larose, Jacob, 56
Lausanne World Conference on Faith and
  Order, 279
Lay School of Theology, 326
Laymen's Missionary Movement, 102
League of Nations, 110, 113
Lebanon Classis, 63
Lederer, John, 4
Lehmann, Timothy, 257–258, 270
Leibnitz, Gottfried Wilhelm, 20
Leich, F. William, 287–288
Leinbach, Paul S., 101
Leitfaden, 128
Leonard, Jacob C., 94, 283
Leutwein, A., 245
Library Society, 155
Liederbuch für Sonntagschulen, 217
Lincoln, Abraham, 80–81, 115
Lippe, 14, 128
Lippe-Detmold, 134
Lipper Settlement, Das, 134
Lischy, Jacob, 36
Liturgical Committee (R), 76

Liturgical Question, The, 76
Livingston, John H., 66, 69
Locher, C. W., 273
Logan, Governor James, 26, 44
Lohans, H H., 259
Lohr, Julius, 251
Lohr, Oscar, 104, 250–251, 269
London, 10, 26
London Missionary Society, 105, 153, 167
Loretz, Andrew, 56
Louis, 8–9
Louis of Baden, 10
Louisiana
New Orleans, 158, 169, 175, 238, 240
Lucerne, 6
Lueder, J., 236–237, 255
L. U. P. O. S. ("Looking Upward, Pressing Onward Society"), 166, 172
Luternau, G. von, 215, 222
Luther, Martin, 13, 148, 230, 281, 336
Lutheran Church, 61, 69, 111, 169, 174, 187, 198, 249
Lutheran Synod of Ohio, 151, 161, 165, 174
Luther's Catechism, 283, 293, 336
Luther's Smaller Catechism, 179

McClure, Norman Egbert, 96
McDonnell, Mrs. William F., 267
Magyar Synod, 90
Mahasamund, 270
Mahnenschmidt, John Peter, 57, 117
Maine, 58
Makassar Theological Seminary, 311
Malplaquet, 10
Mangold, J. G., 243
Mann, Jonathan, 160
Manneheim, 6
Manrodt, M., 259
Marburg, 21, 68
Marburg Colloquy, 70
Marburg Hymnal, 54
Marcus, E. H., 283
Marshall College, 68, 71, 74, 90-91, 95, 97
Marthasville Seminary, 181, 183–184, 206–209, 222–223, 225–226, 228, 231–232, 234, 239, 253, 255
Maryland, 24–25, 27, 31, 56, 58, 117

Baltimore, 47, 61, 65, 76, 87, 107, 201, 266, 281
Frederick, 47, 58, 60, 66, 89, 96, 103
Fredericktown, 31
Hagerstown, 47, 64, 66–67, 86, 98
Monocacy, 31
Williamsport, 98
Maryland Classis, 63, 66, 71, 76
Massanutten Academy, 97, 300–301
Maurer, R., 245
Mayer, F., 258
Mayer, Jacob, 68
Mayer, Lewis, 67–68, 72, 75–76
Mayer, Theodore, 268–269
Meck, Allan S., 93
Mehrtens, Fred J., 267
Meier, Mrs. Wilhelmina, 186
Melanchthon, Philipp, 13, 336–337
Melanchthon Seminary, 206–207, 211
Menzel, Paul A., 271, 274
Mercersburg Academy, 97, 300–301
Mercersburg Classis, 64
Mercersburg College, 91, 96–97
Mercersburg Review, 74, 84, 101
Messenger, The, 294, 316, 333
Messenger of Peace (See *Der Friedensbote*)
Methodist Church, 313
Meusch, Philipp F., 208, 213–214
Michigan, 185, 203, 299
Ann Arbor, 160–161, 168, 262
Detroit, 160–161, 166, 203, 207, 244, 248, 264–265
Freedom, 258
Lansing, 161
Monroe, 161
Saginaw, 161
Mickley, J. Harvey, 90
Middle District, 239
Midwest, the (U.S.), 130, 147, 159–161, 185
Milledoler, Philip, 66
Miller, Charles E., 283
Miller, Henry K., 104
Miller, Mrs. Henry K., 104
Miller, John Peter, 34
Miller, Rufus W., 99–100, 102
Ministers' Retirement Annuity Fund, 319–320
Minnesota, 120, 133, 138, 206, 245, 299

Cottage Grove, 236
Duluth, 236–238
Lake Elmo, 236
Minneapolis, 236
New Schwanden, 236
Osseo, 236
St. Paul, 236, 238
Minuit, Peter, 4, 28
Mission House, 129–130, 133–136, 138–139, 141
Mission House College, 94, 136, 299 (See also Lakeland College)
Mission House Theological Seminary, 127, 137, 299, 316–317, 326
Missionar, Der, 249
Missionary Society (R), 76, 103
Missionsbote, 248
Mississippi, 124
  Biloxi, 267
  Waveland, 269
Missouri, 56, 126, 147, 159, 168–169, 174–175, 177, 181, 184, 211, 219, 240, 243, 248, 274, 299
  Berger, 240
  Bixby, 267
  Bunker, 267
  California, 233
  Femme Osage, 168, 170, 181
  Gladden, 267
  Gravois Settlement, 170
  Holstein, 243
  Kansas City, 89, 234–235
  Lesterville, 267
  Marthasville, 155, 176, 181, 184, 206, 222, 225, 229, 232, 236
  St. Charles, 155, 168, 170, 173, 211
  St. Joseph, 234
  St. Louis, 151, 158, 160, 167–170, 173, 176–177, 181–182, 185–186, 188, 199–201, 215, 224–225, 230, 236, 240, 244, 247–248, 251, 264–266, 272, 308
  Stone Hill, 267
  Washington, 155, 184, 229
  Webster Groves, 132, 258, 294, 316
  Whitmore, 243
Missouri Lutheran Synod, 150, 161, 225
Miyagi (Girls') College, 105
Montana, 245

Billings, 245
Hardin, 245
Moore, Dale H., 96
Moore, Jairus P., 104–105
Moore, Mrs. Jairus P., 104–105
Moravian Church, 111, 247, 249
Mori, J., 108
Moritz, Paul G., 263
Morrison, Charles Clayton, 275
Moss, Robert V., Jr., 93
Muecke, Albert, 231, 247
Muehlmeier, H. A., 130, 133–134, 136
Muehlmeier, Mrs. H. A., 133
Mueller, Gottlieb, 211
Mueller, John W., 282
Mueller, Theophil W., 256–257, 274
Muhlenberg, Henry Melchior, 61
Mullan, James M., 110
Muller, J. G., 243
Musser, Cyrus J., 101
My Church, 314
My Confirmation, 313–314
Mystical Presence, The, 74

Napoleonic Wars, 147
Nassau, 5, 14, 169
National Council of Churches, 111, 300, 322, 328, 330
National Service Commission, 109
National Sunday School Convention, 269
Nazareth Orphans Home, 98
Neander, Joachim, 20
Nebraska, 120, 138, 206, 299
  Omaha, 235
Neckarhausen, 9
Netherlands, The, 12, 14–15, 28, 38–39, 43, 45, 51, 53, 58, 64, 67, 69, 118
Nevada, 299
Neveling, John W. G., 49
Nevin, John W., 62, 68, 72–77, 80, 82–83, 90, 95, 103, 116, 130
New Amsterdam, 4
New Brunswick Theological Seminary, 65, 69
New England, 3, 23–25, 121
New Jersey, 31, 44–45, 58, 298
  Amwell, 31
  Fox Hill, 31

German Valley, 27, 31
Lambertville, 31
New Brunswick, 45, 69
Newton, 31
Princeton, 72
Rockaway, 31
New Measures, 60–62, 117, 121
New York, 24, 28, 31, 38, 44, 55, 57, 69, 117, 176, 203, 296, 298
Albany, 296
Brooklyn, 174, 249, 333
Buffalo, 151, 158, 201, 203, 205, 242, 262, 269
Dunkirk, 269
New York, 19, 66, 70, 107, 129, 166, 182, 274
Rochester, 177, 200–201, 203, 214, 227, 231
Schenectady, 72
Schoharie, 28
Syracuse, 259
New York Classis, 64, 104
New York District, 201, 264
Newmann, J., 245
Nicholas II, 246
Niebuhr, G., 243
Niebuhr, H. Richard, 257–258, 282, 327
Niebuhr, Reinhold, 275, 327
Noehren, H., 274
Nollau, Louis Eduard, 170, 172–174, 181, 186, 191, 199
Nolte, F. W., 232
North, the (U.S.), 24, 56, 87
North Carolina, 4, 24, 30, 55–57, 83, 87–89, 94, 98
Hickory, 94
New Berne, 29–30
Newton, 94
Rockwell, 98
Salisbury, 94
North Carolina Classis, 64, 75, 79, 86–87, 283
North Dakota, 120, 138, 245
Hebron, 242
New Salem, 242–243
North Dakota Synod, 324
Northampton Classis, 63
Northeast District, 204, 218

Northern District, 236, 238
Northern Illinois District, 243, 281
Northwest, the (U.S.), 137, 242, 317
Northwest District, 218
Northwest Synod, 114, 124, 128, 131, 137–138, 140
Noss, Christopher, 92, 105
Noss, Mrs. Christopher, 105
Nottrott, Karl W., 251, 270
Nova Scotia, 58
Nugent, Carl W., 108
Nussmann, Oscar, 267
Nuszloch, 9

Oakwood Institute, 267, 272
Oberlin, John Frederick, 152
Oberwesel, 9
Oel, John Jacob, 28
Ohio, 55–57, 69, 88, 117, 120–121, 124, 131, 134, 137, 171, 203, 205, 262–263, 299
Akron, 102, 132
Canton, 89, 121, 132
Carlton, 132
Cincinnati, 85, 126, 158, 167, 169, 176, 204, 206–207, 209–212, 262, 264, 272
Cleveland, 77, 100, 107, 115, 139, 269, 286, 308, 329, 332, 334–336
Columbus, 132, 257, 296
Dayton, 94, 100, 294
Defiance, 119
Delphos, 125
Galion, 89, 138
Lancaster, 117
New Knoxville, 125–127
New Philadelphia, 118
Oberlin, 332, 334
Tiffin, 94, 105, 125, 132, 135
Toledo, 119
Upper Sandusky, 134–135
Xenia, 102
Ohio Classis, 63–64, 115, 117–118, 130
Ohio Synod (E), 248
Ohio Synod (R), 64, 69, 76, 81–82, 84, 89–90, 107, 114, 118–119, 122–123, 130–131, 136–137
Okinawa, 329
"Old Reformed," 73–74, 84, 86, 101, 114

Olevianus, Caspar, 14, 52
Omwake, George Leslie, 96
Omwake, Howard R., 94
Order of Worship of 1866, 83–85
Oregon, 240, 245
    Portland, 245
Oshikawa, Masayoshi, 105
Otterbein, Philip William, 42, 47–48, 56, 61–62
Otto, Karl Emil, 220, 222–229, 235, 252, 255
Outlook of Missions, 101
Oxford Conference, 322

Pacific Coast, the (U.S.), 138, 265
Pacific District, 243
Page, Kirby, 275
Paine, Thomas, 54
Palatinate, 4–5, 9–10, 13, 52, 150
Palatinate Liturgy, 14–15, 75
Palestine, 104, 161
Paris Mission Society, 310
Passavant, W. A., 185–186
Pastorius, Francis Daniel, 19
Penn, William, 19, 25
Pennsylvania, 4–5, 19, 25–27, 30–32, 35, 39, 42, 45, 51, 53, 55–58, 61, 63–64, 70–71, 89, 98, 101, 116–117, 120, 124, 126, 131, 140, 147, 159, 298
    Allentown, 26, 50, 96, 98
    Allenwood, 98
    Altoona, 113
    Bedford, 66
    Bethlehem, 26
    Butler, 98
    Carlisle, 66–68, 77–79, 90, 98
    Chambersburg, 72, 77, 99
    Collegeville, 84, 94–95
    Dorseyville, 98
    Doylestown, 26
    Easton, 26, 42, 68, 77, 85, 93, 95
    Falkner Swamp, 33, 64–65
    Germantown, 4, 27, 32
    Gettysburg, 71, 167, 182
    Goshenhoppen, 42
    Greensburg, 57
    Greenville, 98
    Hanover, 98

Harrisburg, 62, 69, 118
Huntingdon, 81
Lancaster, 26, 30, 42–43, 51, 53, 59, 63, 65, 68, 78–80, 85, 90–91, 95, 97, 106, 294, 316
Lebanon, 28
Lewisburg, 83
Ligonier, 98
Littlestown, 98
Mercersburg, 68–69, 71–75, 78, 84–88, 90–91, 95, 97, 100, 114, 122, 129, 133–134, 182
Mifflinburg, 62
Myerstown, 84
Neshaminy, 32
Old Goshenhoppen, 43
Philadelphia, 4, 24, 26, 32, 34, 38, 46–47, 50, 55, 59, 62, 65, 76, 82–83, 89, 94, 98–100, 111, 167, 308, 335
Pittsburgh, 72, 79, 82, 89, 169, 185
Pottstown, 313
Reading, 26–27, 42, 49, 73, 82, 96, 101
Roxbury, 32
Schuylkill Haven, 89
Skippack, 32–34
Tulpehocken, 42, 47
Weissenburg, 40
Whitehall, 42
Whitemarsh, 32–33
Womelsdorf, 66, 83, 98
Wyncote, 98
York, 42, 47, 67–68, 71, 73, 76–77, 90
Pennsylvania District, 243
Pension and Relief Fund, 272
Peters, Moses, 93
Petersmann, Werner, 259
Pfeiffer, Friedrich, 239
Pflug, Harold A., 259
Pfrimmer, John G., 61
Philadelphia Classis, 63, 73, 84, 93, 283
Philadelphia Synod, 98
Philip of Hesse, 7, 13
Philip of the Palatinate, 10
Philippines, 330
Phillipsburg, 10
Phoebe Home for the Aged, 98
Pietism, 12, 20, 36, 46, 61, 151–152, 156, 164, 175, 183, 189, 322

Pilgrim Press, 314
Pirscher, K., 231
Pister, Jacob, 202, 273–274
Pittsburgh Synod, 89–90, 92, 96, 98, 102, 107, 114
Plan of Union, 282, 284–286, 289, 296
Pluess, C., 129
Pomp, Thomas, 68
Poorbaugh, Elizabeth R., 105
Porter, Thomas C., 77
Potomac Synod, 89–90, 92, 96, 107, 114
Prakash, Yishu, 270
Presbyterian Church in the United States of America, 49, 69, 106, 182, 249, 283–285, 310, 315
Press, Otto, 220
Press, Paul, 273, 287–288
Press, Samuel D., 232, 258–259, 281
Princeton Theological Seminary, 65, 72, 74
Provisional Liturgy, 75, 78
Prussia, 17, 148, 150–151, 169, 182
Psalms and Hymns, 76
Pulfish, John, 57

Quarterly Review (See *Mercersburg Review*)
Quebec, 129
Queen's College (Rutgers), 45

Ragué, Louis von, 225, 235–238
Rahn, H., 268
Rahn, J. C., 255
Raipur, 251, 270
Rauch, Frederick Augustus, 68, 71–72
Rauch, Henry, 36
Rauhe Haus, 210
Rauschenbusch, August, 177
Rauschenbusch, Walter, 110, 177, 261–262, 273
Reformation, the, 11, 14, 74–75, 148, 283, 285, 325, 329, 336
Reformatusok Lapja, 316
Reformed Church Almanac, 101
Reformed Church in America, 28–29, 34, 38, 44, 49, 69, 104, 106, 111, 249, 283–285
Reformed Church in the United States, 33, 40, 44, 48, 50, 56, 58, 60–63, 67, 69–71,

76, 80, 90, 94–97, 99, 102–104, 106–107, 109–115, 123, 125, 128–129, 160, 169, 174, 221, 249, 279, 282–284, 287–288, 293–294, 297, 310, 312, 319, 327, 329
Reformed Church Messenger, The, 57, 77, 84, 100, 294, 316
Reformed Church Quarterly, The, 84, 101
Reformed Church Record, 101
Reformed Church Review, 102
Reformed Church Seminary (See Lancaster Theological Seminary)
Reformed Churchmen's League, 102, 264
Reformed Commission on Closer Relations and Church Union, 282–284
Reformed Protestant Dutch Church (See Reformed Church in America)
Reformierte Kirchenzeitung, 77
Reid, S. H., 81
Reiff, Hans George, 34
Reily, James Ross, 56, 67
Reily, William M., 91
Reimert, William A., 105
Reineking, Friedrich, 129
"Religious and Missionary Magazine of the Reformed Church, The," 76
Reller, F. A., 244
Repairer of the Breach, A, 90
Revised Liturgy, The, 83
Revolutionary War, 5–6, 38, 43, 49–50, 56, 71
Rhineland, 5, 9–10, 15, 19, 23, 33, 150, 177
Richards, George W., 88, 92–93, 112, 116, 282–284, 288–291, 295, 305, 321–322, 331–332
Rieger, John B., 30–31
Rieger, Joseph A., 166–170, 172, 175, 189, 232
Riess, Johann Jacob, 168, 170, 172–173, 175, 177, 181
Rocky Mountain Synod, 324
Rohrbach, 9
Roos, Ernst E., 191, 209–210, 239
Roos, Mrs. Ernst E., 210
Rotterdam, 42
Rubel, John Casper, 28, 50
Rudy, John, 56
Ruetenik, Herman J., 133, 138–139
Rupp, William, 80, 92

Russia, 115, 246
Ryswick, Treaty of, 9

Saeger, F. S., 231
Saeger, Wilhelm A. H., 215
St. Chrischona Mission House, 248
St. Gall, 22, 37
St. John's Classis, 138
St. Joseph Classis, 137
St. Paul Classis, 64
St. Paul's High School (Raipur), 270
St. Paul's Old Folks Home, 98
St. Paul's Orphans Home, 98
Sakti, 270
Salem Girls' School (Raipur), 270
San Pedro Sula, 270
Sauerbier, William K., 214
Saur, Christopher, 41
Saxony, 7, 9, 148, 151
Schaefer, W., 274
Schaeffer, Charles E., 90, 108, 116
Schaeffer, John A., 95
Schaeffer, William C., 92
Schaff, Philip, 69, 72–76, 91, 95, 116, 130, 134, 139, 182, 223
Schaff Building, The, 100
Schick, Herman J., 256–257
Schild, W. H., 260
Schlatter, Michael, 30–31, 37–38, 42–43, 47, 49, 52
Schleiermacher, Friedrich, 152, 154
Schley, John Thomas, 31
Schlicher, J. J., 134
Schmale, John E., 256
Schmalkaldic War, 7
Schmid, Friedrich, 160–163, 166, 168, 185
Schmidt, E., 269–270
Schmidt, G. A., 244, 246
Schmucker, Samuel, 182
Schneck, Benjamin S., 70, 77
Schneder, David B., 104–105
Schneder, Mrs. David B., 104–105
Schneider, Benjamin, 104
Schneider, Mrs. Benjamin, 104
Schneider, Carl Edward, 258
Schneider, J. U., 274
Schory, Albert, 205

Schroedel, M., 268
Schroeder, Paul M., 296
Schroerluke, O. P., 263
Schuenhutz, A., 243
Schultz, Mrs. Caroline, 266
Schwabe, Johann Gottlieb, 166
Schwope, Benedict, 47
Scotland, 331
Scottish Mission, 310
Sechler, John H., 93
Sects, 4, 34–36, 41, 43, 46
Sendai, 105
Severing, N., 222
Shannondale Ozark Center, 267
Sheboygan Classis, 104, 116, 130–131, 133, 135, 137–138, 141, 143
Shenchow, 105
Shenchow Girls' School, 105
Shenchowfu, 106
Siebenpfeiffer, Karl, 200–201, 205, 214, 227, 273
Siegen, 29
Snyder, D. J., 283
Society for the Propagation of the Gospel in Foreign Parts, 28
Society for the Relief of Ministers and Their Widows, 98
Sommerlatte, Paul, 107
Sonnendecker, Henry, 117
Sorrick, G. A., 255
South, the (U.S.), 24, 86, 147, 265
South Carolina, 3–4, 24, 27, 30, 55–57
South Dakota, 120, 137–138, 245
Yankton, 317
South Dakota Synod, 324
South Illinois District, 238
Southern District, 281
Southwest Synod, 89, 138
Spanish Succession, War of the, 10
Spener, Philipp Jakob, 151
Spires, 5, 9
Spotswood, Governor Alexander, 29
Stacy, John, 143
Stacy, Mrs. John, 143
Stahr, Henry Irvin, 96
Stahr, John S., 95
Stanger, C. C., 255
Statement of Faith, 334–335

Staudt, Calvin K., 106
Staudt, Mrs. Calvin K., 106
Staudt, Genevieve, 256
Stein, J. Rauch, 90
Stelzig, the Reverend, 245
Stephan, Martin, 150
Stibitz, George, 93
Stilli, J. G., 273
Stockholm Conference on Life and Work, 279, 281
Stoelting, Christian, 130
Stoll, Andrew, 251
Story of Our Hymns, 217
Stowe, Calvin, 167
Stoy, William, 42
Strassburg, 10, 13
Streich, H. L., 263
Streich, Paul H., 310
Streich, Mrs. Paul H., 310
Streissguth, Wilhelm, 127
Strong, Josiah, 110
Stucki, Benjamin, 143
Stucki, Jacob, 142–143
Stucki, Mrs. Jacob, 143
Study Committee of 1950–53, 303, 307, 323
Stuttgart, 9, 153, 160
Sueger, Mrs. Helen Enslin, 271
Summer School of Theology, 327
Sunday School Board (R), 99
Super, H. W., 93
Susquehanna Classis, 63–64, 103
Swabia, 10
Switzerland, 5, 11, 13, 24, 32, 37, 67, 111, 117, 127, 129, 131, 134, 153, 160, 165, 203, 208, 237, 248, 331
Synod der Reformierten Hoch Deutschen Kirche in Den Vereinigten Staaten von America, Der (Synod of the Reformed German Church in the United States of America), 51, 54
Synod House, 264
Synod in the East (See Eastern Synod)
Synod of South Holland, 27
Synod of the Free German Reformed Congregations of Pennsylvania (See German Reformed Synod of Pennsylvania and Adjacent States)
Synod of the Interior, 89

Synod of the Midwest, 89–90, 114
Synodal-Ordnung, 51, 54

Tanner, Th., 251
Task of American Protestantism, The, 108
Taylor, Carl C., 126
Templeman, Conrad, 33
Tennents, the, 60
Tennessee
  Chattanooga, 240
Tercentenary Monument, The, 82
Tester, Ph., 244
Texas, 240–242, 251
  Bartlett, 241
  Fort Worth, 241
  Houston, 232, 241
  Temple, 241
  Waco, 241
  West, 241
Texas District, 241
Theological Committee, 314, 325
Theological Magazine (See *Theologische Zeitschrift*)
Theologische Zeitschrift, 220–221, 225–227
Theology and Life, 102, 326
Theuss, Christian, 57
Thirty Years' War, 16, 20
Tiffin Classis, 135
Tilda, 271
Tillich, Paul, 327
Tohoku (North Japan) College for Boys, 105
Tokyo, 105
Toth, Alexander, 108
Tri-Seminary Faculty Conference, 326
Truxal, Andrew Gehr, 96
Twente, Mrs. Almeta, 271

Union, 218
Union of South Africa, 330
Union Theological Seminary (N.Y.), 167
Unitarian Church, 229
United Andean Indian Mission, 310
United Brethren in Christ, 48, 61–62, 282, 284–285
United Church Curriculum, 315
United Church Herald, 316
United Church of Christ, 117, 137, 314–315, 317, 329, 331, 333–337

United Evangelical Church, 284
United Evangelical Synod of North America, 204–205
United Evangelical Synod of the East, 205
United Evangelical Synod of the Northwest, 202, 205
United Mission in Mesopotamia, 106
United Nations, 312
United States, 63, 68, 103, 111, 150, 165, 174, 202–203, 205, 207–208, 224, 235, 241, 246–247, 261, 274, 298, 304, 309, 312, 330
United States Christian Commission, 79
Unpartisan Witness on the New Union, 36
Ursinus, Zacharias, 14, 52
Ursinus College, 84–85, 93, 95–96, 300–301
Ursinus School of Theology, 93–94, 132
Utah, 244
   Ogden, 244

Van Haagen, J., 93
Van Vlec, Paulus, 32
Vindication of the Revised Liturgy, 83
Virginia, 4, 24–25, 27, 29, 55–56
   Germanna, 29
   Germanna Ford, 56
   Germantown, 29, 56
   Harrisonburg, 56
   Jamestown, 4
   Warrenton, 29
   Woodstock, 97
Virginia Classis, 64, 79, 97
Vitz, Peter, 125
Vitz, Mrs. Peter, 125
Vollmer, Philip, 94, 110, 258, 282
Voluntary Service Training Center, 312–313

Wack, Caspar, 54
Wack, John Jacob, 28
Wade, Sylvanus, 116
Wade House, 115–116
Wagner, Abraham, 65
Wagner, Daniel, 47, 61
Wagner, James E., 321, 326, 329, 333
Walburn, Myles H., 311
Walburn, Mrs. Myles H., 311
Waldorf, 160

Wall, George Wendelin, 166–170, 172–173, 175, 177, 181–182, 188, 224, 247
War Emergency Relief Commission, 304–305
War Welfare Commission (E), 275
Washington, 245
   Everett, 245
   Seattle, 245
   Spokane, 245
Washington, George, 51
Washington, D.C., 80, 169, 271
Washington Mission District, 245
Waterloo, 57
Weber, F., 273
Weber, John William, 57
Weimar, 21
Weiss, George Michael, 28, 34, 36, 42
Wentzel, Fred D., 100
Werning, F., 240–241
Wesel, 28
West, the (U.S.), 108, 115–116, 119, 122, 126, 130, 132, 135, 139–140, 158–159, 165–166, 169, 172, 174–175, 182, 189, 194, 206, 234, 247
West Coast, the (U.S.), 108
West Friesland, 43
West Pennsylvania Classis, 63
West Susquehanna Classis, 64
Western Missionary, 100
Westmoreland Classis, 64
Westphalia, 150
Westphalia, Peace of, 8
Weyberg, Samuel, 56, 65
Weygold, Frederick, 210, 212–213
Weymer, Jacob, 47
What Is Church History?, 74
Whitefield, George, 36, 60
Whiterabbit, Mitchell, 143
Whitmer, A. Carl, 107
Wichern, J. H., 210
Wilhelm I, Kaiser, 237
Wilhelmius, John, 42
Wilkinson, J. J., 256
Willers, Dietrich, 57
Willy, Bernard, 56
Winckhaus, John Henry, 54–55
Winebrenner, John, 62
Winger, the Reverends, 245

Winnebago Indian Mission, 115, 141
Winnebago Indian School, 143
Winnipeg, 245
Winter, August, 116
Winter, H. A., 130, 133–135
Wisconsin, 115, 120, 124–125, 127, 129–
 131, 133–135, 142, 179, 225, 299
 Appleton, 282
 Belleville, 128
 Black River Falls, 141, 143
 Butler, 236
 Ellsworth, 238
 Fond du Lac, 115, 225, 236
 Franklin, 236
 Greenbush, 116
 La Crosse, 143
 Madeline Island, 267
 Madison, 128
 Manitowoc, 125
 Milwaukee, 129–130, 224, 235–236
 Monroe, 128
 Monticello, 128
 Mount Vernon, 128
 Neillsville, 143
 New Glarus, 125, 127–128
 Oak Grove, 238
 Onion River, 236
 Paoli, 128
 Plymouth, 94, 316
 Portage, 236
 Sheboygan, 115, 130
 Town Eleven, 236
 Town Herman, 125, 128–129, 134–135
 Town Rhine, 235–237
 Town Russell, 236
 Town Washington, 128
 Verona, 128
 Wauwatosa, 236
Wisconsin Lutheran Synod, 161, 224–225
Wislocj, 9
Witte, C., 217
Wittenberg, 14
Wobus, Paul A., 266
Wobus, Reinhard, 219

Wolff, Bernard C., 90–91
Woman's Missionary Society, 101–102, 143,
 294
Women's Guild, 102, 294, 300, 302, 321
Women's Union, 102, 263–264, 267–268,
 294, 300
World Alliance of Reformed and Pres-
 byterian Churches, 111, 300, 329–330
World Council of Churches, 112, 279, 300,
 322, 328–330
World War I, 107, 109, 112, 197, 247, 256,
 259, 266, 270, 274–275
World War II, 108, 304, 317
Worms, 5–6, 9, 32
Wuerttemberg, 5, 21, 148, 152–153, 162–
 163, 166

Yale Divinity School, 257, 259
Yankton School of Theology, 137, 317
Year Book and Almanac, The, 101
Year Book of the Evangelical and Reformed
 Church, The, 101
Yochow, 105
Yockey, S. B., 102
Yockey, Mrs. S. B., 102
Yokohama, 104
Yoshida, Kametaro, 105
Young, Daniel, 67, 77
Young, Zenith F., 267
Youth Fellowship, 100

Zacharias, Daniel, 76
Ziemer Memorial Girls' School, 105
Zimmermann, John, 200–202, 241, 243,
 259–260, 273
Zinzendorf, Count Nicholas Ludwig von,
 34–35, 151
Zion Classis, 63, 84, 93
Zion's Hungarian Classis, 90
Zubly, John J., 50
Zurich, 22
Zweibruecken, 5, 14
Zwingli, Ulrich, 11, 13, 52, 74, 86, 119, 336